Culture and Management

Selected Readings

Edited by Theodore D. Weinshall

Penguin Books

Penguin Books Ltd,
Harmondsworth, Middlesex, England
Penguin Books, 625 Madison Avenue,
New York, New York 10022, U.S.A.
Penguin Books Australia Ltd,
Ringwood, Victoria, Australia
Penguin Books Canada Ltd,
2801 John Street, Markham, Ontario, Canada, L3R 1B4
Penguin Books (N.Z.) Ltd,
182–190 Wairau Road, Auckland 10, New Zealand

First published 1977

Copyright acknowledgements for items in this volume
will be found on p. 435

Made and printed in Great Britain by
Cox & Wyman Ltd, London, Reading and Fakenham
Set in Monotype Times

Contents

Introduction

This book is primarily intended for students of management, and managers whose roles involve them in work beyond their national boundaries. This would include all those interested in international business, whether they be managers in multinational corporations or in national organizations which come into contact with people of other countries. This book would also be of interest to students of the relation between culture and management and of what is today referred to as comparative management: that is, comparison of managerial behaviour and other aspects of management in different countries. The book could also serve people who are merely interested in culture and in the behaviour of people dissimilar to themselves, either because they travel to other countries (for pleasure, or in connection with their work) or because they are curious about culture and its relation to organizational management.

Its main objective is, therefore, to help people to distinguish 'culture-bound' behaviour from what one could refer to as 'universal' behaviour, namely that part of behaviour which is affected to a lesser degree by the environmental culture. An organizationally appropriate example could be the difference in mode of communication between, say, France and the United States. Let us imagine two similar organizations, in the U.S. and France – each headed by an entrepreneur and managed in an entrepreneurial structure, the chief executive communicating with the managers at various levels of the management, rather than only with those directly underneath him. This is a 'universal behaviour' proposition. However, if we consider the communication behaviour of the two entrepreneurs in terms of the intensity of their oral interactions with their managers, we may fall into a 'culture-bound' trap. We would discover that the American entrepreneur widely interacts with managers throughout the organization, whereas with the French entrepreneur similar interaction is much less frequent. Likewise we would discover that the French chief executive uses much more written communication than his American colleagues. This may lead us to the mistaken impression that the Frenchman is a bureaucratic leader of a formally centralized functional structure, while a closer look would reveal that he actually runs an entrepreneurial structure, but in a different culture of communication behaviour. For this reason, the readings were chosen according to the benefit the reader would derive from them in two ways:

1. Conceptual and analytical tools which could serve him whenever he has to evaluate manifest behaviour and distinguish in it the 'universal' from the 'culture-bound' elements.
2. As many examples as possible of some specific managerial behaviour in several different cultures, measured with the aid of the same analytical and/or research tool.

The importance of studying the relation between culture and management has grown enormously during the last decade. The expansion of the European Common Market, the growing links of the U.S.S.R. and of China with Western countries, the accord between the two Germanies and the involvement of the U.S.A. in other parts of the world, are major trends in world politics and economics, favouring the gradual obliteration of national borders.

The multinational corporation, to which the last readings in the book are devoted, is probably one of the most important phenomena of the second half of the twentieth century and is likely to have a major effect on the pattern of the world in the twenty-first. Its advent has accelerated the obliteration of national boundaries and the movement of people from one country to another. All this has been accompanied by revolutionary innovations in transportation, communication and mass media which are not only permitting quicker, easier and cheaper transit from one culture to another, but bringing different cultures and other managements into homes and organizations. It should be noted that all these are quite recent developments.

Until the nineteenth century, organizations used to be fairly simple entities in which the manager-owner was dominant. He did not have to share his power with decision-making factors such as workers, trade unions, shareholders, bankers, customers, suppliers, and governments. The culture of management was to a large extent that of the country to which the organization belonged, even if geographically it happened to operate outside its borders.

In those days, the only way to find out about the possible effect of a culture on management was to get acquainted with the former through anthropological research. Anthropologists, however, preferred to devote their time and resources to primitive and 'out of the way' cultures rather than to those of industrialized countries. The reasons for this preference were several. First, the more primitive the culture, the easier it is to encompass it and study it as a total system. Second (and closely related to the first reason), was the fact that the far-away cultures were 'pristine' and undisturbed by the influence of colonial or organizational expansion. It was only after the Second World War that anthropologists began to take interest in the more industrialized countries. By that time, organizations had become much more complex in their decision-making processes and much more advanced in their management structures. In fact, it seems nowadays very difficult to differentiate between culture and management.

The book comprises four sections – one conceptual and three devoted specifically to the effects of culture on management and vice versa. The choice of readings for these latter three parts was facilitated by two self-imposed limitations. The first has to do with the boundaries between different cultures. Even without trying to define 'culture' at this stage, it is clear that such boundaries could separate one ethnic group from another, or one locality from another, or even one organization (or sub-organization) from another. However, for the purpose of this book, boundaries between cultures were considered those between nation-states. The second limitation confined the material chosen to writings dealing with differences between at least two countries regarding the topic under discussion.

The four parts of the book are thus as follows:

Conceptualization of the Relation between Culture and Management, presenting the ideas of various writers on the relation between culture and management, as well as their evaluation of the research work done to date in this area.

The Cultural Framework, including some of the research and findings regarding the effects of values, beliefs and manifest behaviour on management, in different countries.

The Managerial Framework – Factors of the Decision-making Process, looking at such human factors in the decision-making process as managers, workers and customers and finding out how different cultures affect them in various ways.

The Managerial Framework – the Effects of Size on the Managerial Structure, covering readings which deal with the cultural effects on two different aspects of the managerial structure – *attitudes* and *relationships*; this part includes a third section devoted to culture and management in *Multinational Corporations*.

The Selected Bibliography which follows the four parts is the bibliography from which the readings for this book were selected, as well as a few additional recommended books.

Finally, in this Introduction, some words of acknowledgement are due. My ever-growing interest in the relation between culture and management has been very strongly linked with my association with INSEAD, the European Institute for Business Administration. It is through my relationships with hundreds of participants and scores of teachers from countries all over the world that I have primarily gathered my first-hand knowledge of the wealth, however problematic, of the effects of culture on management. Of these many friends, the one who played an important part in making me formalize my knowledge in the area was Henri-Claude De Bettignies, to whom I am grateful.

I first started work on this project in the course of a stay in England in 1970–71 and during that period was helped by an anthropologist friend, Dr Joyce Pettigrew, and by my assistants at the Ashridge Management College, Miriam Dunn and Michael Silver, to whom my thanks are extended.

The major part of the work, however, was carried out at Tel Aviv University during 1972–3. But for the tremendous help of Mrs Lilly Malz this work would not have been possible. Her devotion, energy and advice have been a source of constant encouragement to me in screening and editing the material for the book.

I am likewise indebted to Mr Eliezer Goldberg (Scientific Editor at the Technion, Israel Institute of Technology), a friend as well as an exceptional linguist, for his comments and advice on this and the other introductions in this book, and on my article on multinational corporations appearing towards the end of the book.

I would also like to thank my secretary, Mrs Vivienne Miller, for her help throughout.

Last, but not least, thanks are due to my wife, Yonna, and to our daughters, Talia and Yael, for their patient acceptance of my work on the project, which for them meant either my absence from home or sharing my longer trips abroad.

Part One
Conceptualization of the Relation between Culture and Management

The readings chosen for this part represent different approaches to the relation between culture and management. Richman covers the most basic and important principles, central to culture's effect on management. He does this by dividing the cultural variables into sociological and educational constraints, and analysing their effects on the management process.

Webber introduces, in the second reading, the concepts of 'divergence' and 'convergence' in reference to the effects of the level of technology and innovation on the culture of the land. Thus, the condition of 'divergence' denotes a situation in which cultural values and norms persist in spite of the spread of technology and innovation. 'Convergence', on the other hand, implies that cultures are being brought closer to one another, as a result of similarities in technology, innovation and standard of living. Webber sees the factors of convergence as predominating at the macro-economic and the micro-technical levels; and those of divergence on the philosophy and practice of managers at the level of the firm.

In a different vein we have the critical review by Roberts of the research carried out up to 1970. The author maintains that there is a serious problem with the lack of basic definition for the word *culture*. She claims that most of the research reviewed by her was not well thought out, had no strong guiding concepts, reached weak conclusions and did not give adequate coverage of the subject.

Selection of readings for this part was quite difficult because, rather than there being a shortage of material, there exist several very good conceptualizations of the relation between culture and management. As a consequence of constraints on the number of readings that could be included, I regretfully had to omit such excellent readings as Jean Boddewyn's and Musbau Ajiferuke's ' "Culture" and Other Explanatory Variables in Comparative Management Studies' (1970); Stanley M. Davis's 'A Conceptual Framework: Values, Relations, Structure' (1971); Raghu Nath's 'A Methodological Review of Cross-Cultural Management Research' (1968); Hans Schollhammer's 'The Comparative Management Theory Jungle' (1970); and William Foote Whyte's 'An Intercultural Context for Organisational Research' (1969). One other large work that ought to be mentioned is Edward T. Hall's 'The Silent Language' (1959), from which no self-contained material could be abstracted and which is accordingly recommended for reading in its entirety. Some additional readings can be found among those listed in the bibliography at the end of this book.

1 Barry M. Richman

Significance of Cultural Variables[1]

Barry M. Richman, 'Significance of Cultural Variables', *Academy of Management Journal*, vol. 8, no. 4, December 1965, pp. 292–308.

The argument between those who believe that efficient and effective management is based largely on universal principles, practices and general know-how which can (and should) be transferred to any country,[2] and those who advocate that management as a philosophy and/or process is essentially or substantially culture-bound[3] will probably be intensified as a result of current cross-cultural and international research activity in the field of management.

Some tough problems

A major problem is the lack of clarity and consistency in defining and using such critical terms as 'principles', 'culture-bound' and 'management philosophy'. A second problem is the confusion between normative, descriptive and predictive elements of management theory, and the absence of empirical and experimental studies for testing and validating firmly held beliefs and 'hypotheses'. A third major problem is the absence of a basic theoretical conceptual framework within which to hypothesize that certain cultural factors do in fact generally and significantly tend to influence the

1. Modification of paper presented at the International Management Session of the Academy of Management Meetings, Chicago, 30 December 1964, based in part on the thinking that went into Farmer and Richman (1965).

2. This is the general view taken by many of the textbooks dealing with the principles and functions of management, such as the works of Harold Koontz and Cyril O'Donnell, and William Newman. See also Merrill (1963).

3. See Gonzales and McMillan Jr (1961), pp. 33–41; and Oberg (1963), pp. 129–43.

performance of management. Finally, there is a lack of 'developmental research' which would attempt to answer the question 'if this hypothesis about a particular cultural variable is generally true in principle, how does it find expression in the operational context of the real management world?'.[4] That is, what concrete effects does this have on the process and performance of management?

For example, one may hypothesize that a dominant unfavourable view towards private business and its managers in a given country might be expected to have a negative impact on managerial and firm performance in that country. Through further research, convincing evidence may be obtained which indicates that there is a pervasive, highly negative view towards private business firms and their managements in, for instance, Burma, Ghana or Iran. Yet we are still in the basic research stage since we are very hazy about the concrete impact this situation tends to have on the performance and operations of, for example, an oil company subsidiary and its management in Iran. Moreover, we are still not sure what the key underlying conditions for this negative view are.

What is needed is research of the developmental and the applied types. If it can be determined how a dominant unfavourable view of the above sort tends to affect the performance of business firms and their managements in general; and (specifically in the case of the Iranian oil subsidiary), in what way, and to what extent, and what the key underlying reasons are for this view, the often dismal story of conflicts, confusion, inefficiencies, and the slow learning process such managements face, could probably be minimized substantially or eliminated.

In order to further clarify and drive home the point, consider for illustration Maslow's (1943) famous theory of human motivation and the hierarchy of human needs. It has been referred to in a recent article by Keith Davis (1964) in the following words:

Modern psychology reports that new human needs take priority whenever former needs are reasonably satisfied. In other words, man is motivated more by what he is seeking, than by what he already has.

4. The term 'developmental research' and some of the ideas associated with it have been borrowed from Haire (1964).

Human needs are generally recognized to be in some order, with physiological and security needs preceding social and ego needs. In underdeveloped countries, most employees are still seeking basic physiological and security needs. Hence, some of the more sophisticated and elaborate motivational devices of modern industrial management may not be appropriate in these countries. The needs of their workers may be more simply reached by direct motivation – in other words, work must be interpreted in terms of their immediate needs, rather than waiting for indirect results through a complex economic system. Accordingly, action which would be inappropriate in an advanced country may sometimes be workable in the underdeveloped country . . .

This reflects sound basic theory. However, only developmental and applied research can determine, in an aggregate human sense, what level of needs within the overall human needs hierarchy are the most potent during a given period of time among the Italian, Mexican or Indian industrial labour force. Would it now seem wise – in terms of productivity – for the international firm operating in one of these countries to start placing less emphasis on monetary incentives and material gain and more on social or egoistic needs?

Mason Haire (1964) gives a good example of the link between basic and developmental research:

McClelland's [1961 and 1962] studies of the achievement motive in businessmen in different countries belong in the category basic. They extend previous research and theory. They make possible a cultural interpretation of the need for achievement. When he goes on to investigate ways in which the drive for achievement can be increased, he is doing developmental research. It is not applied because it is not limited to specific problems – changing shoe salesmen in a retail outlet or life insurance salesmen. It is not basic because its primary aim is a step towards the application of the basic concept. The work sheds more light on the fundamental problem: lots of developmental research does. That's not the criterion of basic research.

To date, there have been some exploratory or basic research studies which have attempted to identify critical cultural variables that seem generally to have a bearing on business management in different countries. Yet there has been little attempt to follow through with the type of developmental research that is needed to describe, explain and predict the actual impact that these variables tend to have on managerial performance.[5] There have been several interesting studies of the applied research type dealing with case studies which have indicated that various cultural factors in a specific situation have certain effects on managerial performance. However, this type of research usually lacks the leverage of broad theoretical concepts, and as a result, usually fails to develop any generality.

Some vital questions

A vital question for international business management seems to be *to what extent can American management principles, practices and general know-how be transferred effectively to other countries, at what cost, and to what degree and extent is the overall process and effectiveness of management constrained by cultural variables?*

The term 'effective' is meant to imply the achievement of corporate objectives which usually boils down to some basic notion of long-term profitability, efficiency, productivity, as well as survival. The operational expression of these ultimate objectives is also likely to be influenced by cultural factors. For this discussion, management principles in their broadest form are effective guides for action. For the building of discipline and operationality in advancing research and practice, the term 'culture-bound' has far less potential than 'cultural variables' or 'cultural constraints'.

This paper concerns *two broad classes of cultural constraints*, those defined as '*sociological*', and those defined as '*educational*':

(1) The former class corresponds to the dominant human attitudes, values and beliefs in a given country, and the way they tend to influence the motivation, behavior, and performance of individuals employed by business firms. Since there may be various sub-cultures in a particular country, research in this area can be very difficult and complex. The concern here is not with the impact of culture on the political, legal or economic systems of different countries, although this may also be a very important area of research for international management.

(2) With regard to educational constraints, concern is only with those

5. Richard Farmer and I have been guilty of this charge in our article 'A Model for Research in Comparative Management', *California Management Review*, Winter 1964, pp. 55–68.

formal educational and training programmes in a given country which are not run by business firms – domestic or foreign. The overall educational system of a given country has a direct and significant bearing on the types and quality of people potentially available to business firms.

To answer the vital question stated above it is necessary to determine how we can tell when a certain aspect of management is in fact constrained by cultural variables, and in what way. It is also necessary to consider carefully what the critical cultural variables and their underlying conditions may be, how they can be identified and measured, and how they are interrelated with managerial performance in terms of their effects. Moreover, we must ascertain what concrete evidence exists, or how much evidence might be generated. It is evident that this line of attack entails an inter-disciplinary approach. Persons with backgrounds in anthropology, sociology, psychology, possibly theology and education, as well as management can play a major role in providing pertinent information and insights, and in designing and conducting tests, experiments and empirical studies in this area of research.

Set up some givens to start

An initial step in this research process is to hypothesize that certain key cultural factors directly influence the performance of management generally. Such factors may be derived, as a first approximation, from various research studies indicating which cultural variables have seemed important in different situations and countries that have been studied, through additional exploratory studies, through observation and practical experience, or even through insightful intuition and deductive reasoning. Only further research can then lead to more refined selection and definition of the variables that seem significant.

Once the key cultural variables have been identified, research of the developmental and empirical type would be required to describe, explain and eventually predict the actual impact that these variables tend to have on management practices, behaviour and performance with reasonable accuracy. Business firms in different countries could be studied using the same basic classification of cultural variables.

In undertaking cross-cultural research of this type, one must also have a common denominator or classification scheme which can be used for comparing the management process and managerial performance in different countries. In other words, if a given cultural variable or constraint tends to influence managers' activities in general, one must have some useful description of the things that managers do that are affected.

Comparative and international

Based on research in comparative management, it appears that managements of business enterprises virtually everywhere perform the same basic managerial functions, if such functions are defined as planning and decision-making, controlling, organizing, staffing and direction or supervision. These can be broken down and classified into descriptive elements common to the management process in any fairly complex business firm.[6] It would be theoretically possible to compare and even measure significant differences in the way the various elements of the management process tend to be performed in firms in different countries by using a common classification scheme.

It also appears that business firms everywhere operate – either consciously or unconsciously or by default – in accordance with a common framework of policy decisions pertaining to the different enterprise functions such as marketing, production, research and development, procurement, finance, personnel and so forth.[7] For example, some common policy decision areas pertain to pricing, product line, make or buy, sources and uses of funds, number and types of suppliers, employee services and so forth.

Even in poorly managed business firms in underdeveloped countries or in Soviet business enterprises,[8] managements engage in the above basic functions and operate in accordance with a

6. Most of the elements of the management process have been taken from standard textbooks on management theory, such as those by Koontz and O'Donnell, and William Newman.

7. See Newman and Logan (1959).

8. See Richman (1965), especially chapters 3 and 4.

common classification of policy decisions – at least to some extent – although this may not be very evident at first glance. However, the specific ways and degrees of effectiveness in which the overall management process tends to be performed by firms in different countries differs substantially in many cases. There appear to be some dominant patterns of managerial activity in various countries, particularly among similar branches of industry.

Does this situation mean that firm managements in various different countries tend to perform their jobs differently because their way tends to be more effective, because they are pursuing different objectives, because certain cultural or other types of environmental constraints – (e.g. political, legal, economic) – are operating on them, or because of ignorance or lack of interest in other more effective ways to manage?

If the answer proves to be ignorance or lack of interest this may also imply that the firms and their managements are affected by various educational and/or sociological constraints. It seems that these questions need serious pondering and answering before we can assert with confidence that certain management practices are significantly constrained by certain cultural variables, or that others can be transferred successfully and with greater effectiveness by U.S. or other companies to their foreign subsidiaries.

Significant cultural constraints

This implies that research in comparative management is closely related to the field of international management, particularly with regard to cultural constraints. It may be prudent for international firms to make some assessment of the dominant management process and its effectiveness in local firms operating in those countries where they are contemplating the establishment of fairly large-scale subsidiaries. If there are some apparently successful U.S. firms already operating in a particular foreign country, merely studying and copying the management process of these firms may lead to significant operational difficulties for new foreign-based firms.

It may be wise for the new firms to attempt to analyse the adjustments required and undertaken, as well as the costs entailed, before the established international firm successfully introduces management practices which differ substantially from dominant local patterns of business management, assuming that it does so. For example, if a U.S. competitor of Colgate-Palmolive decides to set up a firm in India, it may be dangerous initially to pattern its management process closely after Colgate's, since Colgate has been operating in India for a long time, and has probably adjusted its management process rather slowly, and at substantial costs in many cases, because of various cultural constraints.

In our comparative research, we have tentatively identified and hypothesized the cultural variables (or constraints) presented in Table 1 as having a significant impact on the management process

Table 1

Sociological constraints

$C_{1\cdot1}$: View towards business and its managers.

$C_{1\cdot2}$: View towards authority and subordinates.

$C_{1\cdot3}$: Inter-organizational cooperation – which involves the interaction among business firms, labour unions, government agencies, and educational institutions.

$C_{1\cdot4}$: View of achievement.

$C_{1\cdot5}$: Class structure and individual mobility.

$C_{1\cdot6}$: View towards wealth and material gain.

$C_{1\cdot7}$: View towards scientific method.

$C_{1\cdot8}$: View towards risk-taking.

$C_{1\cdot9}$: View towards change.

Educational constraints

$C_{2\cdot1}$: Literacy level and primary education.

$C_{2\cdot2}$: Specialized vocational and technical training and general secondary education (not under the direction or control of firms).

$C_{2\cdot3}$: Higher and advanced education.

$C_{2\cdot4}$: Special management training programmes (not run by business firms).

$C_{2\cdot5}$: Attitude towards education.

$C_{2\cdot6}$: Education match with human requirements of productive enterprises – which is essentially a summary category. Depending on the type of job involved, different C_2s would be more important.

and managerial effectiveness in general.[9] They would seem to have an impact on both foreign-based and domestic firms in a particular country. The argument is that if these cultural constraints differ significantly among different countries, the process and effectiveness of business management, and hence the achievement of corporate objectives would be directly affected. Further, the quantitative expression of the operational objectives themselves is also likely to be affected.

It is obviously easier to measure or quantify the pure educational constraints than the attitudinal or sociological constraints. However, it is theoretically possible roughly to measure the sociological constraints by focusing on the dominant characteristics, values and behaviours of the population in a given country, and a growing amount of fruitful work is being done in this area by various types of social scientists.[10]

Cultural constraints and elements of the management process

As a further step, we have tentatively classified various common elements of the overall management process. Each element in the process can be labelled a P, and some of them are presented in Table 2.

A few highly suggestive hypotheses indicating relationships between various Cs and Ps are presented in Table 3 in the form of equations. They are based largely on our comparative management research, including a limited number of interviews, and discussion with executives of various international and foreign business enterprises. Only intensive empirical research of the developmental and applied types can lead to the verification of these hypotheses. In all cases there may be other significant factors

9. These constraints are defined more fully in Farmer and Richman (1964a). Since the article was originally written, we have made some refinements in our classification of constraints. In our comparative management research we deal with political, legal and economic constraints, as well as educational and sociological variables.

10. As an example of an outstanding work of this type which makes extensive use of other relevant empirical and experimental studies see McClelland (1961).

affecting a particular P, but our concern here is only with cultural variables that may have a significant impact.

At this point it seems desirable to elaborate briefly on a few of the Ps for illustrative purposes. Let us take P_5, P_{12} and P_{15} since

Table 2

P_1 : Methodologies, techniques and tools used in planning.
P_2 : Time horizon of plans.
P_3 : Degree to which the organization is mechanical (pre-programmed).
P_4 : Types of performance and control standards used.
P_5 : Degree of centralization or decentralization.
P_6 : Degree of work specialization.
P_7 : Spans of control.
P_8 : Grouping of activities and departmentation.
P_9 : Extent and use of committees.
P_{10}: Selection and promotion criteria used.
P_{11}: Nature and extent of formal company training programmes.
P_{12}: Degree of participative vs authoritarian management.
P_{13}: Communication structure and techniques.
P_{14}: Techniques used for motivating personnel.
P_{15}: Nature and extent of employee welfare services and facilities. (This is likely to be reflected by the degree of paternalistic management.)

Table 3

$P_1 = f(C_{1\cdot7}, C_{2\cdot1}, C_{2\cdot2}, C_{2\cdot3}, C_{2\cdot4}, C_{2\cdot6})$*
$P_4 = f(C_{1\cdot2}, C_{1\cdot4} \ldots$ various C_2s)
$P_5 = f(C_{1\cdot1}, C_{1\cdot2}, C_{1\cdot4}$, all C_2s)
$P_8 = f(C_{1\cdot2}$, all C_2s)
$P_9 = f(C_{1\cdot1}, C_{1\cdot2}, C_{1\cdot4}, C_{1\cdot5}, C_{2\cdot6})$
$P_{10} = f(C_{1\cdot3}, C_{1\cdot5})$
$P_{11} = f(C_{1\cdot4}$, all C_2s)
$P_{12} = f(C_{1\cdot1}, C_{1\cdot2})$
$P_{14} = f(C_{1\cdot2}, C_{1\cdot3}, C_{1\cdot6})$
$P_{15} = f(C_{1\cdot2}, C_{2\cdot1})$
* Depending on level of plans, different C_2s would be more significant.

there has been a substantial amount of research and evidence pertaining to these in different countries.[11]

From our own research studies and those of others, it appears that there are dominant views of authority and subordinates in different countries which are shaped largely by various underlying cultural conditions. In turn, such dominant views tend to result in dominant patterns of managerial authority and superior-subordinate relationships in business firms. Such patterns can be theoretically represented by continua which indicate the degree to which managements tend to be autocratic or participative in business firms in different countries. Moreover, in some countries management is typically highly paternalistic because of various cultural (or sometimes other) environmental conditions, and this results in a wide range of employee welfare services. In other countries, there tends to be a low degree of paternalism in business enterprises.

If empirical research reveals that local personnel tend to expect, prefer and perform better under a system of highly authoritarian and/or centralized management, then newly established foreign-based firms may be wise to adjust their practices accordingly, at least initially. If, for some reason, the firms want to move in the direction of greater participative management and/or greater decentralization of authority involving local personnel, it would probably be prudent to estimate carefully the overall costs and benefits and time entailed in implementing such a change successfully and effectively.

For example, it may be much more costly, time consuming and risky to introduce substantially greater participative management effectively in Saudi Arabia, Peru or even Germany, as compared to the U.S., Canada or Yugoslavia. In fact, empirical research studies based on interviews and questionnaire surveys conducted in business firms in the U.S. and Peru strongly suggest that authoritarian management tends to be more acceptable and effective in Peru, as compared to the U.S. If participative management were to be applied in a fairly short period of time in a firm in Peru, it is

11. Cf., Haire, Ghiselli and Porter (1963), pp. 101–4; Whyte and Williams (1963), pp. 481–8; Harbison and Myers (1959).

likely that productivity would decline and employees would tend to lose respect for their superiors.[12] Similarly, in countries where, because of various cultural conditions, employees tend to expect, desire and perform better under a system of highly paternalistic management – such as Japan and various Latin American countries – it may be very costly and possibly dangerous – in terms of efficiency and productivity – for the international firm to deviate substantially from such a pattern of management, particularly in the short run.

Cultural constraints, dynamic managerial problems and managerial effectiveness

Even if the relationships between various Cs and Ps can be determined with a reasonable level of confidence, this still may not

Table 4

D_1 : Ease or difficulty of obtaining personnel with the desired skills and abilities.

D_2 : Ease or difficulty of motivating employees – both managers and workers – to perform their jobs efficiently and effectively, and to improve their performance.

D_3 : Degree of identification that tends to exist between the interest and objectives of individuals, departments and the overall firm.

D_4 : Degree of frustration, morale, absenteeism and turnover that tends to exist among enterprise employees.

D_5 : Degree of cooperation or conflict among employees.

D_6 : Degree of information distortion and ineffective communication within the enterprise.

D_7 : Degree of unproductive time expended in unmeaningful bargaining, restrictive practices, etc . . .

D_8 : Ease or difficulty of introducing changes and innovations in enterprise operations.

D_9 : Degree to which scientific method is applied by enterprise employees – both managers and workers – in dealing with causation and futurity problems.

D_{10}: Degree of organizational flexibility in causing or adapting to changing conditions.

12. See Whyte and Williams (1963).

yield a broad insight into the impact of cultural constraints on managerial effectiveness. The elements of the management process are essentially static, and managerial effectiveness is determined in large part by dynamic behavioural factors or conditions operating within the enterprise. Some of these dynamic factors may be identified and evaluated through analysing the static elements of the management process – for example, overburdened spans of control, delays and red tape in decision making because of overcentralization – but it appears that many cannot be.

In general, common dynamic variables or conditions generally conducive to a high or low degree of managerial effectiveness tend to be difficult to identify and categorize. We have, however, attempted tentatively to classify some dynamic variables, which we refer to as 'dynamic managerial problems' or Ds, in an exploratory way as a first approximation. Some of the suggestive categories which seem relevant to international management are presented in Table 4. If we could determine with a reasonable degree of confidence what the actual relationships between the Ds and Cs are in a given situation, it would probably be possible to ascertain, either deductively or inductively, the impact on managerial effectiveness within a reasonable range of accuracy.

In some instances these dynamic problems could be entirely or partially controllable through an effective management process in a given firm. However, in many cases, it appears that management does not have much, if any, control over various negative

Table 5

$D_1 = f(C_{1\cdot1}, C_{1\cdot5}, C_{1\cdot6}, C_{2\cdot1}, C_{2\cdot2}, C_{2\cdot3}, C_{2\cdot4}, C_{2\cdot5}, C_{2\cdot6})$ Depending on the type of personnel in question, different educational constraints would tend to be more significant.

$D_2 = f(C_{1\cdot1}, C_{1\cdot3}, C_{1\cdot4}, C_{1\cdot5}, C_{1\cdot6}, C_{2\cdot5})$

$D_3 = f(C_{1\cdot1}, C_{1\cdot2}, C_{1\cdot3}, C_{1\cdot4})$

$D_6 = f(C_{1\cdot1}, C_{1\cdot2}, C_{1\cdot4}$ . . . various C_2s)

$D_8 = f(C_{1\cdot1}, C_{1\cdot3}, C_{1\cdot4}, C_{1\cdot7}, C_{1\cdot8}, C_{1\cdot9}$ . . . various C_2s)

$D_9 = f(C_{1\cdot4}, C_{1\cdot7}, C_{1\cdot8}$ . . . various C_2s)

C-D relationships in the short run. Table 5 presents some highly suggestive hypotheses indicating possible significant relationships between various Cs and Ds.

At this point a few qualitative examples which serve to illustrate possible significant relationships between various Cs, Ds and managerial effectiveness seem to be in order. In some cases, certain Ps also seem to be inter-connected with certain Ds.

On achievement motivation

There is some convincing evidence to suggest that in various countries (because of dominant cultural values, religious beliefs or ideologies rigidly adhered to, and/or the class structure), the general population tends to have a fairly low achievement drive; while in other countries, the reverse tends to be true.[13] For example, where people adhere closely in their behaviour to the values associated with the Protestant ethic and Calvinism, they tend to have higher achievement motivation than those who behave in accordance with orthodox Hindu, Moslem, Buddhist and even Catholic religious values and doctrines.

If the international firm decides to engage in fairly extensive operations in a country where high achievement human resources are critically scarce, it may prove extremely difficult to motivate many locally recruited personnel to perform their jobs effectively and efficiently, even where the firm's managers are competent and able leaders. In such a situation, it may be best for the firm to undertake training programmes that emphasize changing basic attitudes and values, rather than focusing only on the improvement of skills or new techniques which may not be utilized effectively because of lack of proper motivation.[14]

There are also some indications that the achievement drive among members of minority groups or sub-cultures isolated from the dominant cultural mainstream in various countries is often significantly higher than that of the general population. The

13. See McClelland (1961), especially chapters 2, 3, 9 and 10; and Farmer (1964), pp. 47 ff., and footnotes 17, 18 and 32.

14. For a relevant study indicating the ineffectiveness of management training programmes in Turkey, see Brodburn (1960); also cited in McClelland (1961), p. 415.

Chinese in Indonesia, the Armenians in the Middle East and the Lebanese in various African countries appear to fall into this category. It may prove very useful for the international company in its recruiting if these high achievement sub-groups can be identified, particularly where the firm is operating in countries scarce in high achievement human resources.

One other aspect of achievement is worth noting here. In some countries, such as Japan, it seems that it may be wise for the firm to emphasize group or collective achievement, rather than individual achievement as is typically done in U.S. industry and business.

The cultural view of change

The dominant view towards change in a particular country may have considerable relevance for international business management. Again, research can help. Where locally-recruited personnel in a given country are generally inclined vigorously to resist changes in operations and certain underlying cultural conditions are largely responsible for such behaviour, then management would be in a much better position to anticipate and overcome this problem.

It is true that people employed in business firms throughout the world often tend to resist managerial and technical changes that directly affect them and their work, for a variety of economic and personal reasons. However, there are some indications strongly suggesting that purely cultural factors tend to result in significantly greater opposition to change in some countries than in others. For example, it is likely that human resistance to change in India tends to be significantly greater than in the U.S., largely for cultural reasons.[15]

The degree to which resistance to change is the result of certain cultural constraints might be ascertained by comparing the time, costs and training entailed in introducing similar changes in U.S. based firms and in different foreign subsidiaries. If a significant number of personnel must be recruited from outside a particular country in order to implement an innovation or change in opera-

15. See Sundaram (1963), pp. 495–8; and Rice (1958).

tions successfully, this too may indicate that there is a high degree of cultural resistance to change.

Scientific method, cause and effect

It appears that the dominant attitude towards scientific method varies substantially among different cultures and countries, even with regard to individuals having a considerable amount of formal education. Here again the values associated with Calvinism, if adhered to in practice, tend to be associated with a favourable view towards scientific method.[16] Where the international firm must recruit local personnel in various countries who frequently have little pre-training in or notion of scientific method, basic training in scientific methodology and thinking may be required in order substantially to reduce serious errors, waste and inefficiencies in company operations.

My colleague, Richard Farmer, managed a business firm in Saudi Arabia for two years and quickly learned that one of the most difficult problems confronting him was to try to get locally-recruited managers and workers to work out causation problems. This can range from an apparently trivial but real life problem such as, 'if tyre pressures are not checked regularly, tyre damage is likely', to 'if operating schedules are not made, the firm may be unable to adjust to changing conditions'. The former statement may indeed seem trivial – until $3,000 worth of truck tyres are ruined on a single forty-mile trip, as was the case on several occasions.

View of private enterprise

Our preliminary research in comparative management suggests that in various countries – particularly in Africa and Asia – the dominant view of private business firms and their managements is highly negative, and that such a general unfavourable view may have various adverse impacts on both foreign based and domestic firms. For example, it may prove very difficult to recruit competent personnel locally; more so if the educational and skill level of the

16. See Farmer (1964), pp. 50 ff; and McClelland (1961), chapters 9 and 10.

population is quite low. It also seems likely that the more unfavourable this view, the more closely local personnel may have to be supervised and controlled, since there would tend to be considerable distrust, antagonism and conflict between top management in particular, and locally-recruited employees. If this negative view of business management persists, a rather destructive informal organization might evolve within the enterprise. Moreover, in a country where much of the population has small regard for business managers and business activities it is not likely to have government or labour organizations or many potential investors who are sympathetic to business problems.

Hence it would seem very important for the international firm to have a good insight, based on some concrete evidence, into how private business and its managers are generally viewed in countries where they have or are considering the establishment of subsidiaries. Where there is a dominant negative view, if the real underlying reasons for this attitude can be determined, the firm would be in a much better position to deal effectively with this problem.

Significance of educational constraints

Thus far we have been chiefly concerned with cultural variables of the sociological type, but educational constraints may also be very significant for international business management.[17] One intuitively expects that a firm able to recruit high school and college graduates in the United States will be quite a different type of organization from one which must depend largely on illiterate or barely literate human resources, as is typically the case in such countries as Saudi Arabia or the Sudan.

In general, it appears that the overall educational system in any country affects virtually every important aspect of managerial and business life. For example, it tends to have a significant bearing on the entire staffing function and goal setting and decision-making process; the size of firms and their overall organization structure including degrees of centralization or decentralization, degrees of work specialization, departmentalization and grouping

17. A major study on education throughout the world has been carried out by Harbison and Myers (1964).

of activities; the specific types of operations, techniques and technology employed; costs of production; managerial effectiveness and the overall productivity of firms.

There is substantial evidence that there are large discrepancies in the number, types and quality of personnel employed in similar types of industrial firms, producing a given level of output, in advanced as compared to less developed countries. These discrepancies appear evident not only among unskilled workers, but through the entire vertical skill and occupational structures. Such discrepancies are often due chiefly to differences in the overall educational systems found in different countries.[18]

In countries where formal educational and training systems are not properly geared to the needs of modern industry, the number of personnel required to produce a given level of output, even with the same basic technology, tends to be substantially greater than in an advanced economy which typically has a high quality, diversified system. Often three, four, and in some cases more than ten times as many employees are required in a less developed as compared to an advanced country.[19] In numerous cases more productive technology cannot even be employed, and/or many positions and activities remain unfilled and unperformed, because of the lack of suitable manpower.

Even among the developed countries there are often significant differences in the organizational structures and staffing effectiveness of similar types of firms, due in large part to differences in educational systems. For example, a large company in Great Britain a few years ago had been trying to recruit a person with a background in both economics and psychology to head up its recently established marketing research department. In the U.S., high-talent people of this type can usually be found if the firm is willing to pay the price, but this company could not recruit such a person in Britain even after a costly, extensive and lengthy search. A less qualified man was finally selected, and top management is convinced that the job is not being performed nearly as efficiently

18. See pertinent data presented in *Training of National Technical Personnel for Accelerated Industrialization of Developing Countries* (1964). See also Kuin (1963), p. 436 especially.

19. See Kuin (1963).

or effectively as it might be. A similar problem was experienced by another firm in Britain that tried in vain to recruit locally a well-qualified man to head up its data processing and electronic computer operation. This second company also experienced great difficulty in obtaining competent computer programmers and operations research experts.

Executives of several multinational firms interviewed by this author have assented that educational constraints, particularly in less developed countries, often have a substantial negative impact on managerial effectiveness and firm operations and results. In many cases the educational system of a particular country has been the major limiting factor with regard to establishing a subsidiary operation in a particular country. It is possible for the foreign-based firm to import manpower from other countries to staff its operations, and/or to send promising nationals abroad for study. But there are usually limits as to how far a company will go in this direction. In the final analysis, the local educational system tends to play the paramount role in determining the types and quality of human resources available to the international firm.

Comments on research methodology

In general, if a given set of cultural constraints can be isolated, and if their impact on the management process and managerial effectiveness – i.e. the achievement of corporate objectives – can be determined even in an approximate way, the international firm may have a fairly powerful body of knowledge to apply to many of its problems. Research of the developmental type is clearly needed to determine which Cs generally tend to affect which Ps and Ds, in what ways, to what extent, and the impact of these relationships on overall managerial effectiveness. Research of the applied type can help individual firms improve operations and results or avoid potentially very risky foreign ventures, especially once the general relationships between various Cs, Ps and Ds are determined with a significant level of confidence.

The *extent* to which a given pattern or problem of management is determined by cultural constraints may be reflected by the proportion of comparable firms in a given country that follow the same pattern quite closely, or are affected by the same problem.

The *degree* to which a given pattern or problem of management is the result of various cultural constraints may be theoretically ascertained and measured by the time, expense, and/or proportion of non-nationals entailed in successfully and effectively deviating from the existing pattern, or in overcoming the problem, assuming it can be overcome.

For example, if a U.S. firm abroad – or even a local firm – finds that it must undertake a very costly and time consuming training programme in order successfully and effectively to deviate from a pattern of authoritarian management and/or highly centralized authority, to a pattern of more participative management and/or decentralization, this may imply that the existing pattern is constrained by various cultural variables to a fairly high degree.

Similarly, if the overseas firm must recruit a sizeable number of personnel from the U.S. in order successfully to implement a new management practice or technique or a new production process, this could mean that certain cultural constraints are quite potent. Or if a substantial amount of time and money must be expended in order to alleviate another type of problem which proves to be due to the dominant value system or deficient abilities and skills of the local population, this too would indicate that various cultural constraints are present to a high degree. One way to cross-check the degree to which certain cultural constraints are responsible for a particular management problem might be to estimate the time and expense required by the company to overcome a similar problem – or to implement a similar new practice or technique – in its U.S. operations, as compared to its foreign operations.

Only factual empirical evidence can reveal whether a different or new pattern of management is more successful with regard to the achievement of corporate objectives; and only intensive empirical research can determine whether the overall costs entailed in overcoming a problem due to cultural constraints are more than offset by benefits to the firm. If some of the questions, issues and problems discussed in this paper are dealt with effectively through empirical and experimental research of the developmental and applied types – instead of just talking about things rather superficially – it may be much easier for the foreign-based business enterprise advantageously to manipulate and adapt to the local cultural environment.

A fruitful research procedure to use in the area of international management might be a comparative case study model which is somewhat similar to the classical Latin Square experimental design. For our purposes we could intensively study over a period of time a U.S. company, its subsidiary firm in a particular foreign country, and a roughly comparable competing firm or group of firms – including if possible the most successful one – in this foreign country. For example, we might study Colgate-Palmolive in the U.S. and India, and one or more competing domestic Indian firms such as Tata; or IBM in the U.S. and Japan, and one or more roughly comparable Japanese firms.[20] For the firms to be comparable they all must employ roughly similar technology, and they must all be pursuing roughly the same basic objectives. Another necessary condition for this type of study would be that the U.S. international company chosen would prefer to implement a similar management process in its foreign subsidiaries, if possible, with a minimum of costs and unsought consequences.

The variables in the overall model would consist of the cultural environment represented by cultural constraints (Cs), elements of the management process (Ps), dynamic managerial problems (Ds), and managerial effectiveness (Es). The factors which make up the managerial effectiveness rating would probably include, in part, rate of return on invested and possibly working capital, market share, productivity as reflected by units of output produced and/or sold per employee per year, unit cost of production for major items in the product line, employee turnover, and so forth. It would be more meaningful if the factors determining managerial effectiveness were analysed over a period of, say, five years, since this would take into account the rate and effectiveness of innovations and/or improvements implemented, and hence the level of both short-run and long-run operating efficiency. The research model can be depicted as shown in the table on page 36.

The degree to which cultural variables tend to constrain various

20. This research approach was first suggested to me by my colleague at U.C.L A., Dr Anant Nagandhi.

	Cultural Constraints	*Elements of the Management Process*	*Dynamic Managerial Problems*	*Managerial Effectiveness*
U.S. Company	Cx	Px	Dx	Ex
U.S. Subsidiary in India or Japan	Cy	Py	Dy	Ey
Comparable Domestic Firm	Cz	Pz	Dz	Ez

elements of the management process in the overseas firm may be determined by analysing the difference between Px and Py as compared to the difference between Py and Pz, and/or by evaluating the overall costs and time entailed in deviating successfully from Py towards Px. Similarly, the degree to which various Cs affect various Ds may be ascertained by analysing the difference between Dx and Dy as compared to Dy and Dz, and/or by estimating the overall costs and time entailed in going from Dy to Dx, where this seems desirable. By using this model it may also be possible to determine, at least roughly, the effect that various Cs, through their impact on various Ps and Ds, have on managerial effectiveness in each case.

If research of this type could be successfully undertaken in several diverse countries. there would be promise of substantially greater insight into the vital question posed earlier: *To what extent can American management principles, practices, and general know-how be transferred effectively to different countries, at what cost, and to what degree and extent is the overall process and effectiveness of management constrained by cultural variables?*

Concluding remarks

It is evident that a vast amount of work remains to be done in the cultural sphere of international business management. However, there appears to be no conceptual reason why considerable progress cannot be made by energetic and able scholars with the help of business practitioners – and research funds.

Many in the field of management contend that, in the long run, there will be a convergence of cultures, as well as applicable management principles and practices, throughout the industrial world.[21] However, this type of convergence is likely to take decades, generations, and even centuries in some extreme cases. In the interim it seems apparent that cultural constraints will continue to have varying, and often major, impacts on managerial performance and the achievement of corporate objectives in international business firms, throughout much or most of the world.

References

BRODBURN, N. (1960), 'The managerial role in Turkey, A psychological study', unpublished doctoral dissertation, Harvard University.

DAVIS, K. (1964), 'Managing productivity in developing countries', *Management International*, vol. 4, no. 2, pp. 71–2.

FARMER, R. N. (1964), 'The ethical dilemma of American capitalism', *California Management Review*, Summer, pp. 47 ff. and footnotes 17, 18 and 32.

FARMER, R. N., and RICHMAN, B. M. (1964a), 'A model for research in comparative management', *California Management Review*, Winter, pp. 55–68.

FARMER, R. N., and RICHMAN, B. M. (1964b), 'Ownership and management: the real issues', *Management International*, vol. 4, no. 6.

FARMER, R. N., and RICHMAN, B. M. (1965), *Comparative Management and Economic Progress*, Richard D. Irwin, Inc., Illinois.

GONZALES, R., and MACMILLAN, C., Jr (1961), 'The universality of American management philosophy', *Journal of the Academy of Management*, April, pp. 33–41.

HAIRE, M. (1964), 'The social sciences and management practices', *California Management Review*, Summer, pp. 3–10.

HAIRE, M., GHISELLI, E., and PORTER, L. (1963), 'An international study of management attitudes and democratic leadership', *CIOS/XIII: International Management Congress*, 16–20 September, Council for International Progress in Management Inc., New York, pp. 101–4.

HARBISON, F., and MYERS, C. (1959), *Management in the Industrial World*, McGraw-Hill Inc., New York.

21. See Likert (1963), pp. 110–14; and Richman and Farmer (1966).

HARBISON, F., and MYERS, C. (1964), *Education, Manpower and Economic Growth*, McGraw-Hill Inc., New York.
KUIN, P. (1963), 'Meeting economic and social needs in a variety of countries', *CIOS/XIII: International Management Congress*, 16–20 September, Council for International Progress in Management Inc., New York, p. 436 especially.
LIKERT, R. (1963), 'Trends towards a world wide theory of management', *CIOS/XIII: International Management Congress*, 16–20 September, Council for International Progress in Management Inc., New York, pp. 110–14.
MCCLELLAND, D. (1961), *The Achieving Society*, Van Nostrand, Inc., Princeton, N.J.
MCCLELLAND, D. (1962), 'Business drive and national achievement', *Harvard Business Review*, July–August.
MASLOW, A. (1943), 'A theory of human motivation', *Psychological Review*, vol. 50, pp. 370–96.
MERRILL, H. (1963), 'Listening post', *Management News*, vol. 36, no. 1, January.
NEWMAN, W., and LOGAN, J. (1959), *Business, Policies and Management*, Southwestern Publishing Company, Cincinnati, Ohio.
OBERG, W. (1963), 'Cross-cultural perspectives on management principles', *Journal of the Academy of Management*, June, pp. 129–43.
RICE, A. (1958), *Productivity and Social Organization: The Ahmedabad Experiment*, Tavistock Publications, 1958.
RICHMAN, B. (1965), *Soviet Management: with Significant American Comparisons*, Prentice Hall Inc., Englewood Cliffs, N.J.
RICHMAN, B., and FARMER, R. (1964), 'Ownership and Management: The Real Issues', *Management International*, vol. 4, no. 6, 1964.
SUNDARAM, K. (1963), 'Social and human problems in introducing technical change', *CIOS/XIII: International Management Congress*, 16–20 September, Council for International Progress in Management Inc., New York, pp. 495–8.
UNITED NATIONS ECONOMIC AND SOCIAL COUNCIL (1964), *Training of National Technical Personnel for Accelerated Industrialization of Developing Countries*, Parts II and III, E/3901, Add. 1 and 2, 3 June, New York.
WHYTE, W., and WILLIAMS, L. (1963), 'Supervisory leadership – an international comparison', *CIOS/XIII: International Management Congress*, 16–20 September, Council for International Progress in Management Inc., New York, pp. 481–8.

2 Ross A. Webber

Convergence or Divergence?

Portions of this article are adapted from the author's *Culture and Management: Text and Readings in Comparative Management* (Richard D. Irwin, Inc. Illinois, 1970). It also appeared in *Columbia Journal of World Business*, vol. IV, no. 3, May–June 1969.

Spectre

'A spectre is haunting Europe.' In such chilling terms over one hundred years ago Karl Marx and Friedrich Engels announced the doomed future of capitalism and the glories to come of communism. Today, equally frightening spectres haunt Europe as well as Asia, Africa and the New World. They are the dual terrors of instant annihilation in a nuclear Armageddon or gradual starvation on an overcrowded planet. In recent years these two concerns have produced more international cooperation than any other. Both the Soviet Union and the United States have attempted to limit the spread of nuclear weapons. Every nation and international institution encourages economic development. If anything, more has been done on the latter than the former. As never before, mankind sees salvation in economic development.

The peoples of the world share a great common force – their human nature. Whatever myriad and bizarre forms the pursuit of wants takes, we all share certain needs. As soon as one need is relatively satisfied, a new one emerges. The hierarchical model of these human needs implies motivational dynamism. To be sure, some of the more somnolent societies have not yet started to climb this ladder, but eventually they too will set out on what is a never-ending quest. The underlying dynamism of man's needs is apparent. Increasingly, mankind is becoming united in the belief that economic growth is vital for satisfaction of the full range of human needs. Religious and secular alike now see economic development as a worthy task for the best brains and toughest muscles.

Whether the ultimate objective of this growth is sensual enjoyment or spiritual fulfilment is irrelevant – at least in the short run. 'Greed is the tie that binds,' according to the cynic. Whatever the moral implications, economic interests are exerting powerful unifying pressures. In 1968 the World Council of Churches (Protestant and Orthodox) and the Roman Catholic Church announced 'the most advanced and ambitious Christian unity experiment yet undertaken'. What was it? A conference on world cooperation for economic development held in Beirut, Lebanon. The director of the programme was a Catholic priest who was paid by both sponsors – the first time this had been done. The Reverend Dr Eugene Carson Blake, Secretary General of the World Council, was quoted as having remarked when the idea of the joint appointment was first raised that 'you really discover mutuality when you start *paying* together'.

The forces for convergence in managerial philosophy and practice stem from this common economic orientation. In recent years, a number of articles and books have suggested that such convergence is taking place.[1] Nonetheless, it is a subject which should be stated in the form of a question, the answer to which depends upon cultural factors and the organizational level under consideration. This distinction is frequently ignored. At the top of the firm and in the relationship of man to machine, there does seem to be convergence. Governments are playing larger economic roles in capitalist countries; markets more in socialist countries. In both, managers and many large firms have gained substantial power and autonomy. Similarly, the basic technology of the industrial age is very much alike in Oshkosh, Minsk and Brazzaville.

In the middle, however, where managers communicate, motivate and make decisions, convergence may be less dramatic, for it is here that cultural differences have their sharpest impact. Here, there are forces both of uniformity and diversity. A common economic motivation is manifest in technology, education and

1. Kerr, Dunlop, Harbison and Myers (1961); Haberstroh (1961); Tinbergen, Linnemann, Pronk (1966); Thompson (1965); Moore (1965).

philosophy; diversity is found in time, natural resources, demography and, most important, culture. The factors fostering uniformity appear to dominate at the macro-economic and the micro-technical levels – the place of business in the nation and the use of modern technology in the plant. The forces of divergence, however, assert stronger influences on the philosophy and practice of managers within the firm.

Technology

Whether macro or micro, the most common argument for convergence is the imperative of industrialization itself. Technology – like the language of mathematics – is universal. By obeying laws of reason and science, men of varying cultural and ideological positions presumably can agree on the best machine design or most desirable production system. For the most part, this technology is Western. The hardware of Europe and the United States is spreading over the globe so that the machine tended by the U.S. worker may be more modern, but it is not fundamentally different from that of the Indian or Brazilian workers where industrialization is just taking place. Demands for attention, response and care exerted by the machines on their human operators are essentially identical.

If there is only one best technology, and if a country desires to industrialize, the resulting engineering of work tends to affect occupations similarly. Traditional manual systems of power and manufacture are eliminated or reduced to marginal importance. Elaborated division of labour and graduated skill levels emerge. The unskilled 'hired man', 'handyman' or 'millhand' all tend to become irrelevant; witness how difficult it is for unskilled minority groups in cities to find jobs – jobs they could usually obtain in rural areas years ago. The dumb, phlegmatic, ox-like Schmidt that Frederick W. Taylor made famous fifty years ago has become the literate and fairly articulate Smith with skills that management needs and for which substitutes are much harder to find.

As skill rises, power rises also. Employees are given responsibility for more expensive equipment and more critical decisions. Since a manager in this situation finds it difficult to supervise everyone, his subordinates' commitment to work conscientiously becomes more important. The need for subordinate consent gives them influence. Power may become less unilateral and management less autocratic.

The imperatives of the machine cannot be confined to the shop. Off the job, a man's position in society tends to change and the social structure becomes more open. Choosing one's parents is still important, but it should become less so. What a man does takes on increasing importance instead of what a man is. This leads to convergence.

> The same technology calls for much the same occupational structure around the world – in steel, in textiles, in air transport. The occupational role of a man gives him a place in society that affects his behavior in many ways. Also, there comes to be a growing diversity of occupations and of levels of management, and no really clear cut dividing lines are visible to all. The occupation takes the place of the class.[2]

In corroboration, it has been demonstrated that industrialization tends to be associated with greater opportunity for the relatively modest-born.[3] The performance of the high achiever becomes the determinant of success, rather than nepotism.

More sophisticated technology and greater educational requirements give workers more mobility. With skill there is additional freedom to move – as has occurred in the U.S.S.R. in the post-war era. When Ivan has a skill which the state needs, and for which a number of plant managers are willing to pay, it is not easy to limit his mobility without recourse to expensive and inefficient policing.

Technology, therefore, exerts a major force towards making work and society more similar wherever industrialization occurs: fewer unskilled jobs, greater division of labour, less paternalistic or autocratic management, social level defined by occupation and greater opportunity for the son to move higher up the occupational and social ladder.

Education

Industrialization must be served, and education becomes a servant.

2. Kerr, Dunlop, Harbison and Myers, op. cit.
3. McClelland (1961).

Complex technology and sophisticated organization require training in a variety of specialities. Vast expansion of the educational system is required to support this industrialization, but subsequently, people demand education as a right over and above any contribution it makes to economic growth. The way of life facilitated by industrialization calls for other specialists to attend to needs off the job.

In short, an industrial society must educate its people. Workers must be literate so that they can understand instructions, follow directions and keep records; and so that managers, engineers and civil servants can be trained to operate the new mixed public and private production system. Beyond that are the needs for doctors, lawyers, scientists, professors and other professional personnel.

The correlation of educational development and per capita income suggests that higher income is associated with expanded education – although cause and effect are not entirely clear.[4] The demand for education and educated people supplements and coincides with management's demand for capable people regardless of their origins. One result: a levelling of economic and social disparities. The scarcity of skilled persons is gradually reduced, lessening their economic advantage; a greater number of intelligent people are needed; the advantages of the highly born are undermined.

With industrialization the gap between managers and workers does not disappear. Managers will remain substantially more educated than workers, but the workers' education will improve. The relative gap between a high school and college education in an industrialized country is less than that between the 'no education' of workers and the 'some education' of managers in less-developed nations.

Philosophy

Jet-set is the term applied – partly enviously, partly critically – to the modern élite flying among the capitals of the world. They may be a force for uniformity. If the élite of the economic world become a true élite – the most effective and productive people

4. Harbison and Myers (1964).

regardless of birth or advantage – they may become more alike in their pragmatism. Ideology should fade because of its irrelevancy to the problems faced. Man has a great ability to maintain belief in false ideology in the face of contradictory evidence, but realism may replace it.

It is probable that the aims of economic development (elimination of poverty, greater choice in business occupation, a better life) are more universally accepted today than ever before. This commitment to economic development tends to undermine adherence to ideological principles – to the dismay of dogmatists of both left and right who with equal indignation cry out that we are sacrificing our integrity (be it capitalist or socialist), compromising our principles (be they Marxian or Smithian), and flirting with the devil (be he solid red, or red, white and blue striped) – all in the name of economic expediency.[5]

Ideologies change

'No one can touch the United States in industrial management,' a Communist official of the Czechoslovakian Institute of Management has stated, echoing what many Eastern European economists elsewhere have believed but dared not say. The Institute presents an unabashedly U.S.-influenced programme of case studies, industrial games, marketing, sociology, psychology, research and development and other Western techniques that until relatively recently were either unknown or unmentionable in the Communist world. Jaroslaw Jirasek, the director of the programme, says, 'We are in a very bad position after those years when entrepreneurial decisions were made by centralized management. It is not easy to change men's minds,' he maintains, 'but if we cannot change men's minds, we must change the men because one clever man cannot be replaced by a thousand idiots.'

The reason for these changes? Economics. Faced with serious economic problems, Czechoslovakia 'has no choice but to change and in a very short time. Otherwise, we will not be able to keep in the front of the European Movement.'

5. See Marko (1968); Terestchenko (1967); Pethybridge (1967).

Most managers, owners, politicians and customers want efficiency. Hindering ideologies, beliefs and dogmas surrender to economic pragmatism. In obtaining this efficiency, knowledgeable men – rather than family members or political appointees – are needed to make the important decisions. This implies managerial autonomy. The large-scale production characterizing industrialization requires enormous capital accumulation and complex technology involving elaborate organization. Risk must be minimized in order to facilitate and safeguard the expenditure of time and money to initiate the operation. Communist enterprise managers and corporate executives all desire to minimize uncertainty; they want to control everything that can adversely affect their organization. As John Kenneth Galbraith has said, this means autonomy and control: autonomy from uncontrollable pressures be they market or bureaucratic in origin; as much control as possible over prices, supply and demand.

To manage this organization effectively, executives must be free of interference from incompetent owners or ignorant politicians. In the Galbraithian thesis it is assumed that only professional managers and specialists have the knowledge necessary to run modern complex enterprises. The result: organizational decisions are increasingly centralized in professional management. For a socialist country this implies decentralization from state decision making; for the capitalist nation, it means increased central control by human decision makers (usually corporate planners and executives) versus impersonal control of the market. In either system, the central government has responsibility to decrease uncertainty stemming from economic cycles – especially by ensuring a high level of total economic demand.

National implications

Observing these economic developments, a prophet might maintain that national societies will become more alike because nations are irrelevant and will disappear. In politics, we have heard these arguments for a long time from Communists, Nazis, United World Federalists and super United Nations supporters; from men as different as Karl Marx, Adolf Hitler, Wendell Willkie and Pope John XXIII. All have argued that national governments and boundaries divide men, promote war and compound the human tragedy. Always, however, economic interests, as well as military and political factors, presumably contradicted their unrealistic and, in some cases, frightening arguments.

Exploitation of markets, protection of industry, enrichment of the mother country, insulation from foreign depressions or inflations, and, frequently, defence of liberty itself have all called for strong national boundaries. Currently, however, the economic pressures may be changing – or are starting to change. Adam Smith's old fear of corporations growing and spreading beyond the control of market and government apparently is coming true. It is suggested that we are moving towards a world of very large multinational firms and very small entrepreneurial firms of the one-man-show variety. For many reasons the middle-sized concern will wither or be gobbled up by the monster multinationals – so much so that by 1985 some 300 multinational companies may dominate the world economy.[6]

In short, modern business firms, capitalist or socialist, are transcending national boundaries. Governments only get in the way. A veteran observer of international developments wrote in 1968:

> An industrialized world is held together by the large number of corporate bodies and by their widening role. The corporation groups the nationals into a new loyalty – a functional identity across all borders. The day may well come when the majority of people in all nations will have their functional loyalties to one or more supranational corporate bodies. They may well become conscious of basic commitments, values, and interests unrelated to the state or the nation.[7]

It was the dream of Marx and the early Socialists that workers everywhere would perceive their common interests, throw out the anachronistic nation-states and institute a Communist society in which national boundaries would disappear. These dreams were consumed in the fires of the First World War when the working men of the Western world marched to battle in the names of their respective fatherlands. They went willingly and even happily if

6. See Perlmutter (1968).
7. Tannenbaum (1968).

the accounts of the era can be believed. It is ironic that now the more potent forces for internationalization are the business interests so hated by early Socialist reformers.

The forces of uniformity in economic activities and management are potent. Does this mean inevitable similarity around the globe?

Inevitable is a vague term. 'Inevitably' there will probably be convergence in managerial, economic – and even political – philosophy and practice. Nonetheless, it is a long way off for there are forces of diversity as well. Time, basic resources and demography may be touched on briefly. Culture requires more consideration.

Time

Modern technology is grafted on to societies at different times, when the societies are at different states of economic development. When this technology is introduced into a culture, it is not automatically accepted. Stresses are produced. These may be suppressed, but the tensions spring up elsewhere. Society may adapt to suit the technology, but unintended changes also occur in other institutions. This cycle of stress, accommodation and new stress may dampen out, but the process is undoubtedly gradual. Thus, the introduction of modern technology and industrialization into Japan produced factories and machines very like Great Britain. Nonetheless, life within the plants has not been identical. The countries were different at the onset of development so the stresses produced in the two countries were different: family-centred in Japan, class-centred in Great Britain. The unanticipated and uncontrolled propagation of this stress affects different aspects of each culture producing new diversity at the same time that the forces of uniformity are being felt.

Basic resources

The natural resources of countries differ, and this limits the pace and direction of development. Technology may eventually diminish the importance of natural resource differences: atomic power can substitute for water power, plastics for wood, man-made materials for natural. However, these differences are real, and they cause management to differ because each industry lends a characteristic style to its managerial philosophy and practice. Thus a textile-dominated nation will tend to develop different management from that of a petroleum-rich country.

Demography

The density of population obviously varies and exercises a divergent influence. A relatively empty country is likely to have a different course of development than a heavily populated one. The United States has always had higher wages, and labour recruitment was more difficult than in Europe. Labour efficiency was more critical, and a significant increase in the standard of living was made easier. High valuation of the individual worker and the attention that he deserves were more common. Barriers to immigration and man's uncertain ability or unwillingness to control births suggest that these differences will not soon disappear.

Culture

We are immersed in a sea. It is warm, comfortable, supportive and protecting. Most of us float below the surface; some bob about catching glimpses of land from time to time; a few emerge from the water entirely. That sea is our culture.

Most of us act, think and dream in terms of the norms and standards we have absorbed from the culture in which we are reared. That which our culture values, we value; that which our culture abhors, we abhor. By education or experience, some of us become aware that there are other values and beliefs that make sense too – as much or more than our own. But we see them hazily and, all too often, with age the awareness slips away. A few, very few, are able to escape, overcome parochialism and see the world more objectively. But escape is by no means entirely desirable. We can feel alone and unsure when the comfortable values of our old culture fall away, become irrelevant and are replaced by nothing.

What is 'right'?

Culture is a great source of security that tells us frequently what is 'right' and 'good'. The problem, as numerous anthropologists have pointed out, is that what is right and good may appear irrational and unpredictable. Kissing is an example. In Micronesia, the idea of putting mouth on mouth is unthinkable. For the anti-oral Micronesians, the 'female breast has no sexual significance; it is an organ for providing food for the nursing infant'. The U.S. mammary culture 'must seem very queer to non-breast-loving cultures'.[8]

Culture influences what behaviour is approved or disapproved. This in turn affects management. Consider two students who are playing a game of interpersonal conflict.[9] Each contestant has two strategies from which he may choose with the following results: If both choose Strategy A, each receives $3.00; if both choose Strategy B, each receives $2.00; if they split on Strategies AB or BA, each receives $1.00.

		Player No. 1 A	Player No. 1 B
Player No. 2	A	$3.00	$1.00
	B	$1.00	$2.00

Given this matrix, upon repeated plays Master of Business Administration candidates from the United States tend to stabilize on Strategy A and earn $3.00. Such is not the case for students from Korea. Korean students at the same school tend to select strategy B and earn $2.00. Why?

Perhaps cultural factors cause the difference. It would appear that the Koreans will not cooperate. Either they distrust each other, or they want to minimize the earnings of their competitors even more than to maximize their own. Depriving another would seem to be more important than individual gain – in contrast to the U.S. attitude.

Of course, this experiment does not prove that personal non-cooperativeness is characteristic of Korean society, If it were, however, it would have implications for management. Organization size might have to be limited to facilitate central control

8. Bates (1968).

9. For this information, I am indebted to Professor David W. Conrath of the Wharton School of Commerce and Finance.

since unsupervised cooperation is not likely. Top management might be afraid to delegate authority because they are not sure that subordinate managers will work in the organization's interest. Whatever the actual situation, cultural factors can influence organizational behaviour and management.

In all cultures, existing institutions, ideologies and practices have lives of their own. They are persistent in the face of change. Bare bottoms are an issue in Tanzania, where President Julius Nyerere has ordered the Masai tribe to alter their mode of dress. The haughty Masai, who have long considered themselves

Table 1 The elements and their relationships

Forces of Uniformity	*Managerial Interfaces*	*Forces of Diversity*
Technology	Man – Work	Cultural Inertia
Education	Man – Man	Time and Stage of
Pragmatic Philosophy	Firm – Environment	Development
		Natural Resources
		Demography

superior to their more advanced countrymen, are strongly resisting the government directive to cover up the one buttock that they proudly bare. The Masai's vanity will probably give way to the demands of a more sophisticated state, but it will not be an easy battle. Attitudes towards life and acceptable behavioural patterns are slow to change even under the pressures of economic necessity. They will probably change only as little as necessary to adapt to the new technology of modern industrialization. Residual cultural differences will remain for a long time.

Uniqueness is really the basis of diversity. At any moment, every country is unique in its cultural factors, economic development, natural resources and demographic characteristics. Some of these may be similar to other countries, but the net mix is unique. The values, beliefs and habitual behaviour patterns strongly resist change because they impart security.

The impact of these forces on management as a whole cannot be analysed. Because the factors of uniformity and diversity affect the various aspects of management differently, we need to distinguish among three relationships in management. These are the three levels or interfaces: (1) man and his work, (2) man and man (superior-subordinate, lateral and diagonal relations) and (3) organization and its environment. Table 1 summarizes the elements.

Arithmetic does not help. At present, there is no way of totalling the forces for uniformity and those for diversity in a single country to obtain a net number sugggesting the rate or direction of movement. The arguments for convergence and divergence vary on the three interfaces.

Man and work

The case of convergence in the relationship between man and his work – especially man and the machine – is compelling. Technological and economic pressures are so clear and strong that work for the average man will tend to become more alike. His equipment, his portion of the task, his training for the job, the expectation that he appear and be on the job not at his own volition but that of the employer – all will tend to be similar in the not very distant future.

Firm – environment

Similarly, the forces of convergence are strong on the relationship between the firm and its environment – customers, competitors and government. The growth of professional managers administering fairly autonomous firms is widespread in both capitalist and socialist countries. They must be relatively free from interference by ignorant owners, politicians and bureaucrats. Managers must also be responsible to customers and know what goods are needed. As the Russians found out, managers can produce unwanted goods which pile up in warehouses. In 1968, Premier Aleksei N. Kosygin called on Soviet industry to overcome the gap in consumer goods between the Soviet Union and the United States. Invoking the example of 'capitalist monopolies', he urged Soviet management to reduce delays in producing and marketing new consumer products. 'In the capitalist countries,' he said, 'the monopolies are obliged to react quickly to the needs of the customers and produce modern types of products and search for new rational forms of organization of production and its control.' Just how monopolistic firms are 'obliged' is not entirely clear. If the market forces them to respond, then they must not be completely monopolistic. Still, the point is valid: some avenue of influence from customers to managers is essential and is apparently developing in the Communist states.

Man – man

Less clear is convergence in the man to man, superior – subordinate, and peer relationships within the organization. There is a possible trend towards strengthening of the subordinate's importance and bargaining power through his increased knowledge and the more intricate technology he operates. This implies greater responsiveness by superiors to subordinates. More democracy may be inevitable in economic organizations because of the two-way flow of influence arising out of technical sophistication and employees' skills; fear and power become less effective.[10]

Equality in decision making and harmony of interests is not implicit in this evolution of influence processes. If the prediction has validity, conflict and bargaining between interest groups will undoubtedly characterize the more democratic business firm just as they do every democratic state. The hierarchical structure may change, but the general shape will remain. Differentiated positions in a hierarchy are probably essential because they reflect fundamental functions in the managerial process.

Superiors and subordinates will remain, but the basis of motivation may have to be shifted. With industrialization, government-generated security and improved living standards, management can no longer concentrate its appeal on low-level physical and security needs. Higher drives for competence, achievement and autonomy become relevant. If the manager wants to tap the ability of skilled subordinates, he must gain their commitment. This means he must provide opportunities on the job to satisfy higher needs. At least among managers, there seems to be a universality of higher level drives for self-actualization in several nations and

10. See Slater and Bennis (1964).

various cultures.[11] As man gains freedom from slavery to basic needs, he will attempt to satisfy drives higher in the hierarchy of needs.

These higher needs are not necessarily more noble; striving for ego satisfaction or power can be brutal. But management must respond to them. Satisfied needs are irrelevant for motivation. To obtain commitment and effort, management must motivate by appealing to the next appropriate level of unsatisfied needs. If the hierarchy of needs is truly universal, management the world over will have to provide opportunities for participation, competence and autonomy. From civil rights to education, from poor ghetto dwellers to affluent students, in Washington and Warsaw, the most profound social revolution in the world today is the struggle for democratic processes in decision making.

In addition, in the drive for efficiency there are pressures to impersonalize the managerial process. Family membership, social class, religion, perhaps even colour may tend to lose their centrality as criteria for hiring and promotion decisions in favour of judgement about ability and potential.

Slow process

Despite these forces for uniformity in managerial philosophy and practice, however, the process will be slow. Managerial leadership is affected by demographic conditions causing labour shortage or excess. If excess, management is unlikely to be overly concerned about employees. Even more important, the diversity of cultural values, beliefs, habits and traditions exerts profound influence on managerial relations. Patterns of respect, awe, contempt and deference are deep-seated. What is thought desirable or worthy in life will influence inter-personal relations, especially leadership style.

A comparative study of similar U.S. and Norwegian factories demonstrates that a positive worker's response to more participative management in the United States is not matched in a different cultural setting.[12] In Norway the workers are suspicious and antagonistic. Other studies indicate the different values attributed

11. See Haire, Ghiselli and Porter (1966).
12. See French, Israel and As (1960).

to direction versus persuasion as managerial tactics in different cultures.[13] German managers place high value on the former, low on the latter; Japanese managers vice versa; and Americans in between (although closer to the Japanese). Cultural factors also influence the methods and directions of communications in South American and North American organizations. Complaints, suggestions and criticisms just do not flow upward in a Venezuelan company.[14]

Cultural factors such as attitudes towards authority, achievement and personal risk exercise more influence on the interpersonal aspects of management than on the man-technology or firm-environment interfaces. The forces of uniformity are less clear and imperative on the methods management uses to communicate, coordinate and motivate. The sharp differences existing in these processes between U.S. and foreign companies, and indeed between domestic firms, testify to the divergence in managerial philosophy and practice that exists, and may always have, within organizations. For a long time at the least, cultural factors will exert a strong and differentiating influence upon managerial philosophy and practice: less on technological and production decisions, less on the relations of man and job, less on the firm's relationship to its customers and society; but more on the methods of motivation, patterns of communication and styles of leadership.

References

BATES, M. (1968), *Gluttons and Libertines: Human Problems of Being Natural*, Random House, New York.

FRENCH, J. R. P., ISRAEL, J., and AS, D. (1960), 'An experiment in participation in a Norwegian factory', *Human Relations*, no. 18.

HABERSTROH, C. J. (1961), 'Organizational structure – social and technical elements', *Industrial Management Review*, March.

HAIRE, M., GHISELLI, E., and PORTER, L. (1966), *Managerial Thinking*, John Wiley, New York.

HARBISON, F., and MYERS, C. (1964), *Education, Manpower and Economic Growth*, McGraw-Hill, New York.

13. See Haire, Ghiselli and Porter, op. cit.
14. See Whyte (1961).

KERR, C., DUNLOP, J. T., HARBISON, F., and MYERS, C. (1961), 'Industrialism and World Society', *Harvard Business Review*, January–February.

MCCLELLAND, D. (1961), *The Achieving Society*, Van Nostrand, Princeton, N.J.

MARKO, K. (1968), 'Soviet ideology and Sovietology', *Soviet Studies*, University of Glasgow.

MOORE, W. E. (1965), 'Global sociology: the world as a singular system', *The American Journal of Sociology*, March.

PERLMUTTER, H. (1968), 'The 300: some reflections on the future of the international business firm', a lecture given at Chief Executive Conference, *Business International Roundtable*, Bermuda, January.

PETHYBRIDGE, R. (1967), 'The assessment of ideological influence on east europeans', *The Public Opinion Quarterly*, September.

SLATER, P. E., and BENNIS, W. G. (1964), 'Democracy is inevitable', *Harvard Business Review*, March–April.

TANNENBAUM, F. (1968), 'The survival of the fittest', *Columbia Journal of World Business*, March–April.

TERESTCHENKO, V. (1967), 'Advertisingwise, here's looking at you', *Industrial Marketing*, August.

THOMPSON, E. H. D. (1965), 'Is a world-wide philosophy emerging?', *Management International*, April.

TINBERGEN, J., LINNEMANN, H., PRONK, J. P. (1966), 'The meeting of the twain', *Columbia Journal of World Business*, Summer.

WHYTE, W. F. (1961), *Men at Work*, Richard D. Irwin, Illinois.

3 Karlene H. Roberts[1]

On Looking at an Elephant: An Evaluation of Cross-Cultural Research Related to Organizations

Research and discussion related to cross-cultural studies of organizational behaviour are reviewed. Of the 526 publications originally uncovered, selected articles are assessed. The literature is categorized into twenty-six substantive areas: attitudes and values; attitude change; bibliographies; conflict resolution and ethnocentrism; decision making and bargaining; economics; education, creativity, and intelligence; efficiency and productivity; general; international business; inter-personal behaviour; labour; language and communication; leadership (small group); management; management development; motivation and achievement; national character and stereotypes; occupational prestige; organizational structure; perception; personality; personnel selection and testing; satisfaction; social and technical change; training for cross-cultural contacts. The literature is further classified on the bases of whether entries offer micro or macro data, and the vantage point from which research questions are asked. Thus, findings concerned with the characteristics of individuals in organizations, organizational sub-units, organizational totalities, and organizational interactions are considered. The author invites the reader to consider the available work in terms of three questions: (a) from this research, do we know anything new; (b) are investigations guided by theoretical principles that suggest relevant questions; and (c) are the methodological approaches useful? An attempt is made to answer these questions. The problem of defining 'culture' is discussed, and some of the variables that should be looked at in future work are suggested. A few substantive and methodological approaches that might be helpful are mentioned.
Excerpt from *Psychological Bulletin*, vol. 74, no. 5, 1970, pp. 327–50. Also published by *Institute of Industrial Relations*, Reprint no. 349, University of California, 1971.

The purpose of this paper is to provide a non-exhaustive analysis of cross-cultural research related to organizational behaviour.

1. The author would like to thank Professors Claude Faucheux, Harold Leavitt, and Donald Roberts for their helpful comments; the author alone, however, is responsible for the contents of the paper. Manuscript typing by the Institute of Business and Economic Research, University of California, Berkeley, in the preparation of this paper is acknowledged.
Requests for reprints should be sent to Karlene H. Roberts, School of Business Administration, University of California, Berkeley, California 94720.

While the author originally reviewed as much of the available literature as could be found, the paper is not comprehensive. It briefly summarizes the area and draws from key studies examples of important problems.

The problem of evaluating this kind of research is a little like the exercise of looking at an elephant – what one sees depends on one's vantage point. Students of organizations come from many disciplines. It is, therefore, virtually impossible to think simultaneously about the multitude of problems and research strategies addressed by anthropologists, economists, educators, psychologists, political scientists, sociologists, and students of business. The problem is magnified by the tendency of all these people to avoid talking to each other or trying to understand each other's concerns. The point of view taken here is necessarily psychological. The author's biases determine the kinds of questions covered and the methodological strategies discussed.

The study of organizations

Blau (1968) defined a formal organization as 'the existence of procedures for mobilizing and coordinating the efforts of various, usually specialized subgroups in the pursuit of joint objectives [1968, p. 298]'. He reminded us that social interactions and activities in organizations never correspond perfectly to official prescriptions. Organizational roles and sub-units can be replaced or changed. That is, organizational forms can change to meet changing internal or external conditions. Organizations are affected by internal phenomena, technology, the prevailing economy, and the socio-cultural milieu in which they exist. To systematize our knowledge, 'a theory of organization should not only establish the prevailing relationships between organizational features but also elucidate them in terms of underlying processes that produce them [Blau, 1968, p. 303]'.

That we are far from comprehensive theories about behaviour in organizations is illustrated by the many, often unrelated, concerns of various disciplines studying organizations, and by their lack of agreement about what questions are important. Educators and business people tend to be interested in some practical goal with respect to organizations. Psychologists and sociologists frequently examine internal-role and structural characteristics, and are beginning to think about organizational interrelations. Economists are concerned with interrelations among organizations, but their considerations are generally grounded in purely rational models of behaviour. Political scientists most frequently view policy development in organizations and the effect of policy on other variables or relationships. Finally, 'since formal organizations are largely a modern phenomenon and exist only in rudimentary form, if at all, in simple societies, anthropologists have been little concerned with them [Blau, 1968, p. 299]'. A few exceptions to these generalizations do exist.

The literature review

The literature review of the present paper followed the general strategy of searching publications that might aid researchers initiating cross-cultural behavioural investigations relevant to organizations. The primary criterion for inclusion of any report was that it suggest or test the notion that 'cultural differences' are related to some other variable. Second, the report had to provide data from, or discuss differences among, two or more cultures.[2]

The literature review covered the years 1962 to 1969 and included a few important earlier works. Most of the cited work originated in the United States. Primary resources were *The Psychological Abstracts*, *The Abstracts of the American Sociological Association*, *The American Political Science Review*, and appropriate business and educational journals. Language difficulties and limitations on available materials mean, of course, that coverage of existing work is incomplete. It is known from a number of sources (Campbell, 1968; Kelman, 1967; Tajfel, 1968) that most comparative behavioural research is initiated by Americans. Still, it would be beneficial to survey better such work conceived in other cultures.

In general . . .

The literature search of this review uncovered 526 publications

2. A few single-culture studies were included because they provide insights for cross-cultural researchers or because they are replicated in another country.

which were categorized into twenty-six substantive areas (see Table 1). Some publications were cross-classified. The categories were arbitrarily established after inspecting all entries. The 'general' category includes publications that do not fit neatly elsewhere. Examples of entries here are Ford, Prothro, and Child's (1966) comparisons of aesthetic judgements across cultures, and Casagrande's *In the Company of Man* (1960), a collection of portraits of individuals in rapidly changing societies. All entries were further sub-classified on the basis of whether they were simply discussions or anecdotal accounts, or whether they were examples of empirical work. About 46 per cent fell in the first category, and about 54 per cent provided empirical work containing at least some data.

The work can be even further classified on the basis of the vantage point from which a question is asked. Some researchers are concerned with individual behaviour or roles in organizations, others with organizational sub-units (either hierarchical or functional) or properties of entire organizations. A few are interested in the interactions of organizations with one another or the relationship of organizations to other aspects of their environments.

The research reviewed is a morass. Generally, it represents two traditions, but manifests very little communication between the two groups. One group of workers is interested in the effect of 'culture' on individual attitudes or behaviour in organizations (micro data). If they become interested in macro variables, such as characteristics of total organizations, they tend to aggregate individual measures to obtain organizational measures. The other group is preoccupied with the effect of 'culture' on organizational, structural, environmental and transaction variables. Data, if drawn at all, are from sources such as summaries of organizational, production or national economic statistics (macro data). This tradition is paralleled in American organizational research where one group of workers has been interested in the people without the organizations and another group in the organizations without the people (Bass, 1965, p. 240). Table 1 indicates the approach common in each substantive area. Some substantive areas are characterized by collection of both micro and macro data.

Table 1 Distribution of entries

Category	*Reviews, discussions, anecdotes*	*Empirical*	*Total*	*Micro data*	*Macro data*
Attitudes and values	5	46	51	X	
Attitude change	1	8	9	X	
Conflict resolution and ethnocentricity	10	2	12	X	
Decision making and bargaining	4	4	8	X	
Economics	3	4	7	X	X
Education, creativity, and intelligence	10	10	20	X	
Efficiency and productivity	3	4	7	X	X
General	15	9	24	X	
International business	13	5	18	X	X
Inter-personal behaviour	4	14	18	X	
Labour	11	4	15	X	X
Language and communication	15	16	31	X	
Leadership	5	6	11	X	
Management	35	28	63	X	X
Management development	15	4	19	X	
Motivation and achievement	2	16	18	X	
National character and stereotypes	18	16	34	X	
Occupational prestige	4	5	9	X	
Organizational structure	13	11	24	X	X
Perception	6	20	26	X	
Personality	13	30	43	X	
Personnel selection and testing	7	5	12	X	
Satisfaction	0	7	7	X	
Social and technical change	20	4	24		X
Training for cross-cultural contacts	5	2	7	X	
Bibliographics			9	X	

Where this occurs, micro data are usually collected on the independent variable (i.e. attitude measures of members of various cultural groups), and macro data on the dependent variable (i.e. organizational productivity data or statistics on gross national product).

What to look for

When examining the literature, three questions should be kept in mind: (a) Do we know anything new from the research? (b) Are investigations guided by principles which suggest relevant questions? (c) Is the methodological approach useful?

Based on the cross-cultural research, what do we know?

The literature offers such a wide variety of discussion and data that this question is difficult to answer and is left to the end of this review. A helpful strategy may be to look at the cross-cultural data in terms of our knowledge of a single culture. If we understand a single culture in its own terms, and its institutions and behaviours as products of that culture, then simply comparing behaviours across cultures has no meaning. We can, however, compare behaviours occurring in different cultures when they are shown to be functionally equivalent in the sense that the aspect of behaviour in question represents attempts of the compared culture to solve the same recurrent problem (Berry, 1969). Behaviour in one society may not initially appear related to its counterpart in a second society. Functional equivalencies are naturally occurring phenomena that are discovered, rather than created or manipulated.

As an example of what currently exists in the literature, what does it mean to say that steel factories on two continents differ in the education required at different managerial levels (Harbison, Kochling, Cassell and Reubman, 1955)? Can we assert that this difference is culturally caused? Do we first have a broad enough range of knowledge about managerial education and function in steel factories in a single culture to discuss the meaning of the differences across cultures? Second, is the question of differential management education across cultures the right question to ask?

What principles guide research?

This question asks whether we have good theories and definitions of terms. Anthropologists direct more attention to 'culture' than any other group. That even they are not in agreement on the meaning of the term is amply illustrated. Kroeber and Kluckhohn (1952) defined culture as

> patterns, explicit and implicit of and for behavior, acquired and transmitted by symbols constituting the distinctive achievement of human groups including their embodiment in artifacts; the essential core of culture consists of traditional . . . ideas and especially their attached values; culture systems may, on the one hand, be considered as products of action, on the other as conditioning elements of future action [p. 181].

In his discussion of the definition of a case, Whiting (1968) suggested that culture is best conceptualized in terms of the problem we wish to study. Observations of political differences may necessitate a different definition of culture than understanding weaning behaviour.

Finally, Hall 'treats culture in its entirety as a form of communication [1959, p. 37]'. Despite their diversity, the anthropologists strive to reach a theoretically useful description of culture. Psychologists, on the other hand, fail entirely to address the problem. They view culture as a vague entity, cast it as their independent variable, and forget it. Consequently, they do not know what aspects make up the domain 'culture', how they can be expected to influence anything else, or how various cultural groups in their samples differ. Culture is still a reality to be explained and as such cannot yet explain other realities.

Moving to the 'chicken and the egg' problem, or the attempt to link causally independent and dependent variables, gets us into even deeper trouble. We tend to search for cultural traits that cause other traits. Rather than search for cultural traits or phenotypical variables, we need to search for a set of genotypical variables that can be used to explain other variations. The search for differences in traits among cultures is futile as an explanatory device. Rather, the underlying functions which produce traits should interest us so that we can develop explanations of phenomena operating together and apart.

Whiting's argument was (1954) and is (1968) that through cross-cultural research we extend our knowledge of the range of variation in many variables. This range (the dependent variable) is supposedly influenced by culture (the independent variable). One underlying assumption is that we have a fairly adequate understanding of the variability in the dependent variable within a single culture, and that we have some reason to be interested in its range across cultures. Another assumption is that we know what the independent variable means. At least we should be able to define 'culture', for without this definition, a theory of culture is impossible to derive. Without some theoretical notions explaining culture and predicting its effect on other variables, we cannot make sense of cross-cultural comparisons. The problem is to explain the effects of culture on behaviour, not to make inferences about behaviour in spite of culture.

The cross-cultural findings of the cultural anthropologists originally interested psychologists because 'they provided evidence concerning the basic nature of man and the possible role of instincts in determining his behaviour [Wesley and Karr, 1966, p. 257]'. From the results, it was thought that one could modify or discount the universality of these instincts. In fact, Wesley and Karr (1966) stated that all that was needed was an example of the 'absence of a trait or behaviour in a different culture to provide a basis for rejecting a given instinct hypothesis [p. 257]'. There were theoretical bases on which to expect certain similarities between cultures, however coarse the theories. It is important that we are not fascinated by similarities *or* by differences in behaviours among cultures, but by both simultaneously. Ultimately, our research must reflect a view of culture as an intervening variable modifying and being modified by other phenomena. Campbell (1961) suggested that cross-cultural studies be used to prune and modify existing theories in order to minimize our own ethnocentrism.

Is the methodological approach useful?

Much of the cross-cultural work is in the form of impressions or anecdotal observation. Publications based on these approaches are not emphasized in this review since they provide less than adequate observations. Such work can, though, aid in hypothesis formation. Other design approaches should be examined for appropriateness to the question asked.

The review which follows classifies findings on the basis of the level of abstraction from which the organization is viewed. Observations of individual behaviour are assessed first, while studies of organizational sub-units and comparisons of total organizations are assessed later.

Characteristics of individuals in organizations

Discussions and studies of attitudes and values, management, perception, and personality variables comprise a large proportion of the literature (see Table 1). A few of the entries in any one of these categories are cross-referenced in some other categories, thus inflating the tabulation somewhat. If we combine these areas with entries under attitude change, leadership, motivation, national character, and occupational prestige, we see an extensive literature (both anecdotal and empirical), broadly concerned with roles as they exist or are perceived to exist in various cultures, however defined. Most of the investigations here are case studies or surveys, and although many of the data were not collected in organizational settings, the results often seem applicable to individual behaviour in organizations.

It is not surprising that the problems studied are those generally examined by behavioural scientists in American organizations. There are numerous cross-cultural studies of attitudes (Cortis, 1962; Granick, 1962; Haire, Ghiselli, and Porter, 1966; Knox, 1964; Lauterbach, 1961; McMillan, 1965; Porter and Siegel, 1965; Whitehill, 1964; Whyte and Williams, 1963), many investigations of leadership (Blake and Mouton, 1965; Chemers, Fiedler, Lekhyananda, and Stolurow, 1966; Chowdry, 1960; D'Antonio and Form, 1965; Fiedler, 1967; French, Israel, and Ås, 1960; Ganguli, 1963; Likert, 1963; Misumi and Takasaki, 1965; Philipsen, 1965; Whyte and Williams, 1963; Williams, Whyte, and Green, 1965), and some studies of motivation (Heller and Porter, 1966; Herzberg, 1965a, 1965b; Lazarus, Kessel, and Botha, 1969;

McClelland, 1961). The investigations tend to compare individuals at a single organizational level, but some cross-cultural work does compare individual characteristics across two levels (Desai, 1968; Granick, 1962). These areas are briefly covered, as well as a key area almost totally neglected in cross-cultural organizational considerations – communication. This final category is added because its current status offers a springboard for important future work.

All studies of individual behaviour are, of course, based on micro (individual) data collection.[3] Some theoretical guidance perhaps comes from individual psychology. However, considering attitudes, leadership, or motivation, do we know enough about their aetiology and behavioural variations in a single culture to engage in cross-cultural research?

Taken alone, attitude theory is probably the most researched area in American social psychology over the last few years (McGuire, 1966, pp. 475–7). This massive bombardment has resulted in a proliferation of theories, but little progress towards unification. Similar cases can be made for leadership and motivation research. The present evaluation, then, is carried out under the limitations imposed by inadequate theoretical underpinnings and poor explication of the independent variable (culture). It would require a separate treatise to evaluate adequately studies of individual behaviour relevant to organizations. Only a few instructive examples are offered.

Attitudes and values

The studies of attitudes and values rest on varied underpinnings or were carried out to find answers to specific, practical issues. Many are inextricable from leadership or motivation. Because of this, they are impossible to evaluate as a group. The investigations are generally descriptive of attitudes in different countries, but offer little in terms of explanation or prediction. Two diverse studies are offered as examples.

Haire *et al.* (1966) sought a cross-cultural description of mana-

3. Both micro and macro data are seen in studies classified under 'management'. Macro data, however, are either dependent-variable data or exist in studies of management systems, not of managers as individuals.

gerial motives and attitudes towards leadership and managerial role. They asked 3,641 managers from 14 nations to complete an attitude questionnaire. The instrument contained a number of questions about managerial style and measured the degree of need fulfilment, supposedly in terms of Maslow's need hierarchy. Managers from various countries were surprisingly alike in their responses to questions. One cluster of high-agreeing managers was composed of respondents from Norway, Denmark, Germany, and Sweden. Another included managers from France, Spain, Italy, and Belgium; and a third, Argentina, Chile, and India. Japan stood alone. The authors stated that these national clusters form because of 'strong bonds of similarity in language and religion . . . and many common elements in their cultural background [Haire *et al.*, 1966, p. 11]'. The study was descriptive of the way a particular set of managers answers a particular questionnaire. It focused on phenotypes, and one wishes the authors had devoted more attention to cultural genotypes. They may have been simply offering evidence that business is business, that managers in highly industrialized societies meet their problems in exactly the same ways, and that cultural differences on the dimensions observed do not exist. Finally, the authors sampled on the dependent variable – a problem which is discussed later in this review.

Knox (1964) reported a study of Argentine and American student attitudes towards government and corporations. Questions were asked about recommended action by governments towards corporations. More Argentines believed that governments should take some action either to stimulate or to eliminate corporations, and this finding was status-related for Argentines but not for Americans. Some reasons were offered for Argentine and American perceptual differences about the role of government, but no relevant data were given. Other than suggesting an answer to a specific question raised at a specific time for two narrowly defined samples, the study is not very useful.

Leadership

Of all the cross-cultural studies of individual behaviour relevant to organizations, more are devoted to participative management (or leadership) than to any other single topic. For example, the aforementioned Haire *et al.* (1966) study is appropriately catalogued here, as are the research programmes conducted by the Likert, Whyte, and Fiedler groups.

The basis for testing the Likert group's propositions overseas rests on their early work in the United States (Kahn and Katz, 1960; Likert, 1961). Likert and his colleagues were concerned with 'closeness of supervision'. Their American studies showed that supervision varied on this dimension and that work groups under general (as opposed to close) supervision exhibited a higher productivity and had more favourable attitudes towards job, supervisor, and company than work groups under close supervision. The American data suggest that the nature of supervision causes certain employee attitudes and outcomes, yet the authors offered only correlational data. The cross-cultural studies (Likert, 1963; Misumi and Takasaki, 1965) generally followed the same strategy and provided similar findings. Overall, the Likert group described processes and showed how to measure them. Like so much other work in the area, reasons for expecting cross-cultural similarities or differences are unclear.

Whyte and his co-workers (Whitehill, 1964; Whyte and Williams, 1963; Williams *et al.*, 1965) offered contrasting cross-cultural evidence about supervision. For instance, in their Peruvian study (Whyte and Williams, 1963; Williams *et al.*, 1965) they found worker satisfaction related to supervision which is understanding of workers, and there was a high correlation between closeness of supervision and satisfaction. This investigation rests on suspect data because questions were not back-translated, and samples were not comparable in terms of the kinds of organizations studied or the power in position of respondents.

Whyte, though, took a necessary step towards adequate conceptualization. In a recent book (Whyte, 1969, Chapter 32), he discussed the inter-cultural context of organizational research. He focused on three countries – Japan, Peru and the United States – using the latter as a basis for comparison. His stated reasons for selecting these cultures were his understanding of Peru and the United States, and the striking contrasts that Japan offered. He may have been approximating an ideal of initial cross-cultural research – selecting countries that are understood and that are known to be at extremes on a dimension of interest. Whyte interpreted business activity in terms of language meaning and cultural socialization of the three countries. For instance, based on his cultural analyses, he offered reasons to expect different relationships between closeness of supervision and satisfactions among workers in the three countries.

Fiedler's work (1965) must also be mentioned here because of his attention to simultaneous identification of situational and inter-personal leadership variables affecting output. He manipulated or observed natural differences in leader – follower relations, task complexity, and power position, and noted the interaction effect of these variables on group performance. In contrast to other cross-cultural researchers concerned with supervision, Fiedler used culture as a moderator variable which produced desired changes in his independent variables. For instance, he varied inter-personal closeness between supervisor and subordinate by using culturally homogeneous or heterogeneous groups. Culture was not explicated except to say that some relationship between national groups produces a situation such that, when these groups interact, there is a predictable effect on inter-personal relationships, etc. Fiedler's overseas study (1967) could have been carried out in virtually any setting in which the independent variables could be manipulated. It was probably unnecessary to go overseas.

Motivation

In the motivation literature one of the most exciting cross-cultural approaches in psychology can be found. McClelland (1961) and his colleagues worked towards explaining and predicating differences in entrepreneurial achievement based on cultural factors. They then used time-lag correlations to predict economic growth from the level of achievement motivation found in a culture. The basic problem here was explaining why some societies grow and others do not.

McClelland began by offering several theories of cultural growth and noting that tests of these explanations are wanting. He suggested that human motives may be related to economic development and that we should concern ourselves with economic growth throughout history, not simply at one particular time. The McClelland group worked towards a systems approach which said that cultural values foster need-achievement motivation, which, in turn, influences economic development, which modifies culture.

McClelland discussed the effects of some aspects of culture, such as core religious values and child-rearing practices, on the development of need achievement. Need-achievement motivation is defined as a dominant motive to excel, to work hard, to take calculated risks, to plan ahead, to set goals, and to rely on periodic feedback. It is said to foster economic development. In suggesting motives as a key variable, differentiating the need-achievement motive from others (need power and need affiliation), and then looking for causes of differential motivation, McClelland began to engage the problem of defining culture. Unfortunately, he did not stay long enough.

Originally, need achievement was measured by content analysing doodles and stories concocted to TAT pictures. However, if one is to look at historical relationships, it is not possible to ask people to draw random figures or tell stories. Thus, twentieth century (1925 and 1950) children's readers from many nations, and traces left from other periods (art work and literature from ancient Greece, literature from the Spanish middle ages, and literature and ballads from Tudor England) were content analysed for need-achievement themes.

Interrater reliability is high (·92–·98) for the readers, although it is difficult to say whether the stories chosen are representative of their culture's values. For most other indices of achievement, interrater reliabilities are sufficient, but the number of raters is usually two and the number of products (stories, art objects, etc.) is usually low.

Many of McClelland's dependent variable measures are even more innovative, but probably suffer in terms of validity. For the 1925 and 1950 periods, economic growth of countries was operationalized as per capita income and kilowatt hours of electricity produced. A regression line was established so that nations could be looked at in terms of their deviations from expected growth. Economic growth for various periods in ancient Greece was an index of area of trade. Since wine and olive oil were the major exports, the area of trade was delineated by the earthen jars uncovered abroad representing different time periods. For Spain in the Middle Ages, economic growth was indexed by shipping tonnage leaving various ports for the New World, and for Tudor England it was indexed by coal imports to London. Other societies have been studied in addition to those mentioned.

While both the independent and dependent variable measures suffer problems of reliability and validity, and although the single correlations between representations of need achievement (micro data) in a culture at one time and later economic development (macro data) are not startling, the amount of evidence supporting the prediction is overwhelming. That economic development does not predict need-achievement motivation is also shown.

McClelland and his group have converged on their propositions from a variety of directions, adding building block to building block. Each block is subject to unique error, which hopefully randomizes out over the set. The sampling problems in the combined set are enormous. It is impossible to know whether the independent variable sampling is representative of the cultural values at the time. An attempt was made at least to sample as many nations as possible in the investigations of modern development (1925 and 1950).

McClelland and Winter (1969) recently described an attempt to test the efficacy of a course designed to increase need-achievement motivation in Indian small industry and in commerce leaders. They reported a number of studies supporting the value of such training for American and other businessmen. The authors suffered great difficulty in obtaining and training Indian subjects, but did show differences in business activities and economic performance for trained and control groups. Dependent variable scoring was highly susceptible to both subject and investigator bias. In light of McClelland's original implication that need achievement is culturally trained throughout the early years of life, it is somewhat surprising that a ten-day training course can achieve similar ends.

Regretfully, another recently reported cross-cultural observation of need achievement (Lazarus *et al.*, 1969) did not build on the innovations of the McClelland group, but merely sought to find differences in achievement motivation in two cultural groups.

Besides Maslow's need hierarchy, which was referred to under attitudes (in the Haire *et al.* study), another motivation theory subjected to cross-cultural scrutiny is Herzberg's. *A priori*, Herzberg's (1966) notions offer no reason to expect cultural differences relating motivation and satisfaction. He did not suggest that differences in socialization lead to different expectations of need satisfaction, or that his hygiene factors and motivators were to be defined differently across cultures. It is difficult to know what to expect of cross-cultural application of the theory, and that the results of these studies generally support the American work (Herzberg, 1965a, 1965b) does not add incrementally to our knowledge.

Communication

A critical topic, when considering the behaviour of individuals in organizations, is communication. Yet cross-cultural communication studies actually done in organizations are non-existent. Existing studies are a potpourri and devote little attention to synthesizing concepts and principles. For instance, the effects of source on retention have been touched on (Lorimore, 1967; Lorimore and Dunn, 1968; Whittaker and Meade, 1968) with varying results. Some studies deal with the effects of stereotyping on communication (Campbell, 1967; Mishler, 1965; Scott, 1965) and others with the effects of communication on stereotyping (Pool, 1965; Triandis, 1967; Triandis and Vassiliou, 1967).

One of the more theoretically useful aspects of cross-cultural communication is concerned with meaning (Greenberg, 1966; Kumata and Schramm, 1956; Osgood, 1965; Tanaka and Osgood, 1962). The findings generally indicate that some cultural groups judge themselves similarly but view outsiders as different from themselves. Thus, Japanese and Korean descriptions of self are similar, but when each group describes the other, descriptions are clearly different from self. There are also aspects of language (particularly the way it represents affect, and the way affect mediates metaphor and symbolism), that appear to be universal. Extension of these findings is critical to the understanding of intra- and inter-cultural understanding.

Analyses of non-verbal as well as verbal communication (Hall, 1959, 1966; Little, 1968; Sommer, 1966, 1968) can help us to understand better organizational behaviour in various cultures because it will better enable a definition of culture. This is particularly true if Hall's (1959) definition of culture as communication is accepted, even with reservation. Better knowledge of the methods people use in communicating (facial expressions and gestures, as well as verbalizations), and what is communicated cannot help but increase our understanding of how inter-cultural organizational plans and activities are formulated and understood. Ekman's (Ekman and Friesen, 1968, 1969; Ekman, Sorenson, and Friesen, 1969) research programme looks particularly useful as a base for work related more directly to behaviour in organizations. The Ekman group described micro units of non-verbal communication, and suggested universals and idiosyncrasies in these, across cultures. Facial-effect displays from pre-literate peoples, not yet exposed to mass media, were compared with effect displays from members of modern cultures. Ekman and Friesen have done extensive work developing and refining their concepts and methods, and are concerned with functional equivalencies across cultures. Their findings support Darwin's notion that facial expressions of emotion are evolutionary and consequently similar among all human beings.

Problem areas

There are numerous examples of studies that are both difficult to classify and that suffer from other substantive and methodological problems. As an illustration, Triandis' (1967) investigation of 'interpersonal relations in international organizations' can be examined. Whether this study should be thought of as one concerned with individual behaviour in organizations or with organizational sub-units is questionable. International organizations are defined as organizations whose members are from several nations. Triandis' work, though, initially derives from the finding that workers and managers in a factory in a single culture, who perceive their environments similarly, have fewer communication problems than those who perceive their environments differently. Most of the work reported then goes on to deal with cognitive differences in various types of people, but not necessarily persons representing different units in a single organization. It is assumed that the way people perceive one another in international organizations will determine organizational effectiveness.

As a test of the proposition that people representing different cultures view each other differently, Triandis assessed the perceptions of Greeks and Americans towards each other. His sample consisted of Americans working in Athens, Americans living in Illinois, Greeks from Athens, and Greeks living in Illinois. There are differences in the way Greeks and Americans perceive each other. These differences, according to Triandis, are based on reward systems, competitive-cooperative training, and bureaucratization in the two cultures. While Triandis mentioned these variables and some of the methodological flaws in his study, he did not delineate what he meant by 'culture', which might have allowed him to systematize better the expected interactions of the various factors he considered. Furthermore, since he had not randomly sampled in either culture, or even paid very much attention to the characteristics of his sample, we do not know the probability of finding (right across the street in Illinois) a group of Americans rewarded, trained and bureaucratized like the Greek subjects. Neither do we know the probability of finding samples of Americans and Greeks who do not perceive each other differently.

In another treatise, Triandis (Triandis, Vassiliou and Nassiakou, 1968) addressed the topic of behaviour norms and intentions across cultures (Americans and Greeks). Why Americans and Greeks should be compared at all is unclear. Triandis hypothesized that the factor structure of behaviour norms is similar to the factor structure of behaviour intentions, and that cultures differ in their perception of the meaning of social behaviours. The hypotheses receive partial support. Massive attention is devoted to methods of data analyses, but less reflection is afforded conceptualization.

Summary

Taken together, the cross-cultural studies related to individual behaviour in organizations tell us little. While there is some consensus on the substantive issues that should be pondered, and some steps towards adequate conceptualization in these areas, there is little explanation of why cross-cultural investigations are necessary at all. The area is characterized by little innovation in research approach, which might help to develop new and important foci, nor is there standardization in design to facilitate comparison among studies.

Organizational sub-units

Past work that might improve our understanding of the operations and interactions of functional or hierarchical sub-units across cultures might be expected to be tied to the small group literature in sociology and psychology. However, Claude Faucheux[4] recently pointed out that social psychology in America has moved from observing social reality (intergroup processes), to viewing intragroup processes, to concern with interpersonal processes, and finally to an obsession with intrapersonal processes. While Lewin's (1947) investigations clearly dealt with the total cultural milieu, more recent social psychologists are apt to look at such intrapersonal behaviour as cognitive processes (Festinger, 1957; Zimbardo, 1969a, 1969b). Understanding organizational sub-unit behaviour, then, will not be helped much conceptually by turning to social psychology.

Some work in political science is relevant. Investigators here, however, tend to concern themselves with large systems, and their concepts should be tested in smaller organizational units.

In this diverse literature, one might expect to find cross-cultural discussion and research on those areas which have received greatest attention in the American literature. We might look for coverage of management styles in various functional units or at various levels, conflict and cooperation within and between units, group decision making, deviance and conformity, efficiency, hierarchical and lateral communication. We find that cross-cultural empirical work on organizational sub-units is meagre. It is possible, however, to draw some insights from related studies. These studies tend to aggregate individual data in discussions of group behaviour. Although surveys are most frequent, some laboratory and field

4. Claude Faucheux, personal communication, March 1969.

experiments also exist. These, of course, prune hypotheses better than do surveys.

Management styles

The leadership literature previously mentioned is relevant to considerations of sub-unit behaviour in various cultures. The effects of increasing worker participation in decision making are usually emphasized. One problem is understanding the findings from studies comparing highly technical industries in cultures with different values. Does the technology, the value system, some other variables, or a combination of variables, determine leadership style? And, then, how does style influence unit operations?

At a slightly more macro level, Nagandhi and Estafen (1965) proposed that management philosophy (determined by culture) determines management process which, in turn, determines management effectiveness. They offered a broad scheme which is neither a model nor a theory, and this breadth may be one of the reasons their scheme has not been testable in the field. Not only is there the problem of operationalizing broad hypotheses, but the difficulties of testing 'models' offering broad propositions is increased when they are concerned with cross-cultural organizations, because it is difficult to sample numerous organizations in different environments. A more theoretical framework might evolve from the approach Nagandhi and Estafen suggested, with better explication of independent and dependent variables, and thoughtful consideration of the expected interactions among them, and reasons for these interactions.

In a similar vein, Harbison and Myers (1959) described management systems across cultures and looked for correlates of economic activity in various countries. They supposedly confirmed the hypothesis that relative economic activity and achievement are a function of socio-economic conditions which manifest themselves in management utilization, authority, and relative prestige in a country. However, the confirmatory evidence is drawn from case studies that rely on individual reports. It is known that these are usually considered hypothesis-generating rather than validating techniques.

Perlmutter (1965) and Thorelli (1966) discussed three management philosophies (ethnocentric, polycentric, and geocentric) that can be adopted by multinational firms. They then predicted the kinds of relationships that firms and their branches will have under each of these three systems. Management philosophy is the independent variable (obviously affected by culture), and organizational efficiency the dependent variable. Culture is not well defined and is looked at only in the sense of being the same or different for host environment and parent company.

One report might be helpful in developing hypotheses regarding the relationship of units in organizations from different cultures. Steiglitz (1965) provided organizational charts for forty-two companies from various nations, and showed how these companies are organized and integrated with the parent company. Studying charts such as these might aid identification of variables that seem to influence the structure and interaction of organizations in different locales.

Conflict and cooperation

The vast cross-cultural literature on conflict and cooperation is directed primarily to the question of international peace. Perhaps it is not surprising that a systematic cross-cultural analysis of labour – management relations is non-existent, when bargaining systems, sanctions applicable to each side, and desired outcomes differ so from culture to culture. Neither is there a sufficient cross-cultural literature concerned with conflict within groups of workers.

A few studies of collective bargaining do exist (Oxnam, 1965, Porat, 1969; Rimlinger, 1959). One of these is of particular interest because it draws from the data bank of the International Research Groups on Management (IRGOM; University of Rochester). The IRGOM has developed a set of exercises (covering attitudes, compensation, supervision, etc.) which can be given to managers attending training courses around the world. A number of studies have used this data resource.

Using the negotiations exercise, Porat (1969) asked teams from five Western European nations to assume management or union roles in group negotiation. For each national group, data were collected on time to reach settlement, the ability of the team to balance competition and cooperation, and the distribution of settlement costs over five bargaining issues. The question of whether this is really a study of inter-unit bargaining is appropriate. Teams were composed of managers, and those assuming union roles were hardly socialized in the same manner as their real union counterparts. The possible cultural determinants of results were only guessed at, and no suggestions were offered as to expected differences or similarities across national groups.

Group decision-making

Some of the cross-cultural decision-making literature is also directed to the larger area of international relations. Principles developed here should be tested in smaller units. Some of the work is from the small group literature and employs experiments or quasi-experiments (Campbell and Stanley, 1963) to test hypotheses.

As examples of the larger scale work, elite decision making is focused on by Bauer, Pool, and Dexter (1963), personal experiences which affect international political decision making by Robinson and Snyder (1965), and strategies and goals in negotiation by Sawyer and Guetzkow (1965). D'Antonio and Form (1965) discussed community decision making in an American and Mexican city. Finally, McCann (1967) compared decision making in Latin America and the United States, and concluded that the scientific method of inquiry and analysis is missing in Latin America. These studies might be looked at for clues to variables that should be observed in organizations.

An example of the small group studies is Blake and Mouton's (1965) field investigation of managerial grid training in Indonesia and Aruba. This investigation is offered here because of the American popularity of the technique. The study is deplorable in terms of sampling and poor data quality. The managerial grid seminar is a device for teaching managers about the problems of integrating people and productivity. A one-week seminar was conducted for supervisory groups of Americans and Nationals in Indonesia and Aruba. Why these locations were selected is unexplained. Questionnaires concerned with course effectiveness in increasing interpersonal understanding and decision-making competence were given to participants only after completion of the course. Respondents overwhelmingly replied that they had changed as a result of the course. The limitations of after-only designs are obvious, and surely these data cannot be seriously accepted as evidence of the usefulness of grid training abroad.

While the available literature may improve our thinking about aspects of conflict, cooperation, and decision making that should be considered, as yet there is little systematization of principles or methodological rigour. Little is known about bargaining and related areas within and between organizational sub-units in a single culture, so it is difficult to know what to observe across cultures.

Deviance and conformity

The cross-cultural literature on deviance and conformity is still only suggestive (Meade and Whittaker, 1967; Milgram, 1961; Schachter, Nuttin, de Monchaux, Maucorps, Osmer, Duijker, Rommetvaitj and Israel, 1954). Schachter *et al.* replicated Festinger, Schachter and Back's (1950) work in seven Western European nations. The independent variables were valency of membership in the group and probability of the group's reaching its goal. The dependent variables were desirability of the deviant as a group member and rejection of him. In three of the countries, the experimental manipulation did not appear to work, suggesting to the authors the possibility that people in those cultures do not perceive uniformity as desirable in order to reach their goal. This study points to an important problem. When experimental replications in foreign lands obtain the same results as the original work, there is little difficulty in interpretation. When the results differ, and the strategy cannot be replicated across national boundaries, there is little hope of interpretation, particularly when we have no clear definition of culture. The manipulation did not work in some cultures in the Schachter *et al.* study. What does this mean? Better understanding might evolve from first knowing more about the meaning of deviance in a particular culture, and then studying deviance cross-culturally.

Efficiency

An avalanche of macro statistical data on production is available for various nations (Russet, 1965; Textor, 1967). The pertinent cross-cultural behavioural literature usually considers production or efficiency as the dependent variable, influenced by some aspect of culture. Functional sub-units of organizations are rarely compared cross-culturally. However, Starbuck (1966) developed a model to compare the efficiency of British and American retail employees. He found that British clerks sell faster but specialize more and, hence, are less transferable and, consequently, less efficient than their American counterparts.

In Great Britain, Chaney (1966) replicated a United States study of research performance among scientists. Scientific output was judged on three performance criteria: (a) supervisor ratings on creativity, (b) number of patent specifications, and (c) number of technical publications. Chaney developed, from questionnaire responses of the scientists, keys to predict the three types of performance. Similar predictors apply to both American and British scientists.

Communication

Communication within and between organizational sub-units, whether considered from the point of comparing inter-unit communication in a single culture, or comparisons among units from different cultures, is a virgin area. Since we know little about organizational communication intraculturally, this comes as no shock.

The communication net studies (Bavelas, 1950; Leavitt, 1951) have been replicated cross-culturally (Mulder, 1960). The latter study generally supports and extends the former work. Here is an example of cross-cultural replication done because workers in different places happened to be interested in the same problem, and not because they sought experimental differences based on cultural determinants. In fact, in studies such as these, the effect of the imposed structure probably overwhelms the effect of any other independent variable. This may be generally instructive to organizational researchers because it is possible that in modern industrial organizations the effect of technology-produced structure simply overwhelms the influence of more subtle cultural variation on the dependent variable. The network studies tell us nothing about the communication structure usually adopted, given a particular task in a particular culture, nor do they improve our understanding of communications within and between cultures.

Other available work, once again, offers disparate thoughts and findings, and is only sometimes relevant to the behaviour of organizational sub-units. Some may be useful in developing systematic principles that can be tested. Gardner (1962) pointed out that actors in a cross-cultural situation may draw contrary inferences from common situations. He offered a research plan for examining this possibility. Keller (1956) looked at aspects of diplomatic communication deriving from social factors of which diplomats are unaware. The survey of Bauer *et al.* (1963) is distinguished by its emphasis on communication flow. Goodfriend (1967) assessed the effectiveness of the United States Information Agency in achieving understanding of the United States' national character and purposes in thirteen countries.

Summary

Discussion and observation relevant to cross-cultural organizational sub-units lack adequate coverage in almost all areas. There is no coverage in some areas. In addition, there is no attempt to view sub-units as composed of or composing integrated functions which operate together smoothly and efficiently to determine unit functioning. Inter-relations with other units, total organizational functioning, decision making, communication, etc., should be simultaneously considered and observed as pieces that make up the organizational puzzle.

Organizational totalities

Many of the issues and investigations mentioned in the last section are applicable here. If we limit ourselves to the comparison of entire organizations across national boundaries, we find most studies deal somehow with organizational structure.

A broadly conceived and well-known research programme is Udy's (1959a, 1959b, 1961, 1962). Initially, Udy assumed the inter-relationship of technology, administration, and social structure. By using a large number of cases (150 non-industrial production organizations), he could approach his data from a variety of theoretical perspectives. He refined and explicated his basic assumptions and emerged with specific propositions. Concepts like organizational rationality and social involvement were explicated and operationalized. The problem of culture was handled tenuously through discussing societies and social settings rather than attempting rigorously to define culture. As an example of the research strategy, Udy (1962) measured thirty-four pre-industrial production organizations on structural requisites of rationality and involvement with their social setting. He supported his prediction that rational organizations will be found in societies in which they can be relatively independent of their social settings. Unfortunately, he provided little description about what is produced by the various organizations. Since Udy observed non-industrial organizations, he contributed base-line data for increasing our knowledge about what the influence of technological development on organizational behaviour may be.

Udy's work is highly commendable. One problem deserves mention, for it occurs in many other anthropological studies. Like many of his colleagues, Udy drew his data from the Human Relations Area Files. The files offer a broad compendium of data on numerous societies, but original data collections were undoubtedly influenced by the differences in bias and lack of systematization on the part of contributors to the data bank. Udy mentioned (1962, p. 303) the problem of coding data which were inconsistently collected across cultures. Naroll (1962) and Whiting (1968) offered excellent discussions of data quality control.

Another well-known investigation in this category is Abegglen's (1958) analysis of the Japanese factory. He observed and interviewed in 19 large and 34 small factories on 3 of the 4 major islands of Japan. The study is an exploratory case study of data aggregated from the various firms. Abegglen provided tables, each with data from only one factory, as examples of trends in all factories. He noted two major factors differentiating American and Japanese factories: (a) lack of differentiation of factory organization and other social groups in Japan, and (b) difference in American and Japanese organizations in the extent to which there is individualization and impersonalization in the relationships in Japan. Do these differences hold for most Japanese factories or just for some? Taira (1962) pointed out that Abegglen selected only the most highly technical firms in Japan, and one surely questions the validity of generalizations to all Japanese industries supported only by a case study of such firms.

Fouraker and Stopford (1968) illustrated yet another kind of interest in organizational structure. Using United States Census Department and Department of Commerce survey data, they supported the proposition that organizations with a single or a few related product lines and a high degree of vertical integration are capital-intensive and have centralized structures. This kind of organization concentrates on domestic markets. Organizations with diversified-product lines tend towards decentralized structure and overseas investment. A counter-intuitive hypothesis is supported here, as one might think that the most capital-intensive, integrated organizations will dominate foreign investment. This investigation compared organizations with home offices in a single society, but was instructive of the aggregate variables which should be considered in multinational work. The work hinted at how various organizational structures might determine lifetime-member activities in production and management.

A final relationship of organizational structure to other variables was illustrated by Porter and Siegel's work (1965). They measured the relationship of structural characteristics and member satisfaction. Some structural characteristics (i.e. size, span of control, tall versus flat, etc.), which might profitably be considered in future work, were considered, but the authors offered little in the way of explaining how these variables relate to one another or how they might differentially influence satisfaction in different cultures.

Other entries deal with structural characteristics across cultures (Armstrong, 1965; Business International, 1965; Granick, 1962; Harbison *et al.*, 1955; Hartmann, 1959; Heller, 1968), but where data do exist, they are not very rigorous. At the most macro level, Gibb (1968) used United Nations Statistical Office industrial development data for a study of national changes in industrial structure. Industrial structure is defined as proportion of manpower devoted to various industries in a culture. Gibb indicated the problem of differential definition of concepts (even straightforward terms) across countries, low reliability, and the difficulty of finding a sample of nations on which comparative economic data exist. He then related changes in overall industry structure to technological efficiency. The study is descriptive and offers no conceptualization about causes of national change in industrial structure. In fact, it seems gratuitous.

One task that might be taken to aid in developing concepts about organizational variation across cultures is to ask systematically how environment acts to influence organizations. Farmer and Richman (1964, 1967) attempted this. They discussed environmental constraints on managerial efficiency and ultimately on organizational effectiveness. However, their differential weighting system for environmental factors seems drawn from thin air. They offered a descriptive first step, lacking in explication of the dependent variable (managerial effectiveness), and failing to discuss how constraints differ from situation to situation. More detailed analysis of what environment means and comparisons of organizations in different environments would be appropriate here. Farmer and Richman's sweeping generalizations have, no doubt, contributed to their inability to test parameters.

Summary

It is interesting that as we consider more macro variables in the cross-cultural organizational work, there are increasingly fewer conceptualizations and observations to guide us. Those concepts that do exist are often not testable. Perhaps this is because 'culture' itself is not defined well enough to predict its influence on organizations, or perhaps it is because at least business organizations are thought to be somewhat alike, regardless of where they exist. If this is true, then it makes no difference from where the samples are drawn.

Organizations are looked at by cross-cultural researchers as static entities, and this review has no examples of measurements taken at more than one point in time.

The various human relations and behavioralist [sic] theories of management focus on the persons in a given firm in a stated environment . . . the decision theorists, the students of bureaucracy, and social system theorists, with few exceptions, view the firm as fixed in space and time [Farmer and Richman, 1967, p. 223].

Since it is difficult to solicit entire organizations for research purposes, comparisons among them, particularly across national boundaries, are rare. Where discussion does exist, it is almost always descriptive and characterized either by total lack of evidence or by presentation of a few macro data.

Organizational interactions

One aspect of an organization's environment is other organizations in the same location. The relationships of organizations with each other are not generally considered in the cross-cultural research.

Two different approaches which might be further developed are mentioned briefly here. Estafen[5] used the aforementioned Farmer-Richman 'model' as a base, and saw external environmental variables as limiting or establishing a ceiling for the maximum firm effectiveness. The system transfer characteristics were focused upon. These characteristics were defined as the normal patterns of flow of men, money, materials, and information across the firm – environment interface. Estafen's is descriptive effort, and while some predictions are suggested, the 'whys' are not considered.

Roberts and Pinfield (1968) postulated environmental causes of organizational interactions. Their scheme was developed from the analogue of parent-organization–branch-environmental relationships to the parent-child–sibling-peer relationships. Their statement lacks isomorphism and, like so many others, fails to define environmental or cultural differences adequately.

Almost no conceptual work or even descriptive observations are available here. It is curious that more work does not exist, because a major practical reason for cross-cultural organizational research is understanding how new organizations come into cultures, develop, and interact with one another. The growth of

5. B. D. Estafen, personal communication, June 1969.

overseas branches of educational institutions and businesses, and the initiation of governmental activities in foreign lands are dependent on such knowledge. The importance of beginning to understand how organizations view and respond to their settings (or each other) cannot be overemphasized. A theory of culture would greatly aid the determination of environmental influences that should be observed. Obviously, the demand characteristics of environments differ and these determine, to some extent, the activities of the organizations in them. Attempting to define the proportion of variance in organizational behaviour accounted for by outside factors may be a timely first step.

Finally, if it is true that today's social psychologists are primarily interested in some form of cognitive behaviour, it might be appropriate for some of these people to turn their attention to the problem of how organization members, because of their particular memberships, view the outside world. What do organizational participants look at in the environment, and how does this influence their behaviour?

General summary

Table 2 summarizes the state of affairs in cross-cultural organizational research. Initially, we asked three questions of the research: Do we know anything new from it, are concepts well developed, and are methodological approaches adequate? The answer to the first question comes only from answers to the others.

At the moment, the kinds of research questions asked and the answers obtained are illustrated by a quote from Harbison *et al.* (1955) concerning their study of German and American steel factory management.

> The problems of organizations and personnel have been highlighted by the contrasts which come to light in cross-national studies of this kind. For example, after analyzing the findings of this survey Inland Steel raised the question as to whether or not its investment in supervision might be too great [p. 38].

This reflects interest in practical application, rather than a more fundamental interest in developing generalizable linked propositions.

More on theoretical guidance

'A theory is a systematically related set of statements, including some law-like generalizations, that is empirically testable [Rudner, 1966, p. 10].' A model is 'an alternative interpretation of the same calculus with which the theory itself is an interpretation [Rudner, 1966, p. 24]', and its strength lies in isomorphism and the ease of visualizing the model's subject matter. Employing a model belongs in the context of discovery rather than validation, because models function as heuristic devices.

The terms 'model' and 'theory' share a melancholy lack of uniformity in the vocabularies of scientists and others who talk about science. Sometimes the two are employed simply as synonyms; sometimes model is used to refer to *any* theoretical formulation other than a theory [Rudner, 1966, p. 23].

This seems particularly true of the cross-cultural organizational literature. The importance of developing systematization through theory building should be obvious. It is only through theory building that we can move from simple description to the asking of relevant questions involving explanation and prediction.

The problem of looking at culture in systems terms has not been tackled. Culture is undoubtedly composed of, determines, and is determined by a multitude of factors. Only McClelland's (1961) work has been noted as a beginning in this direction. 'Mini'

Table 2 **Summary of conceptual and methodological state of affairs**

Research	*Approach sufficiently developed to test?*	*Data*	*Most frequent research approach*
Organizational roles	some	micro	case studies, survey, some field studies
Organizational sub-units	some	micro, some macro	survey, some field studies, some lab studies
Organizational totalities	generally not	macro	case studies
Organizational interactions	no	none	none

theories of culture are inadequate. Theoretical systems must be developed which can handle many and diverse variables.

Currently, the questions asked bear a 'made in U.S.A.' stamp. They examine organizational behaviour in other cultures from an American point of view. Campbell (1968) stated:

> increasingly high research standards mean increasingly high research budgets which further increase the predominance of U.S.A. initiative. We need machinery which will make possible the distribution of research initiative among all nations, at the same time achieving the value of multinational comparison [p. 256].

By spreading the wealth this way, we may find that what is a significant and researchable question in one culture is simply no mystery in another. Berrien (1966) offered several examples of the fact that issues studied in one culture may be of such trivial consequence in another culture as to be meaningless. This brings us back to the appropriateness of focusing on genotypes rather than phenotypes, functional equivalencies rather than behaviours which only on the surface resemble one another.

The present author is considerably impressed by the scholarly provincialism in this area. If a researcher incorporates into his work any notion developed outside his immediate group of colleagues, he generally limits himself to the work of others with his discipline identification. The body of scientific presuppositions and beliefs is not consistent across disciplines. According to Kessel (1969), these beliefs provide tacit rules governing the choice of admissible problems of concern. As such, they limit the view possible for any one discipline, and we are caught with a set of mutually exclusive, but potentially parallel, approaches to the problem of understanding organizations and the cultures in which they live. This seems an inefficient stance from which to develop sound theoretical principles.

The answer to the second question – are concepts well developed? – is negative.

Method

Is the methodology of cross-cultural research appropriate to the questions asked? The preponderance of casual observation and case studies indicates that it is not. Surely, we should be beyond the mere hypothesis-suggesting stage to a time when testing hypotheses is fruitful. Since a measure of a science is its method, this section mentions a few of the more obvious problems specific to this review of the cross-cultural organizational literature, and offers some thoughts about what might be done once the crucial questions to be asked are decided upon.

Sampling

One of the most blatant problems of the research is sampling. Instances of more than one organization per culture are rarely found, and the reliability of results that compare data matrix cells with single entries is suspect. It might be advantageous to sample cultures systematically, or at least people or organizations within any single culture. This is rarely done, and although it is a difficult task, it is not impossible (Naroll, 1962).

Another approach might be an exhaustive, clinical, theoretical analysis of a few cases (Rice, 1955a, 1955b; Trist and Bamforth, 1951). From such analysis there is the possibility of gaining greater insight into the genotypical configurations of organizations.

Currently, research organizations are those with good university relationships, because these are the organizations we are able to measure. More is known about steel factories and hospitals, for instance, than about textile manufacturers or hamburger stands. As stated in this review, the main effect of technology on any other organizational variable (i.e. structure, interactions, etc.) is possibly of such strength that the visibility of the impact of any second-level variable, such as culture (even if we could define it) is simply wiped out. The literature is replete with work on industrial organizations, and the only way to mitigate the influence of the overwhelming impact of technology is to study organizations in non-technical cultures (Udy, 1959b), and then, perhaps, a broader sample of organizations reflecting different levels of technology. An example of what can happen as a result of this review's current approach is Abegglen's study (1958). Since he observed only the most Americanized Japanese factories, his generalization to other kinds of Japanese industry is questionable.

Investigators seem, also, to be choosing cultures because of location, not because of their standing on some variable. Better conceptualization of the independent variable (culture) and the dependent variable (organizational structure, managerial efficiency, or whatever) might reduce this problem. If we thoroughly understood the independent variable, culture, and sampled only at the extremes along various dimensions of this variable, we could better determine the impact of culture on any dependent variable.

Better conceptualization of variables might help avoid sampling on the dependent variable, and then testing it, as has been known to happen. Haire *et al.* (1966) reported no significant differences in attitudes among their 3,641 managers from 14 nations. Their sample, though, was drawn from managers attending training courses, and this strategy reads as if selection was done on the dependent variable, attitude, which drove managers to the course in the first place.

Replication

There are several examples of studies originally done in the United States and replicated overseas. Cross-cultural replication only makes sense where there is some reason for doing it. If another culture looks similar with regard to a problem, it will probably not be more instructive to replicate there than at home. If it looks different, replication can raise problems in translation.

> Strict replication is not only an inappropriate way of finding out whether the culture is 'similar' or not but if similar it is pointless and if really different it is bound to fail without providing necessarily a clue about why it is so.[6]

Again, we are back to the phenotype versus genotype problem.

The well-known Coch and French (1948) study of participative versus authoritarian supervision was replicated in Norway (French *et al.*, 1960). The authors offered no particular reasons for replication in a different culture and no specific reasons for selecting Norway as the second culture. They stated: 'a secondary purpose is to discover whether the general results of the Coch and French experiment, which was conducted in the United States,

6. Claude Faucheux, personal communication, March 1969.

will hold in a different culture [p. 3]'. French *et al.* offered a tentative cultural hypothesis as to why the results do not replicate in Norway, but they have not isolated culture well enough to demonstrate how their findings are related to it. There are plausible hypotheses other than the one they suggest.

The object in cross-cultural research is to find relationships among variables, rather than simply to describe variables. In repetition, more than one entry per cell (i.e. more than one organization per nation) is requisite, and the samples should represent known differences in behaviours on the independent variable(s). The French *et al.* work meets neither of these conditions. Furthermore, the conditions cannot be met without better description and some theoretical notions about culture. The results of the American and Norwegian studies are further confused by the influence of other variables that were supposedly unrelated to culture but probably influenced variation in the dependent variable. Harwood Manufacturing, the United States setting for the original study, was a unique firm because the employees there had been exposed to novel management techniques for some time prior to the experiment. This was not true of the Norwegian firm which also employed over 26 per cent of the inhabitants of the town in which it was located. It had recently fired 5 per cent of the town's people. This surely affected the employees' view of the 'credibility' of participative management for them. The sample ($N = 1$) for the Norwegian replication was possibly very different from that of the original study, and no one knows what aspects of the differences are related to 'culture'.

Design

We have seen few cross-cultural investigations related to organizations which use a convergent-discriminant validity (Campbell and Fiske, 1959) approach. The necessity for converging on constructs of interest and differentiating those from other constructs should be apparent. Assuming that the conceptual groundwork for any future study is relatively sound, multiple indicators of both independent and dependent variables are in order.

If there are multiple indicators which vary in their irrelevant attributes, and if these all agree as to the direction of the difference or the theoretically intended aspects, then the number of tenable rival explanations becomes generally reduced and the confirmation of theory more nearly certain [Campbell, 1961, p. 345].

(See also Campbell, 1957, p. 310; Campbell, 1959; Campbell and Fiske, 1959; Roberts, 1969; Webb, Campbell, Schwartz and Sechrest, 1966).

Most of the available data have been collected using questionnaires or interviews, but with little thought given to design strategies. Since random selection of organizations and cultures is probably not possible, and maybe not even desirable, and field studies are required because of the nature of the most interesting organizational problems, the area lends itself to strategies such as the quasi-experimental designs discussed by Campbell and Stanley (1966). For instance, cross-cultural problems in organizational change might be investigated by an extension of the equivalent-time-samples design (Campbell and Stanley, 1966, p. 43), or a counterbalanced design (Campbell and Stanley, 1966, p. 51). The non-equivalent control-group design (Campbell and Stanley, 1966, p. 47) offers an approximation of a true experiment and can be used to study the effect of some variable introduced in one group but not another within and across cultures.

Instrumentation

The problems of instrumentation are simply magnified when studies are done across national boundaries. An extremely large amount of literature (Berrien, 1967; Ervin and Bauer, 1953; Hudson, Barakat, and Laforge, 1959; Moore, 1961; Rommetvaitj and Israel, 1954; Schachter, 1954) deals with these problems. It need only be pointed out here that 'too often instruments . . . are designed more or less *de novo*, and, therefore, comparisons between studies are difficult and sometimes impossible [Doob, 1968, p. 81]'. If at all possible, standardized measures should be used. 'No one's reputation for originality is injured when he employs a standardized thermometer to measure the temperature of the body [Doob, 1968, p. 81].' Back translation of all paper-and pencil devices is a minimum requirement.

The present author questions the value of measuring structural characteristics of organizations solely by asking members about them, and then relating these characteristics to member attitudes of some similar individual variable. This is not a problem unique to cross-cultural research (Tausky, 1967), but it has been found that cross-cultural work often relies on the easiest methods for obtaining data. Picking up information on the independent and dependent variables from the same source, at the same time, is certainly easier than some other strategies might be. However, it might not be as adequate.

The lack of systematization in instrumentation is possibly the best indicator of how unscientific the area actually is. The discipline is not structured around a paradigm, and standardization can only come with such structuring.

What to do?

Going back to the first question, Do we know anything new from the available cross-cultural work? The increment in knowledge seems minimal and possibly not worth all the effort thus far placed in cross-cultural work.

What to do? First of all, we might retrench. The exercise here should be one of deciding what problems to study. We can best do that from a thorough understanding of our own behaviour. According to Faucheux,[7] until we stop avoiding the question of who we are, it will be impossible to understand others. In trying to understand our own culture, we might assume that 'the best array of phenotypical cultural variables are produced by the genotypical interplay of a few basic variables which can be grasped from anywhere'. It should be easier to infer the processes mediating our observations of behaviour within our own culture than to attempt to do so from cross-cultural data. This exercise should lead us to groups of questions or series of concepts that will necessarily be examined comparatively, because there is some reason to believe they are affected by environmental attributes. We must, then, carefully delineate those attributes. Smelser (1968, p. 65) reminded us that we must walk the fence of avoiding concepts that are so specific that only few instances of them can be found anywhere,

7. Claude Faucheux, personal communication, March 1969.

and those that are so general as to have no explanatory value. We should also avoid wholesale application of ready-made models.

When models are transferred to social science simply because they are formal and aesthetic, without sufficient concern for their isomorphism and with the actualities of social relations, their predictive value is bound to be negligible . . . No matter how elegant the model, it forces us into a selectivity in choosing problems, in defining variables – at times to the point where crucial variables are simply cut off [Sherif, 1968, p. 44].

In addition to the organizational behaviour literature *per se*, where can we turn for conceptual and methodological help? There are a number of possibilities. Several are mentioned only in passing, with the hope of titilating those adventurous for new approaches. Micro (individual) behaviour in organizations is probably best helped by strategies and concepts already familiar to most psychologists. Thus, we limit the suggested 'aids' to those which may help us better understand the macro aspects of organizations, how they operate and are related to their environments.

Those who view organizations as changing entities within also changing environments might turn to sociology and anthropology. Some scholars in these areas offer conceptual work concerned with such problems as general and specific evolution, adaptability and stability, cultural dominance, and the evolutionary potential of organisms and cultures (Parsons, 1966; Sahlins and Service, 1960). Two more considerations that may help us comprehend some of the more specific influences of environments on organizations are offered in discussions of 'the behavioural sink', and 'territoriality' (Calhoun, 1966; Sommer, 1966). Together, these and other conceptualizations from the larger behavioural science literature may help us change our myopic views about how organizations develop and function. Maybe they will lead us nowhere. But that leaves us in at least no worse position than we are today.

How, too, do we develop strategies for observing complex organizational phenomena? If we view organizations as systems of interaction, each system within a larger one (Blau, 1968), and we feel the need for descriptive studies to act as bases for developing and refining concepts about these systems, there are at least two places we might look for guidance.

Barker (1968) observed the interaction of behaviour and environment in real life settings and provided concepts, field methods, and analytical programmes for observing behavioural-environmental interactions. He identified the 'behaviour setting' as the central environmental unit.

> A behavior setting has both structural and dynamic attributes. On the structural side . . . [it] consists of one or more standing patterns of behavior-and-milieu, with the milieu circumjacent and synomorphic to the behavior. On the dynamic side, the behavior-milieu parts of a behavior setting, the synomorphs, have a specified degree of interdependence among themselves that is greater than their interdependence with parts of other behavior settings [Barker, 1968, p. 18].

We might be able to extend these thoughts to conceptualizations about how organizations operate in undermanned and optimally manned behaviour settings, differences in behaviour that can be expected, given certain behaviour settings, etc.

A second approach to thinking about, locating, and interpreting naturally occurring complex phenomena is offered by Garfinkel (1967). His treatment is generally confusing, but the struggle through it may be worth the effort. Garfinkel is concerned with investigating the rational properties of indexical expressions and actions, and the ways this rationality is coded in everyday behaviours. He assumed that the actions which demonstrate an event's rationality are those which produce that event. Garfinkel provided a possibly interesting way of thinking about rational decision-making in organizations, an important topic when we are concerned with how organizations establish new overseas branches, keeping them operating, etc.

Admittedly, we are left in a perplexing state. The lack of evidence for propositions concerned with organizational functioning, plus the availability of diverse and exciting work which may offer help, should act as a stimulus to our future activities. The direction they take will depend on our thoughtfulness and ingenuity.

Conclusion

This review of the cross-cultural research related to organizational behaviour reveals a predominance of discussions and studies concerned with individual behaviour in organizations. Most of the studies are based on surveys which are not well thought out. Empirical work concerned with more macro organizational variables is meagre. It is not well guided by theoretical underpinnings, data are often weak, and conclusions are difficult to comprehend. Organizations are rarely viewed as parts of their environments, yet understanding organizational–environmental interactions seems a major practical reason for engaging in cross-cultural research.

The present author suggests that more effort be invested in understanding behaviour in a single culture, developing middle-level theories to guide explorations, and seeking the relevant questions to ask across cultures. A few resources are suggested that may offer new approaches.

References

ABEGGLEN, J. (1958), *The Japanese Factory*, The Free Press, Illinois.

ARMSTRONG, J. A. (1965), 'Sources of administrative behavior: some Soviet and Western European comparisons', *American Political Science Review*, no. 59, pp. 643–55.

BARKER, R. (1968), *Ecological Psychology*, Stanford University Press, California.

BASS, B. M. (1965), *Organizational Psychology*, Allyn and Bacon, Boston, U.S.A.

BAUER, R. N., DE SOLA POOL, I., and DEXTER, L. A. (1963), *American Business and Public Policy: The Politics of Foreign Trade*, Atherton Press, New York.

BAVELAS, A. (1950), 'Communication patterns in task oriented groups', *Journal of the Acoustical Society of America*, no. 22, pp. 725–30.

BERRIEN, F. K. (1966), *Some Methodological Problems in Cross Cultural Research* (Technical Report I, Contract No. 4086 (00)), Group Psychology Branch, Office of Naval Research, Department of Defense, Washington, D.C.

BERRIEN, F. K. (1967), 'Methodological and related problems in cross-cultural research', *International Journal of Psychology*, no. 2, pp. 33–44.

Berry, J. W. (1969), 'On cross-cultural comparability', *International Journal of Psychology*, no. 4, pp. 119–28.

Blake, R. R., and Mouton, J. S. (1965), 'International managerial grids', *Training Director's Journal*, no. 19, pp. 8–23.

Blau, P. M. (1968), 'Organizations: theories', in D. L. Sills (ed.), *International Encyclopedia of Social Sciences*, Macmillan, New York.

Business International Corporation (1965), *Organizing for Worldwide Operations: Structuring and Implementing the Plan*, New York.

Calhoun, J. (1966), 'Role of space in animal sociology', *Journal of Social Issues*, no. 4, pp. 46–58.

Campbell, D. T. (1957), 'Factors relevant to the validity of experiments in social settings', *Psychological Bulletin*, no. 54, pp. 297–312.

Campbell, D. T. (1959), 'Methodological suggestions from a comparative psychology of knowledge processes', *Inquiry*, no. 2, pp. 152–82.

Campbell, D. T. (1961), 'Mutual methodological relevance', in F. L. K. Hsu (ed.), *Psychological Anthropology*, Dorsey, Illinois.

Campbell, D. T. (1967), 'Stereotypes and the perception of group differences', *American Psychologist*, no. 22, pp. 817–29.

Campbell, D. T. (1968), 'A cooperative multinational opinion sample exchange', *Journal of Social Issues*, no. 24, pp. 245–56.

Campbell, D. T., and Fiske, D. W. (1959), 'Convergent and discriminant validation by the multi-trait-multi-method matrix', *Psychological Bulletin*, no. 56, pp. 81–105.

Campbell, D. T., and Stanley, J. C. (1963), *Experimental and Quasi-Experimental Designs for Research*, Rand-McNally, Chicago.

Casagrande, J. B. (ed.) (1960), *In the Company of Man*, Harper, New York.

Chaney, F. B. (1966), 'A cross-cultural study of industrial research performance', *Journal of Applied Psychology*, no. 50, pp. 206–10.

Chemers, M. M., Fiedler, F. E., Lekhyananda, D., and Stolurow, L. M. (1966), 'Some effects of cultural training on leadership in heterocultural task groups', *International Journal of Psychology*, no. 1, pp. 301–14.

Chowdry, K. (1960), *Human Relations, a Review: Background and Current Trends*, ATIRA Human Relations Division, Ahmedabad, India.

Coch, L., and French, J. R. P. (1948), 'Overcoming resistance to change', *Human Relations*, no. 1, pp. 512–32.

CORTIS, L. E. (1962), 'A comparative study in the attitudes of Bantu and European workers', *Psychologia Africana*, no. 9, pp. 148–67.

D'ANTONIO, W. M., and FORM, W. H. (1965), *Influentials in Two Border Cities: A Study of Community Decision-Making*, Notre Dame University Press.

DESAI, K. G. (1968), 'A comparative study of blue collar and white collar workers', *Indian Journal of Social Work*, no. 28, pp. 379–87.

DOOB, L. (1968), 'Just a few of the propositions and perplexities confronting social psychological research in developing countries', *Journal of Social Issues*, no. 24, pp. 71–81.

EKMAN, P., and FRIESEN, W. V. (1968), 'Nonverbal behavior in psychotherapy research', *Research in Psychotherapy*, no. 3, pp. 179–216.

EKMAN, P., and FRIESEN, W. V. (1969), 'The repertoire of nonverbal behavior – categories, origins, usage and coding', *Semiotica*, vol. 1, no. 1, pp. 49–98.

EKMAN, P., SORENSON, R., and FRIESEN, W. V. (1969), 'Pan-cultural elements in facial displays of emotion', *Science*, no. 164, pp. 86–8.

ERVIN, S., and BAUER, R. T. (1953), 'Translation problems in international surveys', *Public Opinion Quarterly*, no. 16, pp. 595–604.

FARMER, R., and RICHMAN, B. (1964), 'A model for research in comparative managements', *California Management Review*, no. 1, pp. 55–68.

FARMER, R., and RICHMAN, B. (1967), 'A model for researching comparative management', in B. Prasad (ed.), *Management in International Perspective*, Appleton-Century, New York.

FESTINGER, L. (1957), *A Theory of Cognitive Dissonance*, Row Peterson, Illinois.

FESTINGER, L., SCHACHTER, S., and BACK, K. (1950), *Social Pressures in Informal Groups*, Harper, New York.

FIEDLER, F. E. (1965), 'The contingency model: a theory of leadership effectiveness', in H. Proshansky and B. Seidenberg (eds.), *Basic Studies in Social Psychology*, Holt, New York.

FIEDLER, F. E. (1967), *A Theory of Leadership Effectiveness*, McGraw-Hill, New York.

FORD, C. S., PROTHRO, E. T., and CHILD, I. L. (1966), 'Some transcultural comparisons of esthetic judgement', *Journal of Social Psychology*, no. 68, pp. 19–26.

FOURAKER, L. E., and STOPFORD, J. M. (1968), 'Organizational structure and the multinational strategy', *Administrative Society Quarterly*, no. 13, pp. 48–64.

FRENCH, J. R. P., ISRAEL, J., and AS, D. (1960), 'An experiment in participation in a Norwegian factory', *Human Relations*, no. 13, pp. 3–19.

GANGULI, H. C. (1963), *Structures and Processes of Organization*, Asia Publishing House, Bombay.

GARDNER, G. H. (1962), 'Cross-cultural communication', *Journal of Social Psychology*, no. 58, pp. 241–56.

GARFINKEL, H. (1967), *Studies in Ethnomethodology*, Prentice-Hall, Englewood Cliffs, N.J.

GIBB, J. P. (1968), 'Change in industry structure: interactional comparisons', *Pacific Sociological Review*, no. 11, pp. 38–48.

GOODFRIEND, A. (1967), 'Intercultural communication in West Africa', *Off. Ext. Res., United States Department of State*, vol. 5, no. 26.

GRANICK, D. (1962), *The European Executive*, Doubleday, New York.

GREENBERG, J. H. (ed.) (1966), *Universals of Language* (2nd ed.), M.I.T. Press.

HAIRE, M., GHISELLI, E., and PORTER, L. (1966), *Managerial Thinking*, John Wiley, New York.

HALL, E. T. (1959), *The Silent Language*, Premier Books, Greenwich, Connecticut.

HALL, E. T. (1966), *The Hidden Dimension*, Doubleday, New York.

HARBISON, F., KOCHLING, E., CASSELL, F. H., and REUBMAN, H. C. (1955), 'Steel management on two continents', *Management Science*, no. 2, pp. 31–9.

HARBISON, F., and MYERS, C. (1959), *Management in the Industrial World*, McGraw-Hill, New York.

HARTMANN, H. (1959), *Authority and Organization in German Management*, Princeton University Press.

HELLER, F. A. (1968), 'The role of management in economic development', *Management International Review*, no. 8, pp. 63–75.

HELLER, F. A., and PORTER, L. W. (1966), 'Perceptions of managerial needs and skills in two national samples', *Occupational Psychology*, no. 40, pp. 1–13.

HERZBERG, F. (1965a), 'Job attitudes in the Soviet Union', *Personnel Psychology*, no. 18, pp. 245–52.

HERZBERG, F. (1965b), 'The motivation to work among Finnish supervisors', *Personnel Psychology*, no. 18, pp. 393–402.

HERZBERG, F. (1966), *Work and the Nature of Man*, World Publishing Co., Ohio.

HUDSON, B. B., BARAKAT, M. K., and LAFORGE, R. (1959), 'Problems and methods of cross-cultural research', *Journal of Social Issues*, no. 15, pp. 5–19.

KAHN, R. L., and KATZ, D. (1960), 'Leadership practices in relation to productivity and morale', in D. Cartwright and A. Zander (eds.), *Group Dynamics: Research and Theory* (2nd ed.), Row, Peterson, Illinois.

KELLER, S. (1956), 'Diplomacy and communication', *Public Opinion Quarterly*, no. 20, pp. 176–82.

KELMAN, H. C. (1967), 'Psychological research on social change: some scientific and ethical issues', *International Journal of Psychology*, no. 2, pp. 301–13.

KESSEL, F. S. (1969), 'The philosophy of science as proclaimed and science as practiced: "identity" or "dualism"', *American Psychologist*, no. 24, pp. 999–1005.

KNOX, J. B. (1964), 'The corporation: some Argentine and American attitudes', *Journal of Social Psychology*, no. 63, pp. 221–32.

KROEBER, A. L., and KLUCKHOHN, C. (1952), 'Culture: a critical review of concepts and definitions', *Papers Peabody Museum*, vol. 47, no. 1.

KUMATA, H., and SCHRAMM, W. (1956), 'A pilot study of cross-cultural meaning', *Public Opinion Quarterly*, no. 20, pp. 229–38.

LAUTERBACH, A. (1961), 'Managerial attitudes in western South America', in A. Lauterbach (ed.), *Managerial Attitudes in Chile*, University of Santiago, Chile.

LAZARUS, J. R., KESSEL, F. S., and BOTHA, E. (1969), 'Cultural differences in need-achievement externality between white and colored South African adolescents', *Journal of Social Psychology*, no. 77, pp. 133–4.

LEAVITT, H. J. (1951), 'Some effects on certain communication patterns on group performance', *Journal of Abnormal and Social Psychology*, no. 46, pp. 38–50.

LEWIN, K. (1947), 'Group decision and social change', in T. M. Newcomb and E. L. Hartley (eds.), *Readings in Social Psychology*, Holt, New York.

LIKERT, R. (1961), *New Patterns of Management*, McGraw-Hill, New York.

LIKERT, R. (1963), 'Trends toward a world-wide theory of management', *Proceedings of the International Council for Scientific Management, Thirteenth International Management Congress*, no. 2, pp. 110–14.

LITTLE, K. B. (1968), 'Cultural variations in social schemata' *Journal of Personality and Social Psychology*, no. 10, pp. 1–7.

LORIMORE, E. S. (1967), 'Effects of source and certain other factors in cross-cultural persuasive communications: a study of two cultures', *Dissertation Abstracts*, no. 28, p. 188a.

LORIMORE, E. S., and DUNN, S. W. (1968), 'Reference groups, congruity theory and cross-cultural persuasion', *Journal of Communication*, no. 18, pp. 354–68.

MCCANN, E. (1967), 'An aspect of management philosophy in the United States and Latin America', in S. B. Prasad (ed.), *Management in International Perspective*, Appleton-Century, New York.

MCCLELLAND, D. (1961), *The Achieving Society*, Van Nostrand, Princeton, N.J.

MCCLELLAND, D., and WINTER, D. G. (1969), *Motivating Economic Achievement*, The Free Press, New York.

MCGREGOR, D. M. (1960), *The Human Side of Enterprise*, McGraw-Hill, New York.

MCGUIRE, W. J. (1966), 'Attitudes and opinions', in P. R. Farnsworth (ed.), *Annual Review of Psychology*, Stanford University Press, California.

MCMILLAN, C. (1965), 'Industrial leaders in Latin America', in W. H. Form (ed.), *Industrial Relations and Social Change in Latin America*, University of Florida Press.

MEADE, R. D., and WHITTAKER, J. O. (1967), 'Social pressure in the modification and distortion of judgment: a cross cultural study', *International Journal of Psychology*, no. 2, pp. 109–33.

MILGRAM, S. (1961), 'Nationality and conformity', *Scientific American*, no. 205, pp. 45–51.

MISHLER, A. L. (1965), 'Personal contact in international exchanges', in J. C. Kelman (ed.), *International Behavior*, Holt, New York.

MISUMI, J., and TAKASAKI, T. (1965), 'A study on the effectiveness of supervisory patterns in a Japanese hierarchical organization', *Japanese Psychological Research*, no. 7, pp. 151–62.

MOORE, F. W. (ed.) (1961), *Readings in Cross-Cultural Methodology*, Burns and MacEachern, New Haven, Connecticut.

MULDER, M. (1960), 'Communication structure, decision structure, and group performance', *Sociometry*, no. 23, pp. 1–14.

NAGANDHI, A. R., and ESTAFEN, B. D. (1965), 'A research model to determine the applicability of American management know-how in differing cultures and/or environments', *Academy of Management Journal*, no. 8, pp. 309–18.

NAROLL, R. (1962), *Data Quality Control*, The Free Press, Illinois.

OSGOOD, C. E. (1965), 'Cross cultural comparability in attitude measurement via multi-lingual semantic differentials', in I. Steiner and M. Fishbain (eds.), *Current Studies in Social Psychology*, Holt, New York.

OXNAM, D. W. (1965), 'International comparisons of industrial conflict: an appraisal', *Journal of Industrial Relations*, no. 7, pp. 149–63.

PARSONS, T. (1966), *Societies: Evolutionary and Comparative Perspectives*, Prentice-Hall, Englewood Cliffs, N.J.

PERLMUTTER, H. (1965), 'L'entrepris international – trois conceptions', *Revue Économique et Sociale*, no. 23, pp. 151–65.

PHILIPSEN, H. (1965), 'Het meten vron leiderschap (the Measurement of leadership)', *Mens en Onderneming*, no. 19, pp. 153–71.

POOL, I. DE S. (1965), 'Effects of cross national contact on national and international images', in H. C. Kelman (ed.), *International Behavior*, Holt, New York.

PORAT, A. M. (1969), 'Cross-cultural differences in resolving union – management conflict through negotiations', *Experimental Publications System*, no. 2, ms. 069A.

PORTER, L. W., and SIEGEL, J. (1965), 'Relationships of tall and flat organization structure to satisfactions of foreign managers', *Personnel Psychology*, no. 18, pp. 379–92.

RICE, A. K. (1955a), 'The experimental reorganization of non-automatic weaving in an Indian mill', *Human Relations*, no. 8, pp. 199–249.

RICE, A. K. (1955b), 'Productivity and social organization in an Indian weaving mill. II. A follow-up study of the experimental reorganization of automatic weaving', *Human Relations*, no. 8, pp. 399–428.

RICHMAN, B. (1964), *Soviet Management*, Prentice-Hall, Englewood Cliffs, N.J.

RIMLINGER, G. V. (1959), 'International differences in the strike propensity of coal miners: experience in four countries',

Industrial and Labor Relations Review, no. 12, pp. 389–405.
ROBERTS, K. H. (1969), *Understanding Educational Research: Some Thoughts on Evaluating Completed Projects* (Tech. Rep. EM–007300), Educational Resources Information Clearing-house Document Reproduction Service, National Cash Register, Bethesda, Maryland.
ROBERTS, K. H., and PINFIELD, L. T. (1968), 'Offshoot international organizational research', *Proceedings of the 76th Annual Convention of the American Psychological Association*, no. 3, p. 734.
ROBINSON, J. A., and SNYDER, R. C. (1965), 'Decision-making in international politics', in H. C. Kelman (ed.), *International Behavior*, Holt, New York.
ROMMETVAITJ, R., and ISRAEL, J. (1954), 'Notes on the standardization of experimental manipulations and measurements in cross-national research', *Journal of Social Issues*, no. 10, pp. 58–61.
RUDNER, R. S. (1966), *Philosophy of Social Science*, Prentice-Hall, Englewood Cliffs, N.J.
RUSSET, B. (1965), *World Handbook of Political and Social Indicators*, Yale University Press.
SAHLINS, M. D., and SERVICE, E. R. (1960), *Evolution and Culture*, University of Michigan Press.
SAWYER, J., and GUETZKOW, H. (1965), 'Bargaining and negotiation in international relations', in H. C. Kelman (ed.), *International Behavior*, Holt, New York.
SCHACHTER, S. (1954), 'Interpretative and methodological problems in replicated research', *Journal of Social Issues*, no. 10, pp. 52–60.
SCHACHTER, S., NUTTIN, J., DE MONCHAUX, C., MAUCORPS, P. H., OSMER, D., DUIJKER, H., ROMMETVEIT, R., and ISRAEL, J. (1954), 'Cross-cultural experiments in threat and rejection', *Human Relations*, no. 7, pp. 403–39.
SCOTT, W. A. (1965), 'Psychological and social correlates of international images', in H. C. Kelman (ed.), *International Behavior*, Holt, New York.
SHERIF, M. (1968), 'If the social scientist is to be more than a mere technician', *Journal of Social Issues*, no. 24, pp. 41–61.
SMELSER, N. (1968), 'Notes on the methodology of comparative analysis of economic activity', in N. Smelser (ed.), *Essays in Sociological Explanation*, Prentice-Hall, Englewood Cliffs, N.J.
SOMMER, R. (1966), 'Man's proximate environment', *Journal of Social Issues*, no. 4, pp. 59–70.

SOMMER, R. (1968), 'Intimacy ratings in five countries', *International Journal of Psychology*, no. 3, pp. 109–14.
STARBUCK, W. H. (1966), 'The efficiency of British and American retail employees', *Administrative Science Quarterly*, no. 11, pp. 345–85.
STEIGLITZ, H. (1965), *Organizational Structures of International Companies*, National Industrial Conference Board, New York.
TAIRA, K. (1962), 'Characteristics of Japanese labor markets', *Economic Development and Cultural Change*, no. 10, pp. 150–68.
TAJFEL, H. (1968), 'Second thoughts about cross-cultural research and international relations', *International Journal of Psychology*, no. 3, pp. 213–19.
TANAKA, Y., and OSGOOD, C. E. (1962), 'Cross-cultural, cross-concept and cross-subject generality of affective meaning systems', *Journal of Personality and Social Psychology*, no. 2, pp. 143–53.
TAUSKY, C. (1967), 'An organizational alienation', *American Sociological Review*, no. 32, p. 118.
TEXTOR, R. B. (1967), *A Cross-Cultural Summary*, Human Relations Area Files, New Haven, Connecticut.
THORELLI, H. B. (1966), 'The multi-national corporation as a changing event', *The Southern Journal of Business*, July.
TRIANDIS, H. C. (1967), 'Interpersonal relations in international organizations', *Organizational Behavior and Human Performance*, no. 2, pp. 26–55.
TRIANDIS, H. C., and VASSILIOU, V. (1967), 'Frequency of contact and stereotyping', *Journal of Personality and Social Psychology*, no. 7, pp. 316–28.
TRIANDIS, H. C., VASSILIOU, V., and NASSIAKOU, M. (1968), 'Three cross-cultural studies of subjective culture', *Journal of Personality and Social Psychology*, vol. 8, no. 4, part 2, pp. 1–42.
TRIST, E. L., and BAMFORTH, E. K. (1951), 'Some social and psychological consequences of the long-wall method of coal-getting', *Human Relations*, no. 4, pp. 3–38.
UDY, S. H. (1959a), '"Bureaucracy" and "rationality" in Weber's organization theory', *American Sociological Review*, no. 24, pp. 791–5.
UDY, S. H. (1959b), *The Organization of Work*, Human Relations Area Files, New Haven, Connecticut.
UDY, S. H. (1961), 'Technical and institutional factors in production organization', *American Journal of Sociology*, no. 67, pp. 247–60.

UDY, S. H. (1962), 'Administrative rationality, social setting, and organizational development', *American Journal of Sociology*, no. 68, pp. 299–308.

WEBB, E. J., CAMPBELL, D. T., SCHWARTZ, R. D., and SECHREST, L. (1966), *Unobtrusive Measures: Nonreactive Research in the Social Sciences*, Rand-McNally, Chicago.

WESLEY, F., and KARR, C. (1966), 'Problems in establishing norms for cross-cultural comparisons', *International Journal of Psychology*, no. 1, pp. 257–62.

WHITEHILL, A. M. (1964), 'Cultural values and employee attitudes: United States and Japan', *Journal of Applied Psychology*, no. 48, pp. 69–72.

WHITING, J. W. M. (1954), 'The cross-cultural method', in G. Lindzey (ed.), *Handbook of Social Psychology*, Addison-Wesley, Mass.

WHITING, J. W. M. (1968), 'Methods and problems in cross-cultural research', in G. Lindzey and E. Aranson (eds.), *Handbook of Social Psychology*, vol. 2 (2nd ed.), Addison-Wesley, Mass.

WHITTAKER, J. O., and MEADE, R. D. (1968), 'Retention of opinion change as a function of differential source credibility: a cross cultural study', *International Journal of Psychology*, no. 3, pp. 103–8.

WHYTE, W. F. (1969), *Organizational Behavior: Theory and Application*, Irwin-Dorsey, Illinois.

WHYTE, W. F., and WILLIAMS, L. K. (1963), 'Supervisory leadership: an international comparison', *Proceedings of the International Council for Scientific Management, Thirteenth International Management Congress*, pp. 481–8.

WILLIAMS, L. K., WHYTE, W. F., and GREEN, C. S. (1965), 'Do cultural differences affect worker attitudes?', *Industrial Relations*, no. 5, pp. 105–17.

ZIMBARDO, P. (1969a), *The Cognitive Control of Motivation*, Scott-Foresman, Illinois.

ZIMBARDO, P. (1969b), 'The human choice: individuation reason and order versus deindividuation, impulse and chaos', *Nebraska Symposium on Motivation*, no. 17, pp. 237–308.

Part Two
The Cultural Framework – The Effects of Values, Beliefs and Manifest Behaviour on Management

Fayerweather's 'Personal Relations' illustrates how some of the values, beliefs and manifest behaviour in different cultures could affect the relation between U.S. executives and the people whom they encounter in other countries. He lists several obstacles to communication – language, customs, environmental conditions, cultural attitudes and façades masking the true character.

The next reading is a short list of differences between French and American businessmen. Eggers presents twelve such differences in a light vein.

The third reading, Howard V. Perlmutter's article, deals with the problems of how the differences between countries, primarily between Western and Eastern bloc countries, will evolve now that business corporations are moving across national boundaries with ever-growing ease. Perlmutter uses four concepts denoting the relation between the cultures of different countries – 'divergence', 'submergence', 'convergence' and 'emergence'. His conclusion is that the multinational corporations will eventually create an emergent culture in the different countries in which they operate.

Finally, in the fourth reading, Weinshall discusses differences in a few areas – communication, education, social stratification and organization structures – between several countries. He brings research results indicating differences in communication behaviour and in social stratification. The main part of Weinshall's reading is devoted to the education of multinational managers, presenting differences in attitudes, values and relationships between students from many countries in an international business school and how they could be brought closer together.

4 John Fayerweather

Personal Relations

Excerpt from John Fayerweather, *Management of International Operations*, McGraw-Hill Book Co. Inc., 1960, chapter 2, pp. 14–36.

The business activities involved in managing international operations cover a wide range of functions – borrowing from banks, making market analyses, negotiating with unions, and so on. Running all through these activities, however, is one common thread – the administrative process, the art of getting things done through people. In establishing policies, making decisions, and taking action, people are an ever-present factor. Whether they take initiative or not, whether they agree or disagree, how they try to accomplish objectives; these and other personal elements play a part in virtually every situation.

In domestic business the human element is of course significant. But in international business it assumes a new character because of the differences in language, customs, and culture which distinguish the peoples of the world. The art of getting things done through foreign people is a skill unto itself requiring capacities for understanding and flexibility well beyond those necessary in domestic business.

This chapter has to be seen in the context of business activities generally, the human element therein and the problems of the administrative process in an assortment of forms. It is provided at the outset to set the stage for consideration throughout the book of administrative methods in various contexts. It focuses on those differences in characteristics which complicate relations between U.S. executives and the foreign people with whom they associate.

Avoiding stereotypes

There is one great hazard in writing and thinking about foreign people which must be emphasized at the start of this discussion. For practical reasons it is common to generalize about people, to say that the 'Mexicans act this way' or that the 'French think that way'. While such generalities serve certain purposes which will be discussed below, their limitations must be clearly understood. Each foreign person is an individual with a distinctive personality. He is unique. Thus the generalities must never be taken as descriptive of the qualities of each individual in a country.

This hazard is in itself a significant obstacle to effective administration abroad. It is all too common for U.S. businessmen to go overseas with preconceived images of various foreign peoples and to treat each person they meet as though he had all the qualities of the stereotype. People are not stereotypes, they are individuals. Each has his own personality, and to be administratively effective the businessman must seek out and work with the unique qualities of each man.

For the businessman, generalities about people are useful in two ways: first, because they indicate the characteristics which are most common among that group of people, they provide helpful initial hypotheses about the qualities which an individual *may* have. In trying to comprehend the meaning of the words and actions of men whom he does not yet know well, the generalizations supply leads to possible explanations. For example, he may have been told that Latin Americans tend to say that they will do something to be agreeable without actually meaning to fulfil the agreement. He may then consider this as a possible explanation if a new Latin American supplier, Mr Gomez, does not ship him some goods on an agreed delivery date. But this can only be a hypothesis, for it may be that Mr Gomez rigorously respects agreements and the problem lay in a linguistic misunderstanding or some other difficulty. It is most assuredly not possible to assume that all Latin Americans do not do what they say they will, only that this is a likely possibility.

Second, the generalities often describe the codes of commonly approved practice in a country, its ideology, and its standards.

As such, they serve as guides for the population as a whole, both in their own actions and especially in judging the actions of others. Knowledge of the codes is helpful to the businessman in understanding how others feel about a situation and how he will be expected to act. For example, since being agreeable is highly valued in Latin America and the precise meeting of delivery dates is not considered so important, Mr Gomez would not be viewed critically by other Latin Americans and probably would not feel very guilty himself. Furthermore, the U.S. businessman would probably be expected to be pleasant about the whole affair even if it turned out that Mr Gomez had been negligent.

Thus the study of national characteristics is a useful pursuit for the businessman, providing him with valuable clues as to traits he may find in his foreign business associates and giving him a picture of the codes which govern their expectations and standards. Used in this manner, rather than as stereotypes to be applied indiscriminately, generalizations can contribute greatly to administrative skill abroad.

Obstacles to communication

The road to satisfactory administrative relations with foreigners is obstructed by a series of potential blocks to communication. In sum these obstacles make up the meaning of 'foreignness', as it applies to each individual. The problem they pose for the U.S. businessman is usually compounded by his deeply rooted orientation to life according to the pattern of his own society. While he recognizes that foreigners are different, he still finds it hard to understand and especially to adjust to the great variety of ways in which this difference manifests itself. Some differences he may not see, the meaning of some that he sees may not be evident to him, and even when he sees and understands, it is often with the greatest difficulty that he determines an effective approach to accommodating for the gap which separates his ways from those of the foreigner.

This subject involves the whole complex of human life with a myriad of individual variations, and as such it is difficult and a bit risky to reduce it to the orderly presentation of the written page. It is possible nonetheless to set out some guideposts which will help men in overcoming the obstacles to communication. The chief obstacles can be grouped together and within each group the main directions in which the characteristics of foreign people differ from those of the general pattern of the United States can be outlined and finally some useful observations may be made about adjusting to the differences. In this manner, the mind of the reader will be set off along paths of exploration which, when applied to particular countries and situations, will bring greater understanding and open the way for effective administration.

Language

Differences in language are readily apparent as obstacles to communication. Most U.S. businessmen recognize that it would be desirable for them to learn the languages of the foreigners with whom they work. But as Americans are generally not linguists, many of them are reluctant to make the effort. Usually they can find a substantial number of English-speaking people among local populations, and it may appear that adequate management can be accomplished by working through them without requiring the considerable effort of learning a new language. However, this approach involves three potentially important impediments to communication.

First, the extent of the effort an American makes to learn the native tongue affects the feelings of the people towards him. If he treats it as an important matter and applies himself to it diligently, he creates a favourable impression and the foreigners with whom he works are more inclined to be receptive to his communications. But if he has a casual attitude towards learning their tongue, the people react negatively. They are inclined to infer from his actions that he does not respect their country and their pride is offended. When feelings like this are aroused, the effectiveness of communication declines.

Second, the actual capacity of foreigners to understand English may be considerably lower than appears on the surface. For every person who has a mastery of English there are probably ten who can carry on a fairly lucid conversation but who only understand a part of what they hear. These people pose a problem because all too often they will say they understand something and then from subsequent events it becomes clear that they didn't really understand. The cultural attitudes which lead them to say they understand when they don't will be mentioned later. Suffice at this point to observe that if the conversation is held in the native language, the chances of misunderstanding are reduced.

Third, the foreigners who know English are likely to be from the more U.S.-oriented part of the population, so there is a danger that communicating through them will result in a slanted and restricted contact with the country. They may themselves be in touch with only a limited section of the population and they may be inclined to tell the U.S. businessman what they think he wants to hear. If the businessman wishes effective communication with labourers, government officials, customers, and others, he must be able to communicate directly with them in their own language.

Customs

The term 'customs' is used here to mean the habitual physical actions of people – the way they dress, their manner of conversing, and so forth – as distinguished from their mental attitudes which will be discussed later. This distinction is artificial in that many of the customs are related to mental attitudes, but for present purposes it is convenient to think of the two separately.

Differences in customs can obstruct communication because they complicate the attempts of individuals to have easy social intercourse. The customs which are most significant for administrative work are those which might be called the stage setting for communication: the form of address people use (first names, Mr, etc.), the form of greeting (hand-shake, embrace, bow, etc.), the tone of voice used in conversation (jocular, subdued, etc.), the distance that people stand from each other while talking (typically closer in Latin America than in the United States), and so on. None of these things are in themselves especially important. In total, however, they make up the physical environment within which the people of each society have grown accustomed to carrying on their social intercourse. When the environment is right they feel at ease, and communication can proceed normally.

When strange elements are introduced, the individual becomes uncomfortable. Often he may not really know what is bothering him but he feels uneasy and communication becomes less effective. Probably everyone has had experiences of this character. What happens at a dinner table when someone's manners are notably different from those of others – as when a man eats with his knife? What happens in a management committee when a female executive is suddenly added to the group? The strange element does not really affect the other people. They should in theory be able to carry on just as though it were not there. In fact, however, they are uneasy, a bit embarrassed, and there is usually a stiffness and reserve which slows down the whole process of communication.

The strange elements in these cases are minor in impact, however, compared to those experienced abroad. The U.S. businessman thrown into foreign groups encounters a variety of customs which disturb him. In Latin America he finds people crowding up close to him to talk and on occasion giving him a warm *abrazo* suggesting an unfamiliar intimacy, or in India he meets men who either won't shake hands or who give him a weak handshake that leaves him doubtful of their manliness. For the foreigner the problem is similar. The Latin American finds the U.S. businessman is ever retreating from him as he tries to converse, and he has an uneasy feeling that the man dislikes him. The Indian shudders at the American's hearty handshake, physical contact with strangers being thoroughly distasteful to him.

The discomforts which experiences like these cause are a daily occurrence in business abroad. For the U.S. businessman they are often just minor problems but sometimes they are of major importance and in total they are a significant impediment to his efforts at communication with foreigners. Overcoming them is not easy. The ideal solution would seem to be to adapt fully to the foreign customs. In fact that is hard to do. Customs are deeply rooted and not readily modified. Most of them are at an instinctive level and changing them requires a conscious and consistent effort which is not readily undertaken by men who are busy all day with pressing business matters.

Furthermore, attempts at adaptation are not always viewed favourably by foreign nationals. Whereas there is a general tendency to appreciate the efforts of Americans to learn a foreign language, even if the results are far from perfect, the reaction to people who copy native customs is more often unfavourable. A recent novel by a noted Indian writer describes with a critical air the efforts of the wife of an American businessman to conform to Indian practice by wearing a sari.[1] Far from being viewed as a compliment or friendly gesture, her actions were considered patronizing and insulting. The extent of such reactions varies greatly among segments of populations according to the types of feeling that they attach to different customs.

So the degree to which one should adopt foreign customs is not a simple question. The solution will depend on the nature of the situation, the country, the individuals involved, and other circumstances. The only safe generalization is that it will help the U.S. businessman to know in advance that differences in customs are a potential source of discomfort both to himself and the foreigners he is with and that if he thinks about them he may, as events unroll, be able to minimize the problems by checking their effect on himself and conforming to the customs of the others when he feels that is wise.

Environmental understanding

A large number of difficulties in communication between U.S. businessmen and foreigners involve disagreements over specific business decisions. In some cases there are deeper personality differences behind these disagreements; problems of that order will be discussed in the next section. In a great many cases, however, the men simply disagree in their intellectually derived conclusions as to what will be the soundest course of action. While such disagreements are found in all types of business, they often have a distinctive character in foreign situations and an awareness of this distinction is essential to the skills of international administration.

For the most part these problems arise because of the inadequacy of men's knowledge of their environment and shortcomings in their analysis of what they do know, combined with the practice of filling gaps in knowledge and analysis with assumptions based on prior experiences. In the changing and poorly documented con-

1. Rau (1956).

ditions of many foreign countries, differences of this nature are extremely common. Such questions as: 'What advertising programme will be most effective?' 'Will government policies force establishment of a factory?' and 'How can we best satisfy the demands of the union?' must be answered on the basis of very skimpy information. Furthermore, the partial data which are available sometimes lead in different directions depending upon how they are weighted or interpreted.

Confronted by such situations, businessmen must fill the gaps in their information as best they can. Their natural tendency is to call upon the accumulation of past experience – memories of previous situations, assumptions based on general knowledge of people and economic conditions, and whatever else their minds can latch on to which seems to be pertinent. The problems which this process creates in foreign situations are immediately apparent. The U.S. businessman, unless he has spent most of his life abroad, will inevitably find that some of the resources he is calling upon are derived from experience in the United States. He may well be quite unconscious of what is happening. Like a great electronic computer he takes in a few facts and the memory relays do the rest, snapping out assumptions and principles producing a conclusion. The result might be entirely sound for that set of facts as applied to the United States, but there is no assurance that it will fit the foreign environment. Avoiding such errors is difficult even for men who are well aware of the basic problem. Under pressure to make decisions and push along with the day's work, it is very hard to check constantly the basic assumptions behind one's thinking.

For the foreign executives, sound environmental assumptions come more easily. They think naturally in terms of the surroundings within which they have grown up and worked. But in the dynamic situations common to many foreign countries their assumptions suffer from another hazard, that of inertia. Their instincts are set on the basis of the way things were. They may consciously try to correct their thinking to see things as they are now and will be, but the past is always there ready to hold them back.

The difficulties of U.S. and foreign executives in understanding the current business environment represent continuing obstacles to communication. There is a tendency for the men on each side to see in broad generalizations a basis for believing that their assumptions are right. The foreigner says that he knows his country and what will work in it. The U.S. businessman says that conditions are changing in the direction of U.S. business practices, which in considerable measure is true, and he is sure, therefore, that he is on the right track.

The best hope for resolving problems of this character is the endless search for new data and the application of ever better thinking to them. But there will always be many problems for which there are not enough data to permit a clear analytical conclusion. It is at this point that the administrative skill of the businessman is tested. He must be ever alert to recognize the assumptions behind his thinking and sensitive to the assumptions of his foreign associates. They may still end up in strong disagreement; but if he has an understanding of why they are disagreeing, he may work out a sensible solution and not allow the argument to degenerate into a collision which is destructive of the whole basis for communication.

Cultural attitudes[2]

The cultural attitudes of a group are broadly defined as the integrated pattern of beliefs, codes, and feelings on the basis of which the group has learned to live with its environment. They include beliefs about nature and the supernatural, attitudes about how men should treat each other, codes of morals, and all the other fundamentals which govern men's lives. The members of a group will not all have the same attitudes as those of the group culture. The earlier observations about stereotypes apply most strongly in this case because each individual is definitely a unique personality. But the cultural attitudes are significant because of the frequency with which they are found in the group and because they compose the ideology of the group.

The ideology aspect is most important for the communications problem. If an attitude held by a man is regarded as normal,

2. The balance of this chapter is based on the findings of a research study reported at greater length in Fayerweather (1959).

proper, and right by his society, it is quite a different matter than it would be if it were simply an individual characteristic. The man has a much greater conviction as to its correctness, and he can readily find explicit reinforcement for his position from people around him. Therefore, when the communications problems of the U.S. businessman are due to culturally based attitudes, he faces a potentially serious obstacle. The problem is a two-sided one because it includes both his own attitudes and those of the foreigner.

To appreciate the nature of the problem it is necessary to step back and view the origin and meaning of cultural attitudes in broad perspective. They are the result of a long process of evolution, representing a formula which the group has developed as a viable system for coping with its environment. The process of evolution is confused and halting and the result is far from perfect. But in broad terms the formula has proved effective in permitting the people to live together and meet the problems with which nature and history have confronted them. The problems change through the course of time, and the cultural attitudes change to meet the new conditions. Inevitably there is some lag between the change in conditions and the formulation of new attitudes at the cultural level. However, for most of the people the cultural attitudes will at a given time serve quite satisfactorily as a set of guiding principles for the life they are leading.

Thus the cultural attitudes draw basic strength from both historical testing and current effectiveness. Their power in the lives of individuals, however, is derived in an immediate sense from the training people receive, particularly in childhood. Each generation passes on a large measure of its attitudes to the next. Children are told what is right and wrong, and through various rewards and punishments the lessons are driven home. They watch their elders and by imitation acquire the skills of social living. As time goes on they may modify their attitudes to meet the requirements of new experiences. But most of their experiences are with people or conditions which are intimately tied to the culture so their early attitudes are more likely to be reinforced than changed. Therefore, while there are many variations among the individuals in a group, there is a strong tendency for the cultural attitudes to be deeply impressed on their personalities.

These are the powerful forces which are in the background every time a U.S. businessman works with a foreigner. Behind each man is a vast accumulation of history, environment, and education supporting the cultural attitudes of his society. Because there is a large measure of common experience in the history of mankind, there are fortunately many similarities among cultures. Some, like the English and others of Anglo-Saxon origin, are essentially similar to that of the United States. But there are also many differences and it is these which are significant as potential blocks to communication.

The types of attitude which are pertinent to business and the variations among them are very numerous. Four groups of attitudes stand out, however, as the more common and troublesome sources of difficulty for the U.S. businessman. They are: attitudes towards other people, values, social status attitudes, and attitudes towards individual work.

Attitudes towards other people. The attitudes with which men approach their relations with other people may be analysed in many ways but for the businessman the most useful approach seems to be the distinction between two types of personality: the 'individualistic' and the 'group oriented'. The patterns of attitudes and actions of these two types are shown in the diagram in Figure 1.

In his essential relationships the individualistic personality walls himself off as much as possible from those around him. The distinction between essential (e.g. work) and non-essential (e.g. recreational, social activities) is significant because he may be sociable and communicative in the latter while isolated and secretive in the former. He is not self-sufficient because that is impossible, but maximum self-sufficiency is his objective. He looks upon those around him as necessary evils. He is distrustful, suspecting them of predatory intentions towards him; and he feels a sense of hostility towards them. In any relationship he is intensely concerned with his own position and not very conscious of the attitudes of others except as he perceives their impact on him. As the size of the circles indicates, he gives much more attention to those above him than those below.

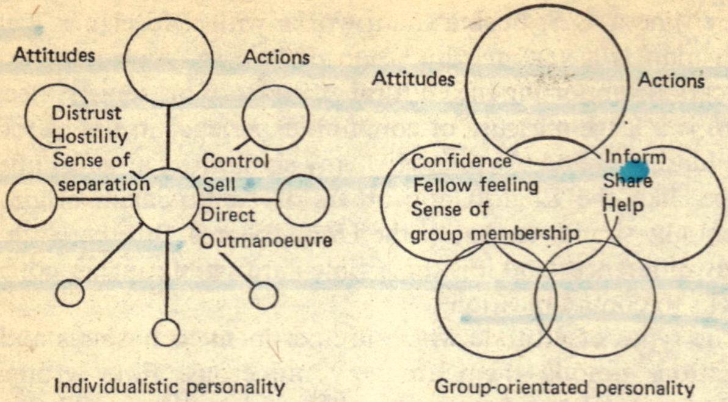

Figure 1 Attitudes and relationships with other men

The group-oriented personality has a feeling of relationship and union with those around him. His satisfactions are in considerable measure achieved as group objectives or just in being a part of a smoothly operating group. He views those around him with confidence, sensing that they have the same group objectives as he. He gives only slightly more thought to his superiors than to his subordinates.

The cultural attitudes in a large part of the world tend towards the individualistic pattern while those of the United States industrial society tend towards the group-oriented personality.[3] The origins of these differences lie in the history of the economic and social patterns in different countries.

The business activities of many countries are dominated by the merchant-trader philosophy. The merchant is essentially a lone wolf. He may make alliances for business purposes, but his stock in trade historically has been his capacity to outbargain and outmanoeuvre other businessmen. He has had to be shrewd and secretive. These are the characteristics of the individualistic

3. These two terms should not be confused with two others which are similar. 'Individualistic' is quite different from 'individualism'. Individualism describes the attitude of independence and liberalism of the man who feels a large degree of freedom in the conduct of his personal life. 'Group-oriented' is not the same as 'group-conforming' or 'group-submissive'. Group conformity is the opposite of individualism, describing the status of the individual whose way of life is dictated by the rules of his society.

personality, and they are strong in the merchant segment of any society. In the United States that segment is today a minor portion of the business community. But it is still the major element in many countries. These attitudes are not restricted to those who are traders, for the factory owners in many countries are simply overgrown merchants, men who have integrated backwards but still retain the basic attitudes of the trading community.

The distinguishing feature of business life in the United States and a few other countries is the dominance of the large, widely owned corporation run by a team of professional managers. The shrewdness of individual executives contributes to the success of the corporation, but equally important is their capacity to produce results as a group. They may compete with each other but only up to a limit. Beyond that, competition must give way to cooperation for the common good. The effective man in this environment is the man who can have confidence in others and can take satisfaction in accomplishing work in common with them. Those are the attitudes of the group-oriented personality.

While attitudes towards relations with other men might be explained solely by these patterns of business activity, other historical differences have also played a part in their evolution. In most countries, opportunities for the individual have been sharply restricted by the scarcity of land, the poverty of the economy, or the rigidity of society. Progress for the individual under these circumstances has often been a matter of getting ahead at the expense of someone else, success going to those who were good at grabbing advantages by whatever means would work: bribing a government official for a concession, squeezing a worker in a company store, and so on. Further influence has come from authoritarian systems in religious, educational, political, and family life. These systems have in many cases encouraged subordinates to compete excessively for the favour of superiors and to escape the will of superiors by lies and evasion. All of these conditions have encouraged the development of the individualistic personality – a man viewing all the world as dangerous and artful in the skills of getting the most he can out of it at the expense of others.

To a degree, similar forces have been present in the United

States, but there have been strong compensating elements. The country has been sufficiently large and wealthy to permit many people to get ahead through their own creative efforts; so cutting the other man out has been less prominent as a road to success. In the frontier conditions which prevailed through much of the country's history, individuals had to collaborate in defence, agricultural, and construction efforts so the habits of mutual confidence and cooperation were encouraged. Despite many authoritarian elements in U.S. society, there has always been a liberal tradition which provided an outlet for the individual. New political parties were permitted to grow, religious deviants were either tolerated or at least able to move to a new area, and even in family life children were given greater leeway than was common in many other societies. All of these elements have encouraged the evolution of group-oriented attitudes – the assurance that others may be trusted and the capacity to cooperate willingly with them.

Men with individualistic tendencies are quite effective in the commercial life of most foreign countries. In fact they are generally more effective than group-oriented executives who are too easily outmanoeuvred. But the individualistic personality is not highly effective as a working associate, especially on the management team of a subsidiary. The relationships that he tends to develop with other men in the organization are not conducive to effective group effort.

He views his superior with a mixture of awe and fear. His chief concern is to keep the superior feeling favourable towards him by being obedient or at least appearing so. If he disagrees with the superior he is not likely to say so. He will either follow instructions without question or, if he feels strongly about his own views, he may evade the instructions. He makes little effort to inform the superior about affairs in his organization, especially if there are problems which may reflect to his discredit. His general attitude towards the superior is one of 'dealing with' him. The superior is feared as a powerful force and tremendous effort is expended in keeping on the right side of him.

Subordinates are viewed essentially as tools to be used for various purposes. As their attitudes are assumed to be individualistic they are not trusted. They are trained only enough so they can do their work. To do more would put them in a position to push the superior out of his job.

Fortunately, the basic lack of confidence which characterizes this sort of atmosphere is often moderated by the paternalistic relationship which carries with it certain responsibilities and obligations. While, as noted above, strongly authoritarian systems seem to encourage excessively competitive and evasive attitudes, they also usually include certain understood ties which hold the members together. The superior has a continuing responsibility for the welfare of the subordinates, and the subordinates are bound to give in return a degree of loyalty and faithful service to the superior. This is the pattern of the family and the large estate. The extent to which it applies to a management organization is extremely variable, depending in large measure on the actions of the head of the organization. As this man is often a U.S. executive it poses a difficult problem for him. Some U.S. executives have assumed a position which is virtually the same as the traditional *patron* while others rigorously avoid it. And many pursue a middle course, no simple task.

The superior – subordinate relationship is troublesome but it at least is a direct carry-over from a system which has been effective in the accomplishment of the basic tasks of authoritarian societies for centuries. Relations with men outside the direct chain of command are another matter. The individualistic personality is highly ineffective in developing the patterns of cooperation and group effort which are expected in management organizations. The heads of other departments and staff men are seen essentially as competitors. The efforts of the individualistic executive are concentrated on making himself look better than the others in the eyes of the boss and pressing every advantage possible for the immediate gain of his section of the company. Manoeuvres and tricks seriously impede the administrative process.

Values. The differences in values which are of primary significance to the businessman are mostly those which are classed as moral standards or codes of conduct. Because social and religious sanctions are associated with such values in most cultures, they are a difficult subject to discuss objectively. This is especially true of the U.S. businessman who comes from one of the most rigorously moralistic cultures in the world. Clearly the whole matter is a very profound one and in this book only a few observations can be made about it.

To start with, the nature of value systems should be understood. There is a basic moral code which is common to practically every civilized nation: stealing and lying are bad, being kind to people and honouring one's parents are good, etc. Systems of values, as the name implies, are concerned with the importance assigned to different elements in the code and not the code itself. They help a man to make the numerous choices between evils with which life abounds.

Furthermore, a system of values is an integral part of a group's whole cultural system. As such, it serves its role in keeping the society functioning effectively. Like other parts of the cultural pattern, it evolved naturally as a useful element in the people's approach to dealing with their environment.

In this perspective, differences in values can be understood even if it is hard emotionally to accept them. Four of the differences which are most disturbing to the U.S. businessman abroad may be taken as examples.

1. There is the tendency in many cultures for subordinates and others to give weight to politeness, form, and agreeableness at the expense of the accuracy and directness which are emphasized in the U.S. ideology. In large part this attitude is derived from the individualistic pattern of relations described in the preceding section. The role of subordinates is to be submissive and obedient and not to embarrass and irritate superiors. In their own interests they do not wish to raise subjects which will make them look bad or cause trouble. So when a subordinate talks to a superior the whole emphasis is on making the occasion pleasant, with direct, accurate reporting having little importance.

Supplementing this attitude is the general view of the people as to what is important and worthwhile in life. In many societies a high value is placed on the enjoyment of the pleasures of the moment. When two people are together, the experience will be pleasant if they are agreeable to each other, and unpleasant subjects are not raised. The U.S. culture is not averse to such pleasantness, but it encourages sacrificing it in many circumstances for the sake of the contribution to industrial efficiency or other causes achieved by accurate and direct reporting of even unpleasant facts and opinions.

2. In many countries bribery is more common than in the United States, a problem which confronts many Americans early in their careers abroad. On the surface there does not appear to be any compensating value judgement involved in bribery but usually there is, at least in part. The complicating factor is that in some countries bribery is almost an institutionalized form of direct taxation. Government workers are grossly underpaid and they earn a decent living only by exacting bribes from those for whom they do service. But in the background is a value decision involving one of those broad ideals which characterize the U.S. culture. The choice is between an irregular and personalized method of administration and a systematized and impersonal approach. In the United States there is tremendous emphasis on regularizing and systematizing life in the interests of efficiency and maximum productivity. By contrast, in many foreign countries these objectives receive far less weight and, given the individualistic approach to life along with the low pay of government workers, the exchange of bribes for special treatment does not meet with the same disapproval.

3. There is the question of stealing. Here it must be noted that the differences in values among countries are diminishing very rapidly, particularly as applied to people in the higher-income groups. Still, it is true that every year a significant number of management men in some foreign areas are reported as having taken company funds, and the proportion seems to be higher than the number of similar cases in the United States. The difference is due in part to the lower standard of living in these countries creating a somewhat greater incentive for stealing. But in the background is another fundamental difference in value systems. In the United States the deterrent to theft is only partly the legal penalty. More important for most people is the social stigma attached to being a thief, and at the back of that is the impact of stealing on the structure of a society in which much depends on a large measure of mutual confidence even between strangers. Such a system cannot exist if dishonesty is common, so the man who

breaks the code carries a heavy load of public disapproval. By contrast, in the individualistic societies, people do not have confidence in each other anyway, so the thief is not hurting society, just the man he steals from. If it happens that he steals from a large, impersonal U.S. corporation, there is little reason why his society should criticize him.

4. There is a range of values which affect relations with people. Americans are great advocates of such codes as 'giving the other fellow a break' and 'playing the game by the rules'. Many of these codes are virtually unknown in some countries, leaving the individual much greater leeway in the methods by which he seeks his own advancement. The background of this difference will readily be evident from what has already been said about individualistic versus group-oriented cultures. In the latter, mutual confidence and cooperation among men requires a code for protection of the individual. If he is to give other men important data, sacrifice his immediate advancement for the common good, and make other group-oriented contributions, he must have assurance that others will not take advantage of his position. Thus general codes of conduct have evolved and are enforced by strong social pressures. In the individualistic society there is no need for such codes, because every one is expected to protect himself.

These four areas of differences in values by no means exhaust the subject but in them can be seen the main elements of the problem – the fact that actions which may in themselves appear 'bad' by U.S. standards are culturally approved choices between two alternatives and that the approval has a sound basis as part of the total cultural pattern.

Social status attitudes. The quest for social status is common to all societies. There are differences, however, in the social objectives of people and the intensity with which they pursue them.

In the United States, social status is relatively less important than in most other cultures. Social distinctions have fallen away rapidly in the last century, resulting in something approaching a classless society. There are, to be sure, differences, but a large mass of people fall into the middle class and their way of life is the standard for the culture. There is a large degree of mobility in the society and people move up and down the social scale without extreme strain. Thus in the minds of the mass of people who live in or close to the middle class, social differentiation is not a major preoccupation.

Similar attitudes prevail only in those few regions where a comparable social levelling has taken place, such as Scandinavia. Elsewhere, extreme ranges of wealth, education, and power are found, and those who have accumulated one or more of these scarce assets guard the status it has given them jealously. Two forms of status are of particular significance to the businessman in these societies: economic level and professional position.

Where sharp distinctions exist between upper, middle, and lower classes the flexibility of management is considerably reduced. A man's pattern of activities is generally restricted to what is acceptable by the standards of his economic class, and it is with the greatest difficulty that he shifts into a different class. For example, a man from the middle class is usually not effective as a sales manager if the job requires selling to upper-class factory owners. He does not know how to handle himself in the new social environment and the men he meets do not readily accept him. Likewise, men are not generally willing to do work which is associated with a status beneath their economic level. A young man from the upper classes, for example, will not serve as a worker on an assembly line in most countries even if it is only for a training period.

Professional position is generally based on degree or type of education and the character of work in which a man is engaged. Among those with substantial education there is typically a hierarchy, and a man's rank in this hierarchy is as important as economic level for his social status. Depending upon the values of the society, one finds the educated élite (doctors, lawyers, and college professors), government officials, army officers, and others at various levels in the hierarchy. But almost always the businessmen are down at the bottom. The low estate of the businessmen arises from their association with the merchant-trader class who are more often than not regarded as money-grubbing, dishonest parasites.

The feelings attached to professional status affect the businessman in two important ways. First, where businessmen are not highly regarded, the best young men typically seek other careers, leaving management work to less able men, and the latter often have a sense of inferiority about their status in relations with government officials and others who stand higher in the hierarchy. Second, respect for symbols of professional status is very important. For the U.S. businessman this may only require giving proper recognition of a man's status: for example, in Mexico, by addressing lawyers as *licenciado*. But often it means being acutely sensitive to situations in which status feelings are important; for example, by assigning a man who always wanted to be a lawyer to serve a semi-legal function in government negotiations or by showing appreciation of the progress of an engineer in a professional society.

Because status is so important in many cultures, social advancement is highly valued. Major progress is generally impossible for an individual but some degree of advancement is often feasible, and the rewards being great, the ambitions of men may run high. The energy with which they pursue those ambitions varies greatly. In some dynamic countries like Mexico, an aggressive drive for progress is common. In many, however, the lack of opportunities and the general lethargy of the culture have combined to discourage energetic efforts, and the cultural standards foster an attitude of resignation and acceptance of one's given lot in life. Still, ambitions are always present in some form and must be catered to if morale is to be sustained.

Attitudes towards individual work. The ways in which the peoples of the world approach their individual assignments vary for many reasons, among which the most important, for administrative purposes, are their attitudes towards innovation, analysis, and discipline.

Attitudes towards innovation. In the U.S. culture great emphasis is placed on innovation. The inventor is a hero; customers are always looking for something new and better; and people in all walks of life are encouraged to apply their imagination and creativity, giving constant stimulus to a dynamic society.

In some cultures similar attitudes are found, notably in relatively new nations which like the United States lack stong traditional roots and have gone through considerable transitions in recent years. The Latin American republics and some of the African countries fit this pattern. Indeed, in these countries the U.S. businessman sometimes finds that people are so eager for new approaches that they will apply U.S. methods without real consideration of whether they are suitable for the local conditions. He then finds himself cast in the role of the conservative holding back the imaginative flights of his associates.

On the other hand, there are many cultures in which the approved standard is not innovation but rather the rigorous adherence to traditional ways. These attitudes prevail through large areas of Asia and to a considerable degree in Europe. In these regions the main patterns of life have been stabilized for considerable periods. Innovations have not been generally productive, so people have grown to regard them as of doubtful value. The wise man has been the man who followed carefully the methods which have been proved sound through endless repetition. The businessman in these societies is reluctant to undertake managerial actions which do not fit established formulae.

Analysis. The scientific management which is so basic to U.S. industrial practice typifies the general cultural attitude of encouraging a thoughtful, analytical approach to all types of action. The U.S. culture is not the most extreme in this respect. Among others, the French and German cultures place even greater stress on extended intellectual effort and precise planning as a prelude to action. The U.S. culture tends to be action-oriented, and there is an impatience with the delays which analysis requires; but it is nonetheless accepted as a vital element in achieving effective action. The origins of this attitude lie back in the period of the Reformation and Renaissance in Europe when men threw off the shackles of a life dictated by dogma. Behind this revolution there also was apparently a temperamental inclination among the people which favoured moderation and deliberation.

In other societies one or both of the bases for the analytical attitude have been lacking. Throughout much of Latin America and related cultural areas like Spain, emotion and tradition have strong cultural support as the bases for action. It is regarded as acceptable, in fact as desirable, for the individual to give immediate expression to his feelings. The analytical approach is disliked because it delays and possibly frustrates the expression of the passions of the moment. Mr Gonzales in the Taylor case is a prime example of such attitudes. In addition, there is greater respect for tradition or superior authority as a determinant of courses of action, especially in situations about which the individual has no personal feelings.

In many of the Asian cultures, the same forces which discourage innovation also restrict the analytical approach to action. Respect for tradition is the dominant attitude, and analysis with its implications of independent thought and critical examination of traditional patterns is not encouraged.

Discipline. Industrial life in the United States is ruled by clocks and schedules, the devices which keep the vast interdependent system tied together in an efficiently productive whole. The cultural attitudes reflect an obedience to the dictates of this system in the form of a pervasive sense of discipline. People feel a compulsion and a responsibility to do a great variety of things which they understand to be their obligations as part of the system – they must get their day's work done, they must be on time to appointments, and so on.

This disciplined attitude towards work is not only not common in other cultures but in most it is specifically deplored. Many foreigners find the pressure and drive of the U.S. pattern of life distasteful. Their cultures have emphasized the search for satisfactions in life which are destroyed by the discipline of the U.S. system. For example, they feel that people should enjoy the company of others according to the feelings of the moment and not according to a pattern set by an appointment schedule. They appreciate a man's desires to make a product which expresses his artistic inclinations and are critical of rigid specifications which frustrate him. And the same philosophy is extended into broader areas covering production planning, government administrative systems, and other phases of life.

Attitudes towards cultural differences. Cultural differences are troublesome for the U.S. businessman, not only because they present him with a strange managerial environment but also because it is difficult to know how he should treat them. There is an inclination to be very respectful of the cultures of other people, to feel that they are something sacred and inalienable which should not be tampered with. It follows from this viewpoint that the U.S. businessman should adjust his actions and methods of management to fit the local culture. But there is a counter argument which is very persuasive when we are talking about relations in foreign business circles as compared, for example, with relations of U.S. agricultural experts in primitive communities. In the latter case the existing cultural attitudes may be regarded essentially as fixed elements, and to be effective the outsider must do all the adjusting.

But the business situation is another story. As was noted earlier, cultures are always changing to accommodate new conditions, and this is apparently just what is happening in the business sector of countries all around the world. The wave of dynamic industrialization is creating conditions which are far different from the relatively stable, commercial communities of the recent past. The large-scale manufacturing organization is replacing the merchant and the small family-owned factory as the dominant factor in economic life. The need for skilled managers and technicians is expanding rapidly. Many new management techniques are being adopted. These and other changes add up to an entirely new environment.

Under these conditions it is not sound to say that the existing cultural attitudes are a fixed element, for there is ample evidence that they are changing and that in many cases the changes are lagging behind the requirements of the conditions at hand. Furthermore, there are good reasons to conclude that they are moving in the direction of U.S. cultural attitudes. The United States has for over a half century been in the midst of the type of dynamic industrial development which is now getting started in most foreign countries. The cultural attitudes with which the U.S. businessman is familiar represent an adjustment to that sort of environment. They are doubtless an imperfect adjustment, but they have provided a relatively satisfactory basis upon which a highly productive industrial system has been built. It seems reasonable to assume that because dynamic industrial societies have much in common, the cultural patterns which other people will evolve to fit their new conditions will resemble those of the United States. Supporting this view are visible evidences of specific attitudes among the apparently more progressive businessmen of other countries which are in fact notably different from those of their native culture and quite similar to those of their U.S. counterparts.

From this the U.S. businessman might conclude that his own cultural attitudes are much more suitable for the problems confronting his foreign associates than their own and his best course should be to change their ways as rapidly as possible. In the extreme this view is usually both unsound and impractical. While foreign cultures appear to be changing in the direction of the U.S. culture, the conditions and background of each country are unique and it is highly improbable that the final outcome will be the same as the U.S. pattern. Furthermore, the difficulties of changing culturally-based attitudes are such that a deliberate effort at rapid change is almost sure to fail and probably will cause much ill feeling in the process. But a more moderate view along the same lines does have merit. If change is taking place, then it is sound practice to help and guide it. Exactly what this means for the businessman inevitably varies from case to case. Some of the men he meets are so fixed in their basic cultural pattern that the only approach is to work with them as they are. Others for practical purposes are so similar in outlook to the U.S. businessman that he does not have to adjust at all. The majority lie somewhere between these extremes. With them he has to adjust to some degree in his own ways and to some extent he is able to help them as they try to develop new approaches to life and their work. This is no easy task.

Attitudes towards U.S. businessmen

The final group of obstacles to communication includes those arising from the attitudes of foreigners towards U.S. businessmen. Feelings about the United States and its people cover a wide range. Some of them are quite favourable. For example, the democracy and generosity of Americans are generally appreciated. But for the businessman three types of attitude are the sources of difficulty in communications.

First, there is the sense of insecurity and inferiority in relations with Americans which is frequently observed in a number of countries. In some cases like India, these attitudes appear to be the result of long colonial domination and a well-developed habit of subservience to foreign masters. In others, like Mexico, they are the result of more complex elements of racial evolution. Where these attitudes are present, the U.S. businessman finds that many of the people are reluctant to take initiative or to disagree with him and that they are extremely sensitive to criticism.

Second, in a great many countries anti-United States sentiment is high. While the United States has done a great deal which is beneficial for foreign countries, there are specific U.S. policies which have irritated practically every country and these tend to attract great public attention abroad. For example, feelings in Mexico have been strongly influenced by the three U.S. military expeditions to Mexico in 1848, 1914, and 1917, and by the adverse economic impact of the U.S. cotton disposal programme and the lead and zinc import restrictions. In the background, of course, is the fear and envy of the United States as a great and rich power able to dominate relations with the weaker nations of the world.

Third, there are the specific attitudes of foreign personnel employed by U.S. companies who often feel exploited or discriminated against. Many workers believe that the companies are making big profits at their expense, an attitude which is encouraged by nationalistic and Communist agitators. At the management level the feelings are more individual in nature. In most companies, U.S. personnel receive compensation in excess of nationals in comparable jobs, either in higher salaries or in fringe areas like better pension benefits or large home-leave allowances. Furthermore, the top positions in U.S. subsidiaries are in a great many cases reserved for Americans. As foreign executives often feel they are, if anything, better qualified for these jobs because of their intimate knowledge of their country, these restrictions are insulting and personally frustrating.

These types of feeling are not always present and they are often outweighed by other influences. In a great many cases, however, they are strong enough to create an atmosphere which is either cool or actually hostile to the U.S. businessman.

The façade

Differences in language, customs, environmental understanding, and cultural attitudes along with feelings towards U.S. businessmen provide the substance for the special problems of communication for the U.S. businessman abroad. In addition there is a different type of problem which arises from a combination of the attitudes discussed above. It is often difficult for the U.S. businessman to understand the true character of the situations which confront him because the words and actions of foreigners convey a confusing impression. This is, of course, a problem in the United States but it is more common and extreme abroad because the attitudes of the individualistic personality, the emphasis on politeness and agreeableness, and the insecurity in relationships with Americans, which are found in many societies, foster a façade of superficial conduct at variance with the true feelings of the individual.

The forms the façade may take vary tremendously. For example, an individualistic junior executive who knows his superior believes in cooperation may go to great ends to appear to be cooperative with other men even though in important respects he is frustrating the development of a cooperative spirit. Another man may be highly respectful of the United States in his comments to U.S. associates, while all the time he harbours strong anti-United States feelings which are expressed in subtle obstruction of company objectives.

The façade presents a challenging problem for the administrator. It requires that he have a thorough understanding of the character of the society and that he be highly perceptive to catch the significance of any evidence that will help him to understand the real feelings which are hidden beneath the front which many people present to him. Furthermore, despite the prevalence of façades he must recognize that many of the people he meets are quite straightforward and to treat them as if they were not would be a serious error.

Patterns of personal action

From the discussion to this point, it is clear that there are many obstacles to developing satisfactory administrative relations abroad. In considering how these obstacles may be overcome, it is helpful to look at the experience of U.S. businessmen who have achieved good working relations with foreigners.

Broadly speaking, it appears that the success of these men is based on an effective adjustment to the foreign conditions and the particular individuals with whom they are associating. This involves a great assortment of adaptations to the variety of things which have been discussed in this chapter and defies most generalizations. Two common threads can be disentangled, however.

First, there is an attitude of respect and interest towards the ways and problems of the host country which removes a significant portion of the binational irritations. These attitudes put the foreigner and the U.S. businessman on common ground in their feelings towards their environment, minimizing the defensive attitudes of the foreigner.

Second, considerable attention is given to building up good personal relations with individuals. The effort in this direction goes beyond that customary in the United States where business relationships can be very impersonal and yet quite satisfactory. In part the difference abroad is an adaptation to a cultural attitude not previously mentioned which is found in Latin America and some other areas, namely, a tendency to emphasize the personal as distinguished from the functional aspects of work. But in large part its value lies in circumventing the wide range of obstacles which have been discussed by building up strong personal bonds. If two individuals like and respect each other, they may differ on many points and still work together satisfactorily.

On the other hand, the successful Americans have a sensitive respect for the integrity of others which results in limiting the extent of personal relations in accordance with the codes of the culture. While the U.S. culture is commonly considered impersonal, the exchange of personal information among Americans is very great. Friends discuss the most intimate aspects of their lives and thoughts. Abroad a much greater reserve is common, especially where the attitudes of the individualistic personality prevail.

The Latin American terms *simpatico* and *sencillo* indicate the type of attitudes which are conducive to good relations. *Simpatico* describes a man who is good company, being pleasant and amusing without offending local codes. *Sencillo* means simple with the implication that the man is unassuming and approachable and does not oppress or embarrass subordinates. In combination their meanings encourage the U.S. businessman to conduct his relationships with warmth and friendliness tempered by considered restraint. In details there will be considerable variation dictated by the range of customs and cultural attitudes in different countries; but an initial attitude of this nature is a good starting point in evolving patterns of action for relations with foreigners.

The cases

The cases in this book will include a variety of the obstacles to relations abroad which have been discussed here: differences in language, customs, environmental understanding, and cultural attitudes, feelings about United States businessmen, and the façade hiding the true character of people's feelings. In each situation the reader is encouraged to search diligently for an understanding of the point of view of both the U.S. businessmen and the foreigners and to question whether the actions of the former could be modified to achieve more effective administrative results.

References

CLEVELAND, H., and MANGONE, G. J. (eds) (1957), *The Art of Overseasmanship*, Syracuse University Press, N.Y.

FAYERWEATHER, J. (1959), *The Executive Overseas*, Syracuse University Press, N.Y.

HALL, E. T. Jr (1957), 'The Anthropology of Manners', in *Plotting a Course for New Profit Horizons*, International Management Association, New York, pp. 277–84.

HARBISON, F., and MYERS, C. (1959), *Management in the Industrial World: An International Analysis*, McGraw-Hill Co. Inc., New York.

LEDERER, W. J., and BURDICK, E. (1958), *The Ugly American*, Gollancz.

OPPENHEIMER, F. M. (1954), 'Notes on Podsnappery', *Harvard Business Review*, July-August, pp. 74–8.

RAU, S. R. (1956), *Remember the House*, Harper & Brothers, New York.

WHYTE, W. F., and HOLMBERG, A. R. (1956), 'Human Problems of United States Enterprise in Latin America', *Human Organization*, Autumn.

5 E. Russell Eggers

How to Do Business with a Frenchman

Condensed from *Harper's Magazine*, August 1965. E. Russell Eggers is President of the Loctite Corporation in Newington, Connecticut.

Obviously, there are problems in measuring Frenchmen by the standards of American industry. And vice versa. As one Frenchman put it, 'You Americans are well-trained executives of well-run corporations in the U.S. But abroad you are not clever enough, not flexible enough, not *débrouillard* (talented, resourceful, literally smart enough not only to pull strings but to disentangle them) enough to really get along in France. You are not French.'

For a more balanced look at the problem, consider the following laws, which pinpoint some basic differences between an American businessman and his opposite number in France:

1. *Whereas the American tries to think in a straight line, the Frenchman insists on thinking in a circle*. The American mistrusts complex things and tends to over-simplify. The Frenchman, by inclination and education, mistrusts simple things and tends to over-complicate. It is for this reason that no Frenchman, by American standards, can ask a simple, straightforward question when speaking in public. By French standards, no American speaker can give a full, sophisticated answer. A Frenchman tries to define the question; the American tries to answer it.

All this might be summed up in a hypothetical translation of Hamlet's soliloquy. In American business jargon, the soliloquy would probably come out: 'To be or not to be? Fine. Let's take a vote.' A Frenchman would say, '*Etre ou ne pas être. C'est là la question. Mais la question est mal posée*' – which freely translated means you cannot put the question that way.

2. *A French businessman mistrusts the very things in which an American businessman has the most confidence*. Examples? The

Frenchman is innately suspicious of the figures on a balance sheet, of the telephone, of his subordinates, of the law, of journalists and of what he reads in the press, of investment banks, and, above all else, of what an American tells him in confidence. The American, *au contraire*, has trust in all these things.

3. *An American executive tends to forget what he's said in a letter. A Frenchman never forgets what he's purposely left out.* This particular law of communication explains why negotiations often break down at a distance. After a meeting in Paris the American will write a letter so factual and so detailed that, in his own mind at least, it doesn't even require an answer. The Frenchman would consider any letter he addressed to a company in the U.S. as the beginning of a long correspondence in which he would gradually elaborate on the nuance contained in the second line of paragraph three. The American will say about the French letter, 'It's very polite but what the heck is he trying to say?' The Frenchman will ponder the American letter. 'There are many details, *mais qu'est-ce que ça veut dire ?*' What's he trying to tell me?

4. *An American will probably lose his typical enthusiasm for a project before a Frenchman gets over his typical reservations.* The business lunch in Paris is a case in point. The American executive rushing through on a two-day stop-over in France wants to talk business and then sit down to a quick snack. His potential French partner wants to eat his way graciously and cautiously to a few business remarks with the coffee. Sophisticated American negotiators know that no Frenchman can digest a new business proposition until dessert or, as the French put it, '*entre la poire et le fromage*'.

5. *A French company prepares its balance sheet and profit-and-loss statement not to show its stock-holders how much money it has made, but to show the tax authorities how little.* An American businessman considers his tax return a legal obligation to pay. But a Frenchman doen't pay, he negotiates his taxes. The tax return is merely his opening offer.

6. *A Frenchman's thoughts are packaged in small and more specific sizes than an American's.* This is due partly to the metric system and partly to the fact that the French economy is only 13 per cent

the size of the American economy. As a consequence, a Frenchman firmly believes that a small company is more efficient than a giant corporation, that custom-built products are of better quality than mass production, that the margin of profits is more important than volume of sales and profits, that details are more important than the big picture in corporate planning. It is no accident that 'economy size' in French – for example, as seen printed on a box of soap flakes that is about the size of a transistor radio – generally means a small, not a large, package.

7. *To a Frenchman, economic prosperity is a series of non-durable pleasures of lasting value. To an American, prosperity is a tangible product with constant model changes.* Two items account for over 50 per cent of the averge Frenchman's budget: food and vacations. Two items account for almost 50 per cent of the average American's budget: housing and the automobile. A Frenchman will not buy and does not really understand American refrigerators (particularly the un-refrigerated compartment for bananas) or automatic washing machines (with one of the special inside racks for the hand laundry). An American does not understand that the Frenchman's only do-it-yourself hobby is eating.

8. *A Frenchman feels as ill at ease with anything mechanical as an American does with a domestic servant.* It is surprising to what degree of suspicion and superstition a Frenchman will go to divorce himself as a person from strictly mechanical objects. To illustrate: in reply to a surprised comment from her American boss that she had been somewhat rude to a client on the telephone, an ordinarily charming French secretary said, 'But, Monsieur, I was not mad at him. I was mad at the telephone.'

9. *An American businessman treats his company like a wife; a Frenchman treats each of his companies like a mistress.* This is particularly true when a firm decides to set up a new subsidiary with a foreign partner. The American wants 100 per cent exclusivity and control over the long run. The Frenchman wants 100 per cent flexibility and freedom over the short.

10. *The word 'immoral' in English refers to what people do; in French it can apply to what companies do.* An American is shocked at the public love affair of a well-known businessman, at the

fudging of tax returns, at taking back under the table what has been formally promised in an agreement. What shocks a Frenchman? A food firm that produces frozen chickens whose growth has been accelerated by hormone injections. A manufacturer in France who closes down his plant and lays off workers without warning to all concerned, especially the government.

11. *When a Frenchman is polite he is very, very polite and when he is rude, he is very, very French.* But a Frenchman is rude only in public places – waiting for a taxi, in a restaurant, behind the wheel of a car. He is supremely polite in private places – in a letter, at a dinner, when he's being introduced. The typical Frenchman can make a prearranged telephone call to a good acquaintance and apologize three times during the conversation for calling. The same Frenchman could dial a wrong number at three in the morning and swear at the person whom he woke up. The two extremes of politeness give a Frenchman a sense of social equilibrium, and he is sure that it is more important to have discriminating manners rather than democratic ones.

12. *To the Frenchman a business career is usually a means to an end. To an American it is often an end in itself.* There are three sharp contrasts between a business career in France and the U.S. (a) The so-called 'poly-technician' – one of France's educated élite, the dominating class in French industry and government – considers his university career the toughest job he ever had; he'll never work that hard again. The American looks at his college days as the best time he'll ever have; he'd better start to work. (b) The ambitious young Frenchman will go to work for his government so that later in his career he can, to use the French expression, 'parachute' into a well-paying job in French industry. His counterpart in the U.S. will go to work for a large corporation so that later in his career he can afford to work in Washington. (3) A Frenchman's idea of real success in Industry is not to have a brilliant career within his company but make a fortune outside it.

6 Howard V. Perlmutter

Emerging East–West Ventures: The Transideological Enterprise

Professor of Industry at the Wharton School, University of Pennsylvania, Howard V. Perlmutter also directs the Division for Research and Development of Worldwide Institutions. Excerpt from the *Columbia Journal of World Business*, September – October 1969.

Consider the following six arrangements between Eastern and Western enterprises:

1. IKEA, a Swedish furniture store chain, supplies to associates in Poland machinery and designs under its technical control for the semi-manufacture of furniture, which is then shipped to Sweden for finishing by IKEA.

2. Italy's Official Meccaniche Gaetana Zocca has set up with Bulgaria's Macheneoxport, the foreign trade organization handling industrial machinery, a 50–50 trading company in Switzerland to sell grinding machines world-wide. Zocca will receive unfinished machines from Bulgaria, add parts (about 40 per cent of final value), finish the equipment and then turn the machines over to the trading company. Zocca will service all sales outside the East bloc, the Bulgarian supplier doing the same within the bloc not only for the grinding machines but also for all of Zocca's other products that are sold to bloc countries.

3. The U.S.-based Simmons Machine Tool Corporation has agreed with Czechoslovakia's Skoda to have the latter produce a line of specialized heavy equipment under the Simmons–Skoda trademark. The U.S. firm has exclusive sales rights in the Western Hemisphere, but there are no other territorial limitations for either side. Simmons reports that delivery time is reduced from 14 months to 3–5 weeks because the Czechs are willing to carry the machines in inventory, a practice contrary to normal free enterprise tenets of doing business at a profit.

4. Krupp of Essen, Germany, and the Csepel machine tool factory of Hungary have jointly developed digitally-controlled short lathes based on German designs and drawings, which are to be exported to Germany and other markets.

5. La Précision Industrielle, a French manufacturer of highly specialized machine tool equipment, signed a full-fledged licensing contract with Hungary's Licencia for the production of hydraulic chucks. The deal consisted of two separate contracts. The first, for sales in Hungary only, contained an option whereby the Hungarians within six months could obtain the rights to sell the tool in other Eastern countries. The option was exercised, and a second contract was signed covering the whole of Eastern Europe except Albania and Yugoslavia.

6. France's Pechiney-St Gobain (PSG) has signed an agreement with Progress-Invest of Belgrade. The principal activity of the joint venture is to be the construction and delivery of turn-key plants for fertilizer, fluoride chemicals, organic chemicals and plastics. The plants will be built in France, Yugoslavia and in third world countries.[1]

How can one reconcile these long-term agreements with present concerns about nuclear balance of terror and East–West ideological incompatibility? Are they a confirmation of the persisting but long-time-perspective claim for the eventual identity of economies, described now as command- or market-oriented?

How do builders of world-wide institutions like the multinational enterprise sort out their own role relative to political and military leaders whose primary concern is with national security and defence? In our view, the builders of world-wide business recognize that it is in the interest of all to understand the prospects for increasing economic interdependence between the East and West. They need to examine on what assumptions the world economic and industrial system is being built. The prospects for building truly world-wide or geocentric enterprises become promising only when the firm can function anywhere in the world.

It is useful to distinguish four different assumptions that under-

1. See *Developing the East European Market* (1966).

pin the building of a world-wide industrial system as they are evidenced in the policies and practices of business leaders in the East and West. These assumptions or conceptions have significant consequences for the success of Western entrepreneurs in East-West ventures, and indeed for the whole planet. They are worthy of analysis and articulation and may be identified as: (1) submergence theory, (2) divergence theory, (3) convergence theory and (4) emergence theory.

Only one side can win

It is inferred from existing policies and practices that the ultimate aims of either or both the Western bloc (United States and its allies) and the Eastern bloc (the Soviet Union and Eastern Europe) are to submerge the other's political system by military and other means. Coexistence, competitive and peaceful, détentes, temporary and long-term are viewed as screening the basic driving force of the other side: to build a world empire in which the other is a subordinate sub-system. However crude, dangerous and provocative submergence theory may appear, the adherents are not few in East and West. Thus the support for pre-emptive war, psychological, political and economic warfare – including incitement to insurrection in each other's territory, are evidences today of the contemporary popularity of submergence theory.

Submergence theorists hold that there are really no common interests between East and West. For them, the world is an arena where power must back up ideology and where softness towards the enemy is seen as potentially disastrous. Thus submergists see Capitalism and Communism as engaged in mortal combat. Few compromises are envisaged in this apocalyptic struggle.

Khrushchev, who was not known for his submergist theory in action – at least compared with Stalin – expressed the essence of this theory in his famous threat: 'We shall bury you.' An equivalent kind of morality is contained in the conclusion by some Western leaders; 'The only good Communist is a dead Communist.'

Stalinism and submergist theory fit together. For submergism of the East feeds on an ideology of revolutionary Marxism, overcoming the evils of capitalistic-bourgeois society through class war and violence.

Obviously submergist theorists are not receptive to supporting joint ventures between the East and West or even conducting trade unless this trade has subversive objectives. Two quotes from U.S. businessmen seem based on the belief that the Soviet Union has submergist assumptions.

The president of a New Jersey manufacturing company said: 'Trade with Soviet bloc nations will come home to roost as our trade with Japan did in 1941. It is our considered opinion that no trade of any sort – import or export – should be carried on with Soviet bloc countries.'

Or another: 'I firmly oppose wheat deals or any other trade with Russia or its satellites. Everything they do has but one ultimate goal – our defeat and subjugation.'[2]

Thus submergists see coexistence as a screen for gaining advantages through bringing the other side's guard down; the ultimate resolution must be based on the power and ideology of one side or the other.

The NATO community was based on submergence theory or at least the belief that in Western unity there is a deterrence against submergist theories of the East. Reciprocally, monolithic Stalinism was a strategy for Eastern unity based on submergist theory.

In game theory terms, submergence theory is based on what is called the zero-sum premises. Between the East and West there can be only one winner. The game is over when the other side 'loses', e.g. all must come around to the kind of thinking that the winner proposes.

Military interventions by the United States and the Soviet Union are seen as evidence for submergence theory. The large expenditure on arms and armies is also consistent with these premises. Under submergist theory, the Eastern European countries can be bound together by the fear of a common 'imperialist enemy' and may be more willing to reduce differences in national view and accept Soviet leadership of a united bloc against imperialistic capitalism.

The mirror image is found in an Atlantic community, spurred on by U.S. leadership 'keeping its powder dry' and bringing former

2. See Goldman and Conner (1966).

enemies like France and Germany together to resist the Communist enemy from within and without.

The submergence theory premises do not always exist at the forefront of consciousness of leaders in times of relative tranquillity. But they are sleeping leopards to be awakened under slight provocation from without. The military intervention by the Soviet Union in Czechoslovakia probably produced new submergence theorists (although fewer than at the time of the Hungarian revolt). Submergists in the West felt justified again to point out that the spots of the Soviet leopard had not changed and never will.

Power is all

Thus under the submergist assumption all contact must be evaluated in politico-military terms. Trade is economic warfare, and the ultimate method for gaining world markets is world conquest. Power must back up ideology. Communism is the next utopia for the East and the scourge of mankind for the West.

A Western submergist believes that the Soviet Union means what it states, repeatedly and officially, that its aim is to destroy the liberal free enterprise system throughout the world and to replace it with an authoritarian, Soviet Marxist system. The Soviet Union's coexistence policy is consequently viewed as an attempt to maintain a hostile, not a peaceful, state of coexistence, with the aim of gradual encroachment and final victory.

In the West, submergist thinking is more likely to be reactive: 'If the Russians say they want to dominate us, we must be prepared to beat them, to make sure that our "free enterprise" economic system is the winner.'

It would appear that to the degree that submergist theory prevails, the prospects for East–West trade are dim and the likelihood of a movement towards developing East–West corporations even dimmer. For the submergist theory flourishes in an atmosphere of mutual suspicion and distrust. Western-based multinational enterprise can only be suspect in the East, as a tool of the home country, a symbol of exploitative capitalism, a purveyor of Trojan horses. Multinational enterprise in our times is unlikely to flourish in a world where political and military leaders of East and West believe that the only way to optimize the use of human and material resources in the world-wide system is to own the system as a whole!

Never the twain

Divergence theory maintains that the United States and the Soviet Union are in fact further away from each other now than in earlier periods. It is based on the assumption that the continued separation of the Western and Eastern socio-politico-economic systems will produce a hardening of differences, and that, rather than move towards one another, the contrasting ideological premises are more sharply held.

The irreconcilability of Eastern and Western ideologies leads to a polarization but with these differences from submergence theory:

1. Divergence theorists do not presume that each system attempts to prevail over the other.

2. East-West relationships do not need to be proselytizing since each recognizes that convincing the other (especially through nuclear war or subversive methods) is either unrealistic, too risky or too costly.

3. In an age of balance of terror, separation of ideological systems is feasible and desirable from a political and an economic view.

4. A world industrial system can be built of two different and isolated socio-political communities.

In fact, a world community based on adaptive segregation of East from West is viable and the best compromise, given the discomforting propensity of submergists on both sides for confrontations. To back up the divergent world view, the West builds EEC and the Atlantic Community, the East builds COMECON.

Divergence theory is based on the proposition that each side has a genuine horror of nuclear disaster and that each side sees submergence efforts are unrealistic, dangerous and provocative. An era of competitive coexistence is not only compatible with divergence theory, it is indispensable. One needs an enemy not for war but as a common base for comparison. Under these conditions the two systems grow more different.

East–West trade should not be constructed as indicating a shift in orientation towards a more international view. It is an opportunity to demonstrate the relative strengths of the socialist and capitalist states but not necessarily how the socialist state will prevail over capitalist countries, or vice-versa.

Divergent theorists consider any similarities between the two systems to be of less consequence than the differences. The recent movement towards Libermanism is seen as very far, as Thorelli puts it, from liberalism, because there is no marked tendency in the Soviet Union to:

1. permit or even force unprofitable state enterprises to go out of business;

2. allow manufacturers of similar goods to compete in selling to the same distributive channels and stores;

3. permit pressure from the market to emphasize consumer goods industries at the cost of heavy industry and producer goods;

4. enact anti-trust legislation;

5. allow stores to integrate backward or allow manufacturers to integrate forward and create their own outlets;

6. permit free labour markets;

7. tolerate such seemingly necessary ingredients of free markets as mass advertising, brands and trademarks.[3]

The characteristics of East – West trade of the 'one-shot deal' variety appear compatible with divergent thinking. Distrust and suspicion are not as intense as in submergist thinking, but there is a strong desire to keep each side ideologically pure. Thus coproduction ventures are likely to be frowned upon by divergists as beginning a dangerous trend towards ideological dilution or being soft by submergist standards.

The ultimate purpose of divergists is to optimize the resources within a network of ideologically compatible countries. For the East this means within COMECON or the 'Socialist Commonwealth' countries; for the West within the Atlantic Community. Each colludes to build a world industrial system of two large blocs whose interdependence is very small.

East is East, West is West, and never the twain shall meet . . .

3. See Thorelli (1965).

Is it still true?

Mutual discovery

In recent times, a recurring theme in East – West relations is based on what might be called convergence theory. Considerable evidence with an admixture of hope has been mustered to demonstrate that communist and free economies show a converging pattern.

The arguments begin by citing the changes that have occurred in the communist system since the Russian Revolution. Jan Tinbergen's observations make this clear:

1. 'The belief that "workers" could take care of management functions is decreasing in prevalence. There is recognition that management is a specialized set of activities.'

2. 'Attempts to equalize incomes did not work. Wages are now dependent on productivity.'

3. For some time planning was done in terms of physical quantities and not in terms of money values. Gradually the use of money as a common denominator penetrated into the planning system and the significance of prices and costs was more and more recognized.[4]

Additional changes in the Soviet system include the introduction of the concept of interest, the increase in emphasis on consumption, the use of mathematical methods associated with capitalists, and changing concepts of international trade to include trade between communist and free economies.

In the meantime, the so-called free economies have also undergone changes:

1. The public sector is now considerably larger than it was in the nineteenth century – especially in Western Europe.
2. Taxes have been used to redistribute wealth.
3. Free competition has been limited.
4. Education has gradually been made available to an increasing portion of the population.
5. Market forces have been eliminated or modified in some cases as, for example, international commodity agreements.
6. Planning has been given a larger role in industry and government.

4. See Tinbergen (1961).

The key idea of convergists is that industrialism imposes its own rules, which lead to uniformities between economies at similar stages of advancing economic development. Industrialism requires similar political, social and economic institutions, regardless of the ideological base. In the long term, it may contribute to a depoliticization and de-ideologization process. Convergence theory is the most threatening to submergist ideologists; in the Soviet Union, it is counter-revolutionary.

Convergence theory implies gradual opening of Soviet society to Western ideas and a more rational evaluation of the Soviets by Western economists: a phase of 'mutual discovery' which must be contrasted with the attitudes of the divergence theorists. Convergence theorists expect that common interests will continue to grow. Convergence will be hastened by the polycentric tendencies in Eastern Europe, which legitimize many routes to communism, from the hard-liners of East Germany to the liberals of Yugoslavia. Because there are many communisms, there should be more similarities than differences between the East and the equally diverse economies of the West. Convergence involves the view that East and West are both on an experimentation course that will evolve into similar if not identical solutions to national economic and industrial problems.

The climate for convergence thinkers is on the whole more ambiguous since the reciprocal borrowing process frequently requires a defensive denial by the submergist ideologists that one can learn much from the other. This is particularly true in the East, despite open admiration for U.S. managerial skills. The kind of world economic system being constructed is based on largely separate systems which are nontheless similar to each other, which learn from each other but will for a long time maintain separate identities. Their underlying similarities are likely, say the convergists, to make them friends, despite the evidence to the contrary between China and the Soviet Union.

To the degree that convergence prevails the entrepreneurial strategies are largely pragmatic arrangements where trade is favoured and communication of knowledge is valued. In a document which caused a major stir in the Soviet Union, Dr Andrei

Four theories of building the world industrial system on the East-West dimension

Parameter	*Submergence theory*	*Divergence theory*	*Convergence theory*	*Emergence theory*
1. Ultimate Objectives, Grand Design	Military and/or Ideological Conquest of Other	Nobody can Win World War But Military Containment Theory Favoured	A Great Variety of Socialisms and Capitalisms Which Come to Resemble Each Other	A World of Economic Interdependence, Ideological Diversity, and International Division of Labour
2. Strategy for Reaching World Markets (Including Eastern or Western Markets)	World Markets Through World Conquest	No Strategy for World Markets: Centred on Regional Markets (COMECON vs Atlantic Community)	Unplanned Strategies; Depends on Individual State	East-West Agreement to Permit Global Strategy for Products with World-wide Competitive Advantage Leading to Lower Unit Costs for World Markets
3. Power/Ideology	Power and Ideology of One Side Must Prevail	Ideological But Not Power Confrontation Hypothesis	Importance of Power and Ideology Reduced Since Systems Approach Identity	Neither Ideological Nor Power Confrontation; Maintenance of Ideological Identity, Development of Comparative Advantage

Four theories of building the world industrial system on the East-West dimension

Parameter	*Submergence theory*	*Divergence theory*	*Convergence theory*	*Emergence theory*
4. Kind of Economic Relations Favoured	Trade is Economic Warfare	Minimal Trade Between, But Concentration of Trade Within Economic Blocs	Trade, During Organic Process of Becoming Similar	Mutual Increase of Balance of Payments and Trade Through the Transideological Zone
5. Function of Détente	Détente is an Opportunity to Build up Strength – But Détente is Not Favoured	To Permit Strengthening of Internal Bloc Relations	Competitive Coexistence But Mutual Borrowing of Elements of Other's System	To Define Transideological Zones, with Transideological Institutions through Transideological Dialogues
6. Definition of Common Interests of East and West	No Common Area of Interest	Minimal Common Interest; Difficult to Find Those Which Do Not Threaten Ideological Cohesion	Common Interests Grow Out of Common Ways of Looking at Problems	Search for Structures in Area of Durable, Reciprocal Interests. International Division of Labour Assumptions Guide East – West Decisions

7. Relocation of Allies or States	States Must Band Together to Defeat Common Enemy Under One Leading State	Free Atlantic Community vs Commonwealth of Socialist States	Polycentrism in East; Loose Alliance Between U.S. and West Europe	Distinctive Competence of Nation States to Reach World Markets Irrespective of Ideology
8. East – West Climate	Chronic Suspicion, Distrust, Envy, Hostility	High Distrust, Suspicion Leading to Avoidance of Other	Cyclical Friendship, Admiration and Distrust of Other's Motives	Moderate Trust Based on Limited Predictable, Functional Actions Based on Objectives and Rules Which are Mutually Acceptable
9. Approach to Building a World Industrial System	The Way to Build a World Industrial System is to Own It.	Build a Self-Contained, Ideologically Homogeneous Sub-system of the World Industrial System	Mutual Learning to Optimize Nation State Sub-systems with a View to Building a Relatively Homogeneous, Unplanned World Industrial System	Build a World Industrial System by Planning for and Defining Shared East – West Geocentric Sub-systems Which Permanently Bind East and West

Printed by permission of the author

Sakharov, known by some as the father of the Russian hydrogen bomb, wrote:

> 1. We have demonstrated the vitality of the socialist cause, which has done a great deal for the [Russian] people materially, culturally and socially, and, like no other system, has glorified the moral significance of labour.
>
> 2. There are no grounds for asserting as is often done in the dogmatic vein that the capitalist mode of production leads the economy into a blind alley or that it is obviously inferior to the socialist mode in labour productivity, and there are certainly no grounds for asserting that capitalism always leads to absolute impoverishment of the working class. . . . The continuing economic progress being achieved under capitalism should be a fact of great theoretical significance for any undogmatic Marxist.[5]

But however frequently the dynamism inherent in capitalism and communism is cited to account for their increasing similarity, it can be matched by a theory which fuses submergence theory and convergence theory. Thus W. W. Rostow's thesis that Marxist society is appropriate only for earlier stages of the industrialization process contains the view that the other economies, especially communist, must necessarily move towards the U.S. model.[6] Convergence theory for U.S. convergists contains a heavy dose of ethnocentrism.

Ideologists from the East do not make public pronouncements about convergence – unless of course by convergence they mean: 'The world will converge . . . into an essentially communist form of government.'

A Russian spokesman, L. F. Ilyichev, expresses the basic spirit of divergence theory and his rejection of convergism:

> Some time ago there appeared a theory according to which socialism and capitalism, in spite of their fundamental differences, are allegedly developing in the same direction – that the compulsory economic imperatives of total industrial development will gradually lead to a hybridization of the two systems, to their synthesis, to the formation of a single mixed society by means of the internal change of socialism and some modernization of capitalism. This is frank social demagogy. The

5. Sakharov (1968).
6. Rostow (1960).

imperialist ideologists speculate on socialist terminology. They are not beyond adapting a few ideas of socialism in order to deceive the working people, to delude them with socialist slogans. . .[7]

On the other hand, Brzezinski and Huntington point out:

> The theory of convergence . . . minimizes or ignores the totality of the Russian and the American historical experience – political, social and economic – and exaggerates the importance of one factor alone . . . The Soviet and the American political systems, each in its own way, have been highly successful. Because they have been successful, they are not likely to change drastically. . . .[8]

A fourth option

Submergence, divergence and convergence theories all recognize that the world political–military system haside ntifiable boundaries between East and West. There appears little doubt that these boundaries are as real as the sentinels along all East European borders. While the submergists, divergists and convergists may vary in influence in both East and West, it is clear that they share a view, held with more passion by the former two than the latter, that the world economy will be divisible by two for a very long time.

But while these propositions provide an explanation for the past and a justification of the present in East – West economic relations, they fail to recognize the character of the evolving world economy as it is understood by multinational corporations. For enterprise has already developed multinational, transnational and global attributes. What remains is to consider a fourth kind of theory of East – West relations.

Those Westerners who have been involved in any professional activity with their Eastern European counterparts will recognize this kind of dialogue:

> Eastern Representative: We believe in the superiority of the socialist mode. How can we trust you capitalists?
>
> Western Representative: We believe in the superiority of our economic system. How can we trust you communists?

7. Ilyichev introduction to Brzezinski and Huntington (1963).
8. Brzezinski and Huntington (1963).

Either: Ideology is irrelevant to the problems we have to discuss. Let us refrain from politics and propaganda and assume that neither can win the other over to his beliefs.

Other: Agreed. Now is it not in our common interest to build a plant in Eastern Europe which will market goods in both East and West Europe?

Eastern Representative: We have good engineers and information about marketing problems in Poland, Hungary and Bulgaria.

Western Representative: We have information about marketing this product in France, Italy, the United Kingdom and Sweden. Your engineers will be able to work with our engineers.

Transideological dialogue typically has these features:

1. Submergist thinking is controlled.

2. Divergist thinking is considered irrelevant to the particular problem at hand.

3. Convergist thinking may occur but is not discussed because its time perspective is so long and can trigger off the submergist and divergist defensive reactions.

4. Emergist thinking is not identified but if discussed provides the basic ground rules for productive discussion.

The transideological dialogues occur in discussions of landing rights in Moscow and New York, air pollution, cures for cancer, international communication systems, exchange of artists, the Olympic Games, increasing tourism, basic research in cryogenics, and in fact all discussions where propaganda, threats and political differences are put aside in the service of an overriding and common objective which is consciously defined as devoid of ideological content. Men meet, not ideologies.

Emile Benoit in commenting on co-production arrangements wrote:

> In such ventures practical results count and ideological differences are pushed into the background. According to a former student of mine who has planned and carried out a number of such operations in Yugoslavia, ideological differences have proved remarkably irrelevant and easy to ignore in this context.[9]

These observations may be discerned in business negotiations between managers of West Europe and those of Czechoslovakia,

9. Benoit (1966).

Hungary and Rumania. Thus we can speak of relationships which cut across and through ideologies (yet which do not claim to be 'above' or 'below' ideologies of 'beyond' in the sense of 'better'). Transideological thinking is beginning to blossom and an amorphous zone is emerging despite the presence of submergists and divergists.

The case for emergence

By ideology we can mean a pattern of beliefs and concepts, both factual and normative, which claim to account for social events. Daniel Bell has argued that the nineteenth-century ideologies, and in particular Marxism, are exhausted.[10] Their credibility is limited. He would regard as inevitable that ideology's force is based on passion, not on empirical tests of propositions about the world. The emotional energy which Marxism musters may exceed that of capitalism, but the claim is clear enough that both world views have a distinct element of faith, sentiment and Utopian simplification of the diversity of man's politico-economic behaviour.

There is by no means agreement on the 'exhaustion of ideologies' theme, the limitations of 'closed' ideologies – rigid, consistent, and universal in character – which, as the British philosopher Morris Ginsberg has put it, 'demand all-or-none commitment of the kind demanded by, for example, Bolshevist communism'. Ginsberg distinguishes 'open' ideologies, which are often criticized from within and which learn from each other, from the one-sidedness of most closed ideologies.[11] When ideologies remain open, they breed new but as yet indefinable forms – emergent systems which, while relatively weak at first and parasitical on their host systems to some degree, gain support if they demonstrate effectiveness.

The case for emergence theory has rarely been articulated. There are three primary reasons. The first is that submergence, divergence and convergence theories all accept the existence of a visible and relatively impermeable boundary between East and West.

10. Bell (1960).
11. Ginsberg (1962).

This is not surprising. There have been no official Iron Curtain-raising ceremonies.

The second reason is that it is convenient to conceptualize the world as a contest between superpowers and their affiliated nations from a military view. NATO versus Warsaw Pact countries is a military reality (with the recent exception of France, perhaps).

The third reason is that the focus of ideologists, political scientists and economists has been on the differences between the political, social and economic systems of the East and West. This comparative approach, even when it is concerned with convergence processes, still uses nations or blocs as units of comparison. The emergence of any sub-system which cuts across the two spheres is likely to be obscured.

Emergence theory holds that interactions between units such as nations, common habits, norms, interests appear covertly at first, and unrecognized interdependencies begin to arise. But among opposing camps it becomes embarrassing to refer to these processes. Each side desires not to set events of a destructive nature in motion, events which could get out of control (as almost happened in the Cuban crisis). Both desire to reduce uncertainty about the other's behaviour in response to a provocative but politically necessary action. Thus the existence of the 'hot line' between Moscow and Washington.

The advantage of these private arrangements is that they do not see the light of day. The submergists do not need to demonstrate that they are tough and have not given up their primary objectives. Besides, emergent theorists may not be in a hurry to move from covert bargaining to legitimized East-West decision-making structures, such as co-production agreements. But emergent theorists can still point to long-term agreements, such as Fiat concluded, as examples of a rather remarkable event involving a Western capitalist automobile company and the leading country of the Communist world.

Emergence theory is supported by at least five persuasive arguments. These arguments have been expressed on private occasions by Western and Eastern managers and, on rare occasions, in a more guarded fashion in the press:

1. The international division-of-labour argument.
2. The world-wide market penetration argument.
3. The geocentric science and technology argument.
4. The balance-of-payments argument.
5. The ideological diversity argument.

The international division-of-labour argument holds that not all products can be developed and produced in each country or within each ideological sphere of influence. Most countries must develop some comparative advantage for the export of their products. The following statement from Moscow put this position rather directly:

> International socialist division of labour takes into account the world division of labour. By expanding their economic ties with all countries of the world, the socialist countries thus strengthen the material basis for peaceful coexistence of the two world socio-economic systems . . .[12]

Exports are not sufficient to maintain a world-wide acceptance for products. Eventually, sales offices, service facilities, manufacturing and development must follow in order that local needs be understood and responded to. This means direct investment overseas and the development of subsidiary structures in foreign economies of different ideological assumptions. For Eastern Europe to reach world-wide markets, Western facilities must be built in the long term. These requirements reinforce emergence theory and the development of a transideological zone. It goes without saying that world-wide markets mean reducing unit costs by reaching billions rather than millions of consumers, and for the East earning the hard currency necessary for trade and development.

To maintain world-wide standards for one's products, world-wide resources in the form of men, ideas and techniques are necessary. Science and technology are geocentric, that is, relevant information can be found in all parts of the world – not just in one country. The Eastern bloc needs access to Western science and technology. And it is probable that the West can learn from Eastern science. This is especially true for smaller countries that seek international division of labour.

12. Quoted in Kaser (1965).

COMECON cannot survive as a closed system. One East European observer wrote recently:

> Big countries, like the Soviet Union or the United States, are not as dependent on the international division of labour as are the smaller countries having a relatively narrow home market in comparison to their level of production. Being poor in raw materials (except its considerable bauxite and manganese resources), Hungary is definitely in need of participating in the international division of labour. The economic development of Hungary cannot do without the influence of the developed Western countries – most of all without that of the West European countries . . .[13]

The Eastern countries badly need hard currency. The best way to earn it is to have products which can be purchased in the West. This requires transideological agreements which increase the design and marketing know-how of Eastern firms and will permit them to export to Western countries. A similar opportunity to improve the balance of payments may exist for Western firms. Transideological enterprises can help achieve these objectives.

In brief, there are many socialisms. Diversity is not likely to disappear even if Soviet pressure is increased in the post-polycentric period. This means a continuation of present creativity in designing East – West joint ventures. Yugoslavia is an example. Creativity here involves building a venture where key decisions can be made by the East–West managerial group despite the legal status of the workers as owners. These examples can multiply and serve as models.

It will happen

There are many other arguments for the appearance of transideological enterprises. Most of them reduce to the proposition that since the world is in trouble, this is the time to experiment with industrial systems which link the East and West in a limited but decisive way in areas of true common interest. The belief persists that because the linkage is necessary, it will happen.

There are only a limited number of licensing, subcontracting, joint ventures between the East and West. Despite recent setbacks

13. See Havas (1969).

for the liberalization process in Czechoslovakia and an air of gloom about the country's future, there are few, if any, examples of contract-breaking or dissolution of East – West co-production arrangements. The driving force towards the transideological enterprise and a wider transideological zone depends on external factors. For both East and West have their share of submergists and divergists. The submergists are committed to casting doubts and suspicions on any deviation from their view that transideological ventures cannot avoid being evil. While the divergists are likely to think of transideological ventures as exceptions which prove the rule, they would caution against binding agreements over the long term. Both submergists and divergists are disturbed by convergist thinking but have not yet made up their minds about the emergist view.

The hard realities of attempting continued economic development without Western markets have been experienced. In the East the convergists and the emergists are being accused of consorting with the enemy. When the smaller countries of Eastern Europe become more and more dependent on trade with the West, the panic among the submergists begins to accelerate. The possibility that Czechoslovakia, Hungary and Romania, like Yugoslavia, will export more to the West than to Eastern countries becomes a nightmare to them.

It is no wonder that polycentrism in the Eastern bloc is increasing the pressures within the Soviet Union (particularly among the ideologists and the marshals) to take measures to 'defend the socialist gains of the Czechoslovakian people' and to remind each Communist party that 'it is responsible not only to its own people but also to all the socialist countries and to the entire Communist movement'.

Pravda, in justifying the Soviet intervention in Czechoslovakia in August 1968, asserts the submergist warning:

> Each Communist party cannot but take into account such a decisive fact of our time as the struggle between two opposing social systems – capitalism and socialism. This is an objective struggle, a fact not depending on the will of the people, and stipulated by the world's being split up into two opposing social systems. Lenin said: 'Each man must

choose between joining our side or the other side.' Any attempt to avoid taking sides in this issue must end in fiasco.[14]

The effort to renew the passionate commitment to ideology is under way.

For polycentrism in the Eastern bloc has produced profound anxieties about the dissolution of the communist system – an event which the submergists have been predicting in the absence of strict intrabloc controls. This is further reinforced by Western submergists, who must justify any rapprochement in terms of a weakening of the communist system. This is perhaps a partial explanation of Soviet anxieties when Czechoslovakia seemed to be moving irreversibly towards too many economic links with the West, coupled with a large dose of liberalization to its political system. Despite Czech claims to be loyal Socialist members of the Socialist Commonwealth, most countries know that commonwealths are notoriously unstable. Allegiance to the Queen, to symbols or to Lenin is a riskier type of arrangement, given the shortcomings of COMECON, than allegiance by fear.

It is in the nature of the evolutionary process that the uncontrolled character of the polycentric phase makes convergence theory less attractive because it implies a total system change and a defeat for the submergists. It may be that the emergists with limited aims, who can point to a moratorium on ideology in specific areas of mutual economic interest – the transideological zone, as it were – may have a stronger case. It may be the time to study the feasibility of defining the transideological zone and of designing a limited number of world-wide transideological firms, which would permit free industrial and commercial relationships between the East and West. It would be foolhardy to underestimate the fragile nature of the neo-natal institutions called transideological and the threatening character of non-ideological activity to submergists, who want people to take sides in the struggle.

Despite the efforts of the United Nations, mankind lacks some crucial institutions to guarantee world order and assure a more equitable distribution of the material wealth of the earth. As the profound implications of nuclear disaster take hold in our minds,

14. *Pravda*, 25 September 1968.

the passionate attachment to ideology is being re-examined in both the East and the West. The results of different approaches to building a world economic system are becoming more apparent, and the interdependence of humanity more concretely felt, in the industrialization process which executives of multinational firms must manage.

There is a painful learning process along the East – West watershed of the world that may result in the legitimization of what we are calling transideological zones, mediated through transideological dialogues and culminating in a greater abundance of already existing transideological licensing, sub-contracting and co-production systems. We have had sufficient time to experiment with the world system based on submergist, divergist and convergist assumptions. Now there may be a role for geocentrically oriented, transideological industrial institutions.[15]

There is growing recognition that the world economic system needs to be whole, that there are true common interests, but that East – West cooperation must be limited and defined by reason of the political and military realities of our present day. There is no other way to keep the planet whole than to recognize that the common ideology that binds mankind to his persisting quest for survival and better conditions of life is the special prerogative of neither East nor West.

We move into an age of universal history, which, as Lord Acton would say, 'is distinct from the combined history of all countries [whose] story will be told not for their own sake, but in reference and subordinate to a higher series according to the time and the degree to which they contribute to the common fortunes of mankind . . .' and which Nikolai Gogol defined as

> not a collection of separate histories of all the nations and states without general connection or common purpose; nor is it a mass of occurrences in a lifeless or dry form, in which it is too often presented . . . it must assemble in one all the nations of the world separated by time, by accident or mountains and seas, unite them in one proportionate, harmonious whole and from them compose one magnificent poem.

15. See Perlmutter (1969).

References

BELL, D. (1960), *The End of Ideology*, Free Press, Illinois.

BENOIT, E. (1966), 'Interdependence in a small planet', *Columbia Journal of World Business*, Spring.

BRZEZINSKI, Z., and HUNTINGTON, S. P. (1963), *Political Power: U.S.A./U.S.S.R.*, Viking Press, New York.

BUSINESS INTERNATIONAL (1966), *Developing the East European Market*, Geneva.

GINSBERG, M. (1962), 'Facts and Values', *The Advancement of Science*.

GOLDMAN, M. I., and CONNER, A. (1966), 'Businessmen appraise East – West trade', *Harvard Business Review*, January–February.

HAVAS, S. (1969), 'Hungary and East – West trade', *The American Review of East – West Trade*, February.

ILYICHEV, L. F. (1963), cited in Brzezinski, Z., and Huntington, S. P. (op. cit.)

KASER, M. (1965), *COMECON*, Oxford University Press.

PERLMUTTER, H. V. (1969), 'The tortuous evolution of the multinational corporation', *Columbia Journal of World Business*, January–February.

PRAVDA (1968), 'Sovereignty and international duties of socialist countries', 25 September.

ROSTOW, W. W. (1960), *The Stages of Economic Growth: A Non-Communist Manifesto*, Cambridge University Press.

SAKHAROV, A. D. (1968), *Progress, Coexistence and Intellectual Freedom*, W. W. Norton, New York.

THORELLI, H. B. (1965), 'Libermanism is not liberalism', *Business Horizons*, Indiana University, Summer.

TINBERGEN, J. B. (1961), 'Do Communist and free economies show a converging pattern?', *Soviet Studies*, April.

7 Theodore D. Weinshall

Communication, Culture and the Education of Multinational Managers[1]

1. This paper is based exclusively on the author's own research. For other publications see under 'Weinshall' in the References.

The *communications study* was first conceived in 1959 during an examination of the managerial relationships and attitudes in a United States company. The analysis concentrates on the different degrees of the use of oral communication in different countries. This in itself is one of the most important differences affecting multinational management, and therefore an appropriate focus.

The *comparative organization behaviour study*, started more recently, drew upon the work of many others. Differences and similarities in the social and organizational behaviour of four countries – France, Britain, Israel and the United States were discussed.

The *multinational management education study* is based on a longitudinal cross-national research project begun at the European Institute of Business Administration (INSEAD) in 1965. This was carried out in three stages:

Research focus	*Started in*	*The three stages* 1 *Before INSEAD*	2 *While at INSEAD*	3 *After INSEAD*	*Publications*
Attitudes	1965–6	+	+	(+)*	Weinshall 1971a
Relationships	1966–7		+	(+)	Weinshall and De Bettignies 1971
Values	1968–9	+	+		Weinshall 1972

* These three stages are discussed in this paper. (+) Planned future research.

As background, the following is an official description of the school: INSEAD was founded in 1958. Its purpose is to prepare future directors and managers for the careers in industry, commerce and banking with a particular emphasis on international business. It provides a practical management education designed to bridge the gap between university and business life. Stress is laid on the cultivation of an international approach to business problems and on the effect of European integration on management decisions. Unique of its kind because of its truly international character, INSEAD provides an exceptional meeting place for students from many countries and teachers of different nationalities. Teaching is in three languages: English, French and German. The programme lasts for one academic year and deals with the most up-to-date techniques of business management. Teaching is primarily done by the case method of instruction. Each student first analyses the case by himself, then discusses it within a discussion group composed of 7 students and, finally, participates in class discussion with 50 other students, led by a professor.

When the present author first came to INSEAD he discovered that the wives of a large number of the married students were of a different nationality from their husbands. Likewise, when interviewing non-directively about twenty students from a variety of national origins, it was discovered that all of them considered the German students to be less mixed with students from other nationalities than the other students. However, all the interviewees mentioned specifically four or five German students who behaved differently from the majority of Germans. All of those specifically mentioned as internationally mixing received their first university degree out of Germany, while none of the other German students had done so.

This suggested that:

(*a*) Some aspects of the INSEAD are 'internationalist', that studying at INSEAD is important not only for students who are only interested in a business administration career, but likewise to students who need such things as mixing with other nationalities and desiring to work in the future in an international setting, in a multinational organization.

(*b*) Were the 'internationalist' students to be segregated from the purely career motivated students and the characteristic personal differences between the two discovered, such characteristics would indicate the background required not only for multinational managers, but for people who wish to promote and maintain better understanding between nations. In other words, such things as the length of time one stays out of one's country and being married to a wife of a different nationality could well be characteristics which are conducive to becoming an 'internationalist'.

This further suggested the three stages of the research, the findings and preliminary conclusions of which are summarized in this chapter.

Excerpt from *The Multinational Company in Europe*, Michael Z. Brooke and H. Lee Remmers (eds), Longman, 1973: University of Michigan Press, 1975.

France, Britain, Israel and the United States: different communication patterns

The existence of different patterns of communication in different countries has often been suggested, but seldom systematically investigated. For greater precision it has been necessary to develop a new analytical tool – the *communication diagram*, or *communicogram* as it is now called. This makes it possible to discern and analyse one of the basic differences in managerial structure between different cultural environments, namely that of communications behaviour. This use of the communicogram became evident by coincidence rather than through testing hypotheses concerning management communication. In 1966 a group of students carried out a communicogram study under the supervision of the present author. The study was conducted in three organizations, one British, and two French; this was done simultaneously with another which explored the relationships and attitudes of the same managers of these organizations who were included in the communicogram study. The chief executives of all three organizations had been promised that they would receive not only the results of their own respective studies, but also a comparison between themselves and the other two organizations. However, when the recorded interactions were fed into the computer, it turned out that while the total number of interactions in the British organization for the fifty participants during two weeks was 2,639, the equivalent number of interactions for the 21 and 26 participants of the two French companies were 128 and 215 respectively, too small for analysis.

When the British chief executive was presented with the results of his organization, an apology was made for not being able to provide him with a comparison with the two French organizations, on the grounds that the French managers failed to report their interactions. He replied: 'The reason is quite clear to me – they just do not interact orally.'

He was right. Going back to the individual Daily Interaction Sheets, it was discovered that while on each British sheet there was an average of some 15 interactions per person per day, only 2–3 interactions per person per day appeared on the sheets of the managers in the two French organizations. The number of re-

Table 1 **Comparison of self-recorded interaction studies in six organizations in four countries**

Type of organization	*Industrial: plastics*	*Marketing: pharmaceutical consumer*	*Industrial: electronic components*	*Industrial: aircraft production*	*Army: ordnance*	*Education: management development*
Data studied Country	USA	UK	FRANCE	FRANCE	ISRAEL	UK
Year	1959	1966	1966	1966	1969	1971
No. of managers						
approached	50	60	26	21	48	32
participated	34	50	26	21	41	27
Length of study (no. of days)	10	10	10	10	10	10
Oral interactions with other participants						
Total reported	1,708	2,639	128	215	672	1,272
% mutually perceived	26%	14%	17%	21%	7%	38%
Daily average per person	5·0	5·3	0·5	1·0	2·6	4·7
% of interactions						
by telephone	22%	45%	73%	29%	19%	14%
Face-to-face	78%	55%	27%	71%	81%	86%
Consensus as to type in mutually perceived interactions	47%	35%	46%	73%	50%	43%
Source	(Weinshall 1966 and 1968b)	(Weinshall, 1970)			(Tzirulnitsky 1969)	(Weinshall, Beal and Silver, 1971)

ported interactions with other managers participating in the study, being usually about one-third of the total recorded interactions, corresponds with the results of 5·3 interactions per person per day in the British organization and 0·5 and 1·0 interactions in the two French organizations. The results of the studies in four countries are shown in Table 1. It can be assumed that the degree of oral communication is not only a function of the type of business. The communicogram results are considered separately for the individual organizations in each of the four cultural environmental settings, so as to segregate the cultural effects from the effects of managerial structure and type of business.

The United States

The study was carried out in the Devon Corporation which has been described in detail elsewhere.* A surprising discovery, demonstrated by the 'Industrial plastics' column in Table 1, was that only 26 per cent of the recorded interactions were mutually perceived. In other words, only 26 per cent of the recorded interactions with other participants in the study were reciprocated by those other participants. However, this low rate of mutually perceived interactions turned out eventually to be the normal rather than the unusual.

We can see that 26 per cent is exactly the average between the two British organizations (14 and 38 per cent), somewhat higher than the rate in the French organizations (17 and 21 per cent) and much higher than the Israeli organization's rate of 7 per cent.

We shall see in the ensuing sections that other communicogram results of the United States organization were also similar to the results in other organizations, except for the 'Daily average oral interactions per person', on which we shall elaborate in the following section regarding the French organizations.

France

All comparisons as to other data studied in the United States, British and Israeli organizations are overshadowed by the relatively very small amount of oral interactions in the French. Indeed some of these comparisons are invalid because of the small and statistically insignificant numbers of interactions. Nevertheless it is interesting to note that in the Aircraft Production organization, where the variations in the manufacturing were larger than in the Electronic Components one, the per cent of face-to-face interactions (71 per cent) was significantly higher than in the other French firm (27 per cent). This should give us some indication as to the effect of the type of organization on communication behaviour.

The United Kingdom

The two organizations studied were of completely different types,

* (Weinshall, 1960).

one in education and the other in marketing. Nevertheless, both were service organizations and both had a strong research orientation. It seems that the difference in type of organization between the two explains the significant difference in the face-to-face interactions (55 per cent as against 86 per cent). The significantly lower rate of those mutually perceived in the marketing (14 per cent) when compared to the education (38 per cent) follows the pattern noticed in the United States company, namely that agreement as to the occurrence of interaction is higher in face-to-face interactions, when the participants see each other rather than only hearing each other's voice on the telephone.

Israel

The figures in this column seem to be dominated by the fact that this is a military organization. This is especially evident when one considers the daily average oral interactions per person (2·6). The managerial structure of this organization, measured by an informalogram,[2] was discovered to be similar to the structure of the French industrial aircraft production organization – to which it is closest in the rate of oral interactions (1·0 as against 2·6). Based on various phenomena of organizational and social behaviour, one could expect Israeli oral communication to be as high as that of the United States. Indeed, in both the percentages of face-to-face interactions and in the consensus as to the mutually perceived interactions, the Israeli organization's results are the closest to the United States. This is why the results in the Israeli organization seem to indicate strongly the effects of the type of

2. The *informalogram* is a technique for establishing the managerial structure based on a comparison between the formal and the informal relationships. It is carried out through the measurement of actual relationships among the managers, as they are perceived by themselves. The data are collected by way of one single sociometric question: 'Name the persons with whom you generally work most closely, regardless of their position in the organization.' The matching of the responses of the various managers provide the mutually perceived working relationships (M.P.W.R.s), i.e. the relationships between managers who mention each other in response to the above-mentioned question. On the basis of the comparison between these M.P.W.R.s and the formal positions of the managers, the managerial structure is established by way of the informalogram.

organization, rather than the cultural effects on communication behaviour. It could be that the low percentage mutually perceived in the Israeli organization is indicative of the high bureaucratization of the military which is used to written communication and therefore perceives low oral communication.

Comparison

Looking at Table 1 as a whole and comparing the six organizations with each other, one is repeatedly drawn back to the 'daily average per person' row. This seems to be the most meaningful measurement by which to compare one organization with the other.

The cultural effects on communication are not measured by themselves, and there is a relationship to the type of organization and to the type of managerial structure. However, even in the communication behaviour of people in this small sample of organizations, different from each other in type and structure, the difference between the United States and British organizations on the one hand, and the French organizations on the other, is unmistakable. So it is useful to discuss the difference in the oral communication between the French organizations and the Anglo-Saxon ones.

A low rate of oral interaction is indicative of the high rate of written communication. Indeed, the higher the bureaucratization of the structure the more the written communication. However, bureaucracies in different cultures such as those of the United States and of France behave differently and have different rates of oral and written communication. The reasons why such cultural differences evolved probably have to do with the fact that French organizational culture has been influenced by and derived from organizations such as the Catholic Church, the army and the government. In the United States, on the other hand, organization culture has been more affected by the development of business organizations which have influenced the Church, the army and governmental organizations, rather than the other way round.

Therefore, while the degree of formalization is an indication of managerial structure, it is also an indication of the cultural effects on management. This is to say that if two identical organizations had been compared as to their scope of decision-making and as to their managerial structure, but operating the one in France and the other in the United States, a significantly higher oral communication would have been found in the latter. The other finding is that comparing oral communication in the three Western countries of the United States, the United Kingdom and France, the United States and the United Kingdom figures are found to be similar to each other (4·7, 5·0 and 5·3 interactions per person per day, respectively), while the French figures (0·5 and 1·0) are significantly different.

The proximity of Britain to the United States rather than to other European countries with regard to managerial behaviour has already been found by others in connection with managerial attitudes and decision-making processes.[3] The almost identical rate of oral communication in Anglo-Saxon organizations on both sides of the Atlantic Ocean is another indication of the cultural affinity between the United States and Britain.

These differences in oral versus written cultures appear in other areas related to the manager's work, whether within or without the organization. Education and teaching is an example. The learning processes in the United States are much more participative than those in continental European countries. Professors in France or other continental European countries hardly ever see students out of the classroom, and within the classroom hardly ever hear what the students have to say. Britain, again, is more like the United States than its European neighbours in that the faculty is closer to the students, through tutoring and other means. Indeed, even the ability of the Anglo-Saxons to spread among the nations and the emergence of the English language as the universal tongue could be attributed to a great extent to their abilities and aptitudes in oral communication. National differences in communications patterns would seem to be the basic and probably the most important cultural characteristic to be overcome in the education of multinational managers.

Let us now turn to some other cross-national differences bearing on multinational management.

3. Especially by Michel Crozier, in Crozier (1964).

Other national differences bearing on multinational management

Four areas in which national differences occur are education, social stratification, organization structure and spoken language. These are not the only areas which affect management and in which one would find national differences; nevertheless these four, along with communications, seem to be the most predominant in so far as they affect multinational management.

Other areas influenced by cultural values, though sometimes crucial for multinational managers, seem to be of secondary importance when compared with the ones chosen for discussion. One such additional area is that of competition and profits, the attitudes to which differ substantially from one culture to another. Attitudes would, likewise, differ substantially with regard to what one might call business morality. This includes such matters as bribery, which in some countries is regarded as outright corruption and in others is accepted. The degree of government intervention and the extent to which this is considered tolerable is another factor which it is important multinational managers should take into account.

The national differences discussed concern primarily countries which belong to what one could refer to as the 'Western culture countries'. This excludes completely different types of culture as, for example, that of Japan. If we had included Japan we would have had to consider the totally different 'business ideology' of that country, when 'ideology' is defined as 'any system of beliefs publicly expressed with the manifest purpose of influencing the sentiments and actions of others'.[4] This term 'business ideology' is used throughout one recent description of the Japanese managerial system.[5] In this the personal and cultural background and practices of Japanese management are summarized for a period of over 100 years. Communications, education, social stratification and organization structures are covered together with a comprehensive discussion of the historical development of Japan's business ideologies. This whole study shows that the ways of thinking and the decision-making process are being conducted in

4. See Sutton (1956), p. 2.
5. See Yoshino (1968).

an environment that is in no way derived from Western culture. Hence the following discussion will only be concerned with Western types of behaviour, in which the references to Japan are incidental.

Education

The suggestion has been made that the availability of higher education in a country determines its economic growth.[6] This theory is hard to verify because of the differences in educational methods between countries. Some of these differences affect management style more clearly than the general amount of education available. For instance, the difference between the French approach and that of the United States can best be described by saying that one is dogmatic and the other is pragmatic. The French approach is Cartesian, and stands for the most systematic and quantitative assault possible on every problem, while taking into consideration all factors which may influence it. The Americans, on the other hand, are more interested in the usefulness of the result than in the theoretical side of the method used to approach the problem.

Thus, if the same problem is presented to a French and to an American businessman, the former is liable to discover, say, twenty factors which influence it, think of about fifty alternative solutions and attempt to find the connection between them. Each alternative would be weighed in the light of the conditioning factors. The American, by contrast, would probably look for the three main factors which influence the problem and take these into consideration. He would then decide on, say, five alternative solutions and evaluate them in the light of these factors. This simplifies description points, to a certain extent, to two different ways of thinking; but first and foremost it shows that there is a basic difference of approach to problem analysis, which has its source in the differences in the social, cultural and educational values of the two peoples. Many Frenchmen regard the Americans as efficient and successful economically, but they despise them for what they consider to be their superficiality. Many Americans, on the other hand, regard the French as being highly cultured and educated, but despise them for their supposed inefficiency, dis-

6. See Servan-Schreiber (1967), p. 66.

order and uncleanliness. It is precisely their tendency to specialize – which is so often incompatible with a broad outlook – which seems to enable the Americans to attack their business problems so efficiently. A broad outlook, on the other hand, and a knowledge of the culture of the world, while they may confer an ability to see the whole picture, also give rise to a tendency to include more and more factors in the analysis of a problem.

The separation between faculty and students, of which the French universities have been an extreme example, has been made possible by both the teaching method and the design of the physical facilities. The professor enters the lecture hall from another door than that used by his students and confronts a crowd of hundreds, usually in a hall originally designed to contain a much smaller number. He delivers his lecture, often read from the paper and repeated from year to year with modifications, without enabling subsequent discussion. The students perceive this way of teaching, in many instances, as the pronouncement of the gospel in whatever field of learning this may be.

The physical design of many French universities prevents the faculty from meeting their students out of class, even by chance. Separate facilities exist for faculty and students in their restaurants, toilets and even in their lifts and staircases.

While continental European universities prefer a separation between faculty and students similar to the one described in France, British universities advocate a certain degree of cooperation. This is mainly practised out of the classroom in the so-called 'tutoring'. Members of the faculty, usually junior members, coach the students on the material covered in class, or any other additional material. The consequence of this cooperation *out* of the classroom is that there is also a fair amount of participation inside the classroom.

The third learning method advocates, in principle, cooperation between the faculty and the students both in the classroom and outside. This method originated in the United States, but is spreading quickly to other countries, especially countries like Israel where the ties with cultural tradition are not as strong as those in western continental Europe.[7]

7. For an account of the position in Israel, see Weinshall (1968a).

The purpose of graduate studies in management and business administration is the academic training of managers for middle and higher management levels in economic and public organizations. The former include industry, agriculture, banking, insurance, transport, tourism and other services. The public organizations are governmental, military, municipal, other public services and trade unions. Graduate management studies are not for the training of professional people who might serve public and economic organizations in fields such as engineering, chemistry, law, economics and others. Their purpose is to train people who might fulfil management functions. The training includes finance, control, production, marketing, research and development, personnel, as well as a synthesis which combines all these and is called 'business policy'. As every one of the managers in charge of each of the above-mentioned functions has to be in a permanent relationship with the other functions of the organization, every manager has to receive a thorough and all-round training in them all. In the modern organization the proportion of professional people is increasing from year to year. There are those who believe that within twenty years the number of professional people in an industrial organization will exceed the number of non-professional.

The manager, who has to be a professional himself, finds himself in charge of one or more functions, each of which involves know-how at an academic level, and many of his subordinates are professionals too: auditors report to comptrollers, economists to finance managers, marketing and research people to sales managers, engineers and scientists to the research and development and production managers, sociologists and psychologists to personnel and manpower managers.

This means that the manager in the modern organization has to have a profession *before* he becomes a manager. In many cases, a man acquires a managerial position by working himself up one of the 'functional channels'. Thus, for example, a man starts as a junior engineer in a certain organization, progresses through the various stages of engineering and production and becomes manager of the production or research and development division. When he reaches management in this way, he is well acquainted with his function but does not always know how to manage it. This is why we sometimes lose a good engineer and gain a bad manager. In other instances, an old-time engineer (or old-time auditor, economist and so on) will receive management training through advanced management courses or by way of a graduate school for management, usually being sent and paid by his company for this long leave of absence. Yet not every student training for management has to travel through this lengthy practical route along one of the 'functional channels'. He has to have previous academic training, meaning a bachelor's degree, so that he will have the educational ability to know how to study what is going on in the organization. His bachelor's degree might be in any field.

The case studies included in the learning programme are usually chosen so as to ensure coverage of various situations that have occurred in recent times in business and other organizations which might employ new managers after their graduation. The length of the 'recent times' depends on the circumstances and especially on the rate of the technological changes which dictate the conditions under which the executive operates. The cases studied today in good graduate business schools generally describe situations which have occurred since the Second World War, namely during the last thirty years. Most of the cases cover a period of the last ten, and sometimes of only the last five, years.

The background material, readings, seminars, reports, business games and all other teaching media complementary to the case method, are usually based on the problems to be encountered in the cases. This is why the material studied is very rarely out of context with the situations in which the manager might expect to find himself during his career. In addition, it has been suggested that there is a need for fictional cases, based on expectations of future managerial situations. Such opinions are prompted by the increasing rate of change occurring in organizations today. Thus, for example, even the study of business history is only carried out in relation to those themes that have a direct bearing on what is happening in present situations, and are important for the actual performance of the manager's functions. Such an approach results in a large economy of the students' time. These points are relevant to the training of all managers. However, the participative learning method is of special importance in the training of multinational managers, who will have to operate in different socio-cultural environments.

The possible effects of higher education on multinational management have already been discussed. We have, however, to realize that management is composed of and assisted by people who do not necessarily have a university education. Let us therefore consider the degree of secondary education, in several countries. Table 2 shows the percentage of 17-year-olds in secondary education in different countries.

The following table means that many jobs which are held in

Table 2 Availability of education in various countries

	*% of 17-year-olds in secondary education** (*in early 1960s*)	*% of 20–24-year-olds in higher education* (*in 1966*)	*% in higher education of those with secondary education* (2) (*1*)
Britain	56	5	9
Holland	41	n.a.	n.a.
Israel	27	13	48
U.S.A.	70	24	34

* Including secondary vocational education.

Western Europe by those with secondary educations are held in the United States by university graduates. In Israel, on the other hand, there is a severe shortage of secondary school graduates. A typical example of the different type of people used for the same type of job in the various countries is to be found in secretarial work. Following the differences appearing in Table 2, in Western Europe secretaries generally have a secondary education; in the United States they have at least a secondary education and there are many who have had a higher education. In Israel, however, the secretary with higher or even secondary education is the rare exception and most of them have only finished elementary school.

Social stratification

The differences in learning methods in different countries seem to be related to the degree of social stratification existing in the countries. Israel, which could be considered to be the last socially stratified country in the world, has also democratic and participative learning. This follows the United States, which is the least socially stratified of the larger Western democracies.

One way to measure social stratification in a country is by considering social mobility in that country. Table 3 presents the inequality of opportunities in various countries. The countries can be divided into five groups, moving from those with the lowest to those with the highest inequality ratio.

Table 3 **Educational inequalities**

Inequality ratio	*Countries*
Less than 250	Israel (Haifa), Great Britain, U.S.S.R. (refugees)
250–99	Australia, Denmark, France, India, United States, Brazil, Sweden, Holland, Japan
300–499	Norway, West Germany, Puerto Rico
500–799	Hungary, Finland, Italy
More than 800	Belgium

$$\text{Inequality ratio} = \frac{\text{Non-manual worker sons of non-manual worker fathers}}{\text{Non-manual worker sons of manual worker fathers}}$$

Source. Bendix and Lipset (1966), pp. 582–601.

The effects of social stratification on the management of national and multinational companies in the different countries are dramatic. Some of these effects carry through from elementary, secondary and higher education right to the positions into which people are hired in business organizations. Let us consider the cases of Britain and France.

There is still a correlation between the social class of candidates in both countries and their chances of being admitted into Oxford and Cambridge or the *grandes écoles*. Nevertheless, the admission to these universities is based more and more on achievement rather than on family background.

Similarly to those who graduate in the United States from, say, Harvard, the graduates of Oxbridge and the *grandes écoles* are preferred over other university graduates. At this point, however, the similarity between Oxbridge and the *grandes écoles* ends.

In Britain and in the United States the companies are seeking to employ the top graduates. In France those who are recruiting from the *grandes écoles* are the previous graduates hired by the same organizations, and they usually go all out to hire from the same school as the one from which they themselves graduated. Thus if you meet in a certain organization with a top executive from, say, the Haute Ecole de Commerce, there is a good chance that most of the graduates in the organization are from that school.

Another difference between university alumni in the United States and British as against French organizations is an extension of this relationship between university and job. In the Anglo-Saxon countries a degree from a 'good' university helps to get a first 'good' job, but from then on performance is more important for progress; in France, on the other hand, previous performance has a much smaller significance throughout a person's career. Once a person has graduated from a *grande école* he has in the great majority of cases made it for life. He could be a complete failure, but usually the alumni of his own school would make sure that his career progresses as if nothing had happened. Thus in France one's objective chances to succeed throughout life are much more related to one's education than in Britain.

In Britain the custom of many companies of placing in positions like the board of directors only members of the higher social classes has been gradually disappearing, while it is still common in France. There are still in existence French companies who would not hire a top executive into formal positions of 'directeur', somewhat parallel to a vice-president who is a member of the board of directors, unless he belonged to one of the so called '200 best families' of France. Strong social stratification is evident in other Western European countries as well. In some of them this social stratification seems to be even more polarized.

In most of these countries such things as the way of addressing people in business organizations, and the times at which these people arrive at work and leave it, change according to their social and organizational positions. Thus, while in the United States people usually address each other by their first name whatever their rank, in Western Europe the form of address usually changes from level to level, and is different in both directions between two people in two different organizational levels. Again, while it is customary in the United States for everybody to arrive at work at the same time, though higher ranking executives may leave later, in Europe the higher the person in the organization the later he often arrives at and leaves work.

Organization structures [8]

Organization structures are related to the socio-cultural environment and the emerging educational patterns in the different countries. There is a direct connection between the ability of the organizations to grow, to innovate and absorb new technologies and their propensity to change and adapt their managerial structures to the growing need to absorb broader decision-making processes. However, every managerial structure requires a different type of manager and therefore managers have to move from one company to another. Alternatively, they could be transferred from one part to another, if the organization is large enough to contain different types of structures within it.

The socio-cultural environment affects the processes of growth, change and mobility in several different ways, but primarily in the way that new generations of managers are being educated and formed. The preparation of the new type of leader required for a new type of managerial structure takes at least one generation. Fifty years ago the United States had a very few people who could become chief executives of decentralized structures. However, as the educational system became more participative and to some degree permissive, more and more decentralized leaders were emerging out of American families and educational institutes.

Taking France again as an example, there are few of what might be called 'decentralized leaders' in the country and therefore few decentralized structures. As a result organizations cannot absorb broader decision-making processes than their functional structures permit. This fact hinders developments in more advanced

8. See also Weinshall (1971).

technologies, more diversified product lines and more international activities.

Another environmental effect on the dynamics and adaptability of managerial structures is the 'anti-mobility value' to which we shall return at some length. This anti-mobility value is a constraint on the inter-organizational mobility which is required in order to enable the progression of management from an entrepreneurial structure to a functional one and from there to a decentralized system. The anti-mobility value is quite powerful in European countries. It, likewise, almost completely freezes any movement of managers between organizations in the large corporations of Japan.

However, the appearance of the so-called multistructure organization has enabled countries with strong anti-mobility values to bypass the necessity of inter-organizational mobility. It is interesting to highlight two points regarding the anti-mobility value and the evolution of large Japanese multistructure organizations. The anti-mobility value was inculcated into Japanese business only just before the First World War, in order to stop the enormously high inter-organizational mobility which existed at the time and thought to be contrary to the Japanese aspirations of growth and technological progress.[9] Until now a very strict anti-mobility value has been preserved only among large Japanese organizations. However, in the smaller ones, where inter-organizational mobility is a condition for their survival through a progression from one managerial structure to another, such a mobility exists.

Countries with cultures permitting the establishment of multistructure organizations are able to bypass the anti-mobility value by means of arranging a systematic managerial mobility not between one organization and another, but rather within the various parts of the same organization; such multistructure organizations are in existence in both the United States and Europe. However, they are of special importance for European countries where the anti-mobility value is quite strong. Not all Western European countries have welcomed the appearance of

9. For evidence of this statement see Yoshino (1968).

very large business organizations through growth, merger and acquisition.[10]

Managerial structures can be measured and established by way of the degree of autonomy, centralized or decentralized, and the degree of clarity, informal as against formal, in the existing relationships between the managers of organizations. However, the degree of clarity is not only related to the managerial structure, but also to the culture in which the organization operates. This culture is determined by the country in which the organization functions and the field – business, political, military and so on – in which it operates. Therefore, when one is measuring the relationships in order to establish the managerial structure of an organization, one should be aware of different flavours of relationships describing essentially the same types of managerial structure. Thus an entrepreneurial structure of a French organization could be expected to be more formalized than a similar structure in an American organization; and functional structures in France would be more 'bureaucratic' than the same structures in the United States. One of the reasons for these differences is the relative degree of usage of oral and written communication in the different countries, which has already been discussed.

Conclusion

The differences in education, social stratification, organization structure and spoken languages are interrelated with each other and connected with the differences in communication patterns in the various countries which we discussed in the previous section.

Generally speaking, we could say that the more democratic the culture of the country is, the more one would expect to discover in it participative learning methods, low social stratification, decentralized organizational structures, free mixing with other nationalities and linguistic ability. The world is moving very fast to the merging and unifying of cultural behaviour, social structure, organization practices and language. However, some countries are moving faster than others.

10. The rejection of big business is a theme also in the United States. See, for example, Glover (1954).

Democracy = PARTICIPATIVE Learning Methods

Cross-national values, norms and attitudes

Certain values, norms and attitudes arise from the communication patterns just described, and are in turn subject to influence by multinational education. When a group of people from a variety of countries are gathered into the same formal organization, they bring along with them all the differences in communication behaviour, education, social stratification, organization structure and national spoken languages which have already been discussed. Nobody could better describe the consequences of such a gathering than the author who wrote about the construction of the Tower of Babel:

> Once upon a time all the world spoke a single language and used the same words. As men journeyed in the east, they came upon a plain in the land of Shinar and settled there. They said to one another, 'Come, let us make bricks and bake them hard'; they used bricks for stone and bitumen for mortar. 'Come,' they said, 'let us build ourselves a city, and a tower with its top in the heavens, and make a name for ourselves; or we shall be dispersed all over the earth.' Then the Lord came down to see the city and tower which mortal men had built, and he said, 'Here they are, one people with a single language, and now they have started to do this; henceforward nothing they have a mind to do will be beyond their reach. Come, let us go down there and confuse their speech, so that they will not understand what they say to one another.' So the Lord dispersed them from there all over the earth, and they left off building the city. That is why it is called Babel, because the Lord there made a babble of the language of all the world; from that place the Lord scattered men all over the face of the earth.[11]

One has only to consider a 'language' in its wider meaning and exchange the type of organization from one of construction to, say, a military one defending the Western democracies or to political ones preserving the health and culture of the world. This quotation would then be transplanted from over twenty centuries before Christ to the twentieth century after.

The educational study for this paper was among the students of the European Institute of Business Administration at Fontainebleau (INSEAD). This began with an attempt to find out how

11. Quoted from the Book of Genesis, 11: 1–9, *The New English Bible*, Oxford University Press, 1969.

they differ from each other when they come in. The differences examined were partly their background characteristics: age, nationality, marital status and first university degree. They also included attitudes towards problems related to multinational management, to business and to business education. The differences in values, norms and attitudes of the students were found to be mainly the consequence of their national background, and only to a lesser degree related to other background characteristics.

The data relating to the pre-INSEAD values, norms and attitudes have been collected by way of two methods:

- General attitudes – gathered through a so-called INSEAD motivation questionnaire.
- Attitudes regarding the anti-mobility value – gathered through reactions to the Jim Fairfax case.[12]

12. 'In the U.S.A. a large enterprise finds itself on the verge of bankruptcy. Its charming, debonair General Manager is liked by all, but no longer has full control over the business. Discipline is non-existent. The personnel take an easy-going attitude towards their work. Morale is good, but turnover is going down fast.

'The Board of Directors is becoming concerned. It quickly takes the decision to appoint a new General Manager to put things right. A strong, energetic man is chosen: Jim Fairfax.

'Fairfax is of an extremely sharp intelligence, has a striking personality, is extraordinarily dynamic and ambitious. Discipline is re-established in a short time. The place buzzes with activity. The new manager is indefatigable, leaves nothing to chance, supervises everything, decides everything and makes his personnel work hard.

'Some of the personnel live in continual fear of having misunderstood Fairfax's orders, others complain bitterly of having no real responsibility or of having no powers to use their own initiative. The psychological climate starts to deteriorate. In fact, it becomes very bad. At the end of a trial period of several months, the Board meets again. Fairfax's successes are noted. Business has improved and become profitable again. The Board also notes the worsening atmosphere within the company which is taking on such proportions that it could in the long run cause the complete breakdown of morale amongst the managers.

'In these circumstances, the Board was confronted with the problem of what to do about Jim Fairfax. The possibilities open to the members of the Board were:

a. Fire him.
b. Appoint him as Chairman of the Board of Directors.

Let us consider each of these methods and their findings separately.

General attitudes

A motivation questionnaire has been administered to the INSEAD students at varying intervals in every academic year since 1965–6.

Table 4 includes an analysis of responses to six selected alternative answers, analysed according to the dependent variables of national complexity,[13] age and marital status. Thus, for example, the first answer selected is that of the 'American ways and approach to business administration', which is one possible answer to the question 'What attracted you in coming to INSEAD?' This was the first choice of the respondents when choosing from among nine possible answers. While age did not affect the answers and marital status affected them only to a small degree, the responses were significantly affected by national complexity. 17 per cent of those not nationally complex chose this answer, while only 11 per cent of the nationally complex group did so. The explanation for this difference seems to be that the nationally complex group is less interested in the career aspects of the INSEAD studies.

Table 4 suggests that the background characteristic which most affected the participants' attitudes was their national complexity; marital status came second and age last. It can likewise be seen that the more nationally complex the participant's

c. Leave him in his present position, but appoint one or more deputy managers to help him.

d. Remove him from his post and appoint him as a consultant to the company.

e. Other solutions.

You are a member of the Board of Directors and you have to vote for one of the alternatives. Please explain your choice.'

13. 'National complexity' was a category which included both those who had wives of another nationality and those whose parents were from different countries. It is regrettable that it was not possible to examine those of mixed parentage separately. Recent observations suggest that there may be significant differences among these latter, depending on the political relations between the countries of origin of the parents.

Table 4 **Selected answers from 'The motivation of INSEAD students', questionnaire according to national complexity, age and marital status**

Question	*Selected answer*	*National complexity*		*Age*		*Marital status*		*Total student body*	
		None (%)	*Complex* (%)	*Low* (%)	*High* (%)	*Single* (%)	*Married* (%)	*This Ans.*	*Out of (no. of choices)*
a. What attracted you in coming to INSEAD?	The American ways and approach to business administration	17*	11*	16*	15*	16*	13*	1st choice	9
a. What attracted you in coming to INSEAD?	International composition of participant body	11*	15*	14*	10*	16*	4*	2nd choice	9
d. When you chose INSEAD, what did you primarily want?	Go to an international school	23	35	28	25	24	38	2nd choice (26%)	2 (100%)
e. When you find basic fault in things that happen in your country – what do you do?	Non-conformists ('Speak to people in my own country about it even if they are not close friends', and more drastic reactions)	69	61	70	66	70	64	4 last choices (68%)	7 (100%)
f. What do you really want to do in the future?	Work in a large organization†	8*	12*	8*	6*	8*	2*	3rd/4th choice	9
h. How much of your spare time did you spend with those participants not from your country?	The greater part (during the last term)	43	50	46	40	45	38	1st choice (44%)	4 (100%)

* This is a 'positive percentage', which is arrived at after the percentage of 'Least attractive' is subtracted from the percentage of 'Most attractive'.

† Perceived by many participants to be a multinational corporation. The percentages in this row are also 'positive percentages', arrived at after subtracting 'the least' percentage from 'the most' percentage.

family, the more he expresses international attitudes and is inclined towards multinational companies. Married participants generally manifest the trend in their attitudes as participants with nationally complex families; but this does not always happen as is shown by attitudes towards the 'international composition of participant body' where the trend is reversed. Similarly, young participants express more internationalist attitudes than older ones.

The other background factor which was tested as to its effects on the attitudes and motivations of the students was their length of

Table 5 **The anti-mobility value – reactions to the Jim Fairfax case – (*a*) The original results**

	Distribution of choices	
	French (*managers*)	*American* (*board-members*)
	%	%
a. Fire (sack) Jim Fairfax	2	80
b. Appoint him as chairman of the board of directors	28	—
c. Leave him in his present position but appoint one or more deputy managers	22	—
d. Remove him from post and appoint him as consultant to the company	26	—
e. Other alternatives	22	Almost none were mentioned

(*b*) INSEAD'S results at the beginnings of academic years*

Class	*Total of participants*	*Those who decided to 'fire'* No.	%
1969–70*	214	11	5
1970–71*	223	20	9
TOTAL:	437	31	7

* The statistic *u* of the Poisson Approximation to the Normal Distribution is 2·279, making the difference between the two classes (1969–70 and 1970–71) in those favouring firing significant at better than the 5 per cent level.

(*c*) Reactions at INSEAD – arranged by countries (ordered by favourability towards firing Jim Fairfax – for the two groups at the beginning of 1969–70 and 1970–71

	Total of 1969–70 and 1970–71	
Country	*Total of participants*	*Those who decided to fire (%)*
Subgroup 1		
1. U.S.A.	7	29
2. Israel	8	25
3. Spain	8	25
4. Italy	9	17
	Subtotal: 32	Subtotal: 25
Subgroup 2		
5. Sweden	9	11
6. Great Britain	43	9
7. France	104	9
8. Norway	16	6
9. Germany	78	5
10. Holland	29	3
11. Switzerland	39	3
	Subtotal: 318	Subtotal: 7
Subgroup 3		
12. Belgium	23	0
13. Austria	15	0
14. Denmark	7	0
15. Lebanon	7	0
16. Luxembourg	7	0
	Subtotal: 59	Subtotal: 0
	Total: 437	7

Notes. Only those countries with seven or more participants have been included; this accounts for the totals not corresponding with the subtotals. The statistic u of the Binomial Approximation to the Normal Distribution is 4·76 for the difference in the subtotal for groups 1 and 2, making it significant at better than the 1 per cent level, and for the difference between subgroups 2 and 3, tested by the Poisson Approximation, $u = 4{\cdot}86$, and the difference is therefore significant at better than the 0·5 per cent level.

stay outside their native countries. It was discovered to be an important factor in that the longer the stay of the participants outside their countries, the more 'international' their attitudes. However, this finding, as well as the previous ones, was based on a comparatively small sample; it requires additional exploration.

Attitudes regarding the anti-mobility value

Differences in inter-organizational mobility are likely to account in some degree for the varying amounts of success that business and other organizations have in absorbing innovations and new technologies, as well as in competing and surviving. Inter-organizational mobility has to occur within all the human factors comprising the organization which include the customers, the shareholders, the bankers and the workers. However, the most crucial human factor as far as inter-organizational mobility is concerned is the management. It is important that the styles of leadership of the managers should comply with the structure required to handle the full range of the decision-making process at every stage of its development. Companies are constantly growing, in terms of the scope of their decision-making process, in order to meet their competition. They therefore have from time to time to adapt their managerial structures. These changes involve an exchange of managers, because the styles of leadership required in each managerial structure are different. Often this means managers changing companies. However, when the firm is very large in its scope, it can adopt several different managerial structures at once. This multistructure system makes possible mobility within itself and does not require movement from one company to another.

The difference in the rate of managerial mobility as between the United States and Western Europe has already been discussed earlier in this chapter. Differences in the rates of managerial mobility extend from countries with almost no mobility at all, like Japan, through countries with very little mobility, like France, and those with growing mobility, like Britain and Germany, to countries where the anti-mobility cultural value almost does not exist, like the Soviet Union and the United States.[14]

A test of the anti-mobility value in French culture occurred when

14. For further discussion of this point, see Weinshall (1968a).

the case of Jim Fairfax was given to a group of French managers. The results appear in Table 5*a*.

Next to the distribution of the responses of the French managers appears the *actual* vote of the American members of the board of directors of this company, who considered all the four first alternatives, but voted only on whether to fire Jim Fairfax, a motion which obtained approval from 80 per cent of those present. The French managers gave to this alternative only 2 per cent while the remaining responses favoured almost equally any one of the other four alternatives: (appoint as chairman – 28 per cent; appoint as consultant – 26 per cent; leave him, but appoint deputy managers – 22 per cent; other alternatives – 22 per cent). This is almost as if the French respondents were saying – 'as long as you do not fire him, we don't care what you do. We have therefore chosen at random one alternative from among the solutions which would enable us to retain Jim Fairfax.'

This case study was therefore chosen as a tool for measuring the attitudes of the INSEAD students towards the anti-mobility value. When this was first used at INSEAD, it was only towards the *end* of the academic year 1968–9, and it constituted part of an examination in the field of business policy. However, since then the Jim Fairfax case has been administered to the students at the very beginning of every academic year.

Table 5*b* presents the results for the INSEAD classes of 1969–70 and 1970–71. The main finding to be drawn from this table is that the 1970–71 class had a significantly higher percentage of students who chose the solution of 'Fire Jim Fairfax' (9 per cent), than the class of 1969–70 which preceded them (5 per cent). Assuming that these two classes were equally representative of the cultural values existing among the nations from which the INSEAD students are drawn, one can discern a shift away from this anti-mobility attitude. More people were ready to accept inter-organizational mobility in 1970 than in 1969.

The second analysis which was made of the same figures was by lumping the 1969–70 and 1970–71 figures together and dividing them according to the students' national origins. The countries were grouped into three subgroups, according to the percentages of those who chose the 'Fire Jim Fairfax' alternative in each group

(17–29 per cent subgroup; 3–11 per cent subgroup and 0 per cent subgroup). When doing so it was found that the countries in subgroup 1 included the United States and three out of four Mediterranean countries. The one excluded was the Lebanon, which could be because of the influence of French culture in that country. Subgroup 2 included some of the more economically advanced and more homogeneously cultured countries of Europe, while subgroup 3 included countries with somewhat mixed cultures like Belgium and the Lebanon as well as subcultures of countries in the previous group. These explanations should be regarded as hypothetical and to be explored in future research, in which the growing numbers of respondents from individual countries would enable statistically significant comparisons between single countries, rather than between subgroups of countries.

Summary

One dominant factor which accounts for the differences in the attitudes between a conglomeration of human beings gathered from a variety of nation states is their affiliation to the culture of their countries. The difference between people with regard to communications, education, organization structures, and spoken languages originates from the different cultures of their countries of origin. We have surveyed in this chapter some background characteristics of people which tend to *counter* their national attitudes. This we did by exploring the characteristics of those who manifest internationalist attitudes, as distinguished from attitudes one would expect from non-internationally inclined students who come to INSEAD. The small sample which has been analysed hitherto could only lead to some indications rather than to definite conclusions. The findings of this small sample indicate that two of the most important background factors which are conducive to internationalist attitudes are the national complexity of the student's family, usually when his wife comes from a different national origin, and the length of time he has spent outside his own country. We then regarded the attitudes of the students at the very beginning of the year towards the anti-mobility value, by way o asking for their reactions to a case study in which the attitudes towards inter-organizational managerial mobility are cardin when the student's decision is made. We found that the average anti-mobility attitudes decreased from 95 to 91 per cent, from September 1969 to September 1970. We likewise analysed the subgroups of countries from which the students expressed similar degrees of anti-mobility attitudes. These ranged from the subgroup including the United States, Israel, Spain and Italy, which averaged 75 per cent with anti-mobility attitudes, to the subgroup including Belgium, Austria, Denmark, the Lebanon and Luxembourg, which expressed 100 per cent anti-mobility attitudes.

The effects of multinational education

Having discussed the cross-national values, norms and attitudes of the students who come to a school like INSEAD for multinational education, let us now consider the effects that this type of multinational education has on both their attitudes and social relationships.

In spite of the relatively short period of exposure to the educational and social experience of INSEAD, the findings of the research project show a marked effect on the attitudes and relationships of participants. The findings concerning these attitudes and relationships towards the end of the year at INSEAD will be presented separately for the three phases of the research: general attitudes, attitudes towards the anti-mobility value and the social structure of the students.

General attitudes

In part B of the questionnaire the respondents were asked to rate the various countries and fields of study represented at INSEAD with regard to the degrees of mixing with students from different countries and backgrounds, their contribution to the learning process and how much they benefited from it.

The various countries and professions were subsequently ranked on each of the three scores: mixing, contributing, receiving. The results are presented in a graphic way on the two parts of Fig. 1. Thus, for example, in Fig. 1*a* Belgium scores the highest on mixing, is the third in ranking on contributing and in sixth and seventh place together with Italy on receiving. The average rank order of Belgium is therefore 3·5.

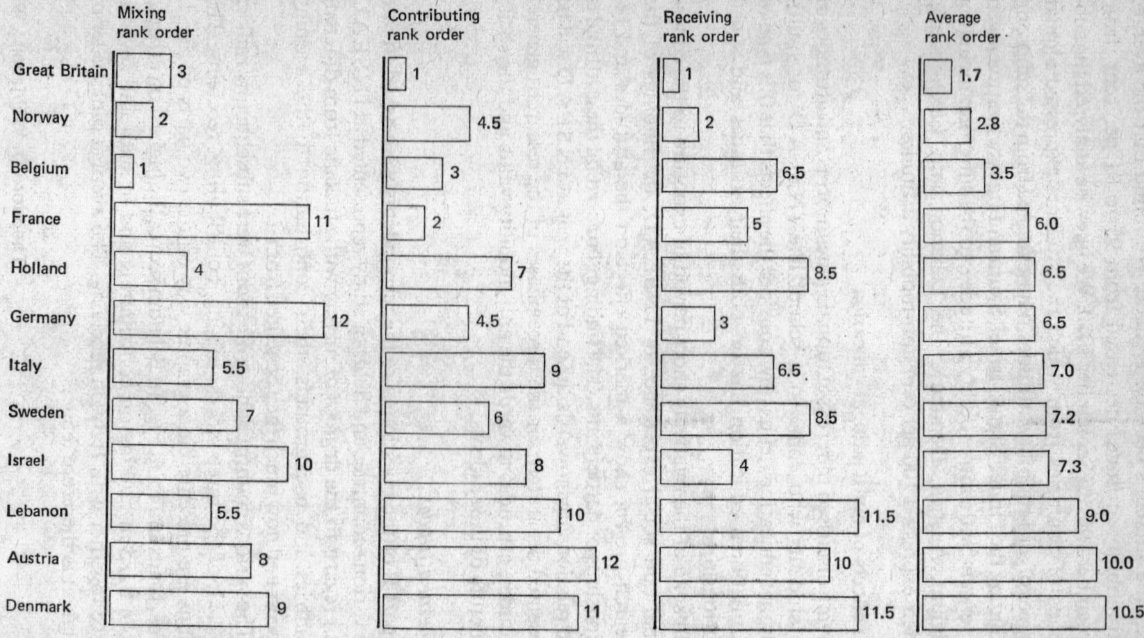

1 (a) The effects of the participants' mentioned origins on their studies

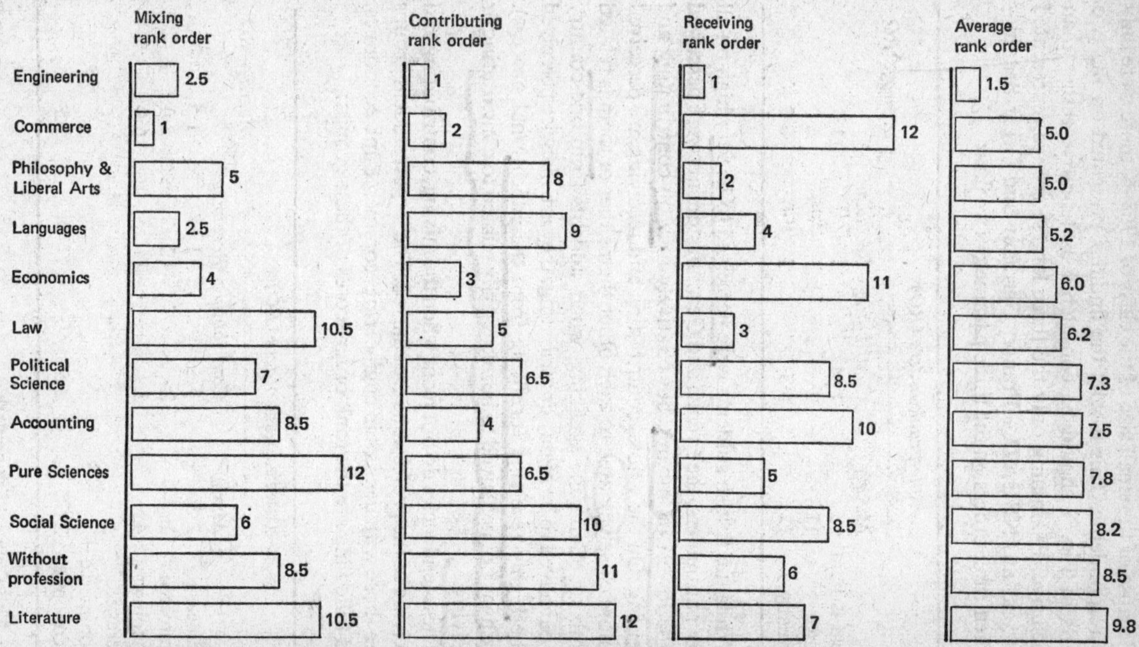

1(b) The effects of the participants' professions on their studies

Because of the small size of the class of 1965–6, there were only 100 respondents. This is why the findings presented on the two charts of Fig. 1 should be considered as tentative rather than conclusive. Examining only the three largest groups represented that year at INSEAD – France, Germany and Great Britain – in their rank orders on the three parameters we find:

	Detailed rank orders (RO)			*Average RO*
	Mixing	*Contributing*	*Receiving*	
Great Britain	3	1	1	1·7
France	11	2	5	6·0
Germany	12	4·5	3	6·5

While the British students were perceived to be very high on all three parameters, the French and German students were perceived as the lowest on mixing, but relatively high on contributing and receiving. On the whole, contributing and receiving are perceived as more closely related to each other than either of them is related to mixing. Generally speaking, when students from one country are perceived to be highly contributing, they are likewise perceived to be highly receiving (profiting from the educational process). Mixing is not perceived to be necessarily related to contributing or receiving.

These tendencies do not recur when the mixing, contributing and receiving of the professions are charted. The largest student groups were those with degrees in engineering, commerce and economics. The following are the rank order scores of these groups:

	Detailed rank orders (RO)			*Average RO*
	Mixing	*Contributing*	*Receiving*	
Engineering	2·5	1	1	1·5
Commerce	1	2	12	5·0
Economics	4	3	11	6·0
Average commerce – economics	2·5	2·5	11·5	5·5

Comparing the engineering with the average of the commerce–economics groups, we see that, in mixing, the engineering graduates are just between those with commerce degrees and those with economics degrees. The engineering graduates contribute more to the educational process than their colleagues with commerce and economics degrees, who immediately follow them in the highest contributions. As to receiving (profiting from the studies) the engineering graduates are perceived to be the highest. Those with degrees in economics and commerce are ranked lowest on receiving. This probably means that the INSEAD studies were perceived to be closely oriented towards commerce and economics, but also to require a high degree of knowledge in quantitative techniques.

These were the perceptions of the 1965–6 respondents as to the relative positions of the three largest national groups (France, Germany and Britain) and the largest professional groups (commerce, economics and engineering), when measured by the parameters of mixing, contributing and receiving. When asked 'To what background factors do you think that mixing or not mixing internationally could be attributed at INSEAD?' they ranked the six alternative factors presented to them in the following order:

1. Mastering the required languages.
2. Being married to another nationality.
3. Having parents of two different nationalities.
4. Social class.
5. Nationality.
6. Profession.

We have already seen that 'being married to another national' does indeed account to a large extent for the 'international' attitudes and motivations of the INSEAD students. As for the national origin having a larger effect than the professional background on mixing or not mixing internationally, we shall see that this is borne out by the social structure which will be discussed later.

Ideas about the anti-mobility value

The Jim Fairfax case was first applied in research with the

INSEAD students at the end of the academic year 1968–9, as part of a written examination. The results of this were compared with the results of the administration of the Jim Fairfax case to the students at the beginning of the following year, 1969–70. It was found that the percentage of those who chose to fire Jim Fairfax at the *end* of 1968–9 (33 per cent) was almost *seven times* more than those who chose to fire him at the beginning of 1969–70 (5 per cent). This comparison appears on Table 6*a* country by country.

Table 6 **Changes in the anti-mobility value – changing reactions to the Jim Fairfax case**
(*a*) From the end of one year to the beginning of the following year

Country	*End of 1968–9* Total of partici-pants	*End of 1968–9* Those who decided to 'fire' (%)	*Beginning of 1969–70* Total of partici-pants	*Beginning of 1969–70* Those who decided to 'fire' (%)
1. Norway	3	67	7	0
2. Germany	35	37	39	3
3. France	50	34	45	7
4. Austria	6	33	8	0
5. Switzerland	12	33	23	4
6. Great Britain	16	31	21	10
7. Holland	9	29	14	17
8. Italy	9	29	3	0
9. Belgium	8	13	15	0
Total	164	33	214	5

Notes. Only includes countries in which there were at least three participants in each of the two years. Hence 'total' varies from sum of countries shown.

The difference between the 1968–9 and 1969–70 totals gives a value of 6·8 for the statistic *u* of the Binomial Approximation to the Normal Distribution and it is therefore significant at better than the 0·5 per cent level.

In the cases of France and Germany, the differences between the two classes in those favouring firing, when tested by the Binomial Approximation to the Normal Distribution, give *u* the same values and significance levels for both countries, namely 5·7 and better than the 0·5 per cent level respectively. The differences could not be tested for other individual countries, because the numbers involved were too small.

The total includes all thirty-seven countries.

(b) From beginning to the end of same academic year

Country	*Beginning of 1970–71*			*Towards end 1970–71*		
	Firing		*No. of participants*	*Firing*		*No. of participants*
	%	*No.*		%	*No.*	
1. U.S.A.	50	2	4	50	2	4
2. Israel	33	2	6	50	3	6
3. Britain	9	2	22	39	7	18
4. Luxembourg	0	0	3	33	1	3
5. Sweden	0	0	3	33	1	3
6. Italy	22	2	9	29	2	7
7. Norway	11	1	9	29	2	7
8. Germany	8	3	39	21	5	24
9. Switzerland	0	0	16	20	2	10
10. Austria	0	0	8	17	1	6
11. France	10	6	9	12	5	43
12. Holland	0	0	15	8	1	13
13. Belgium	0	0	8	0	0	5
14. Denmark	0	0	4	0	0	4
	9·1%	20	220	20·3%	35	172

Notes. Only countries with at least three participants at the beginning and end of the year; arranged by the percentage of the 'firing' at the end of the year.

The total includes also participants from another eleven countries with less than three participants at the beginning and/or end of year.

(*a*) Difference between beginning and end of 1970–71 is significant at the 2 per cent level when treated by the Binomial Approximation to the normal and at the 1 per cent level when tested by the Sign test for two related samples.

(*b*) Difference between beginning and end of year – significant at better than the 3 per cent.

(*c*) Difference between beginning and end of year – significant at better than the 0·5%.

The following academic year of 1970–71 enabled the researchers to compare the change which occurred within the same class over a period of about seven months' studies at INSEAD. The findings appear in Table 6*b*. We can see from Table 6*c* overleaf that the distribution of 'firing' by countries at the ends of the two years are

Table 6 (contd)

(*c*) Distribution of 'firing' responses in beginnings and ends of academic years

	1968/69 (end)–1969/70 (beginning)					*1970/71 (end and beginning)*			
	No. of countries		*% of countries*			*No. of countries*		*% of countries*	
% Firing	*End*	*Beginning*	*End*	*Beginning*	*% Firing*	*End*	*Beginning*	*End*	*Beginning*
More than 37	1	—	11	—	more than 39	3	1	21	7
29–37	7	—	78	—	17–39	7	2	50	14
less than 29	1	9*	11	100	less than 17	4	11†	29	79
Total	9	9*	100	100	Total	14	14†	100	100

* Including four countries with 0% 'firing'.
† Including five countries with 0% 'firing'.

Table 6 (contd)

(*d*) Rates of change in 'firing' responses of country groups from beginning to end of 1970–71

Level of firing at end of year		*Country group*	*Beginning*			*End*			*Rate of change (% firing)*
%	*level*		*% firing*	*No. of pts**		*% firing*	*No. of pts**		
				firing	*total*		*firing*	*total*	
39–50	Very high	U.S.A. + Israel + Britain	19	6	32	43	12	28	×2·3
29–33	Medium	Luxembourg + Sweden + Italy + Norway	12	3	24	30	6	20	×2·5
17–21	Low	Germany + Switzerland + Austria	5	3	63	20	8	40	×4
0–8	Very low	France + Holland + Belgium + Denmark	7	6	86	9	6	65	×1·3

* Participants.

of a bell-shape around an average, while the beginnings of years are moving from about half of the countries at 0 per cent firing to a gradual increase of up to 17 per cent in 1969–70 and 50 per cent in 1970–71. This suggests that education at INSEAD leads to a change in the anti-mobility value for students from different cultural backgrounds. The table also shows that the amount of change varies from year to year.

Analysing in more detail the changes which occurred among students of different countries, we could divide the countries according to the levels of 'firing' responses at the end of the year and find out the rates of change which occurred in each group (Table 6*d*). We see that in the group which registered high on firing (39–50 per cent) and comprised the United States, Israel and Britain, the rate of change was more than doubled (from 19 to 43 per cent). These countries have also been found to be similar to each other in their managerial communication as well as in other aspects of organizational behaviour. The rate of change of the next group, which consisted of Luxembourg, Sweden, Italy and Norway, was at a similar rate (from 12 to 30 per cent). The largest rate of change (from 5 to 20 per cent) occurred in the German group, which included Switzerland and Austria; the smallest (from 7 to 9 per cent) in the group of France, Holland, Belgium and Denmark. The grouping of the countries could be of some significance, considering that the more centrally situated, non-German-speaking countries of Europe behave differently from those located on the outskirts of Europe.

Social structure

The students gathered at INSEAD came from a variety of national origins, had gone through different fields of study for their first degree and had various other different personal characteristics including age, marital status, degree of national complexity and length of time spent abroad. Had INSEAD let its students structure themselves freely, without any institutional intervention, it is probable that they would have structured themselves along one or more of their personal characteristics. In 1966–7 the students were divided as follows:

National language:	12 groups of countries, with an average of 12 participants in each.
Profession:	9 first university specializations, with an average of 16 participants in each.
Family status:	bachelor and married groups, with an average of 72 participants in each.
National complexity:	nationally complex and non-nationally complex groups with an average of 72 participants in each.
Age:	young and old (divided by medium) groups, with an average of 72 participants in each.
Time abroad:	long and short term abroad (divided by medium) groups, with an average of 72 participants in each.

However, the formal structure of INSEAD has been set up so as to counteract the possible effects of the personal characteristics of the participants on their social structure. In other words, the objective has been to mix the students as much as possible. Many other graduate schools of business administration have a similar objective in that they try to mix the students by profession, in order that their different academic backgrounds would contribute to each other, or by age, so that the more experienced will contribute to the less and vice versa. INSEAD adds one other important mixing factor, namely that of mixing the culture, nationalities and languages of its students. This mixing is done through both the learning organization and the living organization of the students. In 1966–7 they were divided as follows:

Case discussion group:	20 groups, with an average of 7 participants in each.
Floor in the residence:	15 floors, with an average of 8 participants on each.
Residence:	6 residences with an average of 20 in each.
Class at entry:	3 classes in the first half of 1966–7 with an average of 45 in each.
Class at end of year:	3 classes in the second half of 1966–7 with an average of 45 in each.

About 17 per cent of the students did not live in INSEAD residences.

The researchers, therefore, set two possibly conflicting hypotheses for their research:

- that the personal characteristics of the students affect their social structure.
- that the formal structure affects the students' social structure.

The social structure was investigated by means of four sociometric indicators, measuring the perceptions of participants as to their relationships with other participants: whom they had meals with, met during leisure time, would like to work with, would like to meet socially. The choices of participants in each of these four indicators were matched and only mutually perceived choices were taken into account. Two sociograms (Figs 2 and 3) were drawn to demonstrate the network of the closer social relations between participants. The lines between participants in these two sociograms indicate mutual choices according to more than one indicator. For the purpose of clarity, only those participants who had such social relationships among themselves, namely, having mutual choices according to more than one indicator, appear. All the isolates according to this definition, those participants who had no mutual choices or had them only on one indicator, were omitted from the sociograms. Fig. 2 shows the social network superimposed on the geographical map of the different countries. Fig. 3 shows this network in relation to the accommodation of the INSEAD participants at Fontainebleau.

In both sociograms the types of lines designate the degrees of closeness of social relations between participants. The closest social relation is found to be between participants who chose each other on all four indicators for social relationships and is represented in the sociograms by the thick black lines. Thus on Fig. 2 two thick lines are inside one country, France, while the other three thick lines cross borders between the following pairs of participants – Austrian and Finnish, British and French, French and Lebanese. In Fig. 3 we see that four thick lines are inside the residences while only one thick line passes outside.

A visual analysis of the sociograms points again to the fact that

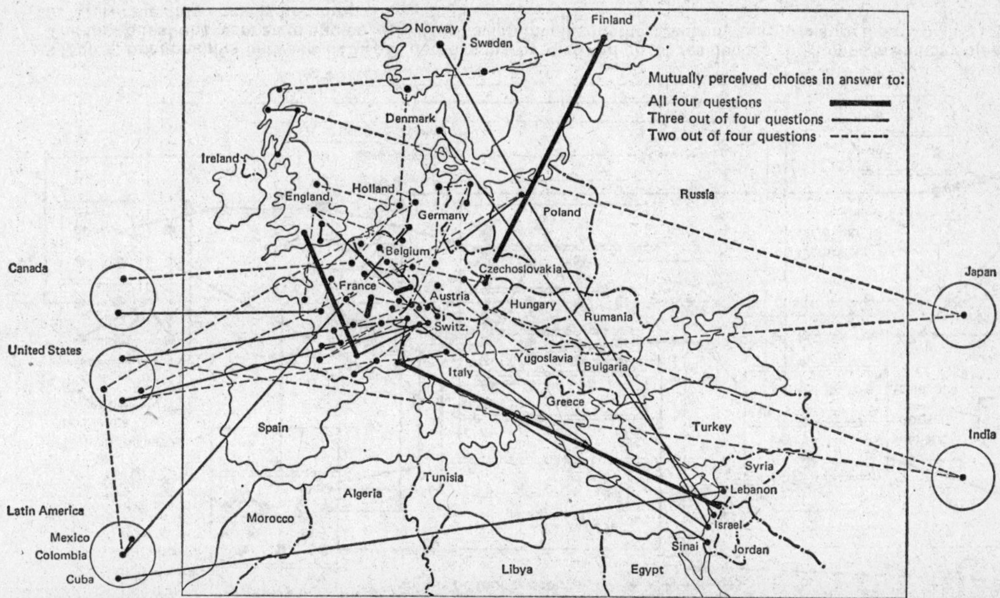

2 The social structure: mutual relationships between INSEAD participants by countries of origin. The four questions were as to choices regarding having meals together: meeting during leisure time: working together in future: meeting socially in future.

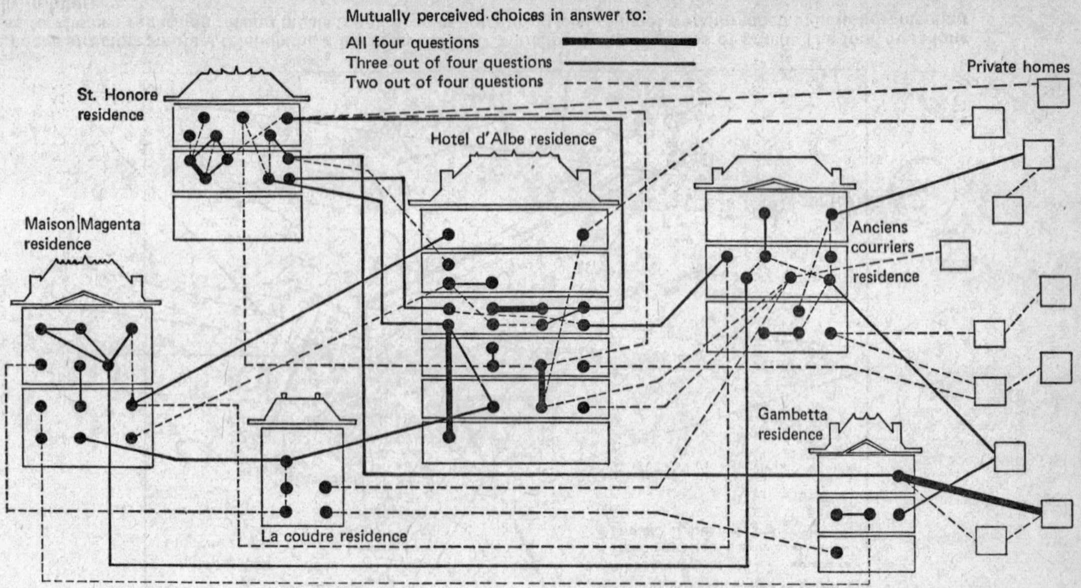

3 Mutual relationships between INSEAD participants by distribution of residences and homes in Fontainebleau, 1967. The four questions were as to choice regarding having meals together: meeting during leisure time: working together in future: meeting socially in future.

the school's framework, the residences in this case, affects somewhat more social relations between participants than the background characteristics, the countries of origin.

Finally, the conclusion of the whole analysis supports hypotheses about the effect of imposed conditions and given conditions on social relations between participants. There is also a clear indication that the imposed conditions had a larger effect on the social structure than the given conditions. This last finding puts a special emphasis on the importance of international schools such as INSEAD, which by its formal structure and teaching methods encourages social relations among participants from different nations and different backgrounds.

An analysis of the correlations between the social structure and the personal characteristics of participants on the one side and the formal structure of INSEAD on the other is presented in Table 7. The analysis presented in this table reveals that the effect of INSEAD's formal structure on the students' social structures is much more dominant than the effects of their personal characteristics.[15]

The most significant factor affecting the social structure was found to be membership of a discussion group. The relationships *between* members of discussion groups exceeded by six their randomness. Next in its effect on the social structure in Table 10 is the residence: relationships between students living on the same floor exceeded by 5·5 their randomness. The next two factors affecting the social structure, exceeding by three their randomness, were the residence itself, as opposed to the floor, and the national origin. The following two factors which had an effect on the students' social structures were their first degree, and the class in which they studied at the beginning of the year. Such a class was usually composed of seven discussion groups. The last two factors appearing in Table 7, as having an effect on the social structure, were the students' class at the time of the research and their marital status.

All other factors tested were below 1 per cent per participant and

15. For the exact method of calculating the figures in Table 7 see Weinshall and De Bettignies (1971).

Table 7 The social structure: summary of effects of independent factors on social structure

Rank order	*Factor*	*Imposed or given conditions*	*% of mutual choices within own factor group*	*Approximate average no of participants in a group*	*Percentage of total mutual choices per participant within own factor group* (%)*	*Relation between % of actual choices within group and % of random choice†*
1	Discussion group	Imposed	30	7	4·3	×6·1
2	Floor in the residence	Imposed	31	8	3·9	×5·5
3·4	Whole residence group	Imposed	44	20	2·2	×3·1
3·4	National origin group	Given	26	12	2·2	×3·1
5	Professional (first university degree) group	Given	31	16	2·0	×2·9
6	Class at the beginning of the year	Imposed	71	45	1·5	×2·1
7	Class at the time of the research	Imposed	55	45	1·2	×1·7
8	Marital status group	Given	71	72	1·0	×1·4

* If we take the discussion group as an example for calculation of percentage and total mutual choices per person, the analysis was done in two stages: it was found that 30 per cent of the mutual choices of the participants were among members of the same group. These 30 per cent were divided by 7 (the number of members in each group) which gives the 4·3 per cent of mutual choices per person.

† The random being – $\frac{100\%}{143 \text{ students in 1965–66}} = 0{\cdot}7\%$

For the exact method of calculating these figures see Weinshall and De Bettignies (1971).

Table 8 The social structure: mutual relationships inside and between country groups*

	No. of participants		*Mutual relationships per participant*					
	Total in	*Appearing on*	*Total*		*Inside country group*		*Out of country group*	
Country groups	*study*	*sociograms*†	*No.*	%	*No.*	%	*No.*	%
1. U.S. and Canada	6	6 (100%)	4·33	100	0·33	8	4·00	92
2. Switzerland	10	7 (70%)	4·60	100	0·80	17	3·80	83
3. Scandinavian countries (3)	6	5 (83%)	4·00	100	0·67	17	3·33	83
4. Mediterranean countries (4)	10	7 (70%)	4·09	100	0·82	20	3·27	80
5. Britain	16	9 (56%)	3·56	100	1·13	31	2·44	69
6. German-speaking countries (6)	18	13 (72%)	4·39	100	1·67	38	2·72	62
7. France	34	23 (68%)	3·47	100	1·82	53	1·65	47
Total	100	70 (70%)						

* Only country groups with at least six participants in the study. These include 100 of the 115 who participated in the study.

† The numbers of participants appearing on the sociograms (Figs. 2 and 3) are smaller than the total number of participants in the study because the sociograms, including only participants with mutual relationships on two, three and all four indicators (i.e. do not include mutual choices for one indicator only).

(3) Scandinavian countries including participants from Denmark, Norway, Sweden and Finland.

(4) Mediterranean countries – including participants from Israel (5 part.), Italy (3 part.) and Lebanon (2 part.).

(6) German-speaking countries – include participants from Austria (4 part.) and Germany (14 part.).

very close to the random 0·7 per cent per participant. It can be seen from the tables that the factors imposed by INSEAD were predominant in their effect on the social structure both in their number, five factors imposed by INSEAD and only three personal characteristics, and in their variance from random, as follows:

Imposed factors: membership in a discussion group, 6 times more than random.
living on the same floor of residence, 5·5 times more than random.
living in the same residence, 3 times more than random.
belonging to class at beginning of year, 3 times more than random.
belonging to class at end of year, almost twice more than random.

Personal factors: originating from the same national group, 3 times more than random.
having obtained the same first university degree, almost 3 times more than random.
belonging to the same marital status group, 1·4 times more than random.

Mixing with participants from other countries

Table 8 represents the mutual relationships inside and between seven country groups. In order to arrive at larger groups, the participants were grouped by countries: three single countries (Switzerland, Britain and France), two double-country groups (United States and Canada, Austria and Germany), one four-country group (Scandinavia) and one three-country group (Mediterranean).

The chance of having more mutual relationships within a group increases, of course, the larger and more monolithic the group is. This is why the comparison should be made separately for the four first country groups and for the larger groups of Britain, German-speaking and France. The United States and the Canadian participants appear at the top of the list in their out-of-group relationships (92 per cent). Next come the Scandinavian and

Swiss participants who should be considered to some extent as a country group (83 per cent each). Very close to them come the participants from the Mediterranean countries (80 per cent). This bringing together of Israel and the Lebanon may seem artificial to outsiders; in reality, however, the Israeli students had, for different reasons, close links with both the Italian and the Lebanese students. As for the larger groups, Britain is the biggest (69 per cent), closely followed by the German-speaking countries (62 per cent), with France lagging behind (47 per cent), which could be explained to some extent by the size of this group (34 participants). Such figures indicate that an institution like INSEAD has to limit the participants from single countries, as indeed it does.[16]

Summary

It has been demonstrated how during a period of only about six months, from September 1970 to March 1971, the attitudes of INSEAD students towards the anti-mobility value have significantly changed. It has been pointed out that those ready to ignore the anti-mobility value had reached 33 per cent towards the end of 1968–9. It seemed that the organization of the curriculum and its contents have a major effect on the way that an institution like INSEAD can affect the attitudes and values of its students.

The findings as to the social structure of the students were at least as impressive as those regarding the attitudes. It has been found that the social structure has been mainly affected by the factors imposed on the students by INSEAD and in the following order – their discussion group, the participants with whom they live on the same floor and in the same building, and the class in which they study. Personal characteristics have less effect and operate in the following order – their national origin, their first degree and their marital status. In other words personal characteristics, which could be expected to affect the social structuring of the same people had they met without the formal intervention of the factors imposed by INSEAD, were pushed aside into second-

16. In 1971 the limit was 25 per cent of the student body for any particular country. In recent years France and Germany have usually had more than 20 per cent each. This might seem a high figure for purposes of integration.

ary importance by imposed factors which had been in existence for only six months.

All these phenomena have been observed and studied under the conditions of the protected environment of INSEAD. The big question mark is whether the observed behaviour lasts after the students graduate from INSEAD and for how long and with what intensity? We have some indications that at least some of these manifestations of internationalization and integration among the students have been perpetuated among the INSEAD alumni.

References

BENDIX, R., and LIPSET, P. K. (1966), *Class, Status and Power*, Free Press, New York.

CROZIER, M. (1964), *The Bureaucratic Phenomenon*, Tavistock Publications.

GLOVER, J. D. (1954), *The Attack on Big Business*, Harvard Business School.

HELLER, F. (1971), *Managerial Decision-Making*, Tavistock Publications.

SERVAN-SCHREIBER, J. J. (1967), *Le Défi Américain*, Editions Denoël, Paris; English edition, Penguin, 1969 (the references in the text are to this edition).

SUTTON, F. X. (1956), *The American Business Creed*, Harvard University Press.

TZIRULNITSKY, D. (1969), 'Quantitative and qualitative measurement of the elements affecting the organizational structure of the MATSLAH military unit' (in Hebrew), unpublished M.B.A. Dissertation, Graduate School of Business Administration, Tel Aviv University.

WEINSHALL, T. D. (1960), 'Effects of management changes on organization relationships and attitudes', unpublished Ph.D. thesis, Harvard University.

WEINSHALL, T. D. (1966), 'The communicogram', in J. R. Lawrence (ed.), *Operational Research and the Social Sciences*, Tavistock Publications.

WEINSHALL, T. D. (1968a), 'Organizational behaviour in Israel and the West', unpublished MS, Tel Aviv.

WEINSHALL, T. D. (1968b), 'The reciprocal perception of communication', in R. Dubin, *Human Relations in Administration*, Prentice Hall, Englewood Cliffs, N.J.

WEINSHALL, T. D. (1970), 'Some uses of communications pattern research', in Barto Rio-Amat (ed.), *La Impresa Multinacional* colection IESE, Serie AC-3, Edicioñes Universidad de Navarro, pp. 301–26.
WEINSHALL, T. D. (1971a), with Beal C., and Silver M., Patterns of communication and organization structure in a management training college', a research report, Ashridge Management College.
WEINSHALL, T. D. (1971b), 'Multinational business education – research methodology and attitudes study', *Management International Review*, vol. II, nos. 2 find 3, pp. 87 ff.
WEINSHALL, T. D. (1972), 'Changing the effects of culture on problem-solving in management education', *Management International Review*, no. 12.
WEINSHALL, T. D., and DE BETTIGNIES, H. C. (1971), 'Multinational business education – the social structure study', *Management International Review*, vol. II, nos. 4 and 5 ff., 45 ff.
YOSHINO, M. Y. (1968), *Japan's Managerial System: Traditions and Innovation*, M.I.T. Press.

Organisational
Inter Linkage

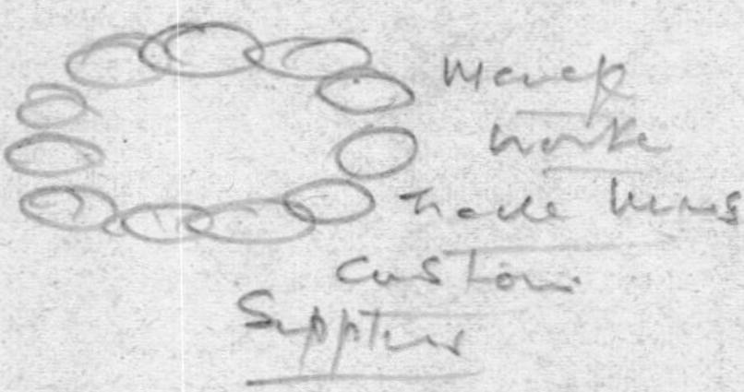

The (+) Greater the
Linkage = the
more complex
the pattern

Part Three
The Managerial Framework–Factors of the Decision-Making Process in Different Cultures

This part includes readings relating to the effects of culture on some of the different human groups within the organization – management, workers, trade unions, customers, suppliers, bankers, shareholders, government, etc. They are the human factors without whose cooperation an organization cannot survive. The behaviour of these different factors in the organizational decision-making process varies from country to country.

The readings in this part describe the differences found in some of these human factors – management, workers and customers – when moving from one country to another. The opening reading is by Harbison and Myers, discussing management as a class or an élite in the enterprise and the industrial society, concentrating on its professionalization and position in the modern state. They bring examples both from the industrialized countries and from the developing ones.

The second reading is by David Carson. He offers some anthropological insights in his comparative system approach to international marketing. In an historical survey he leads us from ancient empires to present-day modern countries, discussing the effects of such cultural aspects as custom, language, religion, taboos and ethnic relationships on the structure of marketing systems.

Sirota and Greenwood, in the third reading, deal specifically with the problem of managing employees in different countries and report the results of a study involving thousands of workers of an international corporation in twenty-five countries.

Finally, De Bettignies and Evans compare in their article the characteristics of chief executives of six Western European countries and of four Scandinavian countries with those of their U.S. counterparts.

8 Frederick Harbison and Charles A. Myers

Management as a Class

Excerpt from Frederick Harbison and Charles A. Myers, 'Management as a Class', *Management in the Industrial World*, McGraw-Hill Book Company Inc., New York, 1959, chap. 4, pp. 68–86.

In this reading, we shall examine management as a class or an élite in the enterprise and in the industrial society. Here the important considerations are the avenues of access to its ranks, its orientation as a class, the trend towards professional management, and finally management's power position in the modern state.

In most industrial societies, only a few are able to gain access to the ranks of management. Frequently, this access has been on the basis of 'whom you know' rather than 'what you know'. Some families or family groups may control important segments of industry, as in Japan in the late nineteenth century or in India at the present time. In the Soviet Union, the government, and more particularly the Communist Party, may retain the prerogative to designate the gatekeepers. Education is increasingly an important entrance requirement in many other societies, whereas in some the opportunity to rise from the lower ranks may be a possibility. Thus, professional training and experience in management become avenues to higher managerial positions. In all cases, the incumbents in the managerial hierarchy seek as new recruits people they can rely upon and trust. They demand that the newcomers be loyal, that they accept authority (of the family, the party, the government, or the professional superior as the case may be), and that they conform to a prescribed pattern of behaviour. In any enterprise, therefore, management is an identifiable high-status minority, just as in an army the officer group is a clearly identifiable class. And, of course, the orientation and outlook of the managerial class in an enterprise and also within the industrial society as a whole usually reflect in one way or another the criteria which govern admittance to it.

A typology of managerial élites

For purposes of analysis, we shall again resort to the device of 'ideal' types to distinguish between different kinds of management. The shorthand terms for our three basic types of management are patrimonial, political, and professional. In this section we shall define these types, indicate their strength and weaknesses, and seek to identify the direction of managerial development in response to the logic of industrialization.

Patrimonial management

Patrimonial management is business management in which ownership, major policy-making positions, and a significant proportion of other jobs in the hierarchy are held by members of an extended family. The effective decision-making authority is centred in the family, and the goals of the enterprise are oriented towards the interests and the aspirations of the family.

Patrimonial management is a common first stage in a country's march towards economic development. In countries where the family is one of the dominating social institutions in the society, the family enterprise is a simple and logical instrument of business activity. Loyalty and trust within the hierarchy are assured. The forces of tradition and religion support the essential integrity of the family dynasty. The enterprise provides the means for safeguarding the security and the reputation of the family.

Thus there are certain clear advantages in an industrializing society '. . . where men cannot rely on strangers to give faithful service, the family may be the most effective unit for large scale enterprise'.[1] The extended family can actually serve as a *sine qua non* of industrial development '. . . where one can neither trust a stranger or an acquaintance as a business associate, nor persuade him to lend one money . . .'[2] The Brazilian experience is typical of circumstances where the initial development is led by an established élite: key posts are reserved for relatives '. . . not only out of a sentiment of family solidarity but . . . Above all they can count on the loyalty of their own kin. It is therefore logically consistent that many business enterprises in Brazil are essentially family

1. Lewis (1955).
2. Hagen (1957), p. 198.

affairs.'[3] Into the Brazilian cotton mills '... were niched the sons, sons-in-law, nephews, the godchildren of the management. To them were confided the methods that had worked for their seniors and were to perform for them ...'[4]

In many European countries, family connections often serve as the main basis for entrance into managerial positions.[5] This is probably even more true of contemporary India, where the important management posts tend to be the closed preserve of a few leading families.[6] However, Japanese economic development probably represents the extreme manifestation of the patrimonial form, as exemplified in the Mitsui code: 'Managers ... are those persons whose essential role it is to guard the business of the house.'[7]

Patrimonial management may be especially effective in the early stages of industrial development. 'In a society where trained skills are scarce and the sons of the wealthy have much of the training, nepotism may be relatively costless.'[8] If the key members of the family dynasty are competent, well educated, and diligent, patrimonial management may be quite dynamic. This is well illustrated by some of the patrimonially oriented enterprises in Germany in which the typical industrialist is usually himself a man with extensive technical or professional education.[9]. He frequently exerts great pressure upon his sons or sons-in-law to prepare themselves for the responsibilities they will be 'called' to assume. Thus, when motivated by a creed of hard work and determination to acquire or maintain a position of power, the family enterprise can be a very effective agent of industrialization.

However, the key members of the family dynasties are often incapable, either by training or psychological inclination, of

3. Bernard J. Siegel, 'Social Structure and Economic Change in Brazil', in Kuznets, Moore, and Spengler (1955), p. 408.

4. Stanley J. Stein, 'Brazilian Cotton Textile Industry, 1850–1950', in ibid., p. 438.

5. Harbison and Burgess (1954), p. 17.

6. M. M. Mehta's careful study of Indian industries led him to conclude that the nine leading families hold nearly 600 directorships or partnerships in Indian industries. Mehta (1955), pp. 260–61.

7. Quoted in Bisson (1954), p. 10.

8. Baldwin (1959), part II.

9. Hartmann (1959), chap. 6. For a more detailed discussion, see Hartmann (1956), pp. 144–63.

leading the march to industrialization. This is well illustrated by the conservatism and rigidity displayed by the old, established merchant families in the early Meiji period in Japan.[10]

The great merchant families ... had become wealthy by manipulating the terms of trade through government regulation. Profits, in their experience, depended on political influence and the dominance of guild organization, upon restricting rather than expanding production ... Indeed, so poorly prepared were they for the new era that two of the three greatest merchant families ... went bankrupt within the first decade [the 1870s] of the Meiji period.

The 'house laws' of the merchant families emphasized that the manager 'must not depart from the business practices of the past handed down through generations, and there was a hint that to do so would be disrespectful to his ancestors. Frequently, he was explicitly warned against venturing into new lines of business ...'[11] Contemporary France provides some mid-twentieth-century documentation of the family firm's preference for vegetating instead of expanding. Landes describes the typical French family firm as placing '... inordinate stress on safety and security. It fears change and is unwilling to borrow for fear that the lender, whether individual or bank, will gain a foothold in the enterprise. As a result, the firm prefers to enjoy its own little market ...'[12]

The family enterprise is usually most effective in small and relatively simple organizations such as retail and wholesale trade, craft industries, and small or medium-sized industrial plants. In such cases it is relatively easy for the family, particularly the extended form, to recruit and generate from within its own orbit most of the managerial resources needed. However, if large-scale and complex enterprise is either required or undertaken, the family is eventually forced to bring in outsiders, whose qualifications are mainly professional training and competence.

Japanese development not only illustrates the extreme of the patrimonial form, but also demonstrates the tendency towards extension of the base for access to management as industry be-

10. Smith (1955), pp. 67–8.

11. ibid, p. 40. Smith concludes that 'fear of taking risks' and of 'venturing anything uncertain ... seems to have been the cardinal principle of the merchant class. With this outlook it is no wonder the merchant did not break new ground for industry'.

12. Landes (1957), p. 336.

comes more complex. The house of Mitsui was able to maintain its supremacy by expanding its patrimonial in-group to include *eleven* families, each of which included within its compass loosely-defined cousins of common ancestry.[13]

The 'eleven families plus cousins' extension of patrimonial access to the managerial hierarchy is but a particular manifestation of a much more universal phenomenon. The group 'within which I identify and among whom I trust' tends to become a 'community' – sometimes defined religiously, other times ethnically, and occasionally just linguistically or geographically. The catalytic potential of such minorities has been recognized ever since Weber put the stamp of economic innovationist on the Protestant reformist. However, the impetus stimulated by a minority is much less unique than suggested by Weber. Present-day Pakistan illustrates a Moslem 'protestant' group providing a major source of industrial entrepreneurship, the Khojas (Ismaelis) who, as followers of Aga Khan, are counselled on sound business practices by their religious leadership.[14]

The distinguished Indian economist, D. R. Gadgil, puts great stress on '... the concentration of trading and entrepreneurial activity in comparatively small sections of the total population' in India and emphasizes that this concentration is accentuated by its narrow caste and geographical dimensions.[15] The Parsis constitute a minute religious minority whose participation in entrepreneurial adventure is wholly disproportionate to their size; the Gujaratis are enterprising entrepreneurs whose 'community' status is based on a combination of ethnic, linguistic, and geographic elements; whereas the Marwari, the most dominant and aggressive of India's business communities, is the most narrowly defined of all – a subcaste group from an arid, thinly populated geographical area.[16]

The economic development of the United States is a tribute to the vitality of waves of religiously and culturally dissimilar minorities. Less recognized, but perhaps even more influential, is the effect of the 'minorities' on Brazil: the Germans in the south,

13. Allen (1940), p. 635.

14. Aubrey (1955), p. 346.

15. D. R. Gadgil, 'Indian Economic Organization', in Kuznets *et al.* (eds.), op. cit., p. 459.

16. See Myers (1958), pp. 21–4.

Syrians in industries such as textiles and steel, and East Europeans in pulp, paper, rayon, and chemicals.[17] We do not attempt to explain the seemingly universal prevalence of a dynamic minority characterized by entrepreneurial initiative. Just as one observer notes but does not explain the 'spirit of enterprise' emanating from Monterey and penetrating throughout Mexico,[18] so do we acknowledge the proliferation of narrowly defined, innovation-attuned 'communities'.

When the family enterprise expands, however, its patrimonial form is undermined. To find technicians, engineers, and administrators with the requisite knowledge, training, and skill, it must go beyond its blood relatives. Significantly, the family enterprise *par excellence*, Japan's house of Mitsui, illustrates this need for the professional most clearly. It was forced to acknowledge that adding respectable families and even their cousins could not develop the required managerial resources. The Mitsui and other *zaibatsu* were forced to seek out and compete for '. . . the best graduates of the Universities and the higher technical and commercial schools . . .' regardless of their social or family origin, with Mitsui itself apparently concentrating its recruitment efforts in the inter-war period on Hitosubashi University, Tokyo's leading university of commerce.[19] Today there is much less significance attached to the old family dynasties in Japan's major enterprises.

As the number of professionals in the patrimonial enterprise expands, the members of the family find it increasingly difficult to control the management. There comes a point where the family interests are better promoted by turning over the operation of the enterprise to a competent professional managerial careerist. This is what happened in the case of hundreds of family enterprises in the United States, and the same trend is apparent in the larger enterprises in England, Germany, and even France and Italy today. In the most advanced industrial economies, therefore, the proprietary capitalist and the family enterprise, though still important in petty trade or small-scale industry, no longer play an influential role in large industrial establishments.

17. George Wythe, 'Brazil: Trends in Industrial Development', in Kuznets *et al.* (eds.), op. cit., p. 57.

18. Mosk (1950), pp. 271–2.

19. Allen, op. cit., p. 636.

Political management

Our second type, political management, is less common in industrial societies, and like patrimonial management, its chances for survival are slim in modern industrial societies. Political management exists where ownership, major policy-making positions, and key administrative posts are held by persons on the basis of political affiliations and loyalties. Access is thus dominated by political considerations, and the orientation and interests of management are coloured throughout by political goals. However, just as patrimonial management may hire professionals to work under its direction, so political management may enlist the services of professionally trained managers and technicians.

Political management is often commonly associated with government-owned and -operated enterprises, particularly in Western Europe.[20] Sometimes, as in the case of postmasters in principal cities in the United States, political managerial appointments are regarded as a sort of pay-off or reward for the politically faithful. Some of the nationalized enterprises in India were at first headed by managing directors whose principal qualifications appeared to be their government connections rather than their proved ability as managers. For many years, the Egyptian National Railways had managements which were essentially political in nature. Indeed, the danger in all socialized industries is that managerial appointments may be made at the outset on the basis of political connections rather than professional competence.

As in the case of patrimonial management, however, there may be an element of loyalty and trust involved in managerial appointments to public enterprises. When a new revolutionary élite seizes power, as in Russia for example, it may feel uncertain as to the loyalty of the old managerial cadre. Political management in the sense of loyalty to the new régime may therefore become a necessity in the eyes of the ruling group, at least in the initial stages. In the Soviet Union, warnings about the necessity for political loyalty in state enterprise management appeared as early as the late 1920s,

20. 'In several European countries the socialization of major enterprises has become an obsession. In these socialized enterprises not the ablest men are commissioned, but rather those having the best connection with the momentarily most influential political party.' Hruschka (1956), p. 18.

and there were official notices of reprimand and discipline by 1934. The 'kill the Kulaks in management' period occurred approximately five years after its appearance in agriculture. The general purges of 1937–8 coincided with the more specific elimination of the politically questionable from managerial authority. Caught between pressures for maximum output and the fear of sedition, therefore, the Kremlin demonstrated an extreme example of political management. Not only were party members appointed to managerial positions, but in many cases, these managers and others were checked by political commissars or representatives with power equal to the technical managers in each enterprise. Eventually, the inefficiency of this system resulted in the establishment of 'one-man management' in the factories, although party membership and loyalty was still an important criterion.[21] This coincided with political stability of the régime, and in post-Stalin Soviet practice, professional competence clearly seems to have replaced party loyalty as the primary standard for managerial appointments.

For varying reasons, a similar trend from political towards professionally oriented management is observable also in countries like France, Italy, Egypt and India, where nationalized enterprises are increasingly being staffed by managers with previous training or managerial experience. As in Great Britain earlier, attempts have been made in these countries to encourage, in one way or another, 'non-political' management. In some cases, all managerial positions are subject to civil service regulations; in others, public enterprises may be given a quasi-independent status in order to free them from political control and also sometimes from unduly restrictive civil service regulations. The development of semi-autonomous public corporations in Britain's nationalized industries is a good example of the way in which 'non-political' management has developed in public enterprises. These corporations are responsible to Parliament on broad matters of policy but are largely self-governing in all other managerial and administrative matters. This same pattern has been adopted in Indian public enterprises.

21. See Berliner (1957), pp. 9, 202.

Political management, as we have defined it, is simply incapable of coping successfully with the intricate tasks which must be performed in modern, large-scale industry. In this respect, it is even less viable, in our judgement, than patrimonial management. But this does not imply that management is likely to be free of all political influence even in the most advanced societies. For example, when the welfare of the enterprise is dependent upon receiving favours or special treatment from the government or from the political party in power, it may be important to have someone in the managerial ranks who is close to the seats of power and who can 'get things done'. In many countries, 'political connections' are indispensable both to patrimonial and professional management. A good example is the inclusion of former highly-placed government officials in the managerial staffs of large French firms. There are cases, too, where private companies may be forced to provide jobs for persons foisted upon them by persons in high political office. This kind of political influence in most cases, would not mean that all major policy-making positions and key administrative posts are held on the basis of political affiliations, and thus we should not refer to it as political management. It does indicate, however, that in practice it may be difficult to find any management which is completely 'non-political' in its orientation and class structure.

Quite apart from this aspect of political management, we should note again the basic similarity between patrimonial and the usual form of political management: the importance of finding managers whom a ruling group can trust and who will be loyal and obedient. But rulers or prime movers in industrialization gradually find that the stress on loyalty and obedience is at the expense of efficiency. It becomes increasingly evident that they must rely on competence rather than connections as the standard for access to managerial positions. This is the logic of the industrialization process. The record of such diverse economic and political societies as Great Britain, Germany, Japan, the Soviet Union, and the United States testifies to the ultimate triumph of professional management in advanced industrial societies. The industrializing societies must follow their lead. We turn now to an examination of this worldwide trend.

Professional management

In a strict sense, professionally-oriented management is enterprise management in which major policy-making positions and nearly all other positions in the hierarchy are held by persons on the basis of alleged or demonstrated technical competence rather than on relationships to a family or to a political régime.

Our definition does not imply, however, that management *per se* is a 'profession' in the sense that law, medicine, chemical engineering, and teaching are professions. According to the late Justice Brandeis, 'A profession is an occupation for which the necessary preliminary training is intellectual in character, involving knowledge and to some extent learning, as distinguished from mere skill . . . which is pursued largely for others, and not merely for one's self . . . and in which the financial return is not the accepted measure of success.'[22] To be sure, within the ranks of management there are members of professions such as engineers, chemists, and lawyers. They are sometimes engaged in the work of their respective professions but they also may hold administrative posts quite unrelated to their previous professional training. Administration, however, is not strictly a profession, nor is organization building. But administrators and organization builders may be careerists and they are more professionally than patrimonially or politically oriented.

Administration and general management increasingly constitute a field demanding some form of advanced training and preparation, as well as development on the job. And management is a distinctive speciality with professional aspects, as is shown by the following partial definition of the work of a professional manager in the General Electric Company:[23]

'*Managing*,' as a distinct and a professional kind of work, is *Leading*:

- By persuasion rather than by command, and by blending thought and action in decision-making
- Through Planning, Organizing, Integrating and Measuring – as the elements in this Work of a Professional Manager –

22. Brandeis (1914), p. 2.
23. See Smiddy (1955), pp. 5–6. See also Cordiner (1956), pp. 40–79.

- In the balanced and effective use of all the Human and Natural Resources
- Of the Particular component, or the whole enterprise, being managed
- With due understanding and balanced application of the skills and knowledge required to manage its particular activities or operations . . .

Part of this definition suggests a particular managerial philosophy, similar in some ways either to the constitutional or the democratic – participative type discussed in the preceding chapter. More often than not, professional management tends to have a managerial philosophy closer to these types than to the authoritarian or paternalistic types. But the correspondence between these two typologies at any one time, or over a period of time, is not identical. It is entirely possible for professional management to be authoritarian, as in some German and French firms, for example, where there is little toleration or acceptance of the opinions or views of subordinates. But more often than not, the growth of professional management brings a view of the management task which is different from the older views of management as having God-given rights which must not be challenged. Douglas McGregor has said of present American management:[24]

> Executives display the kind of confidence characteristic of a respected profession, including a concern for ethics and genuine humility . . . [M]anagements of our big corporations have exercised their power in ways detrimental to society. They have exercised self-restraints. This is a facet of the self-confidence that is making management a real profession today.

The stress upon professional management is found also in countries in the process of industrial development. The Administrative Staff College of India, patterned after a similar institution for middle and upper management in Great Britain, states under 'objects and aims':[25]

> As industrial and commercial enterprises as well as the activities of the Government become increasingly wide-spread and complex, the administrators in charge are required to show a capacity 'to hold in mind

24. Douglas M. McGregor, 'The Changing Role of Management', in Thole and Gibbons (eds.) (1956), p. 14.

25. *The Administrative Staff College, India: The Plan* New Delhi, February 1957, p. 8.

a total and perhaps distant situation, to plan ahead imaginatively and firmly and yet with the necessary margins, to assemble in the right relation and at the right time diverse material and human resources, to take consistent decisions on points of detail and in turn to see that their junior executives in their several spheres know how to do the same.' In short, every large enterprise calls for the constructive skill and technique of leadership, policy making and planning which are not simply gifts of nature. Training is necessary.

This need for professional managers in public as well as private enterprises is widely understood in the advanced industrial countries. This point was effectively made by the top managers of the Tennessee Valley Authority in a paper presented at the Eighth International Management Congress in Stockholm in 1947:[26]

The auspices under which management operates, whether state or private enterprise, do not in the experience of TVA endow the managing organization with any advantage which lessens the necessity for developing methods of scientific management. The search for methods of management that will yield efficient results, whether the auspices are public or private, must encompass and strive to solve the basic questions of how to develop individual responsibility, how to promote the individual will to achieve, how to nourish individual and group desires for freedom, and how to obtain participation by the members of the community.

The need for professional management is no less in a totalitarian state-enterprise economy like that of the Soviet Union. At the time of the Bolshevik Revolution in 1917 there were no communist industrial executives, and Lenin apparently believed that management consisted of 'the extraordinarily simple operations of watching, recording and issuing receipts, within the reach of anybody who can read and write and who knows the first four rules of arithmetic'. He added:[27]

It is perfectly possible ... immediately, within twenty-four hours after the overthrow of the capitalists and the bureaucrats, to replace

26. Lilienthal and Clapp (1947), vol. II, p. 239. In another place, Lilienthal has defined management: 'It is in the process of defining with skill and sense, what is to be done and with it the fixing of responsibility for results, with wide freedom for judgment in the managers as to how it may best be done, that you have the essence of the best modern management.'

27. Quoted in Schwartz (1957), p. 9.

them in the control of production and distribution, in the business of control of labour and products by the armed workers, by the whole people in arms.

How wrong this view was is clearly shown by the subsequent history of industrialization in the Soviet Union. Today, the professional factory manager enjoys high status as a member of the Soviet élite. As one student of the Soviet economy has said: 'It is the resourcefulness, the ingenuity and – not infrequently – the dishonesty of the Soviet organization man that makes the Soviet economy work despite all the blunders of the planners and administrators above him.'[28] One of the reasons for the decentralization of Soviet economic administration and factory management under Khrushchev was said to be the inefficiency of a highly centralized system which handicapped the work of the competent professional manager at the plant level.[29]

Similarly, in other planned socialist economies, the importance of professional management is achieving some of the same recognition that it has long had in the advanced industrial countries of the West. The experience with workers' councils in Yugoslavia since 1950, for example, has emphasized the importance of a competent factory manager. Although these councils apparently perform some managerial functions in policy making, the active

28. ibid., p. 69. See also Berliner, op. cit., chaps. 13–16.

29. See Nove (1957), pp. 19–25. However, there is evidence that the impact of the Soviet system has discouraged independent managerial action, and that decentralization will not work without a change in educational methods.

'Right up to this year the training of students (technical and political) was characterized by the complete absence of the necessity or ability to make independent decisions. All questions and their solutions were offered ready-made. There existed a number of "typical situations" to which there were ready-made solutions which came from above, solutions which answered the "general line" of a given period. However, the decentralization of industry which has been under preparation for several years has confronted the Soviet Leaders with an obvious fact: the inability of administrators to make independent decisions. This trait which has developed over the 40-year period of the existence of the Soviet régime when workers were required to follow one central line is not now so easy to change. That now there is talk of the need for independent decisions to be taken by administrators is in itself alone a fact of considerable significance.' Tschirwa (1957), p. 21.

direction of the plant is in the hands of a managing director or plant manager whom the workers' council has helped to select.[30] In fact, a council will compete actively with workers' councils in other plants for a competent plant manager.[31]

Thus, we see that advanced industrial development – whether in capitalist, socialist, or communist economies – demands a professionally oriented managerial élite. Access to managerial positions increasingly must be based on competence. And competence becomes ever more dependent upon specialized professional training and experience. As a consequence, the managerial class in the more advanced industrial societies inevitably tends to become an élite of competence, which means that education and training, rather than family ties or political connections, must inevitably become the principal avenue of access to its ranks.

We conclude this section with a note of warning: patrimonial, political, and professional management seldom exist as pure types. In the real world, managements are often quite heterogeneous in composition. As we have indicated, the family-dominated enterprise may bring many hired professionals into its ranks. The professionally-oriented top management may select from among otherwise qualified candidates those who come from particular families, races, religions, or political parties. No management is completely free of nepotism, and even the most professionally-oriented organization builders may sometimes favour the persons they know over the ones who have the best education and experience. For purposes of our analysis, however, we are not concerned with the non-existence of professional management in

30. Dunlop (1958), chap. 7. A similar result is reported in Poland; see Rosner (1957), pp. 257–77.

31. The Yugoslav press carries notices such as the following: 'The Workers' Council of the "Kozara" Shoe Factory of Zemun hereby invites applications for the post of factory director. The candidates should hold the degree of Faculty of Law or the Faculty of Economics and they should have at least three years' experience in executive posts in the economy; also eligible are highly skilled leather workers with over 10 years' experience in executive posts in the economy. Applications, accompanied by the candidates' *curriculum vitae*, should be submitted, within 8 days of the present announcement, to the Commission on Applications and the Appointment of Directors and Executives of Economic Organizations, the People's Committee of the Commune of Zemun.' Quoted by Dunlop, op. cit., p. 290.

its pure form. Our argument has been simply that in the logic of industrial development the management of enterprises is forced to move away from a patrimonial or political orientation *towards* the kind of professional orientation set forth in our typology.

The power position of the managerial class

In the preceding section we have identified management as a class. We have examined its varying orientations and also the diverse avenues of access to its ranks. We have concluded that it becomes more professionalized as industrialization advances. These questions now arise: Is industrial management the master of its own fate? Is it destined to become a really dominant élite? Is it likely to wield great economic or political power in the modern state?

Some popular books advance the opinion that the professional managerial élite is destined to rule the state as well as its own industrial empires. Probably the clearest argument for this case is presented in *The Managerial Revolution*, published in 1941.[32] Its author contends that 'the instruments of production are the seat of social domination',[33] and that persons who control production control society. Burnham goes on to show that the big capitalists are moving further away from the economic process and that *de facto* control of production is passing into the hands of professional managers. As he puts it:[34]

> It is the managers, with their allied or to-be-allied political associates, who are taking up the control as it slips from the capitalist grasp. This is not a shift scheduled for tomorrow. It began yesterday, continues today; and the only element of prediction lies in expecting it to be completed tomorrow.

As the managers thus acquire control over the means of production, they 'gain preference in the distribution of the products, not directly, through property rights vested in them as individuals, but indirectly, through their control of the state which in turn will own and control the instruments of production'.[35] Thus, in effect, the state will be 'the property of the managers'. Finally, the control of the state by the managers will be guaranteed by political

32. Burnham (1941).
33. ibid., p. 102.
34. ibid., pp. 110–11.
35. ibid., p. 72.

institutions analogous to those which have guaranteed bourgeois dominance under capitalism. According to Burnham, it is clear that the managerial class is destined to be the ruling élite in modern industrial society.

In a somewhat different vein, C. Wright Mills argues that in the United States large owners and executives in their self-financing corporations hold the keys of economic power and determine the size and shape of the national economy. If the chief executives '. . . do not reign, they do govern at many of the vital points of everyday life in America, and no powers effectively and consistently countervail against them . . .'[36] Mills sees in America not Burnham's managerial revolution but instead a *managerial reorganization* of the propertied classes, together with the chief executives and other high-salaried members of management, into a new corporate world of privilege and prerogative dominated by what he calls the 'corporate rich'.[37] But the 'corporate rich' are dominant only in the economic domain, and as a governing élite they must share their rule with others who control the political and the military domains. 'As each of these domains has coincided with the others, as decisions tend to become total in their consequence, the leading men in each of the three domains of power – the warlords, the corporation chieftains, the political directorate – tend to come together, to form the power élite of America.'[38]

At the first glance such provocative views appear plausible. Both Burnham and Mills correctly describe the gradual demise of the proprietary capitalist and the rise of professional management in Western economies, and both relate this trend to the technology and the complicated organization of modern industrial society. But they both overrate the power which was held by the capitalists, and they greatly exaggerate the actual and potential influence of the managers who are displacing them. The history of management development in industrialized countries throughout the world refutes their basic assumptions, and their failure correctly to understand the processes of managerial development as related to industrialization destroys the essential logic of their analysis. In our

36. Mills (1956), p. 125.
37. ibid., p. 9.
38. op. cit.

view, there is little evidence that the state will become the property of the managers or that the so-called corporate rich are destined to hold the keys of economic power in any advanced industrial society. Let us first look at the record in several countries and then proceed to examine the logic of the potential power position of management.

In the Soviet Union, industrial management is clearly subservient to the political and governmental élite. Management implements but certainly does not control the economic processes. It determines neither the direction nor the pace of the march of industrialization. Management is simply the instrument of the political rulers. To be sure, the rulers may from time to time delegate more authority and responsibility to the managers of industrial enterprises, and they in turn may delegate to their subordinates within the firm. The trend towards some decentralization with greater delegation, however, is nothing more than a recognition that managerial efficiency under modern technology requires greater latitude for individual initiative and broader participation of members of the managerial hierarchy in the decision-making process. But it certainly carries no indication that the managers are becoming dominant in the affairs of state or that they decide even the direction and the emphasis of industrial development. The position of management is similar in other communist societies such as China, Poland, Hungary or Yugoslavia. In all such societies, industrial enterprise and industrial management are the property of the state, and any suggestion by managers that their 'control' of productive processes should entitle them to control of major economic or political decisions probably would lead to their speedy liquidation.

In Japan it is true that, before the Second World War, large-scale industry was controlled by a handful of capitalist family clans called the *zaibatsu*, and their authority within their respective industrial empires was as absolute as that of the feudal lords over their vassals in the pre-Meiji era. Yet, it was the state which initiated the industrialization march and which turned over the management of the enterprises to the private capitalists. Despite their obvious interest in making profits, however, the rulers of the *zaibatsu* were always conscious of their prior obligation to serve nationalist objectives and the interests of the state. Although the *zaibatsu* played an indispensable role in the preparation and waging of war, they invariably acted as servants rather than as masters of the state. With the shift to more professional management after the Second World War, large-enterprise management has sought the help and protection of the government, but it certainly has demonstrated neither the desire nor the capacity to assume responsibility for broad economic and political policy.

One might argue that before the Second World War the German industrialists, with their tightly organized cartels and great accumulated wealth, wielded great power over the economy. And perhaps without their help, Hitler might not have been able to build his Nazi régime. But Hitler subsequently made the German industrialists his vassals and manipulated them as pawns to carry out his grand strategy for Nazi domination of the world. The Nazis, the German Army, and the industrialists were crushed by the war, but the industrialists regained power within their own domain and quickly rebuilt and greatly expanded the nation's industry. As in the case of Japan, German industrialists sought help and protection from the state, permission to re-establish their system of cartels, and a freer hand in the internal operation of their enterprises. Of all the managerial groups studied, the post-war German *Unternehmer* probably have the greatest will to power. But even they are not likely to succeed in achieving the dominant economic and political role to which they aspire.

In France and Italy, industrialization has been retarded, partially because of the inability to develop an effective managerial élite. In both countries, industrial management, in comparison with other élites, has gained neither respect nor power. Though they may get some protection and encouragement from government and though they may be able to buy some friendly politicians to advance their special interests, the owners and managers, with some notable exceptions, suffer from a feeling of social and political inferiority. Far from having a desire to rule, they are content with getting small favours to help protect their personal security. Indeed, in both France and Italy, the managerial class, instead of developing prestige as an élite, has often failed to command even general respect and to attract to its ranks the best young minds.

Certainly, one sees in the post-war development of England and Sweden no prospect either of Burnham's managerial revolution or evidence of Mills's managerial reorganization into the corporate rich. In both countries professionalization of management has proceeded rapidly within the last fifteen years, and as in other progressing industrial societies, the numbers of people in management have been increasing. But certainly their political influence has not been increasing; on the contrary, it can be demonstrated that control over economic processes is passing further into the hands of finance ministries, planning agencies, and other government departments. The wealth of the 'corporate rich' is heavily taxed. The economic decisions of enterprises both public and private are meticulously regulated; the prerogatives of management are limited both by strong unions and by legislation, and as a consequence the private domain of management has been clearly restricted to the organization and technical management of business enterprise.

If managers are ever to dominate modern industrial society, one would expect some clear indication of a trend towards greater power and influence in the most advanced industrial nation of the world – the United States. But there is very little evidence here that such a trend prevails. The large industrial enterprises of America are now run by a predominantly careerist managerial class. To be sure, corporate management wants all the commercial power it can get, and it seeks as much freedom as it can from governmental regulation in its internal affairs. At the same time, a new kind of statesmanship has been developing within professional management which seeks to legitimize its role by recognition of the public consequences of private actions and by exercising considerable self-restraint in the use of economic power to serve its narrow interests. The rising level of business education, the challenge of unions, and the pressure to satisfy consumers tend to orient American business management more towards service to the community than towards exploitation for the sake of maximizing profits. Adolph A. Berle suggests that there are two major forces tending to keep the modern American corporation a serviceable rather than a tyrannical institution: the first is public opinion, and the second the check of oligopoly, or existence of imperfect competition, which causes large enterprise tacitly to limit its competition with its giant rivals but which prevents such limitation from being carried to extremes.[39]

Modern management in the United States stresses the virtues of competitive enterprise and argues with some justice that the market is really the master of the managers. The forces of the market are supposed to put pressure on management to make quality products at competitive prices. To be sure, free enterprise is not always as competitive as it should be; there have been times when business tycoons organized conspiracies to restrict production and restrain trade. But when they have done this, they have invited opposition which invoked anti-trust laws to limit their actions. Whenever management claims to be the leading group or even the most powerful of many leading groups, it is likely to be rebuffed, investigated, and shorn even of some of its legitimate power within its own domain.

But, irrespective of whether markets are genuinely competitive or not, America is a pluralistic society which comprises whole constellations of economic, political, and social interest groups. Enterprise management is only one of these groups, along with organized labour, the farmers, the Catholic Church, the Zionists, the segregationists, the anti-segregationists, the American Legion, and scores of others. In such a pluralistic society, where the interests of different groups frequently offset or conflict with each other, it is extremely dangerous for any single group to attempt to seize the reins of economic power, for to do so would be to unite the others to exercise the political power of the state against it.[40] We agree with Peter Drucker that, although management can be *one* leading group among many, it can never afford to be *the* leading élite or even the most powerful of the leading élites.[41]

The managerial class, in the United States, enjoys great prestige. It attracts intelligent and able people to its ranks. In terms of American values, management has always been held in high esteem and the sharp growth in enrolment in collegiate schools of business in recent years is further evidence of the pull which careers in

39. Berle (1954), pp. 48–58.
40. For elaboration of a related viewpoint, see Galbraith (1952).
41. Drucker (1954), pp. 10–11.

management have on the minds of the rising generation. But, as Drucker has pointed out, the knowledge and experience of a successful manager will not necessarily qualify him for leadership in government, politics, the military, the church, or a university.[42] Indeed, the pressures on the managerial class are likely to turn it inwards. The intricacies of technology and organization of modern enterprises consume the thoughts and energies of the career-oriented manager. He tends to become a conformist, the prototype of Whyte's 'organization man'.[43] The very idea that management should plan and organize society is inconsistent with its creed of the supremacy of the market as the regulator of economic activity. In the United States, management's political objective, if it has one at all, is to keep government out of business rather than to get itself and business into government.

The American managerial class, moreover, has expanded tremendously, as have the avenues of access to its ranks. The proportion of persons coming from the lower ranks via the route of education and upward mobility within the firm is increasing.[44] Although, as Whyte claims, their pattern of behaviour within the firm and even in the community tends to be moulded by the organization, they may at the same time have quite diverse political convictions. Since the members of management have no sense of collective political direction, they really disqualify themselves from becoming a ruling élite. Their allegiance is to the narrow objectives of the enterprise organization, and they seek fulfilment in development of professional competence rather than in any ideological goal or collective will for power.[45]

In conclusion, one cannot say that management in the United States is the property of the state any more than the state is becoming the property of the managers. The truth is that management is philosophically oriented to being a servant rather than a master in modern society. In ideology, and also to a large extent in practice, it subordinates itself to the market which in ritual, at least, it worships as its master, and it is quite sensitive to public criticism

42. ibid., pp. 8–9.
43. Whyte (1956).
44. Abegglen and Warner (1955).
45. Whyte, op. cit., p. 279.

which may be mobilized into political movements potentially hostile to its narrow interest.

Conclusion

Our examination of management as a class has revealed that it must inevitably become more professionally oriented as industrialization advances. The types of patrimonial or political management which may be appropriate in the early stages of industrial development are incapable of controlling or operating modern large-scale enterprise. The managerial élite, therefore, becomes an élite of brains and education, and professional training instead of family or political connections must become the principal avenues of access to its ranks.

The rising careerist managerial class, however, is *not* destined to wield great political or economic power in private-enterprise societies, socialistic economies, or totalitarian states. As it increases in membership and functional importance with the industrialization of a society, the managerial class becomes less exclusive. And the trend towards professionalization turns its interest and its energy ever more inwards as, true to its professional outlook, it becomes increasingly involved in the growing complexities of the operation of modern enterprises.

References

ABEGGLEN, J. C., and WARNER, W. L. (1955), *Occupational Mobility in American Business and Industry*, University of Minnesota Press.

ADMINISTRATIVE STAFF COLLEGE, INDIA: THE PLAN (1957), New Delhi, February, p. 8.

ALLEN, C. C. (1940), 'Japanese industry: its organization and development to 1937', in Schumpeter, E. B. (ed.), *The Industrialization of Japan and Manchukuo, 1930–1940*, Macmillan, New York, p. 635.

AUBREY, H. C. (1955), 'Industrial investment decisions: a comparative analysis', *The Journal of Economic History*, vol. 15, no. 4, December, p. 346.

BALDWIN, G. B. (1959), *Industrial Growth in South India*, part II, Free Press, Illinois.

BERLE, A. A. Jr (1954), *The Twentieth Century Capitalist Revolution*, Harcourt Brace & Co. Inc., New York, pp. 48–58.
BERLINER, J. S. (1957), *Factory and Manager in the U.S.S.R.*, Harvard University Press, pp. 9, 202.
BISSON, T. A. (1954), *Zaibatsu Dissolution in Japan*, University of California Press, p. 10.
BRANDEIS, L. D. (1914), *Business: A Profession*, Small, Maynard & Co., Boston, Mass., p. 2.
BURNHAM, J. (1941), *The Managerial Revolution*, The John Day Co. Inc., New York.
CORDINER, R. J. (1956), *New Frontiers for Professional Managers*, McGraw-Hill Inc., New York, pp. 40–79.
DRUCKER, P. F. (1954), *The Practice of Management*, Harper & Brothers, New York, pp. 10–11.
DUNLOP, J. T. (1958), *Industrial Relations Systems*, Henry Holt & Co. Inc., New York, chapter 7.
GADGIL, D. R. (1955), 'Indian economic organization', in Kuznets, S., Moore, W. E., and Spengler, J. J., (eds.), *Economic Growth: Brazil, India, Japan*, Duke University Press, N. Carolina, p. 459.
GALBRAITH, J. K. (1952), *American Capitalism: The Concept of Countervailing Power*, Houghton Mifflin Co., Boston, Mass.
HAGEN, E. E. (1957), 'The process of economic development', *Economic Development and Cultural Change*, vol. 5, no. 3, p. 198.
HARBISON, F., and BURGESS, E. (1954), 'Modern management in Western Europe', *The American Journal of Sociology*, vol. 60, no. 1, July, p. 17.
HARTMANN, H. (1956), 'Der zahlenmässige Beitrag der Hochschulen zur Gruppe der industriellen Führungskräfte', *Zeitschrift für die gesamte Staatswissenschaft*, vol. 12, January–March, pp. 144–63.
HARTMANN, H. (1959), *Authority and Organization in German Management*, Princeton University Press, N.J., chapter 6.
HRUSCHKA, E. (1956), 'Management functions: organizing', *Management Philosophy and Process: The European Point of View*, Indiana University Bureau of Business Research, p. 18.
LANDES, D. S. (1957), 'Observations on France: Economy, Society, and Polity', *World Politics*, vol. 9, no. 3, April, p. 336.
LEWIS, W. A. (1955), *The Theory of Economic Growth*, Richard D. Irwin, Inc., Illinois, p. 115.
LILIENTHAL, D. E. (1953), *T.V.A.: Democracy on the March*, twentieth anniversary ed. Harper & Brothers, New York, p. 156.

LILIENTHAL, D. E., and CLAPP, G. R. (1947), 'Progress in regional planning in the U.S.A.', *Papers Submitted to the Sectional Meetings of the Eighth International Management Congress*, Stockholm, vol. II, p. 239.

MCGREGOR, D. M. (1956), 'The changing role of management', in Thole, H. C., and Gibbons, C. C. (eds.), *Business Action in a Changing World*, Public Administration Service, Chicago, p. 14.

MEHTA, M. M. (1955), *Structure of Indian Industries*, Popular Book Depot, Bombay, pp. 260–61.

MILLS, C. W. (1956), *The Power Elite*, Oxford University Press.

MOSK, S. A. (1950), *Industrial Revolution in Mexico*, University of California Press, pp. 271–2.

MYERS, C. (1958), *Labor Problems in the Industrialization of India*, Harvard University Press.

NOVE, A. (1957), 'The Soviet Industrial Reorganization', *Problems of Communism*, vol. 6, no. 6, November–December, pp. 19–25.

ROSNER, J. (1957), 'Management by the workers in Poland', *International Labour Review*, vol. 76, no. 3, Geneva, September, pp. 257–77.

SCHWARTZ, H. (1957), 'The Organization Man, Soviet Style', *The New York Times Magazine*, 2 June, p. 9.

SIEGEL, B. J. (1955), 'Social structure and economic change in Brazil', in Kuznets, S., *et al.*, op. cit., p. 408.

SMIDDY, H. F. (1955), 'General Electric's philosophy and approach for manager development', *Fitting Management Development to Company Needs*, American Management Association, General Management Series, no. 174, New York, pp. 5–6.

SMITH, T. C. (1955), *Political Change and Industrial Development in Japan: Government Enterprise, 1868–1880*, Stanford University Press, California, pp. 67–8.

STEIN, S. J. (1955), 'Brazilian cotton textile industry', in Kuznets, S., *et al.*, op. cit., p. 438.

TSCHIRWA, B. (1957), 'Management training in the U.S.S.R.', report prepared for Inter-University Study of Labor Problems in Economic Development, from Russian publications in the U.S.A., August, p. 21 (mimeo).

WHYTE, W. H. Jr (1956), *The Organization Man*, Simon & Schuster, Inc., New York.

WYTHE, G. (1955), 'Brazil: trends in industrial development', in Kuznets, S., *et al.* (eds.), op. cit., p. 57.

9 David Carson

Anthropological Insights

Excerpt from *International Marketing: A Comparative Systems Approach*, John Wiley & Sons, New York, 1967, pp. 57 and 73–90.

In the quest for insights and understanding on the development of marketing, students and marketers have become increasingly aware of the contributions being made by anthropology or, more specifically, *cultural* anthropology. Whereas *physical* anthropology is based primarily on the biology of man, cultural anthropology deals with man's total culture: economic, political, and sociological. The cultural anthropologist studies human communities as a whole, irrespective of time and place, and in his search for abstract or generalized principles, he may turn to ancient, savage, exotic, and extinct peoples.[1]

Cultural reactions

The governments of many newly-formed nations, or of those which have undergone revolutionary changes in administration, have been prone to attack distribution not only on political grounds, but also on the argument that 'foreigners' controlled marketing. Senegal has placed incessant pressures on French-owned trading companies at the same time that it has encouraged the establishment of so-called pure Senegalese wholesale firms. Cambodia has taken similar steps against French and Chinese import–export firms, and set up consumer cooperatives to compete with the Chinese and Vietnamese merchants. Ghana has insisted that management of its two major department stores – Kingsway (owned by Unilever) and Union Trading (Swiss-owned) – be Africanized. The post-independence surge of Filipino nationalism was especially directed against the Chinese who had long domi-

1. Gee (1950), pp. 63–72.

nated retail trade, even in the smallest towns, not to mention the fact that from its founding, National Socialism of Germany had made one of its prime targets Jewish-owned department stores and other retail establishments. Nasserites in Egypt were especially avid in expropriating distributive firms owned by French, Greeks, Italians, and others of non-Egyptian stock. It is still too soon to measure objectively the effects of such repressions on these nations.

Dispositional characteristics

Societies as units tend to exhibit various traits which influence the organization and the behaviour of their group activities, among them marketing. The traditional characteristics of the following two societies will therefore be discussed as an illustration of such relationships: the Indian caste system, and Latin American management.

Indian caste system

Most literature on the Indian caste system has devoted little attention to the economic aspects of castes. Even though castes have been officially outlawed, their influence is still pervasive, particularly in the rural areas, where over 80 per cent of the nation's inhabitants reside. In his study of village life in Northern India, Lewis explained that each caste group was expected to furnish specified, standardized services to families of other castes. A carpenter repaired certain tools, and a barber cut hair, but they were not obliged to perform these services for everyone. Each man worked for a particular family or group of families with which he had hereditary ties. A characteristic of the system was that it operated without the stipulation of the exchange of money. This was not an open-market economy, as in the case of employer-employee relationships in a capitalistic system. Individuals performing the services were compensated by means of periodic payments, usually of grain or cash, but the payments were not directly related to the time services were performed. Despite the increased use of cash in recent years, many of the lower castes still preferred grain, since prices for this commodity had risen so much. A major function of the system was the assurance of a stable supply of labour for the dominant agricultural castes because of limits on the mobility of the lower castes, especially of individuals who assisted in the agricultural work.

In the village of Rampur, for instance, a man of the Camar caste (leather workers) by tradition received one-twentieth of what was produced if he assisted with agricultural labour and also contributed a specified assortment of additional services. If he removed dead cattle from the village, his traditional fee was one-quarter of the produce of the beasts, plus their skins. The system was breaking down, however, largely because of the rise of industrialized tanneries. Moreover, 'mixed' economies were becoming more prevalent. A tailor in Rampur stitched clothes free for certain castes, such as barbers and washermen, but from other families he received fixed fees in money or in kind.[2]

Although the caste system was disintegrating as the urban-centred marketing economies permeated the countryside, traditions continued to affect trade. Suspicions of the middleman and doubts as to the values of *his* services were widespread. The community ostensibly had got along without middlemen for centuries. The idea that a man deserved a certain standard of living because of who he was, rather than what he contributed, also persisted in many quarters and, since market systems are designed to sell to anyone who has the wherewithal, modern marketing has clashed head-on with age-old beliefs.

Management in Latin America

Before the Second World War all worthwhile business in the Latin American nations was generally in the hands of a very limited number of powerful families. Business was commonly carried on in family-knit company groups; for instance, a rancher's produce would probably be processed by a slaughterhouse, a packer, and a shipping representative all run by his kin. Because of a lack of competition, operations were often backward. The individual nations had for centuries been boxed off from one another by topographical features, and the residents of major seaports often had closer contacts with Europe than with the interior sections of

2. Lewis (1958), pp. 55 ff.

their own countries. Universities stressed the European classics, law, and medicine. Women of the middle and upper classes were even more isolated than the men, since they were forced to lead sheltered lives and typically did not even read newspapers. One result was that fashions sometimes remained unchanged for decades. The masses of people (largely Indians, Negroes, and people of mixed ethnic stock) generally lived in rural slums. On the other hand, their 'patrons' usually felt obliged to care for them in bad times as well as good. Following the Second World War, however, the urban slums exploded in size, with the sundering of the traditional ties between patron and peon.[3] Even today these traditions are clearly visible in all aspects of business, where stores still make their major appeals to certain groups, and where great distinctions in merchandise exist between the upper and the lower classes.

In Lauterbach's investigation of managerial attitudes in Latin America (especially in Chile, Colombia, Peru, Argentina, Uruguay, and Brazil), he noted that the traditional emphasis in a country on non-material values was likely to slow down, if not actually prevent, the rise of systematic business management in the American sense.

> A strong influence of caste mentality is likely to have similar effects. So does the concentration of material things on consumption, especially luxury consumption in the upper classes, rather than production and service. Where leisure, contemplation, or merely an unhurried way of going about things and avoidance of worry about the future represent predominant values in life, clockwise split-second decisions or rigid datelines, even for loan payments, may be at odds with cultural assumptions . . . Abstract organization charts are of little effect where management is based primarily on family relations and personal contacts.

In the evaluation of personnel, individual personality was often more important to Latin American executives than ability, since the separation between managerial and other interests and activities was often vague. Office hours were commonly devoted to politics or personal affairs, and many business decisions of major importance were frequently made at home or elsewhere. Accord-

3. Dunbaugh (1960), pp. 3–4.

ingly, personal factors (with family connections ranking high) were of major importance in the choice of one's business associates. Alhough the abstract principle of competition was commonly approved, it was the rare manager who reacted to it favourably in his own field.[4]

Contrasts with the United States

Although most Latin American societies have been considerably freer than the caste system of India in recent years, nevertheless both India and Latin America as a unit contrast sharply with the United States. Greater movement in the United States is perhaps the major difference: mobility of managers and of employees from firm to firm, fluidity of socio-economic status, and the freedom with which ideas are disseminated, sometimes so quickly that fads are as likely to be accepted as more basic developments. The division between business and home life tends to be more clearly delineated in the United States and, while consumption is very important, so are savings and investments. Needless to say, all but a minuscule sector of the economy is monetized. These characteristics of the United States have often been credited with playing a major role in the growth of a forward-looking, entrepreneurial spirit and of a willingness to experiment, especially in distribution.

Ethnic differences

Much has been written about ethnic social characteristics, most of it based upon loose generalizations rather than empirical investigation, because of the difficulties involved in obtaining sound data. By no means the least of these obstacles has been the sensitive nature of the subject.

Fisk remarked, in his study of Malaya made shortly before its merger into the Federation of Malaysia in 1963, that Malaya was actually two countries: one composed of 3·1 million Malays; and the other of 2·3 million Chinese (population for 1957). In addition there were 700,000 Indians, and over 100,000 other people. The urban areas, large estates, and mines were largely in the hands of the Chinese, whereas the Malays tended to live in the poor, back-

4. Lauterbach (1962), pp. 383–5.

ward, peasant-type agricultural communities. Although 68 per cent of the gainfully occupied Chinese worked in commerce, manufacturing, or mining, only 18 per cent of the Malays did so. Even so, most of the Malays classified as working in manufacturing were merely part-time producers in the cottage industries, and those in 'commerce' were generally petty retailers or itinerant tradesmen in the rural districts. Most economic benefits since 1950 have accrued to the urban areas and to large-scale agriculture, manufacturing, and mining – the very segments in which the Chinese have been most prominent.

Because the Malays have controlled the land politically, concerted efforts have been made to balance the situation, but to little avail. Their lower incomes have handicapped their entering commerce. Moreover, they were often unfamiliar with the ways and environment of trade and lacked the formal education to compete in these fields. Since the cities have been predominantly Chinese, it was more difficult for Malays to settle there. Language was another problem, since the Chinese naturally preferred to speak their own tongue. The high level of competition made it mandatory that entrepreneurs employ people with the greatest potential. On the other hand, the better-educated Malays usually preferred government service, and were actually given preference in government placement. Then, too, Malays often had strong ties to the land not only for economic reasons, but also for traditional status. Because the Malays have had little to invest, they have often preferred get-rich-quick schemes to smaller-scale but less risky ventures.[5] The circle seems to be vicious, and efforts to alter the situation have not been markedly successful thus far. Have the Chinese managed to dominate marketing and other forms of business because of inherent abilities vis-à-vis the Malays, or have circumstances (environment) been mainly responsible for the outstanding commercial record of the Chinese in Malaya?

Bauer has tried to explain why certain migrants have made disproportionate contributions to the economic life of their adopted countries.

5. Fisk (1962), pp. 209 ff.

The tendency of migrants to proceed where their skills and aptitudes are most valuable; the stimulating effect of the change in environment; the familiarity with different methods and products, and the inclination to question, compare, and experiment; the comparative freedom from social and customary bonds; the probability that emigrants are a self-selected sample of the more able and enterprising members of the population; the social cohesion of migrants; their exclusion from important categories of noncommercial activities – these are among the more obvious factors. They may help to explain, for example, the remarkable contribution which the Chinese migrants, who came from backward and poor regions in their home land, have made to the economic development of Malaya. The Chinese in China failed to contribute to the development of their native provinces, and so had the Malays in Malaya; but the Chinese in Malaya have made a great contribution.[6]

Bauer also posited that the commercially successful migrants have, in the aggregate, created capital on a massive scale by spending less than their incomes, even when they entered the country without capital; and that they contributed skills not available locally, or at any rate available only at a higher real cost.

There are manifest and striking differences between racial and ethnic groups in such qualities as industry, thrift, enterprise, and the readiness to perceive and exploit economic opportunity, and there are resulting differences in economic performance. The Chinese in Malaya, the Indians in East Africa, the Lebanese in West Africa – usually migrants without capital and without much formal education – have quite soon greatly surpassed the economic performance of the indigenous population ... It seems probable that climatic and other environmental factors play an important part, and also that the differences are not fixed for all time.[7]

Dispositional characteristics of various societies influence marketing in many ways, including product development. Fayerweather has contended that machine maintenance depended less on the intelligence and education of a people than discipline, responsibility, and thoroughness – characteristics which were hard to inculcate into people. The degree to which these qualities were present depended in large measure upon the culture of the society.

6. Bauer (1957), pp. 72–3.
7. ibid., pp. 74–5.

He cited the case of an African government which had been purchasing hand-operated dusters for use in distributing pesticides in the cotton fields. The American-made machine was finely tooled and required regular oiling and good care. Since the native farmers did not follow through on maintenance, the machines froze up and broke. The government therefore went back to an older type of French duster not nearly so efficient, but more durable because it required less care and lubrication.[8]

Receptivity to change

Mention has been made above of the relative disinterest in change exhibited in some of the poorer areas of the world, but this characteristic is also displayed by wealthier, more highly industrialized nations. In contrasting marketing (particularly retail) trends in the United States with those of Great Britain, Hall has pointed out that in the older, settled areas traditions permeate every facet of life, including shopping. Thus the British were more likely to resist new techniques than Americans, as indicated by the lag in the former's mass adoption of the supermarket. Moreover, British consumers were more apt than Americans to be loyal to particular stores. Within the United States innovations were most likely to be welcomed in California, in a sense the 'newest' state in terms of absolute size of population growth.[9]

Another outstanding example of resistance to change in the Western world has been the French retailer, for many years notorious for his strong individuality and great reverence for tradition. He has been slow to adopt such standard retail procedures as advertising and self-service, and he was often more interested in maintaining family control of his business as a way of life than in net profit and accumulated surplus. The typical French customer frequently was also reluctant to alter his habits, clinging to his store as something of a social institution.[10] Socio-economic pressures, however, have forced a break-through to more efficient practices.

In contrast to the above examples of resistance to change in

8. Fayerweather (1965), pp. 60–61.
9. Hall (1961), p. 138.
10. Dunn (1962), pp. 20–21.

Western nations is the enthusiastic manner in which innovations have been welcomed in certain Asiatic societies, which are sometimes considered the stalwarts of the status quo. Social movement towards a more open society has been a prime characteristic of Teheran, not only in recent years but for past centuries. An English visitor to the Iranian city in the early part of the seventeenth century wrote of the search of its inhabitants for 'novelties', and an American businessman reported in 1911 that 'the people are kind and hospitable and capable of rapid development in Western ways'. Contemporary observers in depth have also been impressed by this city's pursuit of modernization.[11]

Illustrations of dispositional characteristics

The group traits of various peoples, like those of individuals, are usually more obvious to others than to the peoples themselves; therefore, one of the most effective ways of understanding these dispositional characteristics is to compare them with those of other groups. Because many of these characteristics set the background against which marketing is conducted, it is especially important for marketers to appreciate these differences.

One of the major differences in national characteristics is the sense of time. To a Westerner, particularly an American, setting deadlines is a way of indicating the urgency of an activity, but in many parts of the world time has another significance. In Ethiopia the time required for a decision is directly proportional to its importance. And in the Arab East, time does not generally include schedules as the better-organized Westerners know them, but is related to personal relationships, with close relatives taking top priority. To set a deadline in the Middle East is considered rude, pushy, and demanding.[12]

Dichter has termed as 'inverted morality' the use of moral suasion for peoples whose cultural traditions are actually the exact opposite.

> The fact that 64 per cent of Frenchmen don't brush their teeth is in part caused by the lack of running water in many communities. But a

11. Bayne (1961), pp. 5–6.
12. Hall (1960), pp. 87 ff.

far more interesting aspect of this behavior could be explained on the basis of what I call 'inverted morality' . . .

In Puritanical cultures it is customary to think of cleanliness as being next to godliness. The body and its functions are covered up as much as possible.

But, in Catholic and Latin countries, to fool too much with one's body, to over-indulge in bathing or toiletries, has the opposite meaning. It is *that* type of behavior which is considered immoral and improper. Accordingly, an advertising approach based on Puritanical principles, threatening Frenchmen that if they didn't brush their teeth regularly, they would develop cavities or would not find a lover, failed to impress.

To fit the accepted concept of morality, the French advertising agency changed this approach to a permissive one. The new approach presented the brushing of teeth as modern and chic but not as an absolute necessity which when neglected would result in dire consequences.[13]

In many societies a particularly wide chasm separates those who keep informed through reading, and those who do not do so because of illiteracy, disinterest, or social conditioning. Until the advent of television it was extremely difficult to reach the Italian working-class housewife, for instance, since she seldom read, and alternate forms of advertising were often too expensive to use on a mass basis. In countries with a high rate of illiteracy, social contact between the classes who read and those who do not is apt to be limited, so that even word-of-mouth dissemination of information from one group to the other is rare. In a nation such as Pakistan, where average illiteracy has been calculated at 15·3% (although it rose to 31·3% in Karachi), advertising has necessarily played a limited and difficult role.[14]

Fine distinctions between people may be exaggerated, however. Tourism, mass communications, and business, professional, artistic, and political relationships are rapidly demolishing cultural borders separating people in various nations, as well as demarcations between groups living in the same land. In order to test the recurrent caution that advertising designed for one nation should not be used in an identical fashion in another, one major international agency devised an identically organized programme

13. Dichter (1962), pp. 113 ff.
14. Dunn (1962), pp. 136 and 588.

on the basis of a single theme, and conducted the campaign with exactly the same material in six nations: Australia, Austria, Denmark, Finland, Great Britain, and Norway. Designed to increase consumer interest in savings and in savings banks, the campaign resulted in increased deposits ranging from 44 to 90 per cent in the six nations over the same bank week of the preceding year. In each country exactly the same ideas, the same material, and the same promotion programmes were used![15]

Religious beliefs

In the earliest recorded civilizations, the forerunners of what we now term religion, law, economics, and philosophy were inextricably bound together, with the dominant element generally being religion. Historians have conjectured that early in Egyptian history, important business transactions were agreed upon formally before one or more priests in a temple: so that the deity of the holy place would be a party to the transaction and therefore make it more binding. As ministers of the gods, priests were expected to remember the most minute details of these arrangements. Since the priests of even the most powerful gods eventually had to admit their human limitations, they started to make notes of these contracts so that they, as well as others, would have a record of these commitments. These notations were believed to be the forerunners of one of the oldest known written languages, hieroglyphics.

... as in the late Dark Ages in Europe, there was a certain safety in the shadow of religious buildings. As the cathedral offered sanctuary to the medieval trader, who held market before it on festival days, so the Greek and Asian temples afforded some guarantee of law and order. In temples, gold might be deposited and treaties filed. Priests acted as caretakers and judges in disputes. The Babylonian Shamash was one of the market-gods; originally, too, Jehovah was market-god of the Tribe of Levi, at whose yearly festivals men of all tribes gathered to barter; Jehovah's priests were judges if altercation arose. The temple of Jerusalem was the center of a financial network in the Near East similar to that cast over Western Europe by the later Christian Church

15. Elinder, 'How international can advertising be?' in Dunn (1964), pp. 59 ff.

Such sacred marketplaces were numerous. In the very midst of the lawless Scythian shepherds, merchants assembled to trade at a spot so holy that no weapons of war were needed; fugitives might find asylum there and umpires adjusted quarrels. The temple of Apollo at Delphi was one of the gold-deposits of antique times and a credit-giving institute as well; the interests of this temple-bank were on the side of peace, and frequently the Pythia, the priestess of Apollo, sought to bring order among striving communities. If, as Goethe says, War, Trade, and Piracy are triune and indivisible, it is also true that Religion, Law, and Trade have been bound together from primordial times, and one evidence of this remains in the Corinthian pillars on bank buildings of Paris, New York, London and Yokohama.[16]

In Scandinavia many of the most famous market sites, which pre-dated the Vikings, had originally been pagan shrines and were sanctuaries from violence against persons and property. Initially people were attracted to these places for the purpose of worship and sacrifice, and the suppliants brought their gifts to the gods. When surpluses of certain goods accumulated, the priests would barter them for other necessities of life. Traders were encouraged to visit the shrines by the assurance of safe transit and of secure repositories for valuable merchandise. As was true in the Mediterranean area, these combined sanctuaries and markets tended to be located at important junctures of sea-lanes and overland routes, generally at territorial borders or in strategic, deep, sheltered harbours. Eventually, formal rules and regulations were developed to govern all transactions and, when trade at certain markets grew to outsized proportions, special market officials supplanted the priests to supervise law and order.

Religion has often been an important factor in trade throughout the ages not only because of the direct roles played by priests and temples as regulatory agencies, but also because of functions performed by certain groups as part of (and sometimes in spite of) their religious beliefs. From the eighth century until the Renaissance, while Jews were persecuted by Christians and by Moslems, they were also thrust into a privileged position of banking and trade. Since neither Christianity nor Mohammedanism permitted

16. Miriam Beard, 'Swordsmen and salesmen in the Homeric age,' in Bursk (1962), p. 167.

its believers to accept interest payments, Jews became both the local and international financiers. Many Christian monarchs forbade their subjects to trade with Islamites, and since the Jews were considered stateless peoples and politically harmless, they were not only permitted, but frequently encouraged, to conduct trade between the Christian and Moslem worlds. Because of the schisms that arose between the Roman Catholic Church and Christian churches of the East, Jews were also trade intermediaries in the Christian world itself.[17]

Medieval Christian theologians formulated fundamental assumptions concerning trade that have more or less influenced the Western world to this day. Economic interests were to be subordinated to the real business of life, namely salvation, and economic conduct was an aspect of personal conduct upon which the general rules of morality were binding.

> It is right for a man to seek such wealth as is necessary for a livelihood to his station. To seek more is not enterprise, but avarice, and avarice is a deadly sin. Trade is legitimate . . . But it is a dangerous business. A man must be sure that he carries it on for the public benefit, and that the profits which he takes are no more than the wages of his labour. Private property is a necessary institution . . . But it is to be tolerated as a concession to human frailty, not applauded as desirable in itself . . .[18]

One of the most virulent attacks on trade was made by the Calvinist-oriented Puritan theocracy during the seventeenth century, especially in Massachusetts. Not only were tobacco, 'immodest fashions and costly apparel' frowned upon, but the New England founding fathers reserved their strongest vehemence for that 'notorious evil . . . whereby most men walked in all their commerce – to buy as cheap and sell as dear as they can'. The authorities not only regulated prices, limited the rate of interest, and fixed minimum wages – such as had been done in England, from where they had fled – but they also tried to limit business profits. The Massachusetts authorities decreed that the price of cattle was to be determined so that it would yield no more than a

17. Postan and Rich (1952), pp. 168 and 256–7.
18. Tawney (1926), pp. 34–5.

reasonable return to the seller but, in the legal prosecutions of profiteering which ensued, the magistrates were forced to admit that it was not easy to determine what profits were fair.[19]

Contemporary examples

Religion makes itself felt in contemporary marketing notably by prescribing and proscribing certain foods and by influencing business hours, especially with regard to religious days of rest and holidays. Moslems are forbidden to eat during daylight hours during the holy month of Ramadan, but there are nightly feasts to compensate. Prices of mutton, sugar, and other necessary foods usually soar at the onset of Ramadan in Arabic countries, as shortages develop and supplies decline. Strongly Calvinist Scotland has insisted that businesses, including the vast majority of retail stores, be closed on Sunday, but in most of the Catholic Mediterranean lands one of the peak periods for food stores is Sunday morning. Town fathers of St Germain-en-Laye, a distant Parisian suburb, were forced in 1964 to institute a complete ban on automobiles in the centre of town on Sunday mornings to alleviate the congestion of the street market.[20]

Although today most religious organizations do not condone active trading in their houses of worship, and they surely do not encourage it, modern history is replete with examples of religious groups that have been deeply involved with the political economy of nations. There is a current tendency among religious organizations in general to disengage themselves from secular activities, but instances of such connections are still numerous. An issue primarily involving merchants flared up in early 1965 between the Baathist (Socialist nationalist) government in Damascus, Syria, and the Moslem Brotherhood, a religious lay group. The government had accused twenty-two businessmen – principally merchants and members of the Brotherhood – of smuggling funds out of the country, and Moslem religious leaders in turn devoted their Friday (the Mohammedan Sabbath) sermons to denouncing the Baath party as atheist and declaring a *Jihad* (holy war) to remove

19. ibid., pp. 111–13.
20. *Retail News Letter*, May 1964, p. 6.

the Baathists from power. The following day shopkeepers of the ancient bazaars went on strike to protest at the nationalization of certain businesses, largely firms in the distributive trades.[21]

Religious attitudes towards economic relations

Tawney has proposed four main attitudes which religious opinion may adopt towards social institutions and economic relations: (1) it may stand on one side in ascetic aloofness; (2) it may take them for granted and ignore them; (3) it may throw itself into an agitation for some particular reforms; and (4) it may at once accept and criticize, tolerate and amend.[22] All of these attitudes have been in evidence in recent years, but in different parts of the world and among various religious groups there has been a general tendency to shift from the first two positions to the latter two; that is, from aloofness to involvement. Marketing systems and practices have not been overlooked in the renewed interest of religious groups in mundane affairs.

In many instances attitudes towards business in general, and marketing in particular, have lost their earlier significance. In a study of entrepreneurship in the Middle East, Meyer concluded that no coherent thesis with area-wide validity could be formulated on the role of religions in shaping economic activity. He noted that in half-Christian, half-Moslem Lebanon, the majority of industrialists were Christian; but in Syria (which was 10 per cent Christian) almost all industrialists were Moslem. In Cyprus they were Christians; but in Turkey, Iran, Iraq, and Saudi Arabia, except for Lebanese, the entrepreneurs were Moslems. Examples abounded of highly efficient, well-run ventures controlled and staffed by Moslems. The pilgrimage to Mecca itself was a major stimulus to business, with sales created for suppliers of goods, transport operators, bankers, and dealers in foreign exchange. Although Islam has continued to prohibit interest-taking within the Moslem community, as in the Christian West in an earlier era, practices by businessmen and actual theology (in the form of a

21. 'Syrians doom 8 opposing régime,' in the *New York Times*, 27 January 1965, p. 7.

22. Tawney (1926), pp. 22–3.

long series of liberal interpretations emanating from Moslem religious leaders) have tended consistently to adapt the Islamic community to the requirements of an expanding capitalism.[23] Contemporary technological demands have apparently elicited adjustments in Islam, as they have in other religions.

In summary, it may be said that religion still plays an important role in marketing, but it is more generally related to the ritualistic and the spiritual than to actual involvement in day-to-day affairs. Whereas specific religious groups appear to be favoured in certain kinds of enterprises in particular communities, these roles change in terms of time and place. And so does the interpretation of religious dogmas in their attitudes towards marketing.

Customs

Customs are the habitual practices of people, either as individuals or as groups. Except for personal selling, marketers are usually more interested in the group than the individual insofar as customs are concerned. Customs refer to the manner in which people are likely to act under given circumstances, often because of long-conditioned habits transmitted from one generation to another. The origins of customs may be a function of the political, nationalist, religious, or social backgrounds. Frequently their origins have been lost in history, and anthropologists and others can only speculate on their evolution. As a rule, however, marketers are more concerned with the pervasiveness, significance, and applications of such customs than with their history.

Colours

Colours frequently vary in their meanings from one group to another. Green has been the nationalist colour of Egypt and is frowned on in that country for use on packages. Black and white have been the colours of mourning in Japan and are not likely to be acceptable on a product. Brown and grey have negative associations in Nicaragua, and purple has been widely unacceptable in most of Latin America because of its association with death.

23. Meyer (1958), pp. 393–4.

A prominent international manufacturer of water-recreation products learned an expensive lesson ... in Malaysia. Its home office received heated requests from its Malaysian distributors to stop shipments on all products coloured green. The distributors reported that numerous customers associated the firm's colours of green with the jungle and illness. As many illiterate customers purchase strictly by colour appeal in this area of the world, it was obvious that the eye – and not the advertising – was the key to expanding product sales.[24]

Colours may also be a positive factor in marketing, especially in advertising. The combination of red and white has been widely regarded in Japan as appropriate to happy and pleasant occasions. It is probably more than coincidental that these are also the colours of the national flag.

Other taboos

Pairs of anything have been disapproved on the Guinea Coast of Africa, and the illustration of feet has been regarded as despicable in Thailand, where any object or package showing feet was likely to be unfavourably received. Since the cow has been a sacred animal to the Hindu in India, it would be very unwise for a manufacturer to extol beef products. On the other hand, the promotion of pork products would be repugnant to a devout Moslem.

The American custom of patting a child on the head would not be considered a sign of friendliness in the Orient, where the head has been held sacred. And the American custom of flicking a cigarette into the hearth would be considered a disagreeable practice in Japan, where the hearth has been regarded as holy. A clock has been considered an ill omen in China, and giving one as a gift has been strictly taboo.[25]

Astrological factors have been important considerations in the time and manner in which business affairs were conducted in many parts of the world for millennia, and they are still significant in many lands. In India and Pakistan the signing of contracts and other legal documents may be influenced by the positions of the

24. 'Key to Asia: respect for difference', in *Printers' Ink*, 21 February 1964, p. 48.
25. Kramer (1959), pp. 272–3.

moon and stars, in the belief that the success of the venture depends upon forces beyond human control. Whereas the first day of the new moon was considered a very poor day for conducting business in India, the Hindu New Year, *Divali*, was believed to augur success.

In many parts of the world, including such relatively advanced nations as Japan and those of Western Europe, husbands and wives still lead relatively separate lives and are seldom seen out together, although the custom is breaking down. Advertising stressing 'togetherness' in a public setting in these lands could backfire among more traditional individuals. American door-to-door firms trying to break into overseas markets have learned that, in contrast to their domestic experiences, they cannot sell goods in many parts of Italy, for instance, unless the husband is at home. It is socially unacceptable for a salesman to be alone with someone else's wife, and the husband might refuse to pay for the merchandise if it were purchased without his prior approval.[26]

An illustration from France

In a marketing research study for a French manufacturer of major household appliances, specifically for the washer market, the researchers learned that French housewives boiled their linens, and therefore required washers which would bring their laundry to a boil. The capacities required had to be larger than those typically sold on the American market, since the French housewife washed less frequently than the American, but in larger quantities. For every 100 households, the frequency of doing household laundry in the two nations was:

Frequency	*France*	*United States*
Less than once a week	24·5	1
Once a week	52	32
More than once a week	23·5	67

Unfortunately, there were no significant comparisons of possible

26. 'Overseas sales grow for American firms peddling door-to-door', in *The Wall Street Journal*, 15 April 1965, p. 1.

motives and of social structures, such as size of family, size of dwelling, climate, and so on. What may be written off as differences in customs may have had more objective bases.[27]

Applications in Canada

Canada has been a favourite subject of study by anthropologists because of the strong cultural and linguistic divisions between its English-oriented and its French-speaking peoples. For the marketer it is additionally significant that these investigations have seriously influenced sales and promotional practices.

One laundry-soap company (selling in French-speaking Quebec Province) had point-of-sale material on its soap describing it as extra strong and the best one to use on especially dirty parts of wash ('les parts de sale'). After sales of the soap declined, an anthropologist who was called in by the company pointed out that the phrase is comparable to the American slang phrase 'private parts'.

... Even the English spoken in Montreal differs somewhat from the English spoken in Toronto, creating potential hazards for the marketers who may not know, for example, that a 'tap' in a 'flat' in Toronto is likely to be a 'faucet' in a Montreal 'apartment'.

... Alertness to taboos was illustrated by an anthropologist's suggestion to a manufacturer of canned fish for changing a series of advertisements which were appearing in Quebec magazines and newspapers. The same advertisement was run repeatedly. The advertisement showed a woman in shorts playing golf with her husband. The caption read that the woman would be able to be on the golf links all day and still prepare a delicious dinner that evening if she used the product. Every element in the advertisement represented a violation of some underlying theme of French Canadian life; the wife would not be likely to be playing golf with her husband, she would not wear shorts, and would not be serving the particular kind of fish as a main course.[28]

Summary and conclusions

Since marketing is part of the social warp and woof of a nation, it is essential to understand all aspects of a people's culture in order to appreciate the structure of their marketing systems and operations. Customs, language, religion, taboos, ethnic relationships,

27. Fournis (1960), pp. 17 ff.
28. Winick (1961), pp. 53 ff.

and dispositional characteristics can significantly add to the professional insights of the marketer. As industrialization spreads throughout the world, people are generally moving from caste-type hierarchies to freer, more democratic societies. The dissolution of peasant marketing systems, offset by the rise of more sophisticated institutions, calls for a new set of abilities. In many instances the indigenous population has been unwilling or unable to cope with this challenge; therefore, people have migrated from other lands to fill the void. These newcomers have at times been integrated into their adopted countries with ease; in other cases serious social, economic, and political friction has resulted. Whatever the situation, merchants as a group are frequently set apart from the mainstream in which they live because of diverse religious, ethnic, national, or social backgrounds.

Throughout history marketing has been one of the major factors of international acculturation, and the process appears to be speeding up because of the growth of tourism, mass communications, and international business ventures. Instead of mere individuals travelling from one land to another, today entire companies cross international borders. The export of (consumer) goods from one part of the globe to another is frequently accompanied by promotional methods which are very broadly based in terms of national and ethnic cultures. The more traditional societies are frequently affected by these ideational infusions in a most fundamental fashion.

Religion is of great interest to marketers not only because of its historical associations, but also because of the influence it has on the vending of foods and other merchandise, as well as when and (sometimes) how business is conducted. In more traditional societies religious organizations sometimes take an active hand in supervising business conduct, especially marketing. In the Western world the influence of religion tends to be more indirect, but religious leaders here appear to be concerning themselves increasingly with the day-to-day ethical practices of their followers.

A major variable among societies is the male – female role, generally most clearly manifest in the husband – wife relationship. Marketing is affected by this in the distribution of work, especially in how small-scale retailing is performed and by whom. It was noted that among the Chiapas Indians, as well as on the west coast of Tropical Africa, women tended to dominate petty trade, but as distribution became more highly sophisticated, men took over. The relative influence of members of the household on purchase decisions is another major factor. It is a far cry from the Hindu woman living in purdah (seclusion) to the alleged mom-mism or teenage tyranny of many American households.

References

BAUER, P. F. (1957), *Economic Analysis and Policy in Underdeveloped Countries*, Duke University Press, N. Carolina, pp. 72–3.

BAYNE, E. A. (1961), *Changing Teheran*, American Universities Field Staff Report Service, May, pp. 5–6.

BEARD, M. (1962), 'Swordsmen and salesmen in the Homeric age', in Bursk, E. C. *et al.* (eds.), *The World of Business*, vol. 1, Simon & Schuster, New York, p. 167.

DICHTER, E. (1962), 'The world customer', *Harvard Business Review*, July–August, pp. 113 ff.

DUNBAUGH, F. M. (1960), *Marketing in Latin America*, Printers' Ink Book Co., New York, pp. 3–4.

DUNN, S. W. (1962), 'French retailing and the Common Market', *Journal of Marketing*, January, pp. 20–21.

ELINDER, E. (1964), 'How international can advertising be?', in Dunn, S. W., *International Handbook of Advertising*, McGraw-Hill Inc., pp. 59 ff.

FAYERWEATHER, J. (1965), *International Marketing*, Prentice Hall, Englewood Cliffs, N.J., pp. 60–61.

FISK, E. K. (1962), 'Special development problems of a plural society: the Malayan example', *The Economic Record*, June, pp. 209 ff.

FOURNIS, Y. (1960), 'The needs of firms', *Market Research on a European Scale*, Organization for European Economic Cooperation, Paris, pp. 17 ff.

GEE, W. (1950), *Social Science Research Methods*, Appleton-Century-Crofts Inc., pp. 63–72.

HALL, E. T. (1960), 'The silent language in overseas business', *Harvard Business Review*, May–June, pp. 87 ff.

HALL M. (1961), *Distribution in Great Britain and North America*, Oxford University Press, p. 138.

KRAMER, R. I. (1959), *International Marketing*, Southwestern Publishing Co., Cincinnati, Ohio, pp. 272–3.
LAUTERBACH, A. (1962), 'Managerial attitudes and economic growth', *Kyklos*, no. 2, pp. 383–5.
LEWIS, O. (1958), *Village Life in Northern India*, University of Illinois Press, pp. 55 ff.
MEYER, A. J. (1958), 'Entrepreneurship and economic development in the Middle East', *Public Opinion Quarterly*, Autumn, pp. 393–4.
POSTAN, M., and RICH, E. E. (1952), *The Cambridge Economic History of Europe*, Cambridge University Press, pp. 168, 256–87.
PRINTERS' INK (1964), 'Key to Asia: respect for difference', 21 February, p. 48.
RETAIL NEWS LETTER (1964), May, p. 6.
TAWNEY, R. H. (1926), *Religion and the Rise of Capitalism*, New American Library, New York, pp. 34–5.
WALL STREET JOURNAL (1965), 'Overseas sales grow for American firms peddling door-to-door', 15 April, p. 1.
WINICK, C. (1961), 'Anthropology's contributions to marketing', *Journal of Marketing*, July, pp. 53 ff.

10 David Sirota and J. Michael Greenwood

Understand Your Overseas Workforce

Excerpt from *Harvard Business Review*, January – February 1971, pp. 53–60.

One of the major problems facing multinational corporations is the need to tailor management practices and styles to the business conditions and cultural milieux of those countries in which they employ nationals. Inability or unwillingness to do so is frequently cited as a primary cause of U.S. business difficulties abroad.

Successful approaches to the problem depend, of course, on access to reliable information about these nations. In addition to what can be observed and easily identified, concerned companies must inquire into what lies behind the observable: the norms, values, aspirations – in a word, the culture – of the countries in which they operate.

Scholarly and popular publications are replete with characterizations of other nationalities, and there are numerous experts on culture, but what, really, do they tell us? We have been told, for example, that –

. . . Frenchmen are the most individualistic people on the earth;
. . . Germans are docile under government;
. . . Mexicans are passionate, aggressive, and warlike;
. . . Japanese minimize the importance of accumulation of wealth;
. . . Americans, more than any other people, view money as the universal standard of value.

While these observations are interesting, and perhaps enlightening, they are generalizations based almost entirely on the subjective, impressionistic experiences of the observers. Acceptance of these conclusions must therefore depend largely on faith – faith both in the observer's objectivity and in the representativeness of the anecdotal evidence he usually presents as proof of his case.

The research method

The company studied in our survey is a large manufacturer of electrical equipment. During 1967 and 1968, an opinion questionnaire was administered to about 13,000 of this company's employees working in forty-six countries. Three different occupations were represented; and, for comparative purposes, the company's U.S. workers in similar occupations were also sampled.

The questionnaire consisted of about 200 multiple-choice items and was administered in group sessions, on site, and on company time. Respondent anonymity was guaranteed. The original version of the questionnaire was written in English and then translated into the twelve other required languages. The translation process was checked both by independent re-translations into English and by exhaustive pre-testing. Only that section of the questionnaire dealing with employee work goals is reported in this article.

While forty-six countries were included in the study, the results presented here are limited to the twenty-five countries which had at least forty employees in all three of the surveyed occupations. (Some such size cut-off was necessary to help ensure the reliability of data.) The following countries were included in our analysis:

Argentina	Israel
Australia	Japan
Austria	Mexico
Belgium	New Zealand
Brazil	Norway
Canada	Peru
Chile	South Africa
Colombia	Sweden
Denmark	Switzerland
Finland	United Kingdom
France	United States
Germany	Venezuela
India	

The history of cross-cultural observation – coloured as it is by power and economic disparities, nationalism, and feelings of ethnic superiority and inferiority – encourages us to place much faith in faith as the basis for adapting management practices to the particular needs of foreign employees. Furthermore, many of the conclusions are contradictory and obviously transient. Consider, for example, how the Second World War affected our views of Germans, Japanese, and Russians and how post-war events succeeded remarkably in altering these concepts.

It is clear that the results of our largely impressionistic efforts to understand other nationalities need to be tested and supplemented by an increased use of scientific methods. This field has an over-abundance of 'wisdom'; what it requires now is the kind of evidence that lends itself to objective verification.[1]

This article presents the results of a research project undertaken to determine the differences and similarities in work goals of thousands of industrial workers employed in twenty-five countries by a large international corporation. We elicited opinions on fourteen work goals from three different occupational sectors: sales, technical, and service (see the ruled insert on page 262). The evidence provided by this study offers objective, verifiable information to those executives seeking to adapt management practices to the cultural environment of overseas operations, and it contradicts some common stereotypes that often dictate attempts to motivate employees of differing national origins. The main findings:

- The most important goals of these workers are all concerned with opportunity for individual achievement.
- Occupational and national comparisons reveal remarkable similarity in the goals of workers around the world.
- Although differences among nations are relatively small, it is possible to identify country 'clusters' within which goals are nearly identical.

1. While cross-cultural observation and research have traditionally been impressionistic in method, the following studies are notable for employing a more objective approach: Haire, Ghiselli and Porter (1966); Bass *et al.* (1967, 1968, 1969); and McClelland (1961).

What do they want?

Before considering occupational and national comparisons, we shall discuss the importance attached to each goal by the overall group of surveyed workers.

Each respondent was asked to rate the importance of fourteen various work-related objectives on a five-point scale ranging from 'of utmost importance' to 'of no importance at all'. Table 1 shows the rank order of work goals, according to average importance scores (starting with the goal assigned the highest

Table 1 **Goal ranking for the total population**

Rank	*Goal*	*Questionnaire wording*
1	Training	Have training opportunities (to improve your present skills or learn new skills)
2	Challenge	Have challenging work to do – work that gives you a personal sense of accomplishment
3	Autonomy	Have considerable freedom to adopt your own approach to the job
4	Earnings	Have an opportunity for high earnings
5	Advancement	Have an opportunity for advancement to higher level jobs
6	Recognition	Get the recognition you deserve for doing a good job
7	Security	Have job security (steady work)
8	Friendly department	Work in a department where the people are congenial and friendly to one another
9	Personal time	Have a job which leaves you sufficient time for your personal and/or family life
10	Company contribution	Have a job which allows you to make a real contribution to your company's success
11	Efficient department	Work in a department which is run efficiently
12	Benefits	Have good fringe benefits
13	Physical conditions	Have good physical working conditions (good ventilation and lighting, adequate work, space, etc.)
14	Successful company	Work for a company which is regarded in your country as successful

average importance). The data allow us to make a set of rough generalizations about the goal-importance pattern of these employees:

◇ The five most important goals concern achievement – in particular, individual achievement. This includes both getting ahead (i.e. advancement and earnings) and job-related accomplishment (i.e. training, challenge, and autonomy).

◇ As the list progresses downward, concern shifts from individual achievement and opportunity to what the organization *gives* its employees. Most of these less important goals pertain to: (a) the employee's immediate environment (efficiency and friendliness of his department), (b) the general features of the organization (its success), and (c) the basic contract of employment (working hours, physical working conditions, and benefits).

This interpretation of the goal hierarchy of employees in different countries and cultures conforms generally with much of behavioural science theory and research currently being applied in U.S. industry. It indicates that asking the perennial question, 'How do we motivate employees?' is as inane internationally as it is in the United States. These employees do not have to be *motivated.* They are eager and ambitious, interested both in having their skills utilized on present jobs and in moving ahead to more responsible and better paying jobs. The task of management – in the United States as well as multinationally – is to create organizational and job conditions that harness, rather than stifle, the considerable energy employees bring to their work.

Some qualifications

Before discussing occupational and national comparisons, there are two qualifications of our findings which should be mentioned.

First, none of the fourteen goals are really unimportant to these employees. Even the lowest ranked goal – successful company – still had an average score close to the middle of the scale (i.e. near moderate importance). Therefore, all the goals are of at least some importance, and the distinctions among them are relative in nature – more important versus less important.

Second, it could be argued that employees in this study responded to the questions not as they really felt but, rather, as the company's values (and perhaps their own) dictated they *should* feel. It is certainly possible that 'social desirability' did affect the results to some extent, but other research conducted in this corporation tends to support the basic validity of our current findings. For example, we found that the best predictors, by far, of whether employees in these occupations leave or stay with the company are job-related satisfaction (challenge, utilization of skills, and so on) and perceived advancement opportunities. Satisfaction with benefits, physical working conditions, and the like showed no relationship whatsoever to attrition.

Occupational influences

The goals of employees in each of the three occupations studied are similar to each other and generally conform to the pattern described earlier for the total population (see Table 2). As the

Table 2 **Goal ranking by occupation**

	Average rank		
Goal	*Salesmen*	*Technical personnel*	*Service personnel*
Training	2	1	1
Challenge	1	2	2·5
Autonomy	3	3	7
Earnings	4	4·5	4
Advancement	5	6	5
Recognition	6	4·5	9
Security	10	11	2·5
Friendly department	9	8	8
Personal time	11	7	6
Company contribution	7·5	9·5	10
Efficient department	7·5	9·5	11
Benefits	13	13	12
Physical conditions	14	12	13
Successful company	12	14	14

data show, the highest-ranked goals in all three groups still tend to be those relating to individual achievement. But, within this pattern of overall similarity, certain deviations do occur. Two of the larger differences concern job security and job autonomy:

☐ Job security is ranked 2·5 by service personnel but only 10 and 11 by salesmen and technical personnel, respectively. This difference no doubt reflects the way goals are influenced by environment – in this case, by labour market conditions. Opportunities for employment outside the company are smaller for those in service positions than for those in the other two occupations. This difference is reflected in the voluntary attrition rates of the three groups; in almost all countries, the attrition rate of service employees is much less than that of sales and technical employees. Clearly, as outside job opportunities increase, loss of present employment becomes less of a threat.

☐ Job autonomy is ranked 3 by salesmen, 3 by technical personnel, but 7 by service personnel. In our view, this variation also reflects differences in environmental conditions. Service personnel – workers with responsibility for equipment maintenance – do, in fact, have less autonomy than the salesmen or technical employees. One might postulate, therefore, that the less autonomy required for effective job performance, the less will be the desire of workers for autonomy. Employees working on routine factory jobs, for example, would probably show even less desire for autonomy than would service employees.

The occupational goal rankings appear, then, to be products of two major influences. On the one hand, the considerable similarity of goal importance for workers in all three occupations indicates a general motivational pattern in which individual achievement needs predominate. On the other hand, certain deviations do appear, which we interpret as reflecting environmental differences.

Of course, even the general pattern may be affected by environment – namely, the internal environment of this company. For example, the great importance placed on the training goal may be a consequence of the company's rapidly changing and advanced technology.

Since we have no comparable data from other organizations, we cannot at this time comment on possible differences between companies. But we do have data on another form of variation, that of nation, and it is to this subject that we now turn.

The national level

Exhibit III presents rankings of the 14 goals for each of the 25 countries surveyed. In all three of the occupational sections of *Exhibit III*, the five most important goals in each country have been shaded in black and the five least important in grey. (Thus, if the most important and least important goals were identical around the world, the top and bottom portions of the charts would be solid blocks of black and grey.)

While it is obvious that perfect identity does not exist in any of the three occupations, the country rankings are still remarkably similar to each other; black-shaded ranks dominate upper portions of the charts and grey-shaded ranks dominate the lower portions. Note that each goal is ranked 75 separate times (25 countries times 3 occupations). Consider the two goals that, overall, were thought to be most important (training and challenge) and the two that were ranked the least important (successful company and physical conditions). Of the 75 ranks received:

- *Training* is listed among the five most important goals 69 times.
- *Challenge* is among the five most important goals 70 times.
- *Successful company* is listed among the five least important goals 71 times.
- *Physical conditions* is among the five least important goals 70 times.

Just as we were able to refer to a general pattern of goals across occupations, so can we speak of a general pattern of goals across nations – in all countries, individual achievement is the main concern of this company's employees.

Table 3 Goal ranking by country

A. Salesmen

	Argentina	Australia	Austria	Belgium	Brazil	Canada	Chile	Colombia	Denmark	Finland	France	Germany	India	Israel	Japan	Mexico	New Zealand	Norway	Peru	South Africa	Sweden	Switzerland	United Kingdom	Venezuela	United States
Challenge	7	2.5	4	3	4	1	4	3.5	2.5	1	2	5	1	1	3	4	1	2.5	5	1	1	1	2	3	1
Training	1	5	2	6	2	3	1	1.5	2.5	2	1	1	6.5	8	9	1	6	1	1	3	2	4	5	1	8
Autonomy	2	5	1	4	7	4	6	1.5	1	3	3	2	3.5	4.5	5	6	4	2.5	7.5	8	7.5	2	4	3	4
Earnings	5	1	5	2	1	5	6	5	4	6.5	5.5	4	6.5	7	1	5	3	6.5	5	2	6	8	1	12	3
Advancement	5	2.5	3	1	5	2	11.5	3.5	6	6.5	4	3	3.5	2.5	2	2	2	6.5	9.5	4.5	3.5	3	3	7	2
Recognition	9.5	7	6	9	10	6	14	9	8	11	7	8	5	10	4	10	8.5	10	12	6.5	11	9	7	11	5
Company contribution	5	9.5	7	9.5	3	9	6	7.5	11.5	10	8	7	2	4.5	11.5	7	7	8	2	4.5	3.5	5	8	3	6
Efficient department	8	8	8	7	8.5	8	9	11	5	4.5	5.5	11	13.5	6	6	8	5	4	9.5	6.5	7.5	10	6	9.5	10
Friendly/department	11	9.5	9	11	6	10	9	6	7	4.5	9	9	11	9	7	9	10.5	12	7.5	11	5	6.5	11	8	9
Security	3	11	10	9.5	12	13	2	7.5	11.5	9	10	6	9	2.5	8	3	12	11	5	13	10	13	10	5	12
Personal time	9.5	5	13	8	11	7	3	11	10	8	11	12	8	14	13	13	10.5	5	14	10	13	6.5	9	13	7
Successful company	12	11	11	14	14	11	13	13.5	13	13	13	13	12	12	10	11	8.5	14	13	12	9	14	12	9.5	11
Benefits	14	14	14	13	13	14	11.5	11	14	12	14	10	10	11	14	12	14	9	3	9	12	11	14	6	13
Physical conditions	11	13	12	12	8.5	12	9	13.5	9	14	13	14	13.5	13	11.5	14	13	13	11	14	14	12	13	14	14

Key: Goals of high importance; Goals of low importance

Table 3 Goal ranking by country (contd)

B Technical personnel

	Argentina	Australia	Austria	Belgium	Brazil	Canada	Chile	Colombia	Denmark	Finland	France	Germany	India	Israel	Japan	Mexico	New Zealand	Norway	Peru	South Africa	Sweden	Switzerland	United Kingdom	Venezuela	United States
Training	1	3	2	2	1	2	1	1	1	3	1	1	2.5	1	4	1	2.5	1.5	1	3	2	2	4	1	3
Challenge	3	1	1	1	3	1	7	2	4	2	2	3	2.5	3	1	2	1	1.5	2	1	1	1	1	2	1
Autonomy	2	2	3	4.5	7	3	12.5	5.5	2	1	3	2	6.5	2	5	4.5	2.5	3	3	7	6	3	5	3	5
Earnings	6	7	5	4.5	9	6	10.5	5.5	5.5	7	6	5	6.5	10	3	7	8.5	4	10.5	5	5	9	7	11.5	6
Recognition	4	8	6	3	6	5	12.5	7	8	11.5	4	6	1	5	6	10	6	8	10.5	5	10	7	2	9.5	7
Advancement	9	5	4	6	4	4	2	3	7	5.5	8	4	4.5	7.5	2	3	4	5	7	2	8	4	3	5.5	2
Personal time	6	4	10	7	2	7	7	9.5	9.5	5.5	5	10	9.5	9	10.5	11	8.5	6	12	10	10	5	6	11.5	4
Friendly department	10	11	11	9	8	10	3.5	11.5	3	4	7	9	11.5	4	9	9	12	9	7	12	4	6	10	9.5	8
Company contribution	11	9	7	11	5	8	7	4	12	10	11	8	8	6	12	7	6	10	5	5	3	8	9	8	10
Efficient department	8	6	9	10	10	9	7	9.5	5.5	8	9	12	13	7.5	8	4.5	6	7	4	8	10	10	8	5.5	11
Security	6	10	8	8	11	11	3.5	8	9.5	9	10	7	4.5	13	7	7	13	11	7	9	7	12	11	4	9
Physical conditions	13	12	13	13	12	12.5	7	14	11	11.5	12	13	11.5	12	10.5	14	10	12	14	14	14	13	12	13	14
Benefits	12	14	12	12	13	14	10.5	11.5	13	13	13	11	9.5	14	14	12	14	13	9	11	13	11	14	7	12
Successful company	14	13	14	14	14	12.5	14	13	14	14	14	14	14	11	13	13	11	14	13	13	12	14	13	14	13

Key: ■ Goals of high importance; ░ Goals of low importance

Table 3 Goal ranking by country (contd)

C. Service personnel

	Argentina	Australia	Austria	Belgium	Brazil	Canada	Chile	Colombia	Denmark	Finland	France	Germany	India	Israel	Japan	Mexico	New Zealand	Norway	Peru	South Africa	Sweden	Switzerland	United Kingdom	Venezuela	United States
Training	1	2	2	3.5	1	2.5	1	1	1	1	3	2	1	1	3	1	4	1	1	2	2	2	3	1	5
Challenge	4	1	1	3.5	3	1	7	2	4	2.5	6	3.5	3	5	4	5	1	2	2	1	3	1	1	8	1
Security	2	3	6	1	12	6	2	3	2	4	1	1	5.5	8	7	2	6	3	8	4	1	11	7	2	3
Earnings	9.5	6	4	2	9	5	6	8	9	6	8	3.5	9	11	2	8	7.5	8	6	7	7	7	5	6	4
Advancement	6.5	4	3	8.5	8	2.5	9.5	4	10	5	4	5	2	6	1	6	2	7	3.5	5	9	3	2	7	2
Personal time	8	5	10	6	6.5	4	8	14	5	2.5	2	9	11.5	2.5	13	13	3	5	9	6	5	5	6	10.5	6.5
Autonomy	5	7	5	5	11	9	11	6	3	8	7	6	8	7	9	9	5	9	5	9	11	4	4	9	10
Friendly department	3	10	9	8.5	2	10	5	10.5	7	9	5	10	7	9.5	6	7	10	6	10	10	4	6	11	3	12
Recognition	6.5	9	7	7	10	8	3	5	12	13	10	8	4	2.5	5	11.5	7.5	10	11	11	13	9	8.5	10.5	8
Company contribution	12	11	8	10.5	4.5	11	13	7	11	12	11	11	5.5	9.5	10	3	11	12	3.5	8	6	10	10	12	6.5
Efficient department	9.5	8	11	11.5	6.5	7	12	10.5	6	10	9	12	11.5	4	8	4	9	4	7	3	8	12	8.5	5	11
Benefits	11	13	12	12	13	13	4	9	8	14	12	7	14	13	14	10	14	11	14	13	10	8	13	4	9
Physical conditions	13	12	13	14	4.5	12	9.5	12	13	11	13	13	10	12	11	11.5	13	13	12	12	12	13	12	13	13
Successful company	14	14	14	13	14	14	14	13	14	7	14	14	13	14	12	14	12	14	13	14	14	14	14	14	14

Key: Goals of high importance (dark); Goals of low importance (dotted)

Overcoming stereotypes

The overall similarity in country goal patterns came as a surprise to many managers of the company studied. Managers, too, are human beings, and thus not completely immune to stereotyped thinking about other nations and people. Stereotypes simplify the world and simplify one's job. They provide automatic and simple explanations for complex problems. If, for example, there is difficulty in a Latin American country, the ready response might be, 'Well, you know those Latins'.

Our research indicates that 'those Latins' (at least those Latins studied) may not be so different in their aspirations from 'those Americans'. However, if people *want* to see a particular group in a certain way, that is the way they will see it. They seek to confirm their preconceptions and tend to ignore contradictory evidence (perhaps even the evidence from this study). Furthermore, managers often act in ways likely to elicit employee behaviour that justifies the stereotype. For example:

◇ Country X employees are believed to have little potential for higher level management positions and are therefore denied the experience and training necessary for developing this potential. Their subsequent very limited advancement provides all the proof management needs that its initial, pessimistic assessment of employees' abilities was correct.

◇ Country Y employees are seen as 'lazy', and, consequently, are subject to stringent controls. They rebel against these controls, often by acting lazy. The appropriateness of management's assumptions and behaviour is thus confirmed and reinforced by the negative employee reactions.

Cultural aggregates

As can be seen in Table 3, no two countries are entirely identical in their goal hierarchies. While goals are similar overall, it is obvious that individual differences do exist. It is impractical to discuss the individual goal orderings of twenty-five countries, but it is possible to look for general patterns – that is, for clusters of countries which can be distinguished on the basis of extremely high goal similarity. We have been able to identify five such groupings (see Table 4). These are:

1. Anglo.
2. French.
3. Northern Europe.
4. Southern Latin America.
5. Northern Latin America.

In addition to the foregoing clusters, six countries stand alone and are labelled 'Independents'. The goal orderings of these six are not closely and consistently related to that of any other country.

The analysis method we used ('Q' version of factor analysis) grouped countries so as to minimize differences within clusters and maximize differences between them. It should be emphasized, however, that the clusters are still quite similar to each other in their goal orderings, and, despite the differences between clusters, the general goal hierarchical pattern is not markedly upset in any of them. For example, while training is less important for the Anglos than for any other group, it is nevertheless one of the most

Table 4 **Country clusters**

1. Anglo	4. Southern Latin America
Australia	Argentina
Austria	Chile
Canada	5. Northern Latin America
India	Colombia
New Zealand	Mexico
South Africa	Peru
Switzerland	6. Independents
U.K.	Brazil
U.S.A.	Germany
2. French	Israel
Belgium	Japan
France	Sweden
3. Northern Europe	Venezuela
Denmark	
Finland	
Norway	

important goals within the Anglo hierarchy. Similarly, while the Japanese rate successful company higher in importance than do the other clusters and nations, this goal is still among the least important to them.

The major differences may be summarized as follows:

□ The Anglo cluster is higher than other clusters on goals pertaining to individual achievement and low on the desire for security.

□ The French cluster is quite similar to the Anglos, except that the French give greater importance to security and somewhat less importance to challenging work.

□ The countries in the Northern Europe cluster seem to be less oriented than the others to the getting-ahead and recognition kinds of goals and more oriented to job accomplishment. Here, people exhibit more concern with the immediate environment (friendly and efficient department) and less with the organization as a whole (working for a successful company and contributing to the company). They place considerable emphasis on their jobs not interfering with their personal lives.

□ The individual achievement goals tend to be somewhat less important in both Latin clusters than in the other groupings. This relative de-emphasis of individual achievement is especially pronounced in the Southern Latin countries. The Southern Latins are also highest of all in their desire for security, and both Latin clusters place considerable emphasis on fringe benefits.

□ Germany exhibits a pattern similar in many respects to the countries of the Latin clusters. It, too, is high on the desire for security and fringe benefits. A difference appears on the getting-ahead goals (advancement and earnings), where the Germans are among the highest.

□ Japan shows a rather unique pattern in that many of the goals which ordinarily relate to one another do not seem to do so in this case. For example, while the Japanese are higher than others in their desire for earnings opportunities, their desire for advancement is relatively low. They are second highest on challenge, but are lowest on autonomy. The one internally consistent pattern for this nation relates to the immediate department environment; the Japanese place relatively strong emphasis on working in a friendly and efficient department and on having good physical working conditions.

Conclusion

The implications of our study may be considered at a number of different levels.

First – at the most general level – our research reinforces the need to put assumptions about people to the empirical test. Organizational policies cannot be more effective than the validity of the assumptions on which they are based. This need to test assumptions is particularly important in international organizations where accurate information is so difficult to obtain and where judgements are so heavily influenced by the preconceptions different nationalities have about each other.

Second, the research data do tend to support the current models of human motivation developed by industrial social psychologists. However, some of these findings suggest that existing models need to be modified. The importance of certain goals – most strikingly, job autonomy and job security – is markedly affected by what we interpret to be environmental conditions. The job autonomy data deserve emphasis because of the key position this variable occupies in so much of modern management theory.

Job autonomy appears in the literature under a number of labels – e.g., 'participative management', 'consultative management', 'democratic management' – and is assumed to be a major goal of most employees. But this emphasis on autonomy may be little more than a projection of the theorists' own goals that stem from their own professional environments. Our data suggest that in some work environments – especially those with tasks that are routinized and predictable – high degrees of autonomy may be neither desired nor appropriate.

Third, and perhaps most relevant to the managers of international organizations, is the considerable similarity we have found in the goals of employees around the world. This finding has an extremely important policy implication: since the goals of employees are similar internationally, corporate policy decisions, *to the extent that they are based on assumptions about employee goals*, can also be international in scope.

It is not only Americans who want money, or Frenchmen who want autonomy, or Germans who want their work skills utilized and improved. A management whose policies and practices reflect these stereotypes (for example, providing few advancement opportunities in some countries or using certain countries as dumping grounds for routine, unchallenging work) should be prepared to suffer the consequences of managing a frustrated and uncommitted work force whose apathy and anxieties it helped nurture.

In this respect, it would be interesting to determine how much of the difficulty experienced in managing employees in other countries is due not to cultural differences at all but, rather, to the automatic and psychologically self-serving assumption of differences that, in reality, may be minor or even non-existent.

References

BASS, B. M., *et al.* (1967, 1968, 1969), *Technical Reports*, Rochester Management Centre, University of Rochester, N.Y.

HAIRE, M., GHISELLI, E., and PORTER, L. (1966), *Managerial Thinking: An International Study*, John Wiley, New York.

MCCLELLAND, D. (1961), *The Achieving Society*, Van Nostrand, Princeton, N.J.

11 H.-C. De Bettignies and P. Lee Evans

The Cultural Dimension of Top Executives' Careers: A Comparative Analysis

Adapted by P. Lee Evans from 'Leaders Across the Ocean: Comparing American and European Chief Executives', H.-C. De Bettignies, *European Business*, 26, Summer 1970; and 'Europe looks North at the Scandinavian Business Elite', H.-C. De Bettignies and P. Lee Evans, *European Business*, 31, Autumn 1971.

Many different ideas and methods are proposed to modernize management in Europe, a majority of them originating in the United States. The company's organization, its personnel policies, its strategy for the future – all the facets of European companies are under review. And most suggestions come back to top management's responsibility for backing change. If the leadership of a company's president can affect the organization and direction of the business, then all the talk about change revolves around one man, the firm's chief executive.

Who are the leaders of big corporations on both sides of the Atlantic? Do different environments have an effect on the men at the top in American and European firms? What lessons can be learned from the experience of others? The debate about the 'American Challenge' and the 'European Challenge' is not settled and may not be meaningful to resolve, except insofar as Europeans ask themselves what they can learn from their American colleagues, and vice versa. A first step in this direction is to ask oneself the question, 'Who is my executive counterpart in this other culture?'

In an attempt to answer these questions, we investigated the personal and professional characteristics of top managers in the largest corporations in ten European countries, namely Belgium, Denmark, Finland, France, Germany, Great Britain, Italy, the Netherlands, Norway, and Sweden (Hall and De Bettignies, 1968; Hall and Amado-Fischgrund, 1969; Hall, De Bettignies, and

Amado-Fischgrund, 1969; De Bettignies, 1970; De Bettignies and Evans, 1971).[1] Although it is difficult to produce a general profile of 'the European top executive', the demographic and career characteristics of these managers were compared with those of Americans, concerning whom independent data were made available.[2]

A given culture will affect the career pattern a businessman is likely to follow, as well as his personal and professional characteristics, and we shall try to specify some of the results of these pressures. They carry a number of sociological and policy-making implications, particularly with respect to the distribution and exercise of power in our political and economic systems. Before considering the career paths of chief executives, let us define and analyse their *personal* characteristics, such as their social class, education and age.

Social origins: a European business establishment?

A peculiar part of the Great American Dream is the Horatio Alger mythology, named after an early twentieth-century author of children's books whose stories had a predominant 'post-clerk to President' theme. The mythology lingers on in a stereotyped view that, regardless of social origins, all people have the chance to attain the ultimate success and prestige of running a corporate empire. We shall look at the social origins of the current business élites in order to assess the extent to which a country's social structure in reality biases opportunities to reach the top level in business organizations. The social origins of executives were

1. A short questionnaire was mailed to the chief executive of the 500 largest companies in these European countries, to a smaller number in Belgium, Denmark, Finland, the Netherlands and Norway, and a total of 985 responses were received. The response rate varied between 32 per cent in France and the Netherlands, and 16 per cent in Sweden, averaging 24 per cent.

2. *Fortune* magazine comments that 'despite their prominence on the public scene, the top executives of very large U.S. corporations remain something of an enigma . . . caricatures aside, who runs big business?' (*Fortune*, May 1970). Heidzick and Struggles, an international management consulting firm who regularly conduct a survey of U.S. top executives, provided us with information on 492 of the presidents of the largest U.S. corporations in 1966.

classified into three groups according to the occupations of their fathers: *Upper class* refers to those chief executives whose fathers were executives or professionals, *Middle class* comprises those whose fathers were white-collar workers, schoolteachers, civil servants and so on, while *Lower class* embraces farmers and blue-collar workers.

Is the self-made man, who rose from rags to riches, as common a figure among U.S. top executives as the Horatio Alger mythology would suggest? (See Table 1A.) When considering the social

Table 1A **Comparison of the social origins of European and American business leaders.**

Social Class	*U.S.* 1900	*U.S.* 1925	*U.S.* 1950	*U.S.* 1964	*Europe 1968–70* (our survey)
Lower Class	12%	16%	12%	23%	7%
Middle Class	42%	48%	52%	66%	18%
Upper Class	46%	36%	36%	11%	75%
	100%	100%	100%	100%	100%

origins of U.S. top executives and comparing these over the past few decades, we note a definite trend towards a more open society, one increasingly dominated by the middle classes and one in which the sons of less privileged families increasingly have access to top business positions. At the beginning of the century, only 12 per cent of the big business executives were sons of blue-collar workers and farmers, while in the post-war era this proportion has risen to 23 per cent.

We do not have longitudinal data of this type for each European country, but given the present situation, progress is obviously much slower. The European business environment offers fewer opportunities to the socially less favoured. Whereas the Weberian analysis of the middle-class business ethic rings strikingly true of the industrial culture in the United States, top management in the Europe of the seventies is more the domain of an upper-class establishment than even in the United States at the turn of the century. The determinism of social origin is heaviest of all in France.

In all countries of Europe, with the notable exception of Denmark, two-thirds or more of the managerial élite are from well-to-do families. France, Belgium and Italy epitomize the upper-class establishment, while only 48 per cent of Danish managers are from the upper classes. (See Table 1B.) With regard to the ability

Table 1B **Social origins of the business leaders**

	B	*DK*	*SF*	*F*	*G*	*G.B.*	*I*	*NL*	*N*	*S*	*U.S.A.*
Top executives from Lower Classes (%)	2	16	10	3	10	7	3	4	4	15	23
Top executives from Middle Classes (%)	20	36	23	15	20	27	17	19	19	15	66
Top executives from Upper Classes (%)	78	48	67	82	70	66	80	77	77	70	11

Total 100%

of persons of working-class origin to penetrate the ranks of the élite corps of presidents, Northern Europe (including Germany, but excluding Norway) is more open than the rest of Europe. The social structure in Britain, which is frequently regarded as a country where the worker on the shop floor can break into the managerial ranks, is less open than in some Scandinavian countries, and is significantly less open than on the other side of the Atlantic. Our data indicate also that Scandinavian society tends to be more open over time. We have more sons of workers today in the younger group of top executives than there were in the past generation. In other countries we find a reverse trend, where the number of workers' sons in the executive ranks was larger a generation ago than now, and where social inbreeding does not contribute to opening the society.

A further indication of the openness of social structure and of the social alliances of top executives is in their marriage patterns. More than half of the presidents in most countries of Europe are sons of businessmen, and outside of Scandinavia more than half of the executives have themselves married daughters of businessmen. The Scandinavians stand out in that one in six of them has married the daughter of a worker. It is interesting to note that not one Frenchman or Belgian in our survey dared to do that! In general, and even in Scandinavia, there appears to be a tendency to marry within the same socio-economic class.

The social structure in Europe is thus quite different from that in the United States, regardless of inter-European differences. Sons of blue-collar workers and farmers comprise more than one in five of the American presidents – a greater proportion than the 16 per cent in the most open country of Europe, namely Denmark. Two conclusions seem justified: firstly, with regard to élite managerial occupations, social origins are less determining in the U.S.A. than in Europe, and there is no clear indication that Europe as a whole is converging on a more open social structure; secondly, it appears that top management in Europe is predominantly the domain of those of upper-class origins, whereas it is overwhelmingly and increasingly a middle-class domain in the United States.

We turn now to consider a variable which may be closely related to social class, namely educational background. Social origins and parental wealth in France, for instance, have an influence not only on social opportunities but also on the type of education received (Hall and De Bettignies, 1968).

Education: Cap and gown or slide rule?

The much debated estimate of Denison that 23 per cent of the growth in real G.N.P. in the United States is directly attributable to education emphasizes the importance of this variable in industrial and commercial practice (Denison, 1962). To run a large corporation would appear to be an increasingly complex job; it requires men of great ability with special skills, and college degrees in the U.S.A. are now seen as an almost essential prerequisite for reaching the top of the organizational ladder. On the other hand, there is an increasing controversy over the extent to which educational qualifications influence or determine success in individual careers such as management. A Fortune article describes a college degree in America as a $40,000 aptitude or screening test which dangerously postpones the student's purposeful contact with reality (*Fortune*, November 1970). A recent study by Christopher Jencks indicates that while occupational status is more closely related to educational attainment than to other measurable factors, there are still enormous differences between people with the same amount of education in the United States; the most significant outcome of the educational process is the 'label' it confers, not the knowledge or content (Jencks, 1972). Many managerial skills, particularly the human and conceptual, can only be adequately developed by on-the-job experience, and in this sense years spent at university have an opportunity cost. Our survey indicates significant differences between countries in the educational profiles of top executives.

A college degree is essential in the U.S.A. It was described in *Fortune* as 'the minimum credential for almost any type of nonroutine work'. If nine out of ten top executives had been to college in 1964, 96 per cent had been in 1968, and while three out of four had obtained a degree in 1964, 83 per cent had at least a bachelor's degree in 1968. An analysis of the European situation is difficult, given the different educational systems in each country. Academic degrees are often not comparable from one country to the other, and within each country institutions may not be comparable. Nonetheless, one out of four European presidents (as against one out of twenty in the U.S.) has *not* attended an institute of higher education. The French and Finnish chief executives have received more university-level education than their European colleagues (see Table 2) and are closest to the United States as far as educational achievement is concerned. There does not appear to be any general relationship in Europe between educational level and variables such as size of company or type of industry.

The least educated of the Europeans are the British, the Danish, the Dutch and the Norwegians, in that order; only half of British and Danish presidents have had some higher education.[3] Whereas

3. Higher education is defined in accordance with UNESCO/O.E.C.D. practice as post-school instruction with an admission requirement of a secondary school certificate.

Table 2 **Comparison of the educational level of European and American business leaders**

	B	*DK*	*SF*	*F*	*G*	*G.B.*	*I*	*NL*	*N*	*S*	*U.S.A.*
% of persons with a higher education in the total labour force (*)	N/A	(2·0)	2·1	2·7	N/A	(3·3)	N/A	1·4	2·6	2·1	19·2
% of presidents with a higher education	85	51	91	83	81	50	78	60	63	77	83
% of presidents who are sons of senior executives	25	14	25	36	16	17	40	20	36	26	N/A
% of such presidents with a higher education	N/A	61	83	60	60	45	64	N/A	36	60	N/A

* From O.E.C.D. 1969.

Figures in brackets are estimates based on the number of years of education of persons in the labour force. N/A means data not available.

the high level of educational qualifications of the total labour force in the United States may help to explain why most executives there have a college degree, availability of education does not appear to be the only explanation for differences in educational profiles within Europe. Relative to the rest of Europe, the availability of education is high in both Britain and Norway (see Table 2).

The explanation for the high proportion of non-graduates in these countries lies more in the value attached to on-the-job experience, and perhaps to the high prestige of careers outside commerce and industry which attract graduates. This can be justified by looking at the educational qualifications of the presidents whose fathers were also chief executives. These men were no doubt brought up in close contact with business life, and by virtue of their social background they have the most complete access to all forms of education, training and experience; their profiles should in a sense reflect the norms of the business establishment in their respective countries. We find that only 36 per cent of the sons of Norwegian executives and 45 per cent of the sons of British executives have a higher education. An intensive study of British industry in the early sixties (P.E.P., 1964) testifies to the misgivings which many British managers have about long years spent in formal education, though such attitudes are found to be more common in less successful, traditionalist firms, and are less prevalent today than when that study was undertaken (*New Society*, May 1972). In Scandinavia, the Danish and Norwegian 'commercial schools', which offer a short commercial education at a School Certificate or Baccalauréat level, have been coming into their own in the post-war years, and account for 26 per cent of Danish presidents today under the age of 45.

Between 1900 and 1964, the proportion of American executives who at least attended college moved from 40 per cent to 96 per cent. The percentage of executives with degrees in science and engineering increased nearly five times and has now reached more than 50 per cent of the total. The top chairs are increasingly occupied by business school graduates who, according to *Fortune*, now head one out of three large U.S. companies (*Fortune*, May 1970). In Europe this picture is markedly different from country to country. For instance, more than six out of ten French, Swedish and Norwegian presidents with a higher education had an engineering or scientific training, while only four in ten of the British majored in these areas.

The trend towards technical training is increasing in Europe. The European business schools are still too recent a training ground to have yielded a significant number of presidents; the vast majority of them were educated at a time when there were no business schools in Europe. In Scandinavia, however, there is a pronounced trend towards a higher education in business/economics, as evidenced by the educational profile of the younger presidents, even at the expense of engineering. In Sweden and Norway the larger companies are predominantly run by engineers, while graduates of business schools tend to gravitate to smaller enterprises, an observation to which we shall return when considering job mobility.

Age

Although there are significant differences between countries in the age of presidents, the average age of the European president is exactly the same as for his American counterpart, 55 years. However, this average belies general differences in distribution between Europe and America. In the U.S.A. a majority (51 per cent) of presidents are in the 50–59 age bracket, whereas in Europe there is a less modal distribution of ages. In all European countries except France there is a higher probability of encountering a younger president than in the U.S.A. and in all except the Scandinavian countries there is a higher probability that a president will be older than in the U.S.A.

The differences in age between countries in Europe is striking. To contrast the two extremes, nearly half of Belgian, French and German chief executives are over 60 (a quarter over 65); in Sweden and Finland only one in ten is above 60 years of age. Scandinavia is clearly the most youthful corner of Europe in top management respects, while the British age distribution approximates the American pattern, midway between the two extremes, with 29 per cent of its chief executives being above 60 years of age (26 per cent for the U.S.A.). The topic of age leads us now from discussing demographic characteristics of presidents to observations on their climb to the presidential suite. In considering the steps for reaching the top managerial level, we consider first the age at which executives became presidents.

The climb to the top

The popular stereotype of American executives as youthful men in their early prime runs counter to our finding that Europeans in *ALL* ten countries reach the top of their companies at an earlier average age than Americans – at the age of 46 in comparison to 50 in the U.S.A. (see Table 3). Half of the U.S. presidents reached this level when they were above 50 in comparison with only a quarter of the Europeans, although the United States has begun to appoint younger presidents now than earlier in the decade of the sixties. Considering that the mean present age of Europeans and Americans is the same, this implies that the European, once in the key

Table 3 Average age of business leaders

	B	*DK*	*SF*	*F*	*D*	*G.B.*	*I*	*NL*	*N*	*S*	*U.S.A.*
Age at which the executive became president	45	41	41	49	48	46	45	42	41	44	50
Present age of the chief executive	58	52	51	59	57	55	54	56	52	50	55
Retirement age of the president	71	66	64	70	70	65	70	64	65	65	N/A

job, will remain there for a longer period of time than his U.S. opposite number.

There is proverbially less 'tenure' associated with a position in an American company, including that of the president. The presidential chair there is not something obtained once and for all, and unlike his European colleague, the American company president will retire earlier or leave for another top job. This difference, as one interesting and recent analysis purports to show (Granick, 1972), may reflect different cultural attitudes regarding policies of promotion and tenure. It may also have much to do with size of company. Britain is the country in Europe with the greatest proportion of large-scale industrial enterprises, and the age profile of the British presidents resembles that for the Americans. By contrast, in Denmark, where 85 per cent of the chief executives took office at under the age of 45 (20 per cent at under 30!), four out of ten of the enterprises in our sample of the top 400 Danish firms have an annual turnover of under $200,000. The smaller scale of industry in some European countries may imply that even the largest companies are entrepreneurial in character; entrepreneurs customarily make young presidents.

Job mobility and functional experience: the transatlantic generalist–specialist debate

We turn now to examine the career path of the executives prior to their presidencies, asking ourselves whether experience in many companies is considered to be a greater asset on the other side of the Atlantic than in Europe, and whether there are differences in functional background.

We read about the 'mobile manager' hopping from job to job, more interested in his career than in his corporation, leaving his employer every other year in search of greener pastures. Do the men who run U.S. companies in reality fit this stereotype?

When asked which factors were involved in achieving their present positions U.S. presidents mentioned their experience in their own company in 81 per cent of the cases, and their experience in another company in 29 per cent of the cases. In 1962, 41 per cent of the U.S. presidents had made their entire careers in the same company, 23 per cent had had experience with another company, 16 per cent with two others and 20 per cent with three or more companies. Four years later a survey with the same population indicated that only 35 per cent had never tried another corporation, while 28 per cent had been with one other, 18 per cent with two and 19 per cent with three or more. American managers are tending to become more mobile, although the degree of mobility is not high. From the composite European figures, we are struck by the similarity of the pattern; however, inter-company mobility patterns, influenced by manpower supply and economic conditions, may be in too constant a state of flux for one to be able to make meaningful assertions. *Fortune* contrasts the cold, pragmatic junior executive of the mid-sixties with the new breed of open, passionate and individualistic junior managers of today and observes that

> when the company makes a commitment to the young executive, he is quick to give loyalty in return. One of the more intriguing insights into his character is the fact that he is apparently less inclined than he once was towards job hopping ... During the mid-sixties many major companies reported losing more than half their newly hired college graduates within the first five years; that costly turnover rate has now begun to slow (*Fortune*, March 1971).

Moreover, the variations from country to country inside Europe are wide, and a 'European' interpretation here, more than ever, is dangerous, as Table 4 indicates. The Europeans appear to divide into three cultural groups with regard to job mobility: the highly mobile Northerners (including Germany, but excluding Finland),

Table 4 **Job mobility of business leaders**

Number of other companies worked for before joining present company (% executives)	*B*	*DK*	*SF*	*F*	*G*	*G.B.*	*I*	*NL*	*N*	*S*	*U.S.A.*
No other companies worked for	34	15	30	32	10	46	34	40	21	17	35
1–2 other companies worked for	51	43	45	40	50	35	40	47	44	42	46
3 or more other companies worked for	15	42	25	28	40	19	26	13	35	41	19
Total = 100%											

where 35–42 per cent of the presidents have worked for three or more companies; the Latin cultures, where mobility is less extreme; and the Dutch and British, of whom more than 40 per cent have made their entire career in a single enterprise. The Americans, in 1966 at least, would appear to be most similar to the middle Latin group.

In all the European countries, the executives who hop from company to company are in general moving from the large organization to the smaller one (see also Willig, 1970). In Scandinavia and Germany, where the phenomenon of high mobility is most evident, this movement appears to be related to the status of various 'élite' graduate schools of engineering and business. The graduate with such a diploma has a much sought-after qualification and is able to search actively for a job which will fulfil his needs. What then are his needs, what exactly is he searching for? One of the most conclusive findings in a well-known cross-cultural study of managerial motivation (Haire, Ghiselli and Porter, 1966) sheds light on this: these researchers found that Nordic managers attach greater prestige to the concepts of 'directing' and leadership than managers in other cultures. On this basis, it would appear that Northern Europeans move from large to smaller companies on the ticket of their élite diploma in search of the highly valued prestige of the direction and leadership of an enterprise. This role is attainable at an earlier age in smaller corporations, and the moves occur despite the fact that the salary level in smaller companies is lower than that in larger industrial corporations (see de Bettignies and Evans, 1971).

We move now to consider the experience of our executives in functional areas, where we do note a 'European' phenomenon. Two-thirds of Europeans have spent the years immediately prior to their presidency in the area of general administration, while only one American in four had such extensive experience in general management. For the Europeans, particularly the Scandinavians, a staff position at top management levels serves as an internship before undertaking the role of heading the enterprise. Americans have a more varied immediate background (29 per cent in general management, 21 per cent in marketing, 15 per cent in finance and 11 per cent in manufacturing), though the pattern in Britain and Germany most resembles that in the U.S.A., with nearly 50 per cent of their top executives making a direct spring from marketing or manufacturing posts.

Respondents were also asked to state what they believe to be the most beneficial area of functional experience for a future president. In the U.S.A. and Europe outside Scandinavia, the profile of these opinions is very similar to that of the actual experience of the chief executives in the respective countries, in the sense that Europeans set forth as their ideal a 'generalist' with experience in many departments and in general administration, whereas American opinions are more heterogeneous. However, for both groups of executives there is a tendency towards advocating experience in marketing and finance at the expense of general management and manufacturing. Opinions among Scandinavian managers as to the most beneficial functional area differ markedly, however, from the background of the present chief executives, which lies primarily in general administration; a clear majority recommend experience in marketing to presidential aspirants. Sweden is unique among the eleven countries in that a large number of presidents advocate manufacturing departments; 25 per cent and 54 per cent of that country's top executives consider manufacturing and marketing respectively to be the departments from where future Swedish presidents are most likely to come. In no other country is there such unanimity of opinion.

It appears that Western and Southern European managers are affirmedly generalist in their orientation, with the British most notably so, in contrast to the specialist Northerners, who see future industrial and commercial leadership in terms of a need for a marketing perspective. Whether these differences in orientation reflect substantive differences in the economic problems of the respective regions of Europe is an intriguing question beyond the scope of our survey (see Nuttall, 1972, for an analysis of the impact of governmental policy and foreign competition on the adoption of sophisticated marketing approaches in Sweden). The United States distinguishes itself for the absence of any consensus as to the most appropriate functional background for a president, perhaps indicating sentiments that the 'man' counts more than his functional background, and that industries and companies are different and consequently require different leadership and management skills.

Compensation: the Atlantic at its widest

There is one truly 'European' feature of the top management scene as to which there can be little doubt – the lower salaries which European companies pay to their chief executives (see Table 5). The median salary for European presidents is approxi-

Table 5 Annual compensation of chief executives

	B	*DK*	*SF*	*F*	*D*	*G.B.*	*I*	*NL*	*N*	*S*
Low: under $24,000 per year	21	23	43	9	10	13	29	18	81	13
Medium: between $24,000 and $48,000 per year	42	60	51	54	43	65	61	42	18	69
High: over $48,000 per year	37	17	6	37	47	22	10	40	1	18

The American chief executive's lowest pay starts at $50,000 with the average between $100,000 and $150,000.

mately $30,000, for the U.S. executive it is $130,000. The lowest American salaries start where the highest European salaries leave off!

Inside Europe, the German and French presidents are mostly in the higher income brackets; the Scandinavians, notably the Norwegians, are by far the worst compensated chief executives in Europe, worse off financially than even the British, who have been the subject of numerous studies commenting on their low level of remuneration. Part of the explanation for the low rates of compensation in these countries is the effect of heavy progressive tax rates which reduce the incentive to claim high salaries. As if to balance the lack of financial incentives, the Swedes have by far the longest periods of paid vacation (thirty working days of paid holiday). In addition, there is a clear relationship that exists in Britain, Scandinavia and the Netherlands between size of enterprise and salary level. The executives with very low salaries may be heading enterprises which are among the top 400–500 in their particular country, but these companies are small compared with the giants of the *Fortune*–500 List.

Conclusion

Europe and the United States share a common status as members of the industrialized society and, when taken as a whole, the European business élite turns out to be less different from the American élite than popular stereotypes would warrant. The cultural stereotypes of the young, highly-qualified, very mobile American executives who are the product of a unique 'career path formula' for success, and the one-company, poorly educated European gerontocrats are not substantiated. In many cases, the differences between European countries are highly significant, and seem to be affected by the broad stream of cultural tradition in a given society. These differences deserve examination in light of the obstacles to communication and understanding which they may present in an economically united Europe.

Although overall European characteristics do exist, such as the social establishment and the generalist tradition, there is no prototype 'European Chief Executive' as such. Europeans tend on the other hand to invent more differences than really exist between themselves and American top managers. These perceptions undoubtedly reflect real differences in attitudes and values, resulting more from environmental and attitudinal climates than from demographic or career characteristics. The Atlantic probably looms at its widest in the attitudinal domain.

References

Birch, S., and MacMillan, B. (1972), 'Managers on the move', *New Society*, 4 May.

De Bettignies, H.-C. (1970), 'Leaders across the ocean: comparing American and European chief executives', *European Business*, no. 26.

De Bettignies, H.-C., and Evans, P. (1971), 'Europe looks north at the Scandinavian business elite', *European Business*, no. 31.

Denison, E. F. (1962), *The Sources of Economic Growth in the United States and the Alternatives Before Us*, Committee for Economic Development, New York.

Fortune (1970), 'Self-portrait of a U.S. executive', May.

Fortune (1970), 'Let's break the go-to-college lockstep', November.

Fortune (1971), 'The accelerated generation moves into management', March.

Granick, D. (1972), *Managerial Comparisons of Four Developed Countries: France, Britain, United States, and Russia*, M.I.T. Press.

Haire, M., Ghiselli, E., and Porter, L. (1966), *Managerial Thinking: An International Study*, John Wiley, New York.

Hall, D., and Amado-Fischgrund, G. (1969), 'Chief executives in Britain', *European Business*, no. 20.

Hall, D., and De Bettignies, H.-C. (1968), 'The French business elite', *European Business*, no. 19.

Hall, D., De Bettignies, H.-C., and Amado-Fischgrund, G. (1969), 'The European business elite', *European Business*, no. 23.

Jencks, C. (1973), *Inequality: A Reassessment of the Effect of Family and Schooling in America*, Allen Lane.

Nuttall, J. (1972), 'Marketing – the Swedish, British and German styles', *European Business*, no. 35.

P.E.P. Reports (1966), *Attitudes in British Management*, Penguin Books.

O.E.C.D. (1969), *Statistics of the Occupational and Educational Structures of the Labor Force in 53 Countries*, Paris.

Willig, J.-C. (1970), 'Organization man or entrepreneur: Europe's "business school" manager', *European Business*, no. 27.

Part Four
The Managerial Framework – The Effects of Size on the Managerial Structure

Managerial structure is considered as a system of attitudes and relationships affected by the *size* of the organization – defined in this context as the scope and complexity of the decision-making process, as it relates to the business strategy of the firm, and the environmental effects on it. As the organization increases in size, its managerial structure in both its above aspects has to be adapted periodically so as to ensure the continued cooperation essential to its survival of all its component human factors – managers, employees, trade unions, bankers, shareholders, suppliers, customers, government, etc. The most advanced stage of growth is reached when the organization extends its operations into other countries or, in other words, becomes a Multinational Corporation.

The readings in this part fall accordingly into two main categories – those dealing with attitudes and those primarily concerned with relationships.

The first two readings deal with cultural effects on managerial attitudes. First Haire, Ghiselli and Porter describe their universal study in which the notion was put forward of clusters of countries with similar managerial attitudes and which has since culminated in Haire's book *Managerial Thinking* (1966). Heller presents, in the second reading a somewhat different approach which is the basis for a large international research project currently being conducted, which measures differences and similarities across countries in attitudes concerning the needs and skills of managers.

Of the two readings concerned with managerial structure the study by Hickson, Hinings, McMillan and Schwitter is concerned with structural differences between the three representative samples of manufacturing organizations matched in size – one British, one American and one Canadian. This is one of a series of studies carried out by Derek Pugh and his collaborators.

The last reading, Weinshall's 'Multinational Corporations – A Total Systems Approach to their Role and Measurement', related the growth processes of multinational corporations to their managerial structure demonstrating the changes developed in the course of evolution from and entrepreneurial structure to a multistructure. He points out how the world is benefiting from multinational corporations and proposes methods for studying their size, structure and attitudes. The first part of this reading presents the conceptual schemes on the basis of which the material of this book of readings on *Culture and Management* was organized.

12 Mason Haire, Edwin E. Ghiselli and Lyman W. Porter (1963)

Cultural Patterns in the Role of the Manager

Mason Haire and Edwin E. Ghiselli are Professors of Psychology and Research Psychologists at the Institute of Industrial Relations, University of California, Berkeley. Lyman W. Porter is Assistant Professor of Psychology and Assistant Research Psychologist at the Institute.
Excerpt from *Institute of Indusırial Relations*, vol. 2, no. 2, February 1963, pp. 95–117.

We have a good many impressionistic reports of national managerial stereotypes, ranging from scholarly summaries through journalistic descriptions to tourist-anthropological anecdotes. Hardly a traveller finishes a whirlwind tour or a scholar a three-day conference at Salzburg or Copenhagen but what he is ready – even eager – to describe the way European managers think. Useful though these insights have been, we also need strictly comparable data – responses to the same questions asked of samples of managers in a number of countries. That was the task of this study: to find an empirical answer to the question of similarities and differences in managers' attitudes. In these days of rapid change in international trade patterns and increased proximity of countries, it is not necessary to emphasize the importance of a further understanding of managers' viewpoints and, if they exist, of national differences in such viewpoints. As a first approach, a questionnaire, asking identical questions, was administered to a sample of managers in each of a number of countries.

Carefully collected objective data offer great advantages, although they are less immediately satisfying than global intuitive impressions. But something must be sacrificed for rigour. In asking identical questions in all countries, one is limited to the questions that apply to all countries. It is difficult to frame a question about pricing, wage-setting, or accounting practices that will apply equally well in the United States, Spain and Denmark. One is forced back, for questions that are relevant to all, to fundamental issues that are common to all, rather than techniques and practices. For this reason, and also because of the investigators' professional interests, the present study focused on three phases of management thinking: (1) views on leadership and how one gets work done well and efficiently, (2) the way in which the role and practices of the manager are seen by managers themselves, and (3) the satisfactions a manager wants and gets from his job.

Before we go on to deal with results, a word must be said about two big problems in this kind of research. Sampling is one of them. The other is omnipresent in cross-cultural research. The thinking of managers is part of the culture itself. The instrument that asks them to express their thinking is, thus, both a part of the culture and the way we study the culture. Each of these points present real difficulties for a cross-cultural study of management.

About 3,500 responses were collected from managers in fourteen countries. We aimed at a minimum of about 200 from each country, and, in general, we roughly fulfilled the goal. The sample for each country is not strictly representative of the total management population of each country. However, the samples are representative of rather large groups. Care was taken to sample different kinds of industries, geographical areas, levels of management, and the like. It seems unlikely that the discerned differences among managers in different countries can be explained by sampling error. With all its limitations, the present sample is probably an adequate first approximation. To have been deterred by the difficulties of sampling would have meant accepting the counsel of despair. These data will add to the growing body of demographic descriptions of management which will eventually lead us to an ideal description.

Another real difficulty arises in translating a questionnaire of this type. Each item must be translated so it is not only literally correct, but also carries the same impression. The first translations were made here by a translator native to the country involved. They were then independently translated back to English, as a check, by a second native. Finally, they were checked in the countries for which they were intended by social scientists and businessmen. The process is arduous and tedious and seems to have been fairly successful.

Incidentally, a good deal comes out of the job of translating itself. For example, *leader* does not translate well except in Scandinavian languages. Even before *Duce* and *Fuehrer* became loaded with special connotations, the word fitted poorly in continental European languages. The word 'manager' with its roots in the Latin *manus*, hand, means one who handles, but in the Romance languages its use is virtually restricted to the rider's management of a horse – a connotation of simple guidance and unilateral control that would probably be unacceptable in industry. Many managerial terms are so specifically American in origin that they have been adopted unchanged in various languages. Finally, many psychological concepts – such as the need for esteem – are so closely tied to what esteem means in the culture that it is difficult to separate the thing measured from the means of measurement. These problems all restricted the things that could be asked about and occasionally involved undesirable circumlocutions.

The present report is a preliminary one in two senses. In the first place, it deals with only 11 countries out of the 14 studied and only about 2,800 managers out of the final total. In the second place, it reports the first analyses of the data. Because the full analysis of the data will not be completed for some time, however, it seemed worth-while to prepare this preliminary report.

In general, the results will be reported in three parts: the section of the questionnaire devoted to leadership first, cognitive patterns and the cultural role of the manager second and, finally, satisfactions of managers.

Leadership

The first section of the questionnaire consisted of eight statements to which managers were invited to respond by checking a point on a five-point scale from 'agree strongly' to disagree strongly'. The items were chosen on the basis of a logical pattern and an attempt was made to cover a fair portion of the gamut of managerial attitudes on leadership. The description of attitudes of this sort as running from 'democratic to autocratic forms of leadership' is too hackneyed and overloaded with meaning to be of great value, but this description is similar to many. To put it in the frame of international studies of management, the ends of the scale resemble the points Harbison and Myers describe as 'dictatorial or authoritarian' on the one hand and 'democratic or participative' on the other.[1] The significance of the scale will become clearer as the results are indicated.

There are two ways one can look at these data: in terms of the substantive meaning of the items and the responses, and in terms of the way the countries group together. Taking up the first point, the eight items concerned with leadership were grouped into four logical categories. These categories were designed to represent concepts in the developing human-relations idea of a manager as a manager of people. They are as follows:

(A) The belief in the individual's innate capacity for initiative and leadership.

(B) The belief in sharing information and objectives.

(C) The belief in participative management.

(D) The belief in internal control (essentially self-control of the individual flowing from the job and from understanding and commitment) rather than external control (punishment, reward, promotion).

In logical terms, the first category seems to be an absolutely essential first step to the other three. The basic reason for adopting shared objectives, participation, and internal control is the contention that individuals have a capacity for initiative and leadership that is untapped by a formal unilateral command form of organization. The logical precedence of category A and its character as a building block for the others makes the results particularly striking. The outstanding first finding is that there is universally more acceptance of what might be called higher order concepts of management than there is of the basic conviction that the individual has initiative and leadership capacity (see Figure 1).[2] By

1. Harbison and Myers (1960).

2. The position of a country on a scale represents the median score of all the managers in that category. In some cases items have been reversed to fit a single scale. The numerical values are unimportant here.

'higher order' concepts, we mean those identified in categories B, C, and D. These (a) logically follow after category A, and (b) deal with management *practices*. No matter how we group the data, this finding stands out. In each country, in each group of countries, in all the countries taken together, the responses to the first category are different from any of the other categories or from all three taken together. The difference is large and compelling.

What can this mean? Presumably, unless one believes in untapped capacity for leadership in subordinates, a classical unilateral directive management is best. Here we find a lack of basic confidence in others and at the same time a leaning towards participative group-centred management. It is at least possible that this result is the effect of the partial digestion of fifteen years of exhortation by the group-oriented consultants and professors of management. These ideas – at the level of management practices – have become common currency among management groups and in executive development programmes and training courses. The data suggest that the ideas dealing with management practice have been persuasive, while the basic conviction about the nature of people remains unchanged. To the extent that this is true, and to the extent that the attitudes expressed in category A do indeed underlie sophisticated management practices, this is an unfortunate state of affairs. It is a little like building the techniques and practices of a Jeffersonian democracy or a basic belief in the divine right of kings.

This finding illustrates a sampling problem in all such studies. It is possible that those who are inclined to cooperate are also those who have been impressed by modern (human-relations ?) management concepts. To the extent that this is true, it probably accentuates the commitment to the higher-order management practices represented in categories B, C, and D. However, even though this response-bias may exist, the fact remains that a large body of managers in each country – and presumably the most advanced – hold the views which have been described.

Among these last three categories of belief there is less difference in level of response. As can be seen from Figure 1, attitudes of managers in all the countries cluster near the same value on all three scales. The belief in participation is perhaps a little weaker

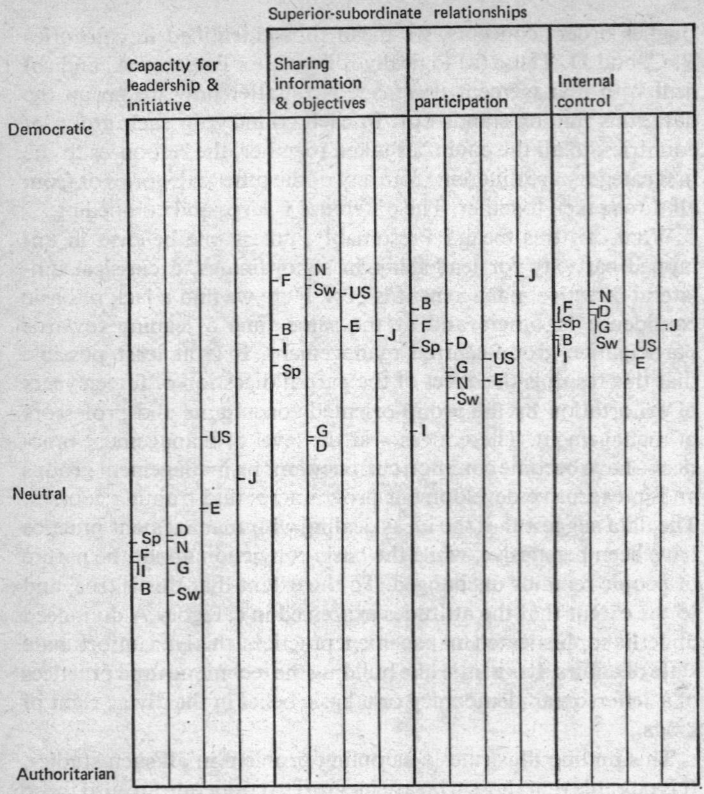

a The following key applies to Figures 1 through 7:
B - Belgium, D - Denmark, E - England, F - France, G - Germany, I - Italy, J - Japan, N - Norway, Sp - Spain, Sw - Sweden, US - United States

Figure 1 Average values on attitudes towards leadership

than in sharing information and internal control, but the difference is small in comparison with the gap between category A and all the others.

One can look at the data in Figure 1 and be impressed by the relatively narrow range of differences among all 11 countries. They all cluster low on category A and roughly together on B, C, and D. Before considering the differences, the similarity is important to notice. In these areas of attitude there are not large, insuperable differences in beliefs about leadership among the countries. We are accustomed to some large differences in prevailing myths about these countries: the icy-eyed Prussian, the fiery, aloof Don, the egalitarianism of the shopkeeper of France and England, Sweden's Middle Way, and the like. At least in their expressed conviction, however, these cleavages do not appear sharply. Managers' views on how to manage people are somewhat similar.

Turning to the differences among countries, Figure 1 again shows the picture.[3] Are there groups of countries? How do they cluster? One way to seek an answer is to observe the way countries shift positions from one part of the chart to another. For example, England and the U.S. seem to shift as a pair. On each of the four scales they tend to be positioned – with respect to all the others – in much the same way. They usually are fairly close in scores, although that may be less useful as a sign of grouping than their tendency to move together relative to all the others. Japan does not fit neatly with any group of countries. It moves by itself. On the four scales, it moves with England and the U.S. twice, with European countries once, and by itself once. It probably must stand alone on the basis of these data. The four continental European countries with a strong Latin background – France, Spain, Belgium, and Italy – move together rather tightly and can probably be usefully distinguished from the Northern European-Scandinavian group of Norway, Sweden, Denmark, and Germany. This gives us four clusters of countries: the Anglo-Saxon pair, Japan, Continental (Latin) Europe, and Northern (Teutonic) Europe.

The difference between the U.S. and all others is largest in category A. U.S. managers express the belief that all men are created equal more strongly than any of the others. Presumably

3. In Figure 1, the countries are divided into four groups. These are the groups that seemed to stand out through all the data. The separation illustrated here is not designed to create clusters, but to make it easier for the reader to see the groups as a whole.

managers think that they themselves have the capacity for leadership and initiative; U.S. managers feel, more than others, that the average person has the same capacities also. On the other categories the U.S. does not stand out from the group in the same way. Our textbooks and lectures may have exported a new concept of management which rests on a concept of man that is less accepted abroad.

Are the clusters ethnic or industrial? The answer seems to be largely ethnic. Norway and Sweden, industrially rather different, are very close together on the basis of these data. Denmark, though somewhat more agricultural than Sweden, tends to move closely with its Scandinavian neighbour. Germany, similar industrially to France, is close to the continental countries whenever the three Scandinavian countries are, but when it differs, it tends to swing with its Teutonic neighbours. France, Spain, Belgium, and Italy, a diverse package as far as industrialization is concerned, tend to swing together. England and the United States stand together, and Japan stands alone.

As far as the logical relationship among the categories is concerned, one might reason as follows. First comes the belief that most people have (untapped) capacities for initiative and leadership. If this idea is accepted, the manager might share information and objectives with them. Subsequently, and to a somewhat lesser extent, subordinates might be invited to participate in decisions. Finally, and to a still lesser extent, measures of self-control might be increasingly decentralized. Thus, the logical order of categories might follow their listing here, with a progressive embodiment in management practice of the basic belief in the individual. We have already pointed out that this relationship does not prevail, since attitudinal support for higher-order concepts of management (categories B, C, D) far outstrips the basic belief in the individual. How does the order work out, considering only the three categories of management practices? Is the logical pattern followed? Not often. Managers in England and the U.S. show more tendency to favour sharing information than eliciting participation or encouraging internal control. This at least approaches the logical model. In other clusters of countries the situation tends to be reversed. The commitment to internalized control tends to be greater than the willingness to share information or invite participation.

What can this mean? On the surface it appears impossible. How can an individual find direction and evaluation of himself in the work process if information and objectives are not shared? If we accept his self-direction, why stop short of participative management? In general, why is the psychological pattern different from the logical? It is perhaps easier to understand the variation in attitudes towards sharing information and objectives if we think in cultural terms and in terms of corporate tradition. In England and the U.S. there is a tradition of knowing and debating national issues and of full and frank disclosure of corporate financial data that differs from the rest of the countries taken as a whole. One can see why managers tend to share more in the Anglo-Saxon countries.

With respect to the category on participation, the three major clusters of countries are substantially the same. Japan favours participation somewhat more. No clue is immediately available to explain this deviation. This leaves only the fourth category. Managers in countries other than the U.S. and England tend to believe more strongly that one finds reward and direction in the work. For the most part, managers in the other countries also believe in this more strongly than they do in either participation or sharing information. It may well be that this belief in work-centred reward and direction arises from the craft and guild tradition, perhaps stronger elsewhere than in the Anglo-Saxon countries. In any case, two things seem clear: first, the patterns of management beliefs about leadership do not follow any simple logical pattern, and second, the pattern is more or less explicable in terms of cultural traditions in the countries. Management beliefs seem shaped more by such traditions than by degree or kind of industrialization.

How do these data compare with the findings of other major comparative studies of management, for example, that of Harbison and Myers? Without being contentious, let us lift a group of relevant statements from their section on 'Comparisons among Countries'.

1. In general, France and Italy have been characterized by a large

number of small enterprises, looked on by the family as a source of personal security and conducted in an atmosphere of widespread absence of trust.

2. The British social system, although much more flexible than it was fifty years ago, still carries over a strong feeling of the virtue of 'aristocratic' values and gives a high mark to the 'right' background in a man. In this respect it may be less egalitarian than that of the Swedes, although in Sweden the business élite is still drawn predominantly from a small group.

3. Japan, among the advanced industrial countries, appears to have retained many of the pre-capitalistic features of an earlier period and has managed to harness many supposedly 'feudal' values to the service of its economic development.

4. The German social system has also a strong authoritarian element, but this has been modified to some extent by the early development of organizations outside of the dominant classes and the need, in a political democracy, for the élite groups to make concessions of various sorts in order to maintain their power.[4]

These views are not exactly mirrored in our data. The absence of trust in Italy is perhaps apparent in the comparative reluctance to share information and allow participation, but France ranks considerably higher on both of these scales. Our data suggest that English managers are slightly less egalitarian than those in Sweden in terms of sharing information and looking for internal control among subordinates. However, in England there is a greater degree of commitment to the basic capacities of man and to participation. The Japanese fit in fairly well with the U.S. and England on everything but participation; here they are more democratic. Finally, the German authoritarianism appears, but is almost exactly matched in Denmark, and fits the same general pattern of the non-Anglo-Saxon countries. The data presented here provide a more differentiated picture, and this perhaps accounts for some of the variations in findings.

Harbison and Myers go on to say:

5. The process of industrialization tends, other things being equal, to limit managerial authority, both as a consequence of its direct effects on the industrial system and of its indirect effects on society as a whole.

4. Harbison and Myers (1960), pp. 123–4.

Directly, the increasing complexity and interdependence of many tasks make it necessary to elicit the cooperation of subordinates; the much larger size of establishment makes it necessary to increase the number of people in key managerial posts and makes it much more difficult to recruit them entirely from a narrow group, such as the family. Indirectly, the broadening of educational opportunities, the assumption of welfare responsibilities by governments or independent institutions, and the growth of rival organizations (such as labour unions), place checks on the power of management and prompt it to seek accommodation rather than arbitrary power.

6. In none of the less developed industrial countries except Israel did we find 'constitutional' management of the type prevalent in Sweden, England, or the United States.

7. Authoritarian and paternalistic practices are also common in France and Italy, despite the presence of labour movements. Centralization of control is characteristic in the French firm, as it is in the Italian or the Indian firm, for example. Despite the advanced stage of industrialization, the same pattern of authoritarian and paternalistic management seems to prevail in Japan – largely because of the social structure which, in prewar Japan at least, emphasized the unquestioning loyalty of subordinates to their superiors, as in the Japanese family.[5]

As has been suggested, the shift from unilateral command to a more participative management does not so neatly follow stages of industrialization in our data. One might roughly identify England, Sweden, Germany, and the U.S. as the most highly industrialized of our group. Perhaps France, Belgium, and Japan would fall in a second group, and Italy, Spain, Norway, and Denmark would be classified as countries still in stages of growing industrialization. Our data on managerial control do not follow such a classification of industrialization (or any other simple one). As has been suggested, we seem forced to turn to cultural traditions to understand managerial beliefs about power and authority.

The argument based on the stage of industrialization has been prevalent for a long time, and this is perhaps true because most of the relevant studies have been done by scholars with a background in economics. The kinds of questions we ask here are determined partly by our base in other social sciences. It is, therefore, not

5. ibid., pp. 125–7.

surprising that we find other-than-economic indicators useful in distinguishing the clusters of countries.

Years ago psychologists began to argue with economists about the 'economic man' concept as a tool for explaining the motivation of the individual at work. In some senses, the 'stage of industrialization' argument is a more sophisticated and more complex form of the same phenomenon. One tries to see, for example, management's view of authority as a function of the level of technological and economic development. The attitude is treated as a dependent variable flowing from independent variables arising from the nature of the business activity. Another possibility – not entirely an exclusive alternative, but partly an enlarging complement – is the view that management's attitude about control is part of a broad web of values and beliefs determined by and part of a stream of cultural traditions outside the business – assumptions about man, political organization, human rights, and the like. The form of the organization, then, determined partly independently of the business, is imposed on a particular level of industrialization, which, in turn, is determined partly independently of the broad non-economic cultural tradition.

When we view, for example, beliefs about control as part of a philosophy of management, it is not so surprising that we need to consider both economic and cultural traditions. We must have room for both the Protestant Ethic and scientific management in our causal texture. The appeal to 'the conscience of the King' influences management's (and the public's) view of control as does the Industrial Revolution. Among our clusters there is a strong cleavage between the generally Roman Catholic countries and the Protestant North. It is not surprising that there are broad determinants of managerial philosophies, values, and the concept of man.

Are the Common Market countries similar on the basis of these data? No more so than the cultural-geographical grouping would indicate. It is possible that they were more different four years ago and will be more similar four years from now, but today they look like separate nations with common cultural streams, rather than a United States of Europe. One is tempted to ask, 'Is England one of the leading Scandinavian countries?' Its isolation from the continent, its leadership in the Outer Seven, and the Anglo-Scandinavian political philosophy suggest the possibility. The answer here is 'No.' England moves with the U.S. and fairly independently of Scandinavia, which tends to move with Germany.

Japan's role in these clusters is interesting. While she stands somewhat alone in this particular family of nations, the difference is not as great as one might expect in a country so recently changed from an absolute monarchy, a cartelized and controlled economy, and a somewhat feudal concentration of capital. Where Japan stands out from the others it is almost uniformly in the direction of a more liberal position. It is perhaps well to remember that the scores represent agreement with statements of belief. There is no way at present to show how closely practice follows expression.

Cognitive patterns in the role of the manager

Another part of the questionnaire attempted to get at the managers' perceptions of the role and practices of the manager. A variety of things depend on these views – what the manager feels is appropriate and inappropriate behaviour in his role as manager, what kinds of values will be seen by one considering management as a career, the degree to which he can wholeheartedly invest himself in the role, and the like. In short, such views reflect the whole cultural assessment of the function of managing. To approach this problem, the more experimental and more projective semantic differential technique was used.

The semantic differential method aims, essentially, at discovering and defining a kind of cognitive map. With a group of concepts, it is possible to say how far each is from every other and in what direction. The meaning of the concepts and their psychological dynamics can be inferred from their positions in this kind of constructed mental space. Quantitatively, this is accomplished by asking respondents to rate each concept on a series of scales which remain the same across all concepts. In this case two groups of concepts were used, one dealing with management functions, and one with the superior – subordinate relationship in the culture. For functions, the concepts *to decide*, *to direct*, *to persuade*, *to cooperate*, and *to create* were used, as well as the more negative *to cheat*, *to reprimand*, and *to make a mistake*. An ordering of these into a cognitive pattern gives us some idea of a nation's view of what a manager does. In addition, hierarchical relationships were compared in three major social institutions: the army, the church, and business.

The detailed statistical analysis of the semantic differential is long and complex and will be reported more fully elsewhere. Preliminary results of this analysis are not as illuminating as in the case of the other two methods, but a brief mention is worth-while because it illustrates further the kind of clustering of countries that occurs. For this brief presentation, four concepts and three scales have been selected. The concepts are *to direct*, *to persuade*, *to cooperate*, and *to reprimand*. Each country's responses are shown in Figures 2, 3, 4, and 5 on the scales of importance, goodness, and difficulty.

Taking all the concepts together, *to cooperate* is thought to be the most important. *To direct* is a close second, *to persuade* is next, and finally, *to reprimand* is the least important (of these four) in the manager's repertory. The same order holds, roughly, for goodness. Cooperation and direction are very, very good, persuasion somewhat less so, and reprimanding the least of all. Difficulty, however, is another story. Directing is the hardest thing to do. Persuading is next hardest. Reprimanding is easier, but cooperating is slightly easier still.

Turning to the way the countries group together, we see essentially the same clusters we saw before. Spain, France, Belgium, and Italy tend to move together in a tight group. (In one case – which will be discussed later – Spain deviates markedly.) England and the U.S. behave alike, again fairly closely linked. In general, Germany and the three Scandinavian countries vary in a similar pattern. Japan, in these data, could be fitted into the (Latin) continental group of countries.

Spain stands out from all others on the function of reprimanding. It is more important in Spain, it is better, and, somewhat surprisingly, it is more difficult. Spain's isolation on this dimension is heightened by another outstanding feature of these data: there is remarkably close correspondence among managers in all the countries in their perception of these functions. While an occasional country stands out – e.g. Denmark finding direction

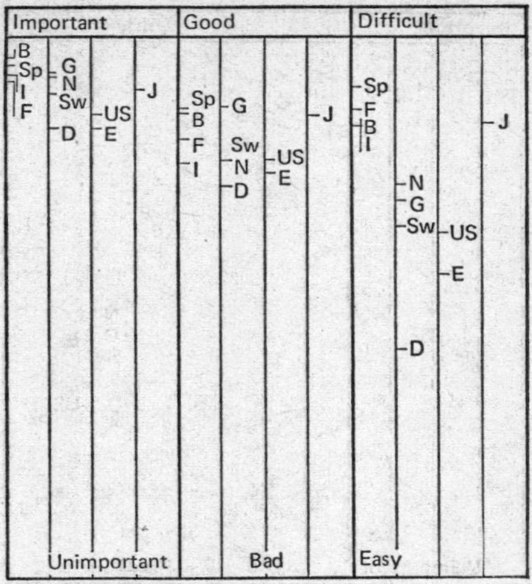

Figure 2 Scaled Responses to the Concept 'To Direct'

Figure 3 Scaled Responses to the Concept 'To Persuade'

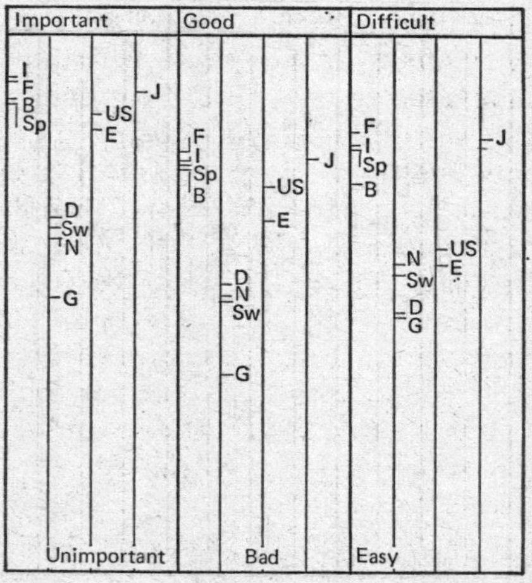

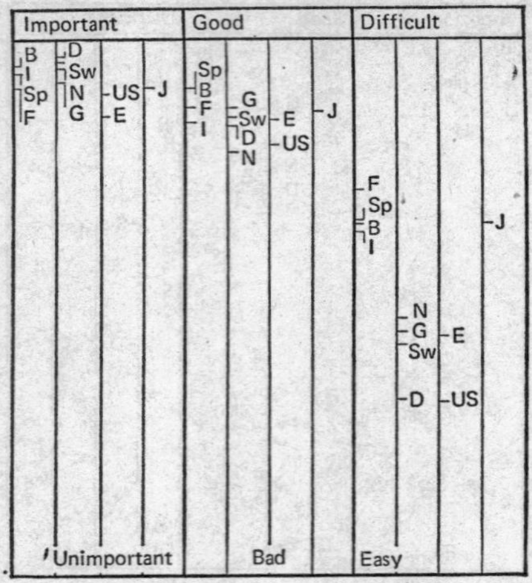

Figure 4 Scaled Responses to the Concept 'To Cooperate'

Figure 5 Scaled Responses to the Concept 'To Reprimand'

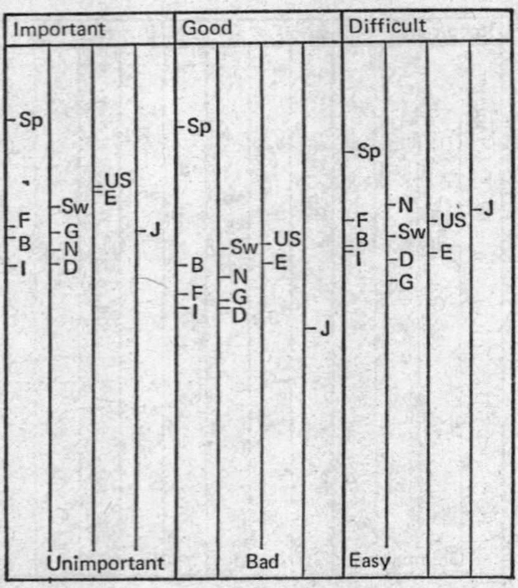

unusually easy, or Germany finding persuasion relatively unimportant, and not very good – still, in general, they shift together. From cooperating to reprimanding, for instance, they tend to move down on all three scales in a bunch.

The broad implications of these data appear less clearly than in either of the other two sections of the study at this stage of statistical analysis. It is necessary to wait until the analysis is completed to give a good picture of cognitive mapping in these areas. Meanwhile, two points stand out in the preliminary clustering. Firstly, there is remarkable agreement among countries in their perceptions of these functions. They are not scattered widely, but tend to bunch together, indicating a strong common thread in the way people view these things regardless of country. Secondly, within this relatively homogeneous set of responses, clusters of countries are still distinguishable. Such variation as there is tends to preserve small tight sub-groups. They are substantially the same ethnic or cultural clusters that appeared in the preceding section.

Motivation and satisfactions

The third section of the study was concerned with the types of satisfactions managers want from their jobs and with the degree to which they feel these different needs are actually being satisfied through their jobs. To obtain information on these points, five types of psychological needs were studied. These needs can be considered as arranged in order from the basic or most prepotent need for security through social, esteem, and autonomy needs to the least prepotent need for self-actualization. This order of needs on the basis of priority or prepotency stems from the theoretical thinking of a number of psychologists and has been used on a wide scale in recent psychological studies of motivation, especially in relation to work. Thus, the results obtained in this study for these different types of needs can be related back to an underlying theoretical foundation.

Before proceeding with a discussion of findings, it is useful to describe briefly the five types of needs. *Security needs* were not defined for the respondent, but were interpreted in a general way as one's feeling of safety and assurance in a particular managerial position. *Social needs* referred to the desire to develop close friendships and the opportunity to give help to other people; thus both ingoing (from others to the person) and outgoing (from the person to others) aspects of needs for social satisfaction were covered in the questionnaire. *Esteem needs* covered both self-esteem and esteem received from other people. *Autonomy needs* referred to the authority connected with the manager's position and the opportunity for independent thought and action. Finally, *self-actualization needs* tapped feelings of self-fulfilment, worthwhile accomplishment, and personal growth.

The specific questions in each of these five need areas asked managers to make three responses: (1) How important is this to me? (2) How much (of the need satisfaction) is there *now* in my position? and (3) How much (of the need satisfaction) should there be in my position? The answers to the first question were used to determine the importance attached to particular needs, that is, what the manager wants to get from his position. To determine degree of fulfilment or satisfaction, or what he feels he *is* getting from his position, the difference between responses to Question 3 and Question 2 was computed for each item for each respondent. Thus, the larger the difference between 'should be' and 'is now', the greater was the indicated *dis*satisfaction.

Importance of needs

The most striking finding concerning managerial feelings about the importance of different needs is the relative similarity of thinking from country to country with regard to a particular need. That is, for example, those types of needs which are considered most important in one country tend also to be regarded as most important in other countries. Likewise, those needs considered least important in a particular country are usually also thought to be least important by managers in other countries (see Figure 6).

Which needs *were* regarded as the most important? In every country, without exception, needs for self-actualization were deemed most important. French, Japanese, and U.S. managers felt most strongly about these needs, but the differences from country to country were very slight. In other words, not only did self-actualization needs consistently rank above other needs, but they were also given quite consistent ratings of importance by the

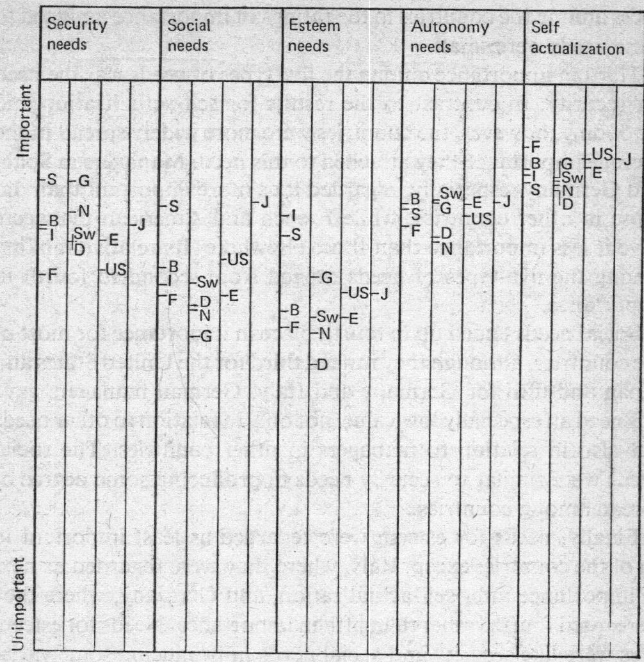

Figure 6 Average values on the importance of various needs

various groups of managers. This means that, at least at the level of response, managers put primary emphasis on opportunities for growth, for realizing their potential, and for worth-while accomplishment. The unanimity of this reaction across countries demands attention.

Needs for autonomy were generally regarded as second in importance, although for certain countries they were third rather than second. Managers in Sweden, Germany, and Japan felt slightly more strongly about these needs than managers in the other countries, while Norwegian and Danish managers attached slightly less-than-average importance to autonomy needs. Again, however, as was the case in needs for self-actualization, the differences among the countries in the ratings of importance assigned to these needs were small.

Third in importance among the five types of needs was the need for security. In contrast to the results for self-actualization and autonomy, however, the countries were more widely spread in the average importance they attached to this need. Managers in Spain and Germany, especially, regarded it as more important than did those in other countries, while French and American managers gave it less importance than those elsewhere. Its relative ranking among the five types of needs ranged from second to fourth in importance.

Social needs ended up in fourth place in importance for most of the countries, although they ranked third for the United States and Japan and fifth for Germany and Italy. German managers gave this need an especially low value, not only in relation to other needs but also in relation to managers in other countries. The social needs were similar to security needs in producing some degree of spread among countries.

Finally, needs for esteem were regarded as least important in all of the countries except Italy, where they were regarded as next in importance after self-actualization, and Germany, where they were rated fourth rather than fifth in importance. Needs for esteem thus were like security and social needs in producing some variation in ratings among countries. The Italian managers gave them a much higher rating than did managers in any other country; on the other hand, Danish managers gave them a particularly low rating.

As pointed out earlier, the most impressive finding in connection with the importance attached to different needs was the relative similarity in the way quite different countries and cultures felt about them. A Spanish manager is not very different from a German manager or each from an English or Japanese manager in the ratings they give to the importance of each need. This similarity, of course, is not complete. Especially for security, social, and esteem needs there was some degree of variation from country to country. But even for these the variation usually was not great except for an isolated case or two. And, for autonomy and self-actualization, the similarity was very close. One should note especially that the similarities were greatest for the two needs self-actualization and autonomy, which were regarded as most important. This suggests that managers feel most strongly about the needs that bring the closest agreement in the value assigned to them. Esteem and social needs produced the least agreement among countries and were thought of as least important.

The overall similarity among managers in different countries in their evaluations of the importance of needs may indicate that what people want from their jobs is relatively unaffected by the cultural environment in which they operate. At least this seems to be true of managers. Whether it is also true of other groups of employees cannot be determined, of course, from our data. Managers, and perhaps all people, seem to be alike in terms of what they regard as important needs to fulfil in their work situations.

The satisfaction of needs

The findings for need fulfilment or satisfaction are in contrast with those previously reported for the importance attached to various needs. Although managers tend to be alike from country to country in what they *want* from their jobs, they tend to be quite different in what they *think they are getting* from their jobs. The absolute ratings of satisfaction for a particular need vary from country to country, and so also do the relative rankings of one or another need in comparison to all other needs. That is, the mean satisfaction for a given need, say esteem, may be high for country A and low for country B, but also country A may regard this need as the most satisfied of the five needs, whereas country B regards it as about third in satisfaction.

Because the absolute and relative satisfaction of most of the five needs varies considerably from one country to another, it is not possible to give any meaningful overall ranking of the needs in terms of the degree to which they are satisfied. The greatest similarity among countries is with regard to satisfaction of the need for self-actualization (see Figure 7). In all countries except Japan, it is considered as the *least* satisfied of all of the five needs. (The results for Japan show a peculiar pattern similar to no other country in that all needs, self-actualization included, are regarded as equally satisfied.) Although the need for self-actualization

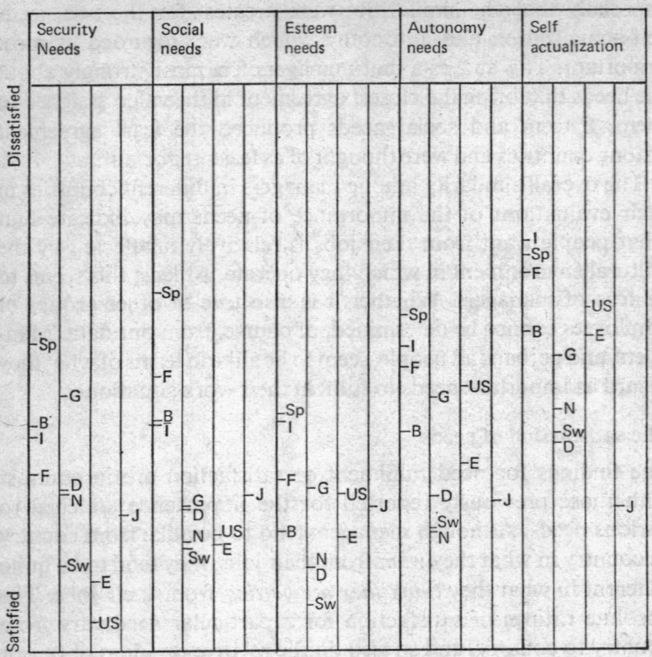

Figure 7 Degree of satisfaction in various needs

produces the greatest dissatisfaction in almost all countries, the dissatisfaction is greatest in Italy, Spain, France, and the U.S. On the other hand, managers in Japan, especially, and in the Scandinavian countries, to some extent, are not as dissatisfied on self-actualization as most of the other countries.

Needs for autonomy are seen as the second greatest producers of lack of need fulfilment in most of the countries. Managers in Spain, France, and Italy indicate somewhat greater dissatisfaction in this area than do those in other countries, while Scandinavian and Japanese managers again indicate slightly less-than-average dissatisfaction.

Needs for esteem rank as the third most unsatisfied needs in some countries, the fourth in others, and the fifth or least dissatisfied in still others. Social and security needs show an even wider variation, ranking in each case from second most dissatisfied in some countries to the most satisfied need in other countries.

Just as in the two major preceding sections of this paper, probably the most meaningful analyses of the data for perceived satisfaction or fulfilment can be made if the various countries are grouped by patterns or profiles of satisfactions for the five types of needs rather than if each need is considered separately. If this grouping is carried out, four fairly clear groups of countries emerge. First are the four countries of mid/southern continental Europe: Spain, Italy, France, and Belgium. The second group includes Germany and the three Scandinavian countries. The third cluster includes the two English-speaking countries, England and the United States. Japan stands by itself, its pattern being completely different from that of the United States or any European country.

The mid/southern continental European group of countries has one outstanding feature in its pattern of satisfactions, and that is the fact that, considering all needs taken together, managers from these countries are more *dis*satisfied than those from any other countries or groups of countries. For four of the five need areas – self-actualization, autonomy, esteem, and social – the managers from these four countries indicate more dissatisfaction than each of the other groups of countries. Only in the security area is dissatisfaction in three of these countries exceeded, and that only slightly, by Germany. Thus, even in the security need area average dissatisfaction in this group of countries is comparatively high. The nation with the most dissatisfied managers by far within this first grouping of mid/southern continental European countries is Spain. Following in order are Italy, France, and Belgium. This group of four countries feels most dissatisfied with self-actualization needs, as do all of the other groups except Japan. Next in order of dissatisfaction for this group are autonomy and social needs. The fact that social needs are almost tied for second in terms of relative dissatisfaction (among the five needs) for this group is noteworthy, for this is a higher relative dissatisfaction for these needs than is the case with any of the other three groups of countries. Security and esteem needs are placed fourth and fifth in dissatisfaction by managers from these four countries.

Germany, in this section of the study, could in some ways be grouped with the preceding four countries of mid/southern continental Europe and in other ways with the group of three Scandinavian countries. Germany is somewhat similar to its four more southern European partners in having a relatively high overall level of dissatisfaction, and is, in fact, closely related to Belgium in this respect. However, in the profile pattern of ranking of the five needs in terms of dissatisfaction Germany seems more similar to its neighbours to the north. Like the Scandinavian countries, it tends to feel relatively well satisfied in esteem and social need areas and relatively less well satisfied on security needs. Security needs for German managers, in fact, are as unsatisfied as autonomy needs.

Scandinavian managers are clearly 'satisfied' managers, at least in terms of their own perceptions of their situations. They are most satisfied of any of the groups of countries on autonomy and, particularly, esteem needs. For the other three need areas – self-actualization, social, and security – they are the most satisfied among the continental European countries. Considering all five needs, the Scandinavian managers are definitely more satisfied than managers from the most southern European countries, Spain and Italy. The Scandinavian managers, like the German managers, feel that security needs are no better satisfied in their jobs than autonomy needs. Thus, among the five types of needs, dissatisfaction in the need for security ranks relatively higher for the Scandinavian countries than for the U.S., England, and the mid/southern continental countries.

The two English-speaking countries have a somewhat different pattern of satisfactions from any of the European countries. For the most prepotent needs, security and social needs, the U.S. and English managers are more satisfied than those in any other cluster of countries (including Japan). For esteem and autonomy needs, the English-speaking managers are more satisfied than German managers and those in most other continental European countries, but less satisfied than the Scandinavian managers. For self-actualization needs the managers from America and England again report more fulfilment – though not very much more – than the four mid/southern continental countries, but less fulfilment than German or Scandinavian managers. The pattern of satisfactions for the two English-speaking countries might be summarized best by noting that the satisfactions decrease exactly in the order in which the five needs are theorized to decrease in priority or prepotency. That is, the managers from these countries report the greatest satisfaction for the most prepotent need of security, less satisfaction for esteem and autonomy, and finally the least satisfaction for the least prepotent need, self-actualization.

Japan presents a picture of the 'inscrutable East', as far as its pattern of satisfactions is concerned. Quite unlike that of any other country, the Japanese pattern shows an equal degree of satisfaction among the five types of needs. Japanese managers feel just as satisfied (or dissatisfied) about self-actualization needs as they do about esteem, security, or any other types of needs. This uniformity of response from one type of need to another was not approached in any other country, is therefore a truly unique response pattern, and is the reason that Japan has been grouped in a category of countries by itself. In terms of amount of satisfaction indicated by the Japanese managers compared to the amount shown by managers from other countries, the Japanese are considerably more satisfied than any other group of countries on needs for self-actualization. On needs for autonomy they are about equal with the Scandinavian countries in having the most satisfaction. For esteem, social, and security needs, Japan is about average in expressed satisfaction. Overall, then, Japanese managers report generally high need fulfilment.

The findings with regard to the patterns of satisfactions among different groups of countries are relatively easy to describe. However, when one moves from description to interpretation, the task becomes more difficult. For example, there is the very clear-cut finding that managers in the northern European countries, especially the Scandinavian countries, are more satisfied than those in the southern European countries, especially Spain and Italy. (There is, in fact, almost a perfect correlation between the overall degree of satisfaction and the median latitude of European countries.) Does this mean that geography or climate somehow influences how much satisfaction managers think they are deriving from the jobs? Can latitude determine attitude? This seems unlikely. Degree of industrialization is somewhat correlated with the north–south geographical axis in Europe, yet it would be difficult to say that this variable is necessarily highly correlated with the satisfaction findings. The lowest group in satisfaction includes, for instance, France and Belgium, highly industrialized, and Spain and Italy. The high group includes the three Scandinavian countries, very different from one another in degree of industrialization.

The answer seems to lie more in social-cultural factors, especially in terms of the role of the manager in occupational status hierarchies and the role of business in the day-to-day affairs of each country. Business organizations are probably more highly respected institutions in the Scandinavian countries and England, and managers who reach middle or top management levels can derive greater feelings of security, social, and esteem satisfactions. Explanations of greater satisfactions in the areas of autonomy and self-actualization, though, do not fit even this theory very well. Perhaps the reason these two needs are so much better satisfied in the northern Teutonic countries lies in the way in which business firms are organized. Middle and top managers in these countries may be given more freedom and more authority to make decisions unhampered by other parts of their organizations or by governmental regulations. This greater autonomy could in turn lead to increased opportunities for self-development and self-fulfilment, that is, to increased self-actualization satisfaction.

One interesting aspect of the findings on satisfaction was the fact that the theoretical classification of the five types of needs according to their priority or prepotency exactly fit the pattern of results for the United States and England, but not for any other group of countries.

It has often been suggested that basic needs – such as for security – are a necessary first step to others. As they are satisfied, and as the assurance grows that they will continue to be satisfied, the others become possible. An hierarchical necessity has been imputed to this ordering of needs. In these data, it appears only in the Anglo-American countries. This suggests, perhaps, that the theoretical formulation is especially relevant to the cultural conditions existing in these two English-speaking countries. It also may suggest that industrial and business firms in these two countries have succeeded in satisfying basic needs first and are currently in a position where employees, at least managerial employees, are directing their efforts increasingly to each higher step on the scale of need prepotency. In other countries than these two, past conditions in business organizations may not have led to such a systematic, step-by-step fulfilment of needs from the most basic to the least basic. In essence, then, this part of the findings for need satisfaction indicates either that the theory of prepotency of needs is particularly well adapted to organizational behaviour in the U.S. and England, or that industrial firms in these countries have created conditions that fit the theory.

It is important to relate the findings for perceived satisfaction of needs to the results reported earlier in this section concerning managers' perceptions of the importance of needs. Needs which which are considered most important by managers, regardless of country, tend to be those needs which are least satisfied in virtually all of the countries studied. This finding should suggest that it is particularly necessary for those who have ultimate responsibility for running a firm to pay special attention to incentives in these areas if they are concerned with managerial motivations. In the event of marked deficits in need satisfaction of the kind reported here, incentives probably must be geared to the deficiencies that are experienced. Where the sense of lack of satisfaction is more uniform, policy regarding incentives would presumably be based on the reported importance of various needs.

There is a fairly uniform agreement from country to country about which needs are regarded as most important and which are least important. But, when the question turns to 'how well satisfied are these various needs?', the findings differ considerably from country to country.

The discrepancy between importance and satisfaction of needs raises a crucial question. These data indicate remarkable similarity in estimates of importance and wide variations in degree of satisfaction. This fact seems to go immediately to the question of whether managerial motives of the kind we have been discussing are general characteristics of people or products of the situation.

The homogeneity of importance across a variety of cultures suggest strongly that the needs arise from the nature of people. Their satisfaction varies with situations. There is little evidence here to suggest that the basic motivational equipment with which the manager approaches his job varies from country to country. What does vary is what he finds there.

Summary

This is a preliminary report of data. More exhaustive analysis will appear later. Meanwhile, some general findings emerge:

1. One cannot help but be struck by the consistent groupings of countries through all three parts of the study. Not only is the grouping consistent, but it tends to follow ethnic lines rather than level of industrialization.
2. The pattern of uniformity and diversity in the data is also striking. It seems possible to identify variables which are enduring and relatively culture-free characteristics of people, and other variables which are more situationally determined. This is outstanding in the uniformity of importance of needs and the great difference in their satisfaction. It also appears in the uniform swings on attitudes towards leadership while preserving national differences and in the similar grouping on the semantic differential.
3. Managers in all the countries studied could profitably examine these data. They might ask themselves if this is the way they see it, if this is the way they want it, and what the differences may mean to their countries' economies.

Reference

HARBISON, F., and MYERS, C. (1960), *Management in the Industrial World*, McGraw-Hill Book Co., Inc., New York.

13 Frank A. Heller, Lyman W. Porter

Two Research Projects on American and British Managers

This reading contains descriptions of two pieces of research on managerial skills and perceptions using American and British samples. The first was carried out in the early 1960s, the second almost a decade later. The first is described fairly fully in a previously published article (Heller and Porter, 1966), the second is presented here chiefly to show a noticeable shift in research theory and field methodology. This shift has led to a more mature understanding of the value of the comparative method (Heller and Wilpert, in press).

The first research project was designed in 1959; at that time very little cross-national managerial comparisons had been published and it seemed reasonable to use validated research questionnaires which were relatively easily administered so that some tentative assumptions about U.S.–U.K. differences could be tested. The samples were chosen from the point of view of easy access rather than for their representativeness. Middle-level executives who attended management courses of a roughly similar kind in America and England constituted the samples.[1]

The second research study started in the United States in 1968 and continued in Britain up to 1974[2]. The U.S.–U.K. findings are not yet fully analysed, although the American results are published (Heller, 1971). This more recent U.S.–U.K. comparison was extended to six other countries and completed during 1975[3].

1. A similar approach was taken a little later with a very much more ambitious cross-national comparison covering fourteen countries and 3,600 managers (Haire, Ghiselli and Porter, 1966). That study used several research instruments including Porter's motivation questionnaire which was used in the Heller – Porter study reproduced here.

2. The British research was supported by two grants from the Social Science Research Council, the American research by grants from the University of California, Berkeley.

3. The participating countries were Germany, Holland, France, Spain, Sweden and Israel.

(a) Frank A. Heller and Lyman W. Porter*

Perceptions of Managerial Needs and Skills in Two National Samples

Excerpt from *Occupational Psychology*, no. 40, 1966, pp. 1–13.

Introduction

Some observers have suggested that a common language tends to minimize differences between British and American managers in their attitudes towards business. Others have held that the considerable cultural variations result in large differences in such attitudes. What are the facts? Most of modern management education has been developed in the United States and exported to the rest of the world, including Britain. An overwhelming proportion of the total literature was produced in America and a considerable amount of it is used with British managerial audiences and postgraduate students. Is this wise in view of alleged differences? Many leading American businesses have established themselves in Britain; some have transplanted American practices and policies while others have allowed the British subsidiaries to develop their own 'local' colour.

One of the objectives of our study was to measure the differences and similarities of attitudes concerning needs and skills of practising managers from these two leading industrial countries. Other objectives were concerned with finding and perfecting useful instruments for measuring incentives, satisfactions and skill requirements in a managerial setting.

A legitimate preoccupation of social scientists working in industry has been with attempts to find measurements of personality and skills which can ultimately be related to business efficiency. Because cognitive skills are relatively easily measured,

* Mr Heller is Senior Expert in Management Development and Productivity, International Labour Office; and Dr Porter is Professor of Psychology, University of California, Berkeley, U.S.A.

the bulk of the work hitherto has been on tests of intelligence and similar capacities and abilities. Moreover, because of an understandable reluctance of senior personnel to submit themselves to psychological investigations and because of a mistaken notion that industrial efficiency is more or less the same as worker or foreman efficiency, there has in the past been an undue concentration on skill requirements at the lower ends of the industrial hierarchy. During the last ten years, however, we have seen a shift of emphasis. Today, social scientists are beginning to look at the work of the senior executives, at the structure of the organization within which they carry out their responsibilities, and at the motivational variables in the work situation.

The parameters which influence business efficiency are extremely difficult to analyse and it is probably for this reason that correlations between any one independent variable and the criterion of efficiency or success have rarely been high. Even if one restricts oneself to social and psychological influences in the total picture, it would be reasonable to consider at least the following five factors: 1. The structure of the organization; 2. The objective role of the individual, that is to say, the work description; 3. The perceived role, that is to say the position as seen from the point of view of the person occupying it; 4. Motivational dynamics – goals and satisfactions; 5. Skills, inherited and acquired, including intelligence and manual and personality skills.

The present research concentrated on middle management levels and covers a number of variables in areas 3, 4 and 5. While it is aimed at obtaining information relevant to these variables, the measuring instruments described here can be used, and have been used, as teaching material. In fact, one of the scales was first devised with the specific intention of obtaining the attitudes of participants in middle and senior management programmes in order to feed back their own group results preparatory to an analysis of the subject of incentives. The other scales have also been tried out as teaching methods; the added ego-involvement and insight produced have been noticeable and offer a range of new possibilities of combining research with participatory teaching techniques.

Measuring instruments and the sample

With one exception, where the English group is 48, the American and English groups consist of 74 to 82 managers each depending on the measuring instruments used. They were middle to senior managers in the 30–45 year age group and came from a considerable range of industry, mainly in middle to large-size firms. It is not claimed that the samples are representative of middle to senior management in the two countries. The businesses whose managers are represented here tend to be among the more progressive and efficient firms in their industry. The majority of the participants were selected to attend the courses during which the research took place because they were felt to possess capacities which would make it likely that they would be further promoted in their respective companies. These biases are equally present in the American and English samples and, far from presenting a statistical embarrassment, contribute to the comparability of the groups and to the interest of the findings.

All the work was carried out by means of five questionnaires which had been developed separately by the two authors. In bringing them together for the purpose of this research it was felt that they would usefully supplement each other and allow for a small amount of overlap which would constitute an internal check on some of the measuring scales. Two of the questionnaires are concerned with the managers' perceptions of their own needs and one of them with their perceptions of the needs of their immediate subordinates. The fourth scale asked the subjects to put into rank-order a number of personality characteristics in terms of their 'importance for success' and the final scale asked them to rank the importance of sixteen managerial skills.

The whole research was carried out during management courses in a selected number of educational institutions. One of the advantages of research done with practising managers attending courses under the control of the investigator is that there are opportunities for questions which help to clarify problems the subjects may have in relation to the measuring instruments. This circumstance helps to produce more meaningful answers.

The results

Need satisfactions. The questionnaire used to obtain the data on need satisfactions was based on the theoretical classification of needs developed by Maslow (1954). Maslow has ordered various needs and motives on the basis of their priority or prepotency. We adopted his systems and developed 13 questionnaire items relevant to five types of needs and two additional items that were not specific to a given need in Maslow's set of categories. Although these 15 items were presented randomly in the questionnaire, they are grouped in Table 1 according to their theoretical order of prepotency.

Example 1 shows a typical item as it appeared in the questionnaire:

Example 1

Questionnaire Item on Need Dissatisfactions

The *opportunity for independent thought and action* in my management position

(a)	How much is there now?									
	(min.)	1	2	3	4	5	6	7	(max.)
(b)	How much should there be?									
	(min.)	1	2	3	4	5	6	7	(max.)
(c)	How important is this to me?									
	(min.)	1	2	3	4	5	6	7	(max.)

For each item the respondent was asked to answer the three questions by circling a number from 1 to 7 'where low numbers represent low or minimum amounts and high numbers represent high or maximum amounts'. Satisfaction was measured by the difference in answers between Part (a) ('How much is there now?') and Part (b) ('How much should there be?') for each item. The larger the difference – (a) subtracted from (b) – the greater the dissatisfaction.

The results (see Table 1) indicate that, on the whole, the English sample is slightly more satisfied with the exception of the two social needs, i.e. 'Opportunity to give help to other people' and 'Opportunity to develop close friendships', where the American group showed higher satisfaction.

Table 1 **Differences between the two samples in percentage of subjects indicating need dissatisfactions**

Questionnaire Items[1]	*% U.S. Sample (N = 80)*	*% English Sample (N = 82)*	*% Difference*
SECURITY NEEDS			
1 The feeling of security in my management position	33·8	26·8	7·0
SOCIAL NEEDS			
2 The opportunity . . . to give help to other people	23·8	30·5	− 6·7
3 The opportunity . . . to develop close friendships	15·0	25·6	−10·6
Average for Category	19·4	28·0	− 8·6
ESTEEM NEEDS			
4 The feeling of self esteem	53·8	35·4	18·4
5 The prestige of my management position inside the company	45·0	45·1	− 0·1
6 The prestige . . . outside the company	38·8	30·5	8·3
Average for Category	45·9	37·0	8·9
AUTONOMY NEEDS			
7 The authority connected with my management position	48·8	43·9	4·9
8 The opportunity for independent thought and action . . .	51·2	41·5	9·7
9 The opportunity . . . for the participation in setting goals	55·0	37·8	17·2
10 The opportunity . . . for participation in determination of methods and procedures	42·5	36·6	5·9
Average for Category	49·4	40·0	9·4
SELF-REALIZATION NEEDS			
11 The opportunity for personal growth and development . . .	56·2	40·2	16·0
12 The feeling of self-fulfilment . . .	60·0	59·8	0·2
13 The feeling of worth-while accomplishment . . .	61·2	61·0	0·2
Average for Category	59·1	53·7	5·4
NON-SPECIFIC ITEMS[2]			
14 The pay for my management position	71·2	67·1	4·1
15 The feeling of being in-the-know in my management position	60·0	47·6	12·4

(*Note:* High percentage indicates more *dis*satisfaction – Low percentage indicates more satisfaction.] For items 4, 9, and 11 the differences are significant at the ·05 level: for item 3 the difference is significant at the ·10 level.

1. Every question employed the phrase 'in my management position'. Dots are used to indicate this.
2. Non-specific to the Maslow-type categories.

Table 2 **Difference between the two samples in percentage of subjects indicating maximum importance of needs**

Questionnaire Items[3]	*% U.S. Sample (N = 80)*	*% English Sample (N = 82)*	*% Difference*
SECURITY NEEDS			
1 The feeling of security in my management position	30·0	23·2	6·8
SOCIAL NEEDS			
2 The opportunity ... to give help to other people	33·8	40·2	– 6·4
3 The opportunity ... to develop close friendships	13·8	6·1	7·7
Average for Category	23·8	23·2	0·6
ESTEEM NEEDS			
4 The feeling of self esteem	18·8	14·6	4·2
5 The prestige of my management position inside the company	20·0	17·1	2·9
Average for Category	17·9	14·6	3·3
AUTONOMY NEEDS			
7 The authority connected with my management position	20·0	30·5	–10·5
8 The opportunity for independent thought and action ...	36·2	39·0	– 2·8
9 The opportunity ... for the participation in setting goals	23·8	37·8	–14·0
10 The opportunity ... for participation in determination of methods and procedures	27·5	30·5	– 3·0
Average for Category	26·9	34·4	– 7·5
SELF-REALIZATION NEEDS			
11 The opportunity for personal growth and development ...	53·8	53·7	0·1
12 The feeling of self-fulfilment ...	43·8	48·8	– 5·0
13 The feeling of worth-while accomplishment ...	55·0	51·2	3·8
Average for Category	50·9	51·2	0.3
NON-SPECIFIC ITEMS			
14 The pay for my management position	22·5	25·6	– 3·1
15 The feeling of being in-the-know in my management position	41·2	28·0	13·2

(*Note:* High percentage indicates more importance – Low percentage indicates less importance.) For items 9 and 15 the differences are significant at the ·10 level.

3. Every question employed the phrase 'in my management position'. Dots are used to indicate this.

The largest differences between the two national samples are concerned with: 'Opportunity to develop close friendships' (with the Americans more satisfied), 'The feeling of self-esteem' (with the English more satisfied), 'Opportunity for participation in the setting of goals' (English more satisfied) and 'Opportunity for personal growth and development' (English more satisfied).

Nevertheless, in the overall picture, similarities between the two national groups are much more noticeable than differences.

Among the five need categories, 'Self-Realization Needs' produced the greatest dissatisfaction for both the American and English samples. Both the American and English groups were most satisfied in the Social and Security Need areas. There are three specific items in relation to which both samples are almost completely in agreement: 'Prestige', 'Self-fulfilment' and 'Feeling of worth-while accomplishment'.

Importance of different needs. Using the same group of 15 need items, all subjects were also asked how important each type of need is to them (see Item (c), Example 1). As will be seen from Table 2, the American and English attitudes are here even more similar than in relation to Table 1.

There are, of course, some differences, most notably in relation to 'Opportunity for participation in setting goals' (which the English thought more important) and 'The feeling of being in-the-know' (which the Americans considered more important).

On a less significant level, the American sample valued more highly 'Security Needs' and the social need of 'Opportunity to develop friendships', while the British sample gave more weight to 'Authority' and the feeling of 'Self-fulfilment'.

In both groups, 'Self-Realization Needs' were thought to be most important and the 'Esteem Needs' least important.

Attitudes to 'Pay' were somewhat ambivalent and this will be brought out again later in relation to Table 3 and the measurement of Incentives. In Table 1 the attitude to 'Pay' showed a high degree of dissatisfaction in both national samples, but from Table 2 it appears that neither group really thought that 'Pay' constituted a need of very great importance.

Incentive preferences of managers. A measurement of the importance of eight incentive preferences for this group of managers, was obtained by using the paired comparison method. The questions were worded as in Example 2.

Example 2

Extract from Questionnaire on Incentive Preferences of Managers

Instructions:

1 In this Questionnaire you are asked to compare *your* preferences for various incentives.
2 Use the enclosed definitions for each incentive.
3 For each question, indicate which of the two incentives you would 'like to have more of' by circling the appropriate word to the right of each question.

Questions:

1 Do you attach greater importance to having more pleasant work companions or to having a more efficient organization?	COMPANIONS EFFICIENCY
2 Would you prefer greater security or more pleasant work companions?	SECURITY COMPANIONS

Etc.

On a similar questionnaire it had been found that people's choices of incentives differ with intelligence scores and occupational preferences[4] as well as with age and levels of responsibility.[5]

However, in the case of the two national samples which are the subject of the present research, there is a considerable similarity of view (see Table 3).

'Prospects of promotion', 'Efficiency' and 'Pay' are the three top-ranking managerial incentives. On the other hand, 'Hours of work' comes last and 'Pleasant working companions' sixth out of eight incentives in both American and English samples. 'Power' as a motivating force in work comes about halfway (fourth out of eight ranks) in both. The correlation between the two national groups is high (Rho = ·88).

The inquiry into managerial needs (see Tables 1 and 2) used a

4. Wilkins (1949).
5. Heller (1956).

different method from that on incentives, but both include 'Pay', 'Security' and 'Prestige'. Although comparison is made difficult by the different nature of the two instruments, it will be seen that the overall weighting of these three factors is not dissimilar.

Estimates of incentive preferences of subordinates. In a second stage of the research on incentives each of the subjects was asked to estimate the preferences of his own immediate subordinate by means of the same scale, but on a separate questionnaire (see Example 3).

Example 3

Extract from Questionnaire on Incentive Preferences of Subordinates

Instructions:

1 In this Questionnaire you are asked to ESTIMATE your *immediate subordinate's* preference for various incentives.

2 For each question, indicate which of the two incentives *your subordinate* would 'like to have more of' by circling the appropriate word to the right of each question.

Questions:

Do you think that the subordinate you have named attaches more importance to:

1	Pleasant work COMPANIONS or a more EFFICIENT organization	COMPANIONS EFFICIENCY
2	Greater SECURITY or more pleasant work COMPANIONS	SECURITY COMPANIONS

Etc.

The results are shown in Table 3.

The correlations between 'Self' and 'Subordinate' are lower than the correlations between the two 'Self' groups; in the case of the American sample, considerably lower (Rho = ·52). Nevertheless, there is a certain similarity of both the English and American managers' estimates of their subordinates' needs, particularly so in the case of their first and second choices. Both English and American managers think that their subordinates' first choice would be 'Pay' (although they themselves have put this incentive in second and third place). Furthermore, they feel that their

Table 3 Differences between incentive preference rankings for self and subordinate

	AMERICAN				ENGLISH*			
	Self Preferences (N=74)		*Subordinate Preferences (N=74)*		*Self Preferences (N=48)*		*Subordinate Preferences (N=48)*	
Incentives	*mean rank*	*ranks*	*mean rank*	*ranks*	*mean rank*	*ranks*	*mean rank*	*ranks*
Prospects	1·89	1	3·33	2	2·03	1	2·78	2
Pay	3·46	3	2·11	1	2·98	2	2·77	1
Security	5·05	5	3·74	3	6·05	7	4·61	5
Prestige	5·81	7	5·17	6	5·40	5	4·10	3
Efficiency	2·52	2	5·10	4	3·17	3	4·64	6
Companions	5·79	6	5·73	7	5·75	6	6·30	7
Hours	6·72	8	5·08	5	6·74	8	6·32	8
Power	4·76	4	5·81	8	3·83	4	4·23	4

Rank-Order Correlation Coefficients (*Rho*):
Between American Self and American Subordinate=·52
Between English Self and English Subordinate=·76
Between American Self and English Self=·88
Between American Subordinate and English Subordinate=·50

* The number of subjects is reduced to 48 in this part of the research as the result of the loss of some original data.

subordinate's second preference would be 'Prospects of Promotion' (although they themselves put it first).

From Table 3 it can be seen that when one compares the 'Self' choices with estimates of 'Subordinate' choices, then one group of incentives is reserved for 'Self' and another for 'Subordinate':

'Self'	*'Subordinate'*
Prospects	Pay
Efficiency	Security
Power	Prestige
	Hours of Work

The Respondents give a more favourable and 'leader-like' picture of themselves compared to their subordinates. 'Prospects', 'Efficiency' and 'Power' are more dynamic choices and are more intrinsic to the job itself, than: 'Pay', 'Security', 'Prestige' and 'Hours of Work'.

There is some evidence to indicate that these 'lower level' estimates for subordinates may be accurate[6,7]. This raises a number of interesting questions about the relationship of needs and incentives to the level of the hierarchy occupied by the Respondents and whether these incentives change with promotion and are therefore anchored in the position itself, or whether they are variables of the personality.

Example 4

Extracts from Questionnaire on Thirteen Personality Traits

Instructions:

The purpose of this inquiry is to obtain a picture of the qualities you believe would best qualify a person for YOUR PRESENT MANAGEMENT POSITION. There are no right or wrong answers.

In each pair of words check the *one* you think is relatively more important for success in your present management position. Although specific words will be repeated, no pair of words will be duplicated. Make each choice a separate and independent judgement, and DO NOT OMIT ANY PAIR.

1
_____ intelligent
_____ sociable

2
_____ flexible
_____ self-controlled

3
_____ energetic
_____ intelligent

4
_____ cooperative
_____ dominant

Etc.

---

6. In the original research design, it was hoped to include the subordinates' own ranking of the same eight incentives. It was found impossible to obtain these results for the whole sample, but in the case of the English group, 26 comparisons are available. These results suggest that the subordinates do in fact put 'Pay' and 'Security' higher than their bosses.

7. The same measuring instrument was used on a group of 500 lower middle English managers whose level of seniority corresponds fairly closely to the subordinates in the present research. While 'Prospects of Promotion' still came first, 'Pay' and 'Security' invariably came second and third. Heller, op. cit.

At the present time, the issue of whether structural or personality variables are more important in affecting such perceptions is unresolved. Considerable future research on this point will be required.

The importance of personality traits in relation to job success. Example 4 shows extracts from a questionnaire listing thirteen personality traits, whose priority was measured by the paired comparison method. The objective was to discover which of the traits was thought to be most important for success in the Respondent's own managerial job.

The rank-order correlation (see Table 4) between the English and American group was very high (Rho = ·87). The two samples agreed that the three most important traits were: 'Intelligent', 'Cooperative' and 'Flexible', in that order. The last two personality characteristics seem to argue for a good 'Human Relations' approach, possibly untainted by 'Sociability' since that item came rather low on the priority scale in both national groups.

Table 4 **Differences between rankings by American and English samples for personality traits in terms of their 'importance for success' in subject's management position**

Traits	*Rank* *U.S.*	*U.K.*	*Mean Rank* *U.S.*	*U.K.*
Intelligent	1	1	1·70	2·30
Cooperative	2	2	2·53	3·77
Flexible	3	3	4·41	3·87
Energetic	4	5·5	4·53	4·53
Persevering	5	5·5	4·96	4·53
Original	7	4	5·95	4·49
Self-Controlled	6	7	5·23	4·69
Aggressive	8	13	6·09	10·02
Poised	9	9	6·47	6·99
Sociable	10	8	7·43	6·55
Independent	11	10	9·17	7·95
Conforming	12	12	9·26	9·17
Dominant	13	11	10·26	9·13
Rank-order correlation (Rho)=·87				

The trait producing the largest mean rank difference between the two samples was 'Aggressive'. The Americans considered this as of eighth or medium importance out of thirteen traits, whereas the English considered it of the thirteenth or lowest importance. The trait 'Cooperative' receives more stress (as measured by mean rank values) in the American and 'Independent' more in the English sample.

Example 5

Extract from Questionnaire of Perceptions of Skill Requirements

Instructions:

Thinking of Management in a general sense, in which order of priority would you think the following functions, skills and qualities, to be important?

Please rank from 1–16.

1 Ability to make rapid decisions .. ..

2 Readiness to accept new ideas .. ..

3 Good Mixer .. ..

Etc.

Perception of skill requirements

Example 5 gives extracts from the questionnaire into perceptions of requirements for managerial skills, functions and qualities carried out by a straightforward ranking of sixteen factors.

From Table 5 it will be seen that the two national groups have virtually identical views on the importance of these factors (Rho = ·96).

The highest ranking qualities are 'Ability to understand people', 'Readiness to accept New Ideas' and 'High Intelligence'. It is interesting to compare these findings with the results of Table 4 which summarizes the results of the inquiry on the same subjects who had decided on the relative importance of thirteen personality traits by a paired comparison ranking method. In the two lists, four qualities can be seen to be related to each other:

Table 4	*Table* 5
Intelligence	High Intelligence
Cooperative	Ability to understand people
Flexible	Readiness to accept new ideas
Sociable	Good Mixer

Table 5 Ranking of functions, skills and qualities in terms of their importance to management

Management Skills	AMERICAN (*N=73*) *Mean Rank*	*Ranks*	ENGLISH (*N=84*) *Mean Rank*	*Ranks*
1 Ability to make rapid decisions	5·21	4	5·20	4
2 Readiness to accept new ideas	5·00	3	3·53	1
3 Good mixer	11·66	13	12·21	14
4 To be available for discussions with workers	9·00	9	10·01	10
5 To observe factory regulations strictly	11·70	14	13·88	16
6 High intelligence	4·18	2	4·91	3
7 Verbal ability (to speak fluently to staff at all levels)	6·52	5	6·35	5
8 Technical ability (i.e. to follow in every detail and assess technical reports)	9·29	10	8·15	9
9 Willingness to admit own mistakes	8·53	8	7·94	8
10 Ability to understand people	3·15	1	3·63	2
11 Not to lose respect through familiarity	11·60	12	11·76	13
12 Willingness to ask other people for their opinion	6·70	6	6·86	7
13 Smart appearance	12·60	15	11·65	12
14 Willingness to pass on information to others	7·75	7	6·38	6
15 Sense of humour	10·58	11	10·10	11
16 Ability to perform operations done by employees	13·36	16	13·57	15

Coefficient of correlation (Rho)=·96.

While 'Ability to understand people' is by no means the same as 'Cooperative', it is probably a pre-condition for being cooperative. Similarly, the personality trait 'Flexibility' is probably a condition of being 'Ready to accept new ideas'. It is therefore a useful check on the reliability of these two measuring instruments to see that these qualities occupy top positions in both tables. The fourth quality which is common to both lists is: 'Sociable' and 'Good Mixer' and these are ranked very low in both inquiries.

Returning to Table 5 it will be seen that, apart from 'Good Mixer', there are two other factors which receive very low priority in both the American and English groups: one is 'Observe factory regulations' and the other is 'Ability to perform operations done by employees' which receives the lowest rank in the American group and is next to the lowest in the English list. This is interesting in view of the frequent speeches of certain senior managers showing pride in having 'come up the hard way' and being still able to turn their hand to any operation carried out in their own factories.

In general, it seems that the higher ranked skills are those dealing with people at work, while the lower ones are concerned with the functional and technical demands of the job. Even 'Technical Ability' is in both groups ranked substantially below 'Verbal ability' (to speak fluently to staff at all levels).

Summary and conclusions

The main conclusion to be derived from this research on 146–64 managers, half of them English and half American, is that their response to five questionnaires administered while they were attending management courses was surprisingly similar.

There was some small difference between the English and American groups in their evaluation of work satisfactions which were now available to them, with the American group feeling slightly less satisfied. Both groups indicated relatively high satisfaction in the 'Social' and 'Security' needs areas. There was considerable agreement on the importance of these satisfactions in absolute terms with Self-realization needs very much in the lead. The American – English agreement on incentives was also high, with 'Prospects of Promotion', 'Efficiency' and 'Pay' receiving top scores.

The managers, ranking of what they believed to be the incentives of their subordinates showed (as one would expect) less consistency and agreement, but in both national samples a picture emerges of the subordinate being thought of as a man with less dynamism and less unselfish dedication to work than his superior.

This considerable similarity in attitudes and judgements of a sample of English and American managers will require further careful analysis.[8]

Although both groups attended courses on management, these similarities cannot be attributed to any effect of 'teaching' since the course subjects were different and a major part of the inquiry was carried out very early in the courses. Nor can it be said, with any measure of conviction, that the similarities in response are due to the subjects giving the kind of answers which they felt that the researchers wanted to get. Most of the results are not at all obvious in the sense that they fit in with stereotyped expectations. On the contrary, some answers go against what can be called the popular view. It is often assumed for instance that a successful manager should be 'sociable', should be able to 'mix well' with different groups and have a 'sense of humour', though he must not 'lose respect by excessive familiarity'. Many people would add that he should be 'capable of doing the jobs which he expects his subordinates to perform'. Such a manager would be a 'pleasant working companion' and would thereby be able to obtain good group results.

However, in the present research, every one of the qualities mentioned in the previous paragraph obtained very low priorities by both the British and the American sample (see Tables 3 and 5).

Both groups in this research are middle managers who come, on the whole, from progressive firms, but they are separated geographically by 8,000 miles and noticeably different socio-economic circumstances (the American group coming mainly from the western parts of the U.S.A. centring on California). One group is the inheritor of an industrial tradition that goes back to the eighteenth century and achieved 'maturity' in terms of Rostow's analysis of the stages of growth[9] in the 1850s while the other group

8. For further evidence see Haire, Ghiselli and Porter (1963).
9. Rostow (1960).

draws on experiences that started more than a hundred years later and whose 'maturity' was delayed until the end of the First World War. Nor can there be much doubt that the pattern of life, consumption habits and business practices of the two managerial groups are very different.[10] One group comes from an area in which industrial development has been rapid and spectacular during the last thirty years (California), while the other operates in a much more sedate economic climate.

In these circumstances, the similarity of expressed attitudes is particularly noteworthy.

References

GORER, G. (1948), *The Americans*, Cresset Press.

GRANICK, D. (1960), *The Red Executive*, Macmillan.

GRANICK, D. (1962), *The European Executive*, Weidenfeld & Nicolson.

HAIRE, M., GHISELLI, E., and PORTER, L. (1963), 'An international study of management attitudes and democratic leadership', *CIOS/XIII: International Management Congress*, 16–20 September, Council for International Progress in Management Inc., New York, pp. 101–4.

HARBISON, F., and MYERS, C. (1959), *Management in the Industrial World*, McGraw-Hill Inc., New York.

HELLER, F. A. (1956), *Motivation and Incentives*, European Productivity Agency Project Paper, no. 289.

MASLOW, A. H. (1954), *Motivation and Personality*, Harper and Bros., New York.

ROSTOW, W. W. (1960), *The Stages of Economic Growth*, Cambridge University Press.

WILKINS, L. (1949), *Occupational Psychology*, October.

10. Most sociological comparisons of the two countries have so far been on an intuitive or descriptive rather than analytical basis. See for instance:
Gorer (1948).
Granick (1960).
Granick (1962).
Harbison and Myers (1959).

(b) Frank A. Heller

Comparing American and British Managerial Attitudes to Skills and Leadership[1]

A working paper, *Tavistock Institute of Human Relations.*

Introduction

The present research has benefited from experience gained in two previous multinational projects.[2] It seemed advisable, however, to make a number of changes. In the first place, the new project adopted a contingency theory which means that findings are expected to vary according to the contingencies of different situations. By contrast, a universalistic theory would expect all managers, or all managers from a given country, to show roughly similar characteristics.

Different habits of thought or role behaviour in America and Britain would form part of a contingency theory, but most other expected differences have no relation to the nationality of the sample. For instance, the experience of managers, their perceptions of what goes on at work, their role expectations and the organization structures within which they work are all put forward as contingencies. These different situations cut across psychological, sociological and technical variables and constitute an open systems approach.[3]

The research is designed to test the relative impact on leadership

1. This article is based on a paper presented to the British Psychological Society's Social Psychology Section Conference in September 1971. The British part of the research has been supported by the Social Science Research Council since 1969.

2. In addition to the Heller–Porter (1966) research, Heller also carried out the South American part of the Haire, Ghiselli and Porter international study in 1966.

3. For a full statement of the variables which are part of the open system theory in this research, see Heller, 1976.

of a variety of situations and environmental conditions. The main research question is as follows: which of the measured variables (and in what combination) account for the largest part of the variance in styles of leadership? (Heller and Yukl, 1969, Heller, 1971 and 1976b). The difference between an open systems contingency theory and the simpler previous research is that the former acts as a check on facile cultural theories. A great deal of cross-cultural research has been correctly criticized (Roberts, 1970) for taking tests or other measurements on samples of managers in two or more countries and concluding that any differences between the samples are due to culture.

The second major difference between the first and the current research project is in the method of data collection. The first project used standardized questionnaires administered by an experienced researcher to groups of people, who filled in the answers in his presence. This method ensured greater motivation and control over the response conditions of the research than is possible by the more frequently used distributed questionnaire method. Nevertheless, the questionnaire method alone has severe limitations which became particularly obvious with complex and controversial subjects like motivation and participation. Multinational research is particularly difficult to carry out with questionnaires alone since subtle cultural interpretations of questions are easily missed. The results have to be explained by researchers who cannot be thoroughly familiar with the background and situations that gave rise to these objections.

To meet many of these objections a new method was developed called Group Feed-back Analysis.

Group feed-back analysis

The research method consists of three stages. The first stage uses standard and validated questionnaires in a single session of one hour, administering them to all the senior managers in a given company, who assemble round a table. An experienced researcher is present to introduce and explain the work and to respond to questions. Standardized tape-recorded instructions are used to reinforce the written words at the beginning of each form. This first session takes place before lunch.

The lunch interval is used by the researcher and an assistant to calculate simple frequency distributions and averages from the three main questionnaires. These results are photocopied. This constitutes the second stage.

During the third stage the summarized results are fed back to the group that provided the answers. The objective is to enlist the experience of the managers in interpreting their own results. The respondents usually supply information about the specific nature of their own job, the company's policy and structure, market conditions and so on which, in their judgements, explain the results. The point about the method is that these interpretations give the researcher a knowledge of relevant situational factors which is not usually available to him.

The feed-back discussion is tape-recorded and later content-analysed. The three stages of the procedure take up only two hours of the managers' time. The method is fairly new and claims to have a number of advantages over the more usual straight questionnaire or interview method (Heller, 1969).

The results of the American feed-back analysis have been reported elsewhere (Heller, 1971, pp. 91–9). An adaptation of Group Feed-back Analysis for cross cultural research is published in Heller (1973).

The samples

The American sample consisted of 260 managers in fifteen large companies which independent judges had classified as successful and 'progressive'. The British sample is made up of 300 managers at a similar level in fifteen companies that were carefully matched to the U.S. firms in size, industry and technology.

The assumptions

The reader may like to consult the references previously mentioned for a review of the literature leading to a number of hypotheses, and for a description of the research instruments. Here we will only state six hypotheses, three dealing with skills and three with leadership.

The research was carried out with two senior levels of management. Level 1 (abbreviated L.1) was one level below the Chief

Executive, and their immediate subordinates were taken as level 2 (L.2).

Hypotheses relating to skill requirements:

1. There will be substantial perceptual differences between two levels of management (L.1 and L.2) when they are asked to describe skill requirements for these two levels of jobs. L.1 managers will see larger differences in the skill required for the two jobs than will L.2 managers.
2. The size of the perceptual differences will vary with the nature of the skill and will be smallest when 'objective' assessment is possible.
3. The perceptual differences will be smaller among American than among British managers.

Hypotheses relating to leadership:

4. Leadership style will vary with the nature of the decision task.
5. Leadership style will vary according to job function.
6. American managers will use less centralized leadership styles than British managers.

Findings

Managers at L.1 and L.2 were asked to describe the skills required at these two levels of management. They were describing differences in the requirements of the jobs, not differences between the actual incumbents of these positions.

As will be seen from Table 1, twelve different abilities and skills were assessed by both levels. Taking the average for all questions, 20·9 per cent of the senior managers (L.1) judged that their level needed very much more skill, 46·4 per cent considered that they needed more skill and only 5·2 per cent thought that somewhat less skill might be required.

The same comparison between levels was made by the subordinate managers. If their judgements had been identical with L.1s, then 20·9 per cent would have said that their level needed much less skill than the higher level. In fact their answer was only 3·3 per cent on that question. Nearly 24 per cent of L.2 managers thought

Table 1 **Analysis of differences of skill assessment by two interlocking levels of management**

U.K. Results

Which job requires more of these skills; your own or the other level?

Answer in %

	As senior level sees it 'I need . . .'					*As subordinate sees it 'I need . . .'*				
	Very much more	*More*	*About the same*	*Somewhat less*	*Much less*	*Very much more*	*More*	*About the same*	*Somewhat less*	*Much less*
1 Knowledge of technical matters	13·6	22·6	33·3	26·5	4·0	14·0	37·3	36·8	10·8	1·0
2 Closer contact with people	10·7	28·2	36·2	23·7	1·1	16·2	40·5	37·3	5·9	0
3 Knowledge of human nature	19·8	56·5	23·2	0·6	0	3·2	14·1	76·8	5·4	0·5
4 Imagination	30·5	58·2	10·2	0·6	0·6	3·2	24·3	59·5	12·4	0·5
5 Self-confidence	18·6	56·5	24·3	0·6	0	0·5	3·8	23·8	60·3	9·7
6 Responsibility	50·8	41·8	4·5	0·6	0	0·5	3·8	23·8	60·3	9·7
7 Decisiveness	22·0	62·1	15·8	0	0	1·6	24·9	53·5	17·8	2·2
8 Tact	11·3	40·1	45·8	2·3	0·6	5·9	41·1	43·8	0	9·2
9 Adaptability	26·5	45·8	24·8	2·8	0	4·3	38·4	41·1	15·1	1·1
10 Forcefulness	18·6	49·1	29·4	2·8	0	2·2	22·2	49·7	23·8	2·2
11 Intelligence	2·8	40·1	55·9	1·1	0	0·5	2·7	85·4	10·8	0·5
12 Initiative	25·4	55·4	18·1	1·1	0	4·3	34·0	49·2	11·9	2·2
Total for all questions	20·9	46·4	29·5	5·2	0·5	4·8	23·9	48·4	19·6	3·3

that they needed more skill, while L.1s' comparative judgements was only 5·2 per cent. However, the averages hide the interesting finding that the differences in judgements were relatively small for three job requirements: knowledge of technical matters, intelligence and responsibility, while for all the other job requirements the differences were very significant.[4] The same pattern applied to the American data.

A summary comparison of the U.K.–U.S. results can be seen in Table 2 which gives averages on a five point scale from 'very much more' to 'much less' skill required. The U.S.–U.K. results are not statistically different. However, the senior and subordinate American managers are almost exactly as far apart in their judgements as British managers.

These findings support hypotheses 1 and 2, but not 3.

The second main assumption applies the contingency theory to the controversial subject of leadership styles. Does a manager use more or less the same method of leadership in all situations?

In this research five alternative methods of leadership were measured.[5] They are described in Table 3. These definitions were used by both levels of management to assess how decisions are made between themselves and the other level. Twelve specific decision situations were used (see Table 4). For instance, both levels described how in their organization they handled subjects like taking on new staff; purchasing a piece of equipment worth £ or $; preparing a departmental budget, etc. Managers did not have to confine themselves to a description using only one style, because that would be unrealistic. They could say that in preparing a departmental budget, for instance, they used methods 2, 3 and 4. They might use method 2 10 per cent, method 3 80 per cent and method 4 10 per cent of the time.

4. The differences were measured by *t* test (see, for instance, Heller, 1971, p. 70).

5. What are here called methods or styles of leadership are probably more accurately described as interpersonal methods of decision-making between different levels of an organization.

Table 2 How senior and subordinate managers judge the skill requirements of their jobs

A U.S.–U.K. Comparison

	L.1		L.2	
	U.S.	*U.K.*	*U.S.*	*U.K.*
Mean	2·26	2·18	3·22	3·15
S.D.	0·37	0·35	0·90	0·37

Results: 1. By test analysis the differences between L.1 and L.2 are significant for both U.S. and U.K. samples.
2. The difference between American and British managers is not statistically significant for either level.

NOTE: The mean score relates to a five point scale. A low score on the L.1 scale means that this level considers it requires more of the skills. On the L.2 scale the scoring is reversed; therefore a high score means that the subordinate considers that he requires more of these skills. A score of three refers to a judgement of 'about the same' amount of skill for both levels.

Table 3 Five alternative leadership styles

Style 1: *Own decision without* detailed explanation
Decisions are made by managers without previous discussion or consultation with subordinates. No special meeting or memorandum is used to explain the decision.

Style 2: *Own decision with* detailed explanation
The same as above, but afterwards managers explain the problem and the reasons for their choice in a memo or in a special meeting.

Style 3: *Prior consultation* with subordinate
Before the decision is taken, the manager explains the problem to his subordinate and asks his advice and help. The manager then makes the decision by himself. His final choice may, or may not, reflect the subordinate's influence.

Style 4: *Joint decision-making* with subordinate
Managers and their subordinates together analyse the problem and come to a decision. The subordinates usually have as

much influence over the final choice as the managers. Where there are more than two in the discussion, the decision of the majority is accepted more often than not.

Style 5: *Delegation of decision* to subordinate
A manager asks his subordinate to make the decision regarding a particular subject. He may or may not request the subordinate to report his decisions to him. The manager seldom vetoes his subordinate's decisions.

If one assumes that the twelve decisions are different managerial tasks, then Table 4 shows how the sample of British managers tackle these tasks by means of the five alternative leadership styles. In handling salary increases, for instance, senior managers use styles 1 and 2 97·3 per cent of the time. By way of contrast, when it is a matter of hiring one of several people to work for their subordinates the same senior managers use styles 1 and 2 only 11·9 per cent of the time. The American managers react very similarly and change their leadership style quite sharply in response to different managerial tasks (Heller, 1971, p. 85).

Some managers work in functional areas like finance, production or marketing. Others have broader general responsibilities. When one compares how these groups make decisions, differences emerge. In the American sample, production and finance managers use a much more centralized leadership style than personnel managers or executives with wide general responsibilities[6] (see Table 5). British results also show significant differences between managerial functions.[7]

If one makes the assumption that the twelve distinct tasks (Table 4) make up a reasonable sample of managerial decision-making, then the scores can be added to produce an overall profile of the average leadership styles used by our samples. The results for the British and American sample are shown in Table 6.

British managers use the highly centralized style 1 a little more than American managers (11·7 per cent compared with 10·7

6. An analysis of variance by three clusters of job function was significant at the 5 per cent level.

7. However, the profile of the functions is different. British production and finance managers use much less centralized leadership styles than their American counterparts.

Table 4 **How two interlocking levels of senior U.K. management see the senior level make decisions in 12 distinct decision areas**

LEVEL 1

Decision Style	*Q1*	*Q2*	*Q3*	*Q4*	*Q5*	*Q6*	*Q7*	*Q8*	*Q9*	*Q10*	*Q11*	*Q12*
1	52·0	5·5	3·9	12·8	13·2	4·4	6·1	14·9	3·5	7·2	8·6	6·8
2	45·3	11·0	8·0	6·6	20·7	8·5	10·5	27·7	9·9	13·7	38·2	27·7
3	2·7	52·5	27·6	18·6	41·7	47·3	33·8	41·4	39·9	42·2	42·5	44·4
4	0·0	28·4	40·7	6·4	17·1	32·5	37·3	15·9	35·9	28·6	10·7	20·9
5	0·0	2·6	19·7	55·6	7·3	7·4	13·0	0·1	10·8	8·3	0·0	0·2

THE DECISION AREAS:

Q 1. To increase the salary of your direct subordinate.
Q 2. To increase the number of employees working for your subordinate.
Q 3. To hire one of several applicants to work for your subordinate.
Q 4. To change the extension number of your subordinate's telephone.
Q 5. To purchase for your department a necessary piece of equipment costing over $100 (or £...).
Q 6. To promote one of the employees working for your subordinate.
Q 7. To give a merit pay increase to one of your subordinate's employees.
Q 8. To increase the dollar allocation for your department during the preparation of the organizational budget.
Q 9. To fire one of your subordinate's employees.
Q10. To change an operating procedure followed by your subordinate.
Q11. To assign your subordinate to a different job (on same salary).
Q12. The decision regarding what targets or quotas should be set for your subordinate.

Table 5 Variations in leadership: six functions of management

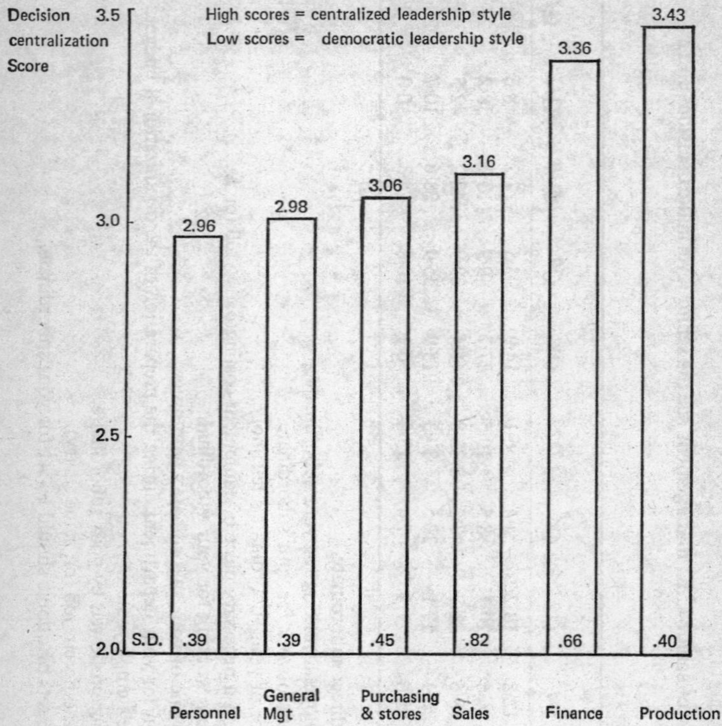

Table 6 Comparative analysis of leadership styles of senior managers (L.1) in a U.K. and U.S.A. sample of firms (in percentage)

		U.K. *N=177*	*U.S.* *N=95*
Style 1	Own decision without explanation	11·7	10·7
Style 2	Own decision with explanation	17·8	17·4
Style 3	Prior consultation with subordinates	36·6	34·2
Style 4	Joint decision-making with subordinates	21·5	23·6
Style 5	Delegation to subordinates	12·4	13·9

per cent), Both groups use Style 2 to about the same extent. British managers use prior consultation somewhat more than Americans (36·6 per cent and 34·2 per cent) but American managers use more delegation and joint decision-making.

Hypotheses 4, 5 and 6 are supported by the evidence. The last mentioned comparison of American and British leadership styles is in the expected direction, but the difference is barely significant.

Summary and conclusions

The purpose of this short account is to show how a very simple type of contingency theory can be applied to research on managerial skills and leadership styles. The theory and field method was first demonstrated on an American sample of fifteen companies and 260 managers (Heller, 1971) while the corresponding and closely matched sample of British companies with 300 managers has not yet been fully analysed. Preliminary comparison is confined to six hypotheses, three relating to management skills and three to leadership styles. Five of these hypotheses are supported by the evidence.

It seems that managerial skills and job requirements are difficult to evaluate. Even if one is concerned with an assessment of the job rather than with the person occupying the job, managers at different levels come to different conclusions. However, this overall picture of uncertainty does not apply to all job requirements. Managers at both levels are moderately agreed on: responsibility, intelligence and knowledge of technical matters. American and British findings are similar.

The contingency differences show up clearly in relation to leadership. The findings show that managers use different leadership styles in different situations. It should be remembered that we are always looking at the same diads of senior – subordinate managers, so that the variations in leadership style can have nothing to do with adjustments to different people.

One of the contingency factors is the nature of the task, while another is the job function occupied by the senior manager. American and British managers respond to these contingencies in a similar way. Nevertheless, in the overall picture it seems that

Americans use somewhat more 'democratic' leadership methods than their British counterparts.

There is a connection between the findings on skill and leadership style. If senior levels of management believe that lower-level jobs require relatively little skill, then participatory leadership styles will be inappropriate.

These findings on two samples of managers have important practical implications. Paramount is the undesirability of training managers in general principles. It may be more useful to make people sensitive to the situational factors which require different kinds of behaviour. In the past this problem has come up most clearly in relation to leadership training, where the so-called democratic style has been widely advocated as superior to more centralized methods. In broad general terms this is undoubtedly true, but failure to draw attention to contingencies which require different lines of approach leads to at least two negative consequences. In the first place it produces ineffective behaviour. Secondly, a credibility gap may be created by managers who pretend to use democratic methods in situations where this is not practicable.[8]

On the subject of U.S.–U.K. differences, the full comparison is not yet available but some differences undoubtedly exist. Research findings up to now, however, have found them to be much smaller than had been expected (Heller - Porter, 1966; Haire, Ghiselli and Porter, 1966; Inkson, Schwitter, Pheysey and Hickson, 1970). Using the same methods and research instruments, comparisons of U.K.–German managerial behaviour has been made (Wilpert and Heller, 1973 and Heller and Wilpert, in press). The results up to now suggest that variance due to contingency factors like task and skill is bigger than the variance due to the national sample. In any case we agree with Roberts (1970) that the term 'culture' should not be used in cross-national studies unless 'culture' is clearly defined and measured (Heller 1976b).

8. See also Vroom and Yetton (1973). The results of their research support our own in most respects.

References

HAIRE, M., GHISELLI, E., and PORTER, L. W. (1966), *Managerial Thinking*, John Wiley, New York.

HELLER, F. A. (1969), 'Group feed-back analysis: a method of field research', *Psychological Bulletin*, vol. 72, no. 2, pp. 108–17.

HELLER, F. A. (1971), *Managerial Decision-making: A Study of Leadership Styles and Power-sharing among Senior Managers*, Tavistock Publications.

HELLER, F. A. (1973), 'Group feed-back analysis: a method of field research in a multinational setting', in Desmond Graves (ed.), *Management Research: A Cross Cultural Perspective*, Elsevier Scientific Publishing Co., Amsterdam.

HELLER, F. A. (1976a), 'Group feed-back analysis as a method of action research', in A. W. Clark (ed.), *Experiences in Action Research*, Plenum Press, New York.

HELLER, F. A. (1976b), 'The decision process: an analysis of power-sharing at senior organizational levels', in Robert Dubin (ed.), *Handbook of Work, Organisation and Society*, Rand McNally, Chicago.

HELLER, F. A., and WILPERT, B. (1976), 'Limits to participative leadership', *European Journal of Social Psychology*, in press.

HELLER, F. A., and YUKL, G. (1969), 'Participation and managerial decision-making as a function of situational variables', *Organisational Behavior and Human Performance*, no. 4, pp. 227–41.

INKSON, J. H. K., SCHWITTER, J. P., PHEYSEY, D. C., and HICKSON, D. J. (1970), 'A comparison of organizational structure and managerial roles: Ohio, U.S.A., and the Midlands, England', *Journal of Management Studies*, no. 7, pp. 347–63.

ROBERTS, K. (1970), 'On looking at an elephant: an evaluation of cross cultural research related to organisations', *Psychological Bulletin*, no. 74, pp. 327–50.

VROOM, V., and YETTON, P. (1973), *Leadership and Decision-making*, University of Pittsburgh Press, Pa.

WILPERT, B., and HELLER, F. A. (1973), 'Power-sharing at senior management levels', *Omega*, no. 1, pp. 451–64.

14 David J. Hickson, C. R. Hinings, C. J. McMillan and J. P. Schwitter

The Culture-Free Context of Organization Structure: A Tri-National Comparison*

Excerpt from *Sociology*, vol. 8, no. 1, January 1974, pp. 59–80.

Abstract. In data in standard form on seventy manufacturing organizations in three countries, consistent relationships are found between variables of organization context or 'task environment' (size, dependence, technology) and measures of structure (Formalization, Specialization, Autonomy). These support the hypothesis that relationships will be stable across societies. Even though culturally shaped variations may occur in some features of organizations, contextual constraints or pressures will persist. Simply stated, if Indian organizations were found to be less formalized than American ones, bigger Indian units would still be more formalized than smaller Indian units.

Cross-national empirical research has received less attention in organization theory than in other areas of social science (Glaser, 1971). From a review of work on comparative management, Nath (1968, p. 56) concludes: 'Cross-cultural studies, being of relatively recent origin, have not been numerous.' Yet organizations are units of analysis which offer a relatively firm foothold in the conceptualization and operationalization of variables, from which

* This research was carried out when D. J. Hickson, C. R. Hinings and C. J. McMillan were members of the Organizational Behavior Research Unit, Faculty of Business Administration, University of Alberta. It was financed by the University and by Canada Council Grants Nos. 670253 and 69–0714. D. J. Hickson and C. J. McMillan are at the Organizational Analysis Research Unit, The Management Centre, University of Bradford: C. R. Hinings is at the Institute of Local Government Studies, University of Birmingham, England: and J. Schwitter is at the College of Business Administration, Kent State University, Ohio. The helpful critical comments of W. H. Starbuck and A. W. M. Teulings on drafts of this paper are acknowledged.

to explore the wider perspective of whole societies. As Bendix (1956, p. 444) said even before the rapid growth of organization theory in the 1960s, the study of the bureaucratization of the 'structure of industrial organizations' (any organizations, indeed) is a focus which 'deliberately eschews a comprehensive theory of society in favour of selecting a problem which, if suitable for comparative analysis, will also lead to an analysis of social structures'.

Most of the studies which have been done have focused on the attitudinal and normative systems of employees in different countries, and the degree to which they feel they participate in organizational activities, rather than on the *characteristics of the organizations as such.* Illustrative examples of work in this category include Lipset's (1963) analysis of value differences between people in English-speaking nations, Granick's (1962) study of the attitudinal characteristics of European and American managers, Fayerweather's (1959) comparison of Mexican and American managers, Haire's *et al.* (1966) extensive study of manager's role perceptions and attitudes, McClelland's (1961) comparisons of achievement motivation, and Form's (1969) research on the job involvement of automobile workers.

There are at least two reasons for the lack of research on the organizations in which these employees and managers work. One may be that most, if not all, prominent writers on organizations ignore possible societal differences and so implicitly take a universalistic view, despite the lack of data. That is, they take it for granted that organizational forms and management principles hold anywhere, regardless of the cultural environment.

A second explanation may have been the absence until relatively recently of acceptable conceptual frameworks on which to base standardized analyses. The development of organization theory has now made available a number of possible frameworks as starting points (e.g. Pugh *et al.*, 1963; Udy, 1965; Thompson, 1967; Landsberger, 1970). The opportunity for comparative cross-national study presented by the operationalization of the 'contextual' and structural variables in Pugh *et al.*, conceptualization (by Pugh *et al.*, 1968, 1969; Hickson *et al.*, 1969; Inkson *et al.*, 1970a) has been exploited in studies in the United States and

Britain by Inkson *et al.* (1970b) and in Canada, the United States and Britain by McMillan *et al.* (1973). These latter studies now make this paper possible.

Cultural or contextual?

Any research is confronted by the question of the effects upon organization of cultural factors which vary between societies, as against the effects of 'contextual' factors of a non-cultural kind such as organization size, ownership, technology and field operation. After surveying effects of both kinds, Eisenstadt (1968, p. 496) comments: 'And just as it has been found necessary to differentiate the pure Weberian model of bureaucracy into its constituent components, it is also necessary to recognize first the great variety of settings in which the Weberian model may develop and to investigate the ways in which such settings influence the structure of the organizations which tend to arise within them . . .'

Are societal differences overwhelming, or are there stable relationships between such contextual factors and the structures of work organizations, relationships which hold good whatever the society in which the organizations are situated? The problem is theoretically important to the understanding of convergence (or divergence) in the social structures of otherwise contrasting societies which are developing large work organizations: and it is critical to decisions on cross-national research designs. The study described here presents some evidence towards an answer, avoiding any assumption that either context or culture 'determines' everything.

A rather subtle distinction has to be made between the contexts of organization structures varying in different societies, and the *relationships* between contexts and structures varying in different societies. As an example of the first possibility, contexts varying, suppose that country A has larger organizations than country B, i.e. size varies. Then *given* that a positive relationship between the contextual variable size and structural features of bureaucratization is the same in both societies, A will have more bureaucratic organizations than B. Only if it can then also be shown that something specific to country A 'causes' it to have larger organizations might this be said to be a societal or cultural difference in bureaucratization, transmitted through the intervening size variable. The second possibility, relationships between contexts and structures varying, is the more fundamental. If, for example, the relationship between size and structural bureaucratization is *not* constant from society to society, then organizational analysis using these variables is only feasible within societal boundaries (i.e. by excluding societal variables). This would be a severe restriction on the development of organization theory, and its contribution to cross-cultural comparative research. This paper is concerned with this second possibility. (It may be noted that stable relationships in all countries between contextual variables and structures would not mean that in all countries organizations must be identical, since the values of the variables may differ as in the example above on differing sizes.)

There is a twofold difficulty. First, the scarcity of data; second, where there are data and/or opinions, knowing whether differences reported between organizations in different countries can be attributed to differences in societal or cultural variables, to differences in organizational contextual variables in these countries, or to changes in relationships between contextual variables and organization structure, which is the concern here.

Some take a view which may implicitly assume the predominance of societal influences. As Crozier (1964, p. 210) says: 'Intuitively, however, people have always assumed that bureaucratic structures and patterns of action differ in the different countries of the Western world and even more markedly between East and West. Men of action know it and never fail to take it into account. But contemporary social scientists . . . have not been concerned with such comparisons.' This may or may not be optimistic about 'men of action', but the shortage of published research bears out Crozier's point on social scientists. Crozier himself suggests that members of French organizations use rules and procedures and differentiated levels of authority as impersonal protections from close personal involvement with the work or with those at other levels. Americans, however, use rules and procedures to obtain 'due process' of consideration for their grievances against those at other levels. The British accept and defer to differential authority. Here Crozier is drawing on Richardson's (1956) comparison of British and American ships. Azumi (1969), developing Abegglen's (1958) study of Japanese and American factories, suggests that members of Japanese organizations are subservient to higher authority levels because the group identification stressed in Japanese society enables subordinates to perceive this authority as rightfully exercised on behalf of the collectivity. Commitment to the organization and hierarchical progression are dominated (though not exclusively) by 'shushin koyo' or lifetime employment and 'nenko joretsu' or rewards by seniority.

Such differences in norms of behaviour between societies might indeed be related to differences in organization *structures*. McMillan *et al.* (1973) compare specialization of functions, formalization of documentation and autonomy of organization in British, Canadian and American factories; and they interpret the lower formalization of some (not all) British units as implying an alternative traditionalistic control of behaviour. Less formal structured documentation is required because of the behaviour norms of British personnel. Similarly, if American personnel at the lower levels of a hierarchy do indeed use rules to obtain consideration for themselves, maybe this keeps their organizations less centralized than are French organizations (as Crozier, 1964, believes they are) or Japanese organizations (as Abegglen, 1958 and Azumi, 1969, believe they are). The same behaviour might also be partly responsible for the greater administrative load of American research institutes as compared to equivalent Soviet organizations (Kaplan, 1961); and for the same structural phenomenon in American hospitals (Glaser, 1963). Again, in the Soviet society with strong small group norms of collective responsibility, organizations incorporate structural 'checking and counterchecking relationships' through political party and other overlapping memberships (Crozier, 1964, p. 229; and Bendix, 1956).

However, the possibility or probability of such culturally 'caused' differences does not mean that they are all-important, and any latent presumption that they are should be avoided. For example, if organizations in Peru have comparatively less specialized role differentiation because of employees' diffuse involvement in the wider society (Whyte, 1968), this might also be due to the organizations being comparatively small. Equally, whilst some British organizations may be less formalized than most American, bigger British units are still more formalized than small British units (Pugh *et al.*, 1969). It becomes plain that any cross-societal analyses must make assumptions as to whether or not relationships between variables such as size and specialization, or formalization, are constant between societies.

Is it possible to formulate an hypothesis? The basis for this can only lie in the strong relationships found within single countries between structure and contextual variables such as stability of market or field of operation, organization size, ownership and dependence on other organizations, and, in some respects, the technology of an organization's own workflow. In effect, these constitute what Thompson (1967) calls the 'task environment'.

With few, if any, exceptions, the salient research on context in this sense has been done on organizations within one or other of two countries only, the United States and Britain. The recent literature is too extensive for simple summing up here, beyond some studies which bring out the main variables.

Burns and Stalker (1961) in Britain emphasize the impact of stability or instability in market, and of the technical know-how required by the product, upon the degree to which an organization structure has mechanistic or organismic (flexible) characteristics. In the United States, Lawrence and Lorsch (1967) also stress stability and certainty or change and uncertainty as critical conditions; and Chandler (1962) traces their effects over time.

In Britain, Pugh *et al.* (1969, p. 109) and Hinings and Lee (1971) show a strong relationship between size and 'structuring of activities' (the latter being a summation of measures of functional specialization, formalization, etc.): and relationships between size and the proportions of employees in various categories are explored intricately in mainly American data by Pondy (1969) and Klatzky (1970).

Ownership if it means just 'who is the owner' may have little relevance. Though Pondy (1969) shows a tendency for the administrative hierarchy to be smaller where there are owner-managers, Pugh *et al.* (1969) find no relations of any consequence between a variety of measures of ownership and of structure. Their position is supported by McMillan *et al.* (1973) who in Canadian manufacturing organizations find no relationship between foreign or domestic ownership and structural features. On the other hand, ownership viewed as links between a unit of organization and a larger organization containing it, and combined with links between a unit and its suppliers and customers into a measure of 'dependence' on others in the environment, has been shown to be critical to autonomy and dispersion of decision-making (Pugh *et al.* 1969; Inkson *et al.* 1970b; McMillan *et al.* 1973). Dependent units or organization have least autonomy and most concentration of authority.

Woodward (1958, 1965) with British organizations first exposed relationships between technology and structure, and is followed by Zwerman (1969) with American organizations. On the other hand, Hickson *et al.* (1969), using British samples, suggest limits to technological effects which may not be important to structural features beyond those linked with the workflow itself, such as the ratio of supervisors or proportions of maintenance personnel.

Thus, to take the simplest position, the principal relationships between structure and context are likely to be with stability/instability of operating field, with size, with dependence, and in some circumstances, with technology. Given that none of the researchers who report these relationships in data on single countries have suggested that they apply only within the country concerned, the boldest hypothesis will be adopted:

> Relationships between the structural characteristics of work organizations and variables of organization context will be stable across societies.

This hypothesis implicitly rests on the theory that there are imperatives, or 'causal' relationships, from the resources of 'customers', of employees, of materials and finance etc., and of operating technology of an organization, to its structure, which take effect whatever the surrounding societal differences. Whatever the society, 'market' uncertainty over 'customers' (commercial or otherwise) forces a flexible and integrated structure. Whether the culture is Asian or European or North American, a large organization with many employees improves efficiency by specializing their activities but also by increasing, controlling and co-ordinating specialities. Organizations in all countries seek secure links with suppliers of materials or money, or with 'customers', and so dependencies arise between organizations which limit the autonomy of some. And the technological equipment of an oil refinery requires much the same operatives and supervisors wherever it is.

Sample

Most research referred to above is in societies with at least a modicum of industrialization. Udy (1961) shows that production organizations in non-industrial societies are unlikely to develop rationally specified objectives and role-segmented participation unless that participation is a positive obligation legitimized by the external society – as it is in industrialized societies. An implication for research on organizations is that the societal level of industrialization should either be measured, or in some way controlled. This first test of the hypothesis uses data from countries which are similar in industrialization, the United States, Britain and Canada. Standardized data are available on these three countries only; but clearly such a restricted sample affords a very limited test. The contextual data are on organization size, dependences and technology, but not on field of operation ('market') where there are no reliable measures of stability or instability.

Data are analysed on seventy manufacturing organizations. In Table 1, the product lines are listed for each national set of firms. American and British data are taken from Inkson *et al.* (1970b) supplemented with more complete information made available by the authors: the data were collected in 1967–8. Some of these data were also treated from a methodological perspective by Inkson *et al.* (1970a). Canadian data were collected in 1969–70, national differences as such being described by McMillan *et al.* (1973).

The first set of firms is in the state of Ohio, U.S.A. There are twenty-one manufacturing organizations ranging in size from a small plant engaged in plastics with 250 employees to a manufacturer of electrical supplies with 25,000. The second set is twenty-five manufacturing firms in Birmingham, England. The size of this set ranges from a firm with 260 employees making paints to a firm with 18,000 employees assembling electrical goods. The

Table 1 **Main product lines**

Org. No.	OHIO, U.S.A.
1.	Office data storage equipment
2.	Electrical wiring
3.	Electric motors
4.	Domestic appliances
5.	Electric light bulbs
6.	Heavy steel goods
7.	Nuts, pins
8.	Sheet and bar steel
9.	Aluminium, etc., castings
10.	Plastic and rubber products
11.	Steel, copper, nickel, etc. (rolled, plated)
12.	Aerospace and defence products
13.	Metal components
14.	Forgings
15.	Packaging
16.	Plastic-working equipment
17.	Steel, copper, nickel, etc.
18.	Fasteners, hoists, chains
19.	Printing and bindery equipment
20.	Tubing, gasketing, linings, etc.
21.	Truck axles
	BIRMINGHAM, ENGLAND
1.	Domestic appliances
2.	Gas and by-products
3.	Aluminium products
4.	Vehicle components
5.	Electrical components
6.	Vehicle components
7.	Building goods
8.	Trucks and vans
9.	Paint
10.	Metal goods
11.	Machine tools
12.	Aluminium castings
13.	Plastics

Table 1 (cont'd) **Main product lines**

Org. No.	BIRMINGHAM, ENGLAND
14.	Control equipment
15.	Paint
16.	Automobile batteries
17.	Large transport and cranes
18.	Automobile components
19.	Automobile steering gear
20.	Civil engineering
21.	Chocolate
22.	Electrical goods
23.	Golf balls
24.	Metal plating finishes
25.	Chemicals
	TORONTO, CANADA
1.	Trailers and containers
2.	Metal finishing
3.	Precious metals
4.	Cartons
5.	Toys
6.	Gears
7.	Wire, sheet metal, nails
8.	Bolts
9.	Alloys and bushings
10.	Auto parts
11.	Motor accessories
12.	Biscuits
13.	Heating, lighting extrusions
14.	Heavy duty construction
15.	Aircraft parts
16.	Stoves
17.	Machine tools
18.	Electric meters and motors
19.	Heaters and pumps
20.	Soups, frozen foods
21.	Office forms
22.	Glass products
23.	Copper sheets
24.	Gears, machine parts

Table 2 **Distributions of sizes of organizations and sizes of parent organizations in each of three countries* (to nearest 50)**

	UNITED STATES N = 21				*BRITAIN N = 25*				*CANADA N = 24*			
	Mean	*Median*	*Standard Deviation*	*Range*	*Mean*	*Median*	*Standard Deviation*	*Range*	*Mean*	*Median*	*Standard Deviation*	*Range*
Size†	5,150	1,700	8,400	250‡–25,000	2,650	1,250	4,000	250–18,200	500	400	350	200–1,200
Size† of Parent Organization	69,000	13,650	144,600	250‡–575,400	33,350	7,700	43,550	300–120,200	5,000	1,850	7,000	600–30,200

* The high mean size of U.S. organizations is partly an artefact of their non-continuous distribution, eighteen organizations being below 9,000 employees but three organizations 23,000 and over. The British and Canadian distributions are also skewed. Medians are, therefore, also given.

† Numbers of employees.

‡ 250 is the smallest size intentionally included: one organization was later found to have only 80 employees, but nevertheless remains in the published data used here.

third set of twenty-four organizations is in Toronto, Ontario, ranging from a small metal goods firm with 215 employees to a glass producer with 1,500. As Table 2 shows, the Toronto set is smaller than the Ohio and Birmingham sets, and are in smaller parent groups (parent size being the number of employees of the parent company to which the organization belongs).

There is a range from independent companies to very small subsidiaries in large groups (as reflected in Dependence scores: see Appendix), the bulk of the organization units being fairly substantial subsidiaries of wider corporations. There are no principal units of independent companies in the Toronto set.

All three sets of data are from large industrial metropolitan areas, i.e. the immediate environment is standardized. The similar ranges of industry in the sets of firms are apparent in Table 1, and in the narrow range of organization Automaticity scores (see Appendix), which mean that most units are of a mechanized batch or mass-production type. Whilst the organizations are widely representative, none of the three sets is claimed to be a *random* sample from its area.

Data collection and measures

As mentioned earlier, Inkson *et al.* (1970b) and McMillan et al. (1973), when gathering the data which is analysed here, took advantage of the relatively standardized methods for organizational research developed by Pugh *et al.* (1968, 1969) and abbreviated by Inkson *et al.* (1970a).

Data were collected on standard schedules in structured interviews with chief executives and, in some cases where the chief executive did not have full information, with other senior managers. Confirmatory material was obtained where possible in the form of company booklets, union contracts, advertising brochures, and organization charts. Interviews were carried out in Birmingham by Hickson and Inkson, in Ohio by Schwitter, and in Toronto by McMillan. No material translations of idiom were required due to the impersonal nature of the data.

The measures used other than size, and score distributions, are given in the Appendix.

Dependence is the degree to which an organization is tied to others in its environment. It is no more important to this paper than, say, size, but it needs more explication. It is here operationalized by three short scales indicating personal (individual) or impersonal (organizational) foundation or origin, the status of the unit of organization (from independent principal unit to a non-distinctive branch of another unit), and the relative size of the unit of organization within any group of which it forms a part. These scales are selected from seven wider ranging scales devised and tested by Pugh *et al.* (1969), which encompass in addition the unit of organization's representation on any controlling body of an owning-group, its reliance on such a group for specialist services (e.g. central accounting department or personnel office) or on external consultants or agents, any ownership links and types of contracts with suppliers and customers, the proportions of its inputs and outputs coming from or going to particular suppliers and customers, and the degree to which its ownership is in publicly accountable form (from the public scrutiny applied to a government department to the comparative obscurity of a company not quoted on a stock exchange). Taken together, these scales signify the dependence or independence of an organization.

The justification of representing, for the sake of economy, this whole range of measures by a selection of a few scales is provided by Inkson *et al.* (1970a), who demonstrate the high intercorrelation of scores from the wider range of data and scores from the selected representative scales. Thus a very dependent score on the three scales in the studies reported on in this paper signifies not only an organization created impersonally as a small branch unit of another, as measured directly, but also implies the likelihood that the organization has no representation in that other, depends on it for specialist functions, and takes all supplies from it and sends all products to it, e.g. the organization in question is a typical local plant of a large combine. At the far extreme would be the company founded and controlled by an identified individual which is self-sufficient in management functions and deals freely with suppliers and customers in the market.

The measures and data available do not yet go as far as showing effects over time, e.g. by discriminating between long-established branch units, and those only recently taken over but previously independent. Like all other cross-sectional research, the studies examined here cannot suggest how long it may take for changes in one variable to be followed by changes in others. However, the recurrent strength of the relationships between Dependence and Autonomy (Table 3) suggests that the measures are powerful as they stand, though data over time should yield further improvement.

The Automaticity measure is derived from Amber and Amber (1962) and represents the degree to which energy and then information are provided by machines rather than by man, being a variable of operations technology defined by Hickson *et al.* (1969) as 'the equipping and sequencing of activities in the workflow'. It is one of a series of technology scales used by Hickson *et al.* (1969); its inclusion in this paper is due to it being common to all the studies analysed, and does not imply that alone it is an adequate measure of technology.

Formalization of Role-Definition is the degree to which intended behaviours are prescribed in writing (in rules, procedures, and instructions), and Functional Specialization is the degree to which the activities of an organization are divided into mutually exclusive sets. Autonomy is the degree to which decisions are made within the unit of organization.

The measures of the latter three structural variables can either be regarded as representing the concepts as defined and nothing more, or as abbreviated indicators of the wider structural dimensions of 'structuring of activities' (indicated by Formalization and Specialization) and 'concentration/dispersion of authority' (indicated by Autonomy), as Inkson *et al.* (1970a) have demonstrated.

The measures are organizational as called for by the hypothesis, and are not concerned with personal values, attitudes, or motivation. The data are directly about organizational features, contrasting with the perceptual type questionnaire responses on organizations employed inter alia by Hall (1963, 1967) and Hage and Aiken (1967, 1969). Thus the data minimize contamination by culturally influenced variations in the perceptions organization members have of their organizations.

The undimensionality of the measuring scales was originally established by Pugh *et al.* (1968, 1969), using a procedure with biserial correlation as evaluated by Levy and Pugh (1969), and is further demonstrated by Inkson *et al.* (1970a) on their fresh British data. Organizations are scored 1 or 0 for possession or otherwise of each item, and scores are added without differential weighting. In the case of technology, inconsistency in the interrelationships among the several scales of technology originally devised by Pugh *et al.* (1969) leads to the use of the single Automaticity categorization separately. Scores can range from 0–5. Dependence is represented by the addition of scores on the three constituent scales shown. Scores on Dependence can range from 0–9, on Functional Specialization from 0–16, on Formalization of Role-Definition from 0–20, and on Autonomy from 0–23. Some score ranges found in the sets of organizations utilized here are narrower since they cover manufacturing only, whereas the scales were designed to cover all forms of work organization.

Results

The product moment correlations between scores on the contextual and structural variables are shown separately for the three countries in Table 3. The organizations in the three countries are similar in Formalization, Functional Specialization and Autonomy, i.e. in levels of scores except for the marginally lower (but significant: $p < 0{\cdot}01$, McMillan *et al.*, 1973) Formalization of British organizations which is examined for its conceptual implications by McMillan *et al.* (1973). This paper is concerned with the relationships between variables rather than with the levels of scores as such.

The pattern of relationships suggested by the correlations is the same in all countries. Two components of these correlations support the hypothesis of stable links between context and structure, namely the constancy of (a) the direction of the relationships, (b) the magnitude of the relationships, especially those between size and Formalization and Specialization and between Dependence and Autonomy, which were highlighted in previous work. These *relationships* are remarkably stable even though there are variations in the *values or levels* of scores on the contextual and structural variables, i.e. Canadian organizations are somewhat smaller in size, and British organizations are rather lower in Formalization.

In more detail, organizational size (logarithm of the number of

Table 3 **Product moment correlations of elements of context with structural variables in three countries separately**

Organizations *United States N=21* *Britain N=25* *Canada N=24*	STRUCTURE *Formalization of Role-Definition*	*Functional Specialization*	*Autonomy*
CONTEXT:			
Size of Organization*			
United States	0·48‡	0·82†	0·37‡
Britain	0·45‡	0·79†	0·01
Canada	0·49†	0·49†	−0·38‡
Size of Parent Organization*			
United States	0·45‡	0·52†	−0·02
Britain	0·60†	0·49†	−0·30
Canada	0·32	0·23	−0·56†
Dependence			
United States	0·11	0·00	−0·54†
Britain	0·57†	0·02	−0·60†
Canada	0·31	0·14	−0·42‡
Operations Technology:			
Automaticity Mode			
United States	0·24	0·42‡	0·27
Britain	0·16	0·13	−0·31
Canada	0·06	0·13	−0·17

* Logarithm of number of employees.

† Correlations beyond the 99 per cent level of confidence.

‡ Correlations beyond the 95 per cent level of confidence.

employees) shows recurring high positive correlations with both Formalization and Specialization. (The smaller coefficient of 0·49 with Specialization in the Toronto organizations may be due to the very narrow range of sizes of firms and to their narrow range of Specialization scores [Table 2, and Appendix] as well as to the possibility of a slightly less linear relationship at the lower end of the size range.) Further, in all three countries, Formalization and Specialization are interrelated (U.S. = 0·72, Britain = 0·41, Canada = 0·39) which supports their use by Inkson *et al.* (1970a) as jointly representing the underlying dimension 'structuring of activities', i.e. the degree to which the intended behaviour of employees is overtly defined.

Though the only data over time on which to base causal inferences are the fourteen organizations on which successive measurements were made by Inkson *et al.* (1970a) it is difficult to avoid a presumption that in all countries size is the overwhelming factor in 'structuring of activities', and that this dimension is the universal fundamental ingredient of organization. As more people are brought together, so economies of scale enable more functions to be specialized into distinctive sets of roles (marketing specialisms, personnel specialisms, etc.) to reap further efficiencies from the development of personal skills and control of behaviour. Simultaneously, as more people are brought together, so problems of control spur the development of control specialisms (inspection, costing, etc.). The knowledge of what is happening in the organization possessed by any one person becomes a progressively smaller part of the whole, so more formalized documentation of what ought to be done and is done is required. Though the *levels* of constituent ingredients of bureaucratization may differ between countries, the pressure exerted by size is the same and in the same direction in each country. Nowhere will traditionalistic custom be adequate for social control once large numbers are gathered. Here is a fragment of a basis in contemporary empirical data from three countries for what Weber (1948) believed so long before.

Attractive though this argument is, it is also possible to argue the other way around, i.e. 'structuring of activities' brings growth to greater size. Decisions formally to routinize and rationalize traditionalistic management would bring control specialisms and formalized control procedures, so that more people would come in to man the specialist departments and to operate the procedures. The fact is that available data can support any causal inferences or none, as the debate on organizational findings between Aldrich (1972), Hilton (1972), Heise (1972), and Pugh and Hickson (1972) shows plainly. Probably size affects Specialization and Formalization and they affect size simultaneously: what is intriguing is whether the first effect is indeed stronger than the second.

A second size effect may be exerted by the size of the parent organization. Organizations in the biggest parent groups show even greater 'structuring of activities' (again, the narrow ranges of scores in the Canadian organizations available appear to affect the magnitude of the Canadian coefficients). The parallel effects of being large and being in a large group tend to occur together since bigger units of organization tend to be in bigger groups (*r* size, size of parent organization = U.S. 0·68, Britain 0·60, Canada 0·43). There is probably some difference here between Formalization and Specialization. Specialization correlates most highly with size, but Formalization correlates as much or more with parent size. It may be speculated that though the growth of an organization itself increases both Specialization and Formalization it has greatest, perhaps prior, effect on Specialization (implying that specialists come first, then generate documentation). But becoming a part of a big parent group has its primary effect on Formalization, by imposed conformity to recording procedures uniform to all units in the same group.

Alongside these effects in Britain and Canada is the positive relationship between Dependence and Formalization. That is, the *relatively* small and dependent units of a large group are even more formalized.

In summary, in all countries a small independent organization is likely to have least Specialization and Formalization: a large organization, also in a large group, which is also very dependent on that group, will have most Specialization and Formalization, especially the latter (*though all these effects do not necessarily occur in the same organization*).

Whichever the country and its policies on corporation activities, the degree of autonomy an organization possesses in decisions is likely to rest on its position relative to an owning organization, as reflected by its dependence/independence score (if it is not connected to any owning group, contracts, etc. with suppliers and customers also affect autonomy: Pugh *et al.*, 1969). Relatively small dependent units have least autonomy: and this is likely to be so also for decentralization of authority within the unit itself, i.e. dependent units also show least decentralization within themselves (Pugh *et al.*, 1969). Using causal imagery to infer an effect from dependence upon autonomy, then it may be argued that owners necessarily retain ultimate financial and marketing decisions, whatever the autonomy permitted once these are taken. So being in a large combine or group of companies limits autonomy irrespective of product or nationality. In hierarchical authority structures, chief executives are finally accountable to any owning group, so being in such a group pressures them, too, into retaining ultimate decisions in their own hands within their own unit, however much else may be decentralized. More than that, the smaller the unit within the owning group, the less it will have its own control and service specialisms, such as finance or training or buying, and the more it will rely for those on group headquarters. Hence the more such specialisms at group headquarters will determine the affairs of the subsidiary or branch unit, and the less autonomy it can have.

This is an interpretation of the negative correlations in each country between Dependence and Autonomy. It suggests that whether the ownership is foreign or national (see McMillan *et al.*, 1973, on American ownership of Canadian organizations), or whether it is dispersed among many individuals or restricted in a few hands, it is of little importance in any country beside the twentieth-century phenomenon of the large parent corporation.

Seen across all three countries, Autonomy has a curious set of relationships with size (Table 3). With size of organization, the relationship is positive in the U.S., drops to nothing in Britain, but becomes negative in Canada: paralleling this, the relationship with size of parent organization is negligible in the U.S., becomes negative in Britain, and strongly negative in Canada (the correlations between size and size of parent are positive and fairly constant, as given earlier).

Thus in Canada especially, larger parent groups grant their subsidiaries least autonomy. Indeed, this tendency by larger groups continues even though their subsidiaries may be larger in absolute terms themselves. It appears to explain the negative relationship between absolute unit size and unit Autonomy in Canada (as compared to the positive relationship in the U.S.). Why is this? For despite the predominantly American and British ownership of the Canadian organizations, McMillan *et al.* (1973) show that they are at any rate no less autonomous than their American and British counterparts. A suggested answer is that the negative relationship between Autonomy and size of parent organizations is due to a few of the biggest American groups granting their Canadian subsidiaries less autonomy than most American groups give their Canadian units, a difference slight in itself but enough for an overall negative relationship when numbers are small. Perhaps it is this tendency by the largest and therefore most conspicuous American corporations which leads to the probably unwarranted belief that this is characteristic of all American ownership in Canada. Data from larger samples are needed before any generalizations can be made.

As stated earlier, Hickson *et al.* (1969) found that contrary to any extreme 'technological determinism', the operations technology of an organization as such is little if at all related to structural features beyond those directly linked with the workflow itself. Of the range of measures of operations technology used by Hickson et al., only the Automaticity categorization is included in the studies reported here, and scores range over three categories only, so the data base is extremely narrow. Nonetheless, the weakness and instability of the correlations between Automaticity and the three structural variables at least do not contradict their view. In none of the countries is technology likely to be important to the wider bureaucratization or to the allocation of decision-making authority. (In the United States set of organizations where positive correlations appear between Automaticity and both Formalization and Specialization, these are reduced to virtually nil when [log] size is held constant by partial correlation.) The presumption is that size has the greater impact on Formalization and Specialization.

Conclusion

The consistency of the relationships between variables of organization context and of organization structure found in data from seventy manufacturing units in the United States, Britain and Canada supports the 'bold' hypothesis that these relationships, notably those between size and Specialization and Formalization and between Dependence and Autonomy, will hold for work organizations in all societies. The hypothesis implies that relationships will be constant in direction; and where they are basically linear as in the data analysed here, they might be constant also in magnitude irrespective of differences in structures or in the contexts of structures (e.g. organization size) between societies. In other words, though organizations in different societies may differ, for example, in deferential behaviour towards higher status ranks, or in role obligations external to the organization, or in traditionalistic custom as a control instead of documentation, all will be subject to the same relationships with their contextual 'task environments'. Even though Indian organizations might turn out to be less formalized or less autonomous than American organizations, bigger Indian units would still be more formalized than smaller Indian units, and dependent Indian units will be less autonomous than relatively independent ones. The links between the contextual variables of size or dependence, for example, and structural features will be of similar magnitudes and in the same directions.

The weakness of this position is that it stands on data from three Anglo-Saxon societies only, and cannot command confidence until tested on reliable data from a much wider spectrum of societies in which levels of industrialization are varied. The numbers of organizations in each country desirably should be greater, and non-manufacturing units should be included. The hypothesis is 'bold' because it is simple, stated in the simplest possible form to offer a starting point for researching the complexities, a prelude to its own modification.

The strength of this position is its base in data from each country which are in standard form, and in the range of organizations covered.

APPENDIX: SCALES USED (in addition to Size, Table 2) (numbered as by Pugh *et al.*, 1968, 1969; and Inkson *et al.*, 1970a).

DEPENDANCE

Scored by the addition of scores on the following three sub-scales (high score = dependence, low score = independence):

		Scoring
Impersonality of Origin	Scale 11.01	
Personal foundation (i.e. founded by a person or persons, not by an existing organization)		0
Foundation by an existing organization		1
Status of Organization Unit	Scale 12.10	
Principal Unit		0
Subsidiary (with legal identity)		1
Head Branch (with headquarters on the same location)		2
Branch		3
Size Relative to that of Parent Organization	Scale 18.07	

The organization's score is its number of employees, expressed as a percentage proportion of the total number of employees in its ultimate owning group, and categorized to correspond with the scoring of the original data reported by Pugh *et al.* (1969), as follows:

over 90 per cent of owning group	0
30–89 per cent of owning group	1
5–29 per cent of owning group	2
under 5 per cent of owning group	3

	Mean	*Standard Deviation*	*Range*
United States	3·8	2·4	0–7
Britain	3·7	2·0	0–7
Canada	3·8	1·2	2–6

Possible Range 0–7

TECHNOLOGY

Automaticity Mode Scale 10.03

Scored according to the 'Yardstick for Automation' from Amber and Amber (1962). Data are collected sufficient only to determine Scale 15.03 'MODE', i.e. an estimate of the automaticity of the bulk of the equipment used by the organization in its workflow activities, bulk meaning the modal or most frequently occurring piece of equipment (e.g. lathes in engineering batch production, or containers and retorts in liquid processing).

	Scoring
Hand tools and manual machines	0
Powered machines and tools	1
Single-cycle automatics and self-feeding machines	2
Automatic: repeats cycle	3
Self-measuring and adjusting: feedback	4
Computer control: automatic cognition	5

	Mean	*Standard Deviation*	*Range*
United States	2·2	0·7	1–3
Britain	2·0	0·6	1–3
Canada	2·2	0·9	1–3

Possible Range 0–5

FUNCTIONAL SPECIALIZATION

Scale 51.01

A function is specialized when at least one person performs that function and no other function. No account is taken of either (a) the specialist's status, or (b) whether an organization has many specialists or only one. For each activity for which there is a specialist the organization scores '1'.

Activities to:

	Scoring
1. develop, legitimize and symbolize the organization's charter (public relations, advertising, etc.)	0/1
2. dispose of, distribute and service the output (sales and service, customer complaints, etc.)	0/1
3. carry outputs and resources from place to place (transport)	0/1
4. acquire and allocate human resources (employment, etc.)	0/1
5. develop and transform human resources (education and training)	0/1

6. maintain human resources and promote their identification with the organization (welfare, medical, safety, magazine, sports and social, etc.) 0/1
7. obtain and control materials and equipment (buying, material control, stores, stock control, etc.) 0/1
8. maintain and erect buildings and equipment (maintenance, works engineer, etc.) 0/1
9. record and control financial resources (accounts, costs, wages, etc.) 0/1
10. control the workflow (planning, progressing, etc.) 0/1
11. control the quality of materials, equipment and outputs (inspection, testing, etc.) 0/1
12. assess and devise ways of producing the output (work study, O.R., rate-fixing, methods study, etc.) 0/1
13. devise new outputs, equipment and processes 0/1
14. develop and operate administrative procedures (registry, filing, statistics, O. & M.) 0/1
15. deal with the legal and insurance requirements (legal, registrar, insurance, licensing, etc.) 0/1
16. acquire information on the operational field (market research) 0/1

	Mean	*Standard Deviation*	*Range*
United States	11·0	4·0	3–16
Britain	11·5	2·3	7–16
Canada	13·0	1·8	10–16

Possible Range 0–16

FORMALIZATION OF ROLE-DEFINITION

Scale 53.01

The degree of formalization of role-definition in the organization is given by the number of specific role-defining documents which exist in the organization, and (in some cases) the extent of their application or distribution. No account is taken of frequency or completeness of use.

Documents		*Scoring*
1. Written Union contract		0/1
2. Information booklets given to	: none	0
	: few employees	1
	: many employees	2
	: all employees	3

3. Number of information booklets	: none	0
	: one	1
	: two	2
	: three	3
	: four or more	4
4. Organization chart given to	: none	0
	: Chief Executive only	1
	: C.E. plus one other executive	2
	: C.E. plus all/most departments heads	3
5. Written operating instructions		0/1
6. Written terms of reference or job description	: for direct workers	0/1
	: for line superordinates	0/1
	: for staff (other than line superordinates)	0/1
	: for Chief Executive	0/1
7. Manual of procedures		0/1
8. Written policies		0/1
9. Workflow ('production') schedule or programme		0/1
10. Written research programme or reports		0/1

	Mean	*Standard Deviation*	*Range*
United States	14·4	3·5	7–20
Britain	10·8	4·5	2–19
Canada	14·3	3·8	7–20

Possible Range 0–20

AUTONOMY OF THE ORGANIZATION

Scale 54.10

An organization scores 1 for each decision on which it has autonomous authority, i.e. on which action can be taken without waiting for confirmation from any level above its chief executive, even if the decision is later ratified at a higher level. Above the chief executive is at the level of the controlling board of a parent company, committee of local council, board of a company if a majority of its members are not executive subordinates of the organization's chief executive, head office department, etc. Inside the organization is any level at or below its chief executive.

Decisions	*Scoring*
1. Supervisory establishment	0/1
2. Appointment of Supervisory Staff from outside the organization	0/1
3. Promotion of Supervisory Staff	0/1
4. Salaries of Supervisory Staff	0/1
5. To spend unbudgeted or unallocated money on capital items	0/1
6. To spend unbudgeted or unallocated money on revenue items	0/1
7. What type, or what brand, new equipment is to be	0/1
8. To determine a new product or service	0/1
9. To determine marketing territories covered	0/1
10. The extent and type of market to be aimed for	0/1
11. What shall be costed	0/1
12. What shall be inspected	0/1
13. What operations shall be work studied	0/1
14. Dismiss a Supervisor	0/1
15. Training methods to be used	0/1
16. Buying procedures	0/1
17. Which suppliers of materials are to be used	0/1
18. What and how many welfare facilities are to be provided	0/1
19. The price of the output	0/1
20. To alter responsibilities/areas of work of specialist departments	0/1
21. To alter responsibilities/areas of work of line departments	0/1
22. To create a new department	0/1
23. To create a new job	0/1

	Mean	*Standard Deviation*	*Range*
United States	17·9	3·5	11–21
Britain	19·2	4·4	7–23
Canada	19·5	4·0	6–23

Possible Range 0–23

References

ABEGGLEN, J. (1958), *The Japanese Factory*, The Free Press, Illinois.

ALDRICH, H. E. (1972), 'Technology and organizational structure: a re-examination of the findings of the Aston Group', *Administrative Science Quarterly*, no. 17, pp. 26–43.

AMBER, G. H., and AMBER, P. S. (1962), *Anatomy of Automation*, Prentice-Hall, Englewood Cliffs, N.J.

AZUMI, K. (1969), *Higher Education and Business Recruitment in Japan*, Teachers College Press, Teachers College, Columbia University, New York.

BENDIX, R. (1956), *Work and Authority in Industry*, John Wiley, New York.

BURNS, T., and STALKER, G. N. (1961), *The Management of Innovation*, Tavistock Publications.

CHANDLER, A. D. (1962), *Strategy and Structure*, M.I.T. Press.

CROZIER, M. (1964), *The Bureaucratic Phenomenon*, Tavistock Publications.

EISENSTADT, S. N. (1968), 'Some reflections on the variability of development and organizational structures', *Administrative Science Quarterly*, no. 13, pp. 491–7.

FAYERWEATHER, J. (1959), *The Executive Overseas*, Syracuse University Press, New York.

FORM, W. H. (1969), 'Occupational and social integration of automobile workers in four countries: a comparative study', *International Journal of Comparative Sociology*, no. 10, pp. 95–116.

GLASER, W. A. (1963), 'Hospital administrators and doctors', in Elliott Freidson (ed.), *The Hospital in Modern Society*, The Free Press, Illinois.

GLASER, W. A. (1971), 'Cross-national comparisons of the factory', *Journal of Comparative Administration*, vol. 3, no. 1, pp. 83–117.

GRANICK, D. (1962), *The European Executive*, Doubleday, New York.

HAGE, J., and AIKEN, M. (1967), 'Relationship of centralization to other structural properties', *Administrative Science Quarterly*, no. 12, pp. 72–92.

HAGE, J., and AIKEN, M. (1969), 'Routine technology, social structure and organizational goals', *Administrative Science Quarterly*, no. 14, pp. 366–76.

HAIRE, M., GHISELLI, E., and PORTER, L. (1966), *Managerial Thinking*, John Wiley, New York.

HALL, R. H. (1963), 'The concept of bureaucracy: an empirical assessment', *American Journal of Sociology*, no. 69, pp. 32–40.

HALL, R. H. (1967), 'Some organizational considerations in the professional-organizational relationship', *Administrative Science Quarterly*, no. 12, pp. 461–78.

HEISE, D. R. (1972), 'How do I know my data? Let me count the ways', *Administrative Science Quarterly*, no. 17, pp. 58–61.

HICKSON, D. J., PUGH, D. S., and PHEYSEY, D. C. (1969), 'Operations technology and organization structure: an empirical reappraisal', *Administrative Science Quarterly*, no. 14, pp. 378–97.

HILTON, G. (1972), 'Causal inference analysis: a seductive process', *Administrative Science Quarterly*, no. 17, pp. 44–54.

HININGS, C. R., and LEE, G. L. (1971), 'Dimensions of organization structure and their context: a replication', *Sociology*, vol. 5, no. 1, pp. 83–94.

INKSON, J. H. K., PUGH, D. S., and HICKSON, D. J. (1970), 'Organization context and structure: an abbreviated replication', *Administrative Science Quarterly*, no. 15, pp. 318–29.

INKSON, J. H. K., SCHWITTER, J., PHEYSEY, D. C., and HICKSON, D. J. (1970), 'A comparison of organization structure and managerial roles: Ohio, U.S.A. and the Midlands, England', *Journal of Management Studies*, vol. 7, no. 3, pp. 347–63.

KAPLAN, N. (1961), 'Research administration and the administrator: U.S.S.R. and U.S.', *Administrative Science Quarterly*, no. 6, pp. 51–72.

KLATZKY, S. R. (1970), 'The relationship of organizational size to complexity and co-ordination', *Administrative Science Quarterly*, vol. 15. no. 4, pp. 428–38.

LANDSBERGER, H. A. (1970), 'A framework for the cross-cultural analysis of formal organizations', in Henry A. Landsberger (ed.), *Comparative Perspectives on Formal Organizations*, Little, Brown & Co., Boston.

LAWRENCE, P. R., and LORSCH, J. W. (1967), *Organization and Environment*, Division of Research Graduate School of Business Administration, Harvard University.

LEVY, P., and PUGH, D. S. (1969), 'Scaling and multivariate analyses in the study of organizational variables', *Sociology*, no. 3, pp. 193–214.

LIPSET, S. M. (1963), *The First Nation*, Anchor Edition, New York.

MCCLELLAND, D. C. (1961), *The Achieving Society*, Van Nostrand, Princeton, N.J.

MCMILLAN, C. J., HICKSON, D. J., and HININGS, C. R. (1973), 'The structure of work organizations across societies', *Academy of Management Journal*.

NATH, R. (1968), 'A methodological review of cross-cultural management research', *International Social Science Journal*, no. 20, pp. 35–62.

PONDY, L. R. (1969), 'Effects of size, complexity, and ownership on administrative intensity', *Administrative Science Quarterly*, no. 14, pp. 47–60.
PUGH, D. S., HICKSON, D. J., HININGS, C. R., MACDONALD, K. M., TURNER, C., and LUPTON, T. (1963), 'A conceptual scheme for organizational analysis', *Administrative Science Quarterly*, no. 8, pp. 289–315.
PUGH, D. S., HICKSON, D. J., HININGS, C. R., and TURNER, C. (1968), 'Dimensions of organization structures', *Administrative Science Quarterly*, no. 13, pp. 65–105.
PUGH, D. S., HICKSON, D. J., HININGS, C. R., and TURNER, C. (1969), 'The context of organization structures', *Administrative Science Quarterly*, no. 14, pp. 91–114.
PUGH, D. S., and HICKSON, D. J. (1972), 'Organizational research design', *Administrative Science Quarterly*, no. 17, pp. 273–6.
RICHARDSON, S. A. (1956), 'Organizational contrasts on British and American ships', *Administrative Science Quarterly*, no. 1, pp. 189–207.
THOMPSON, J. D. (1967), *Organizations in Action*, McGraw-Hill, Inc., New York.
UDY, S. H. (1961), 'Technical and institutional factors in production organization', *American Journal of Sociology*, no. 67, pp. 247–60.
UDY, S. H. (1965), 'The comparative analysis of organizations', in J. G. March (ed.), *Handbook of Organizations*, Rand McNally, Chicago.
WEBER, M. (1948), *Essays in Sociology*, H. H. Gerth and C. W. Mills (eds.), Routledge & Kegan Paul.
WHYTE, W. F. (1968), 'Imitation or innovation: reflections on the institutional development of Peru', *Administrative Science Quarterly*, no. 13, pp. 370–85.
WOODWARD, J. (1958), *Management and Technology*, Problems of Progress in Industry Series No. 3, Her Majesty's Stationery Office.
WOODWARD, J. (1965), *Industrial Organization: Theory and Practice*, Oxford University Press.
ZWERMAN, W. L. (1969), *New Perspectives on Organization Theory*, Greenwood, Westport, Connecticut.

15 Theodore D. Weinshall

Multinational Corporations – A Total System Approach to Their Role and Measurement: Some Reflections on Their Supranational, Intercultural and Multistructural Aspects

The text of the three parts of this reading appeared in the form of two articles in *Management International Review*: 'Multinational Corporations – Their Development and Universal Role' (Vol. 15, No. 2/3, 1975) and 'Multinational Corporations – Their Study and Measurement' (Vol. 15, No. 4/5, 1975). These two articles, however, do not include the footnotes and the full selected bibliography which are part of the present reading.

Introduction

In recent years, much has been written about the phenomenon of the multinational corporation. People have tried to describe it, define it and, on occasions, study it. However, too little has been said regarding the reasons for its advent, or regarding its national and international role.[1] Exploring the development of the multinational corporation will improve our understanding of what it is and where it is headed. Likewise, it would make it possible to discover how the multinational corporation differs from other types of corporations from which it evolved, to size up some of its

1. One of the few to deal with the question, 'Why multinational corporations and why now?' was Raymond Vernon (1971). He, however, belittles the significance of the phenomenon and, in fact, claims that multinational corporations have been in existence since ancient times. Samuel Pisar similarly maintained (in a panel discussion broadcast over the French radio on 11 February 1973) that the first multinational organization was the Catholic Church and that the first clash between a nation state and such an organization involved Henry II, King of England, and Thomas à Becket, Archbishop of Canterbury (of *Murder in the Cathedral* fame). In the latter context, although I have myself pointed out the international scope of the decision-making process in some organizations in ancient times (e.g. Egypt under Joseph – Weinshall, 1973a), I beg to differ on definition rather than on fact. The Catholic Church in Thomas à Becket's days was not a multinational organization in the sense that multinational corporations are defined and described in this article, although it is certainly so today.

major problems, to describe the ways in which it handles these problems, and to contemplate ways of measuring its managerial structures.

Let us start by listing some of the underlying points which will be described and analysed in this article:

- Multinational corporations are an inevitable consequence of the evolution of other types of organizations.
- Like any other organization, a multinational organization can be defined and measured by the scope of its decision-making process and by its managerial structure.
- The main difference between the multinational corporation and its national counterparts lies in its *supranational* approach, tending to disregard national interests.
- In these circumstances the multinational corporation can only be defined in behavioural terms.[2] I have used the following definition since 1966: 'A multinational organization is one in which all considerations related to its growth processes and its survival are based wholly on the interests of the organization itself, national pressures having no influence except insofar as constraints are imposed on it by the country within which it functions.'
- Being a multinational corporation is not an absolute question of 'black' vs 'white', but rather a matter of degree. More and more large corporations approximate to the above definition.
- In order to qualify as such, a multinational corporation must operate in several countries,[3] with control of its constituent

2. Attempts to define multinational corporations without allowance for their behavioural aspects usually end up in confusion (e.g. Aharoni, 1971). This is so because the underlying analyses fail to explore their evolution and dynamics or to compare their behaviour with that of other types of organizations.

3. The actual number is immaterial (Brooke and Remmers, 1970, p. 2), so long as we are concerned with at least two countries which differ with regard to their basic influence on the scope of the decision-making process of the organization. Different researchers have suggested different numbers of countries in which the corporation maintains manufacturing facilities, in order to comply with an 'appropriate' definition of a multinational corpor-

agencies throughout the world combined in a system comprising some elements of a multiple managerial structure.

- This means that we can measure the potential capacity of a given organization for operating as a multinational corporation, through its scope of decision-making process and managerial structure. However, we can only establish whether it is actually multinational on the basis of its world-wide behaviour.
- Finally, it seems that the world-wide role, influence and power of multinational corporations is increasing, mainly at the expense of the nation states. I believe this is a development for the better in terms of the true interests, desires and well-being of individuals and groups throughout the world. Be that as it may, they are probably the most important feature of the second half of the twentieth century – hence the urgency for a conceptual understanding of what they are, as well as for an idea of where they are headed, and at what pace.

The inevitability and particularity of the multinational corporation

Let us consider the advent and evolution of the multinational

---

ation. Thus, John Stopford, following the example of Raymond Vernon's other collaborators in his world-wide research (Vernon, 1971), defines 'multinational corporations with headquarters in the U.S.' as those U.S. corporations which have manufacturing facilities in at least *six* countries (Stopford and Wells, 1972). Seev Hirsch, on the other hand, claims that a multinational corporation could operate even in *two* countries (Hirsch, 1971). It seems to me that this minimum suffices so long as we accept incorporation of the behavioural characteristics of the multinational corporation in its definition.

The fact of the matter is that Vernon's group adopted the minimum of six because they already had a sufficiently large sample, as it were. Hirsch, on the other hand, studied multinational corporations with headquarters in smaller countries and had he not chosen a minimum of two his sample would have been too small. It is strange that writers should try to specify a minimal number without relevance to any pragmatic research considerations or conceptual framework; it sometimes looks like picking a number nobody else has used previously (Aharoni, 1971, p. 35.)

The practice of excluding organizations operating in different environments within the same country is a matter of convenience, just as researchers in the effects of culture on management deliberately make synonymous cultural and national aspects.

corporation in terms of three criteria whereby it differs from other organizations:[4]

- Their scope of decision-making processes, i.e. their size in terms of economic activities and the other aspects which contribute to or ensure their survival in competing with other organizations.
- Their managerial structure, through which they control their decision-making process.
- The attitudes of the management towards the various human groups constituting their decision-making process in the different environments within which the corporation operates, within the framework of managerial responsibility for the survival of the total organization.

The growing size of firms: driving corporations into other countries

1. *Human factors in DMP (decision-making process) and environmental systems.* Ever since the Industrial Revolution, more and more groups (employees, trade unions, suppliers, customers, banks, shareholders, governments) have gained power vis-à-vis organizations in terms of ability to paralyse an individual organization by withholding collaboration. This was the result of the growing competition for their resources and services, without which the organization could not survive:[5] namely:

1. Shortly after the Industrial Revolution, which led to division of labour in organizations,[6] any small group of workers was capable of paralysing the manufacturing process of the entire plant, by stopping work at a single stage. This was followed by

4. The choice of the criteria is, to a large extent, in line with George Homans' description of an organization in terms of the actions, interactions and sentiments of the individuals comprising it (Homans, 1959).

5. The definition of an integral human DMP factor is: 'That human factor of the DMP without the cooperation of which the organization cannot survive' (Weinshall, 1971a, p. 3).

6. The Industrial Revolution led to relative predominance of the cost of equipment in the total cost of the manufacturing process. This, in turn, ended the era of the artisan who carried out all operations on the manufactured product, with tools lying idle waiting for their turn while he contemplated one operation. In the new circumstances, it was essential that machines stay idle as little as possible, i.e. that every machine be attended by a different worker (Weinshall and Twiss, 1973, vol. 1, pp. 12–13).

the advent of trade unions, when individual groups of workers discovered that their power would increase if they joined forces and paralysed an entire industry. In due course, however, workers and trade union officials became separate factors in the DMP, pushing or pulling the individual organizations, occasionally in different directions, according to local employment conditions.[7]

2. The needs of mechanization called for more capital than the managers/owners could afford. They had to turn for help first to bankers and, later, to the general public. Naturally, neither bankers nor shareholders would provide capital without a due share of influence on the DMP, and their power varies with the conditions of the money market.
3. Once organizations began competing among themselves not only for labour and capital but for customers as well, the wishes of the latter regarding price, quality, delivery, servicing, etc., became an integral part of the DMP. Similarly, at some earlier stage of process, suppliers of power and manufacturing materials had also become an integral factor in the DMP.[8]

7. During periods of unemployment the workers would generally support the trade unions, who in turn would exert pressure on management and government to create more employment opportunities.

However, during periods of full employment the managements of individual organizations would often offer their workers wages exceeding current union rates. The unions, committed to equal wages for equal jobs, would not agree to this and would find themselves facing a united front of management and workers.

In cases of overemployment, the workers tend to break off with their unions altogether – being in a position to achieve better working conditions on their own. However, once the stage has been reached when the organization can no longer afford giving in to escalating wage demands, it joins forces with the unions to counteract the pressures of individuals and groups of workers (Weinshall and Twiss, 1973, vol. 2, pp. 166–9).

8. Before the Industrial Revolution, and for quite some time after it, European and U.S. manufacturing organizations operated within a so-called seller's market, in which whatever they manufactured was absorbed by the customers without their being exposed to the products of competing firms. The twentieth century witnessed the advent of the buyer's market and in the 1920s the influence and power of the customers and suppliers within the organizational DMP achieved its present level (Weinshall and Twiss, vol. 1, p. 14).

The relative power of the customers and suppliers in the organization's DMP depend not only on the degree of competition in the specific industry or service, but also on the 'purchasing power' of the consumers at the time.

4. Between the two world wars, the governments in more and more countries became decisive factors in the DMPs of all organizations operating within their boundaries. A classical example is the New Deal era in the U.S.[9]

Figure 1 describes schematically the process of inter-organizational competition, governed by the interplay of environmental systems. Thus, managerial success or failure in any corporation is decided not only by what its immediate competitors do but also by what happens in the overall national environment. While the relative position of a corporation in standing up to its immediate competitors depends on its own actions (new products, services, markets and technologies), it can rarely be, by itself, a decisive factor in the national economy. The employment-, money- and consumer-market systems are primarily controlled by government policies (in turn dictated by conditions in other countries throughout the world) and accordingly alternate between shortage and surplus. By contrast, the technological and socio-cultural systems move as a one-way course (albeit at differing speeds), only marginally affected by State intervention (mainly through education).[10]

9. Large-scale government interference in organizations was common in all countries in wartime. The first four major nation states in which governments decisively 'invaded' the DMPs of all their organizations in peacetime between the two world wars were the U.S.S.R. (1917), Italy (1922), the U.S. (1933) and Germany (1933). After the Second World War, this process spread to all the countries of the world, be they 'socialist', 'capitalist', 'industrialized' or 'developing'.

10. It should be noted at this juncture that different teaching and research approaches are called for in dealing with the two major sub-systems of DMP scope – competing organizations and environmental systems. The first sub-system is dealt with in graduate schools of business administration in such courses as Organizational Behaviour and Business Policy, while the second is covered mainly in the various domains of Economics. Unawareness, in many cases, of the difference between them on the one hand, and of their meeting grounds on the other, is most unfortunate – mainly for the students, who feel either that they are taught the same thing twice, or else

The dynamics of the organizational DMPs, described earlier, accounts for the flood of innovations in all walks of organizational life since the Industrial Revolution. The graph in Figure 2 can only be explained in terms of managerial struggle to secure co-operation by all DMP factors through innovations and changes, either ahead of its competitors or after them.[11]

2. *Growth in scope of DMP*. This means that, if a corporation embarks on overseas operations and is successful in doing so, it will eventually force its immediate competitors to follow suit. This 'chain reaction' is similar to the effect of product/service diversification. There are two main reasons why corporations prefer operations in other countries to continued horizontal diversification or to vertical integration. The first is an obvious one – specialization. Once an organization has acquired expertise in a certain product or service line, it feels that it would be simpler to move to another country than to embark upon a new line. The second reason has to do with the environmental systems. If the relative conditions of one of these systems (or preferably several of them) in a certain country are more advantageous than in

---

that they miss some link between the two streams of learning, or both; as for research, Organizational Behaviour and Business Policy situations are studied with what are essentially economic research tools, or else findings regarding managerial and organizational situations are projected to the environmental systems out of context of the research framework (Weinshall and Shimshoni, 1973).

11. The ever-growing size of business organizations has not been welcomed by the cultures of the countries involved. In France, not only take-overs of local companies by multinational corporations (e.g. Bull by General Electric or Citroën by the Agnelli Brothers, owners of Fiat), but even mergers between French companies have been strongly objected to and, when concluded, most difficult to realize (e.g. marketing cooperation between Renault and Peugeot, mergers in the aviation industry, etc.). Even in the United States there has been a lot of opposition to the growth of organizations (Glover, 1954). That this growth was inevitable has been pointed out both by organizational scientists and by economists who have explored the dynamics of the firm (Penrose, 1959). However, even perceptive economists like Edith Penrose stopped short of realizing that there is nothing to stand in the way of this growth – not even managerial limitations. In fact, at every point in history, when firms outgrew the existing managerial structure, the innovative talent invented an appropriate new structure.

another, at any point in time, this is bound to attract organizations from the latter country.

Let us consider examples of different conditions existing in every one of the five environmental systems (see Figure 1):

- *Employment-market system.* Labour is more available in one country than in another. This may mean that not only is labour easier to obtain but that, in specific trades and skills

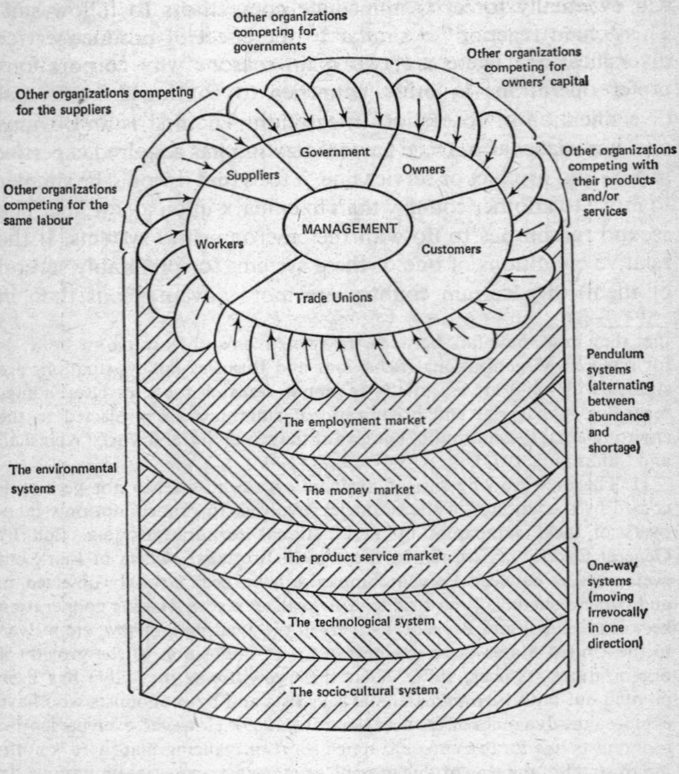

Figure 1 Organizations competing among themselves for the cooperation of their human factors of DMP (decision-making process) within the various environmental systems surrounding them

of both management and workers, one country has more to offer than another. Thus, many organizations in the U.S. and Italy moved part or all of their operations from the North to the South and many started operations in such countries as Spain and Ireland.

- *Money-market system.* If capital is more available and on better terms in one country than in another, this may lead to investments in them. Familiar examples are the oil-producing countries and (more recently) Israel.
- *Consumer-market system.* This system relates both to specific product/service lines where the supply/demand ratio is such that it attracts suppliers from abroad, and in general to an economic situation where all products/services in one country are more in demand than in another because of the higher so-called purchasing power of customers.

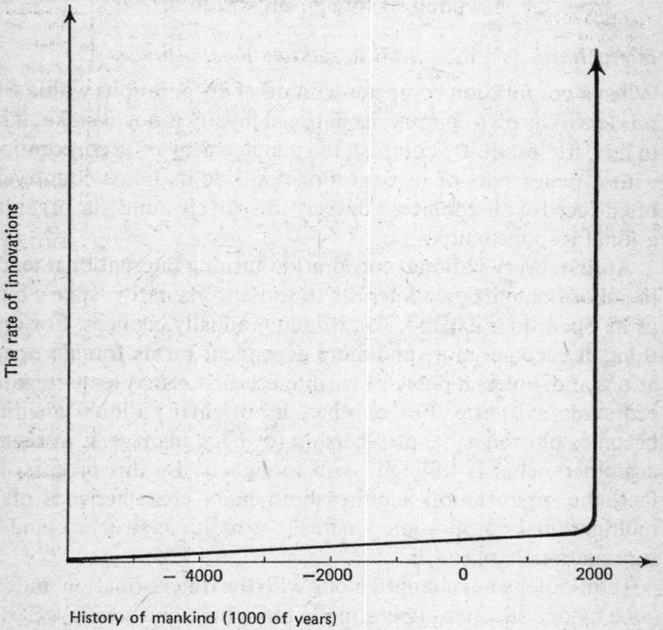

Figure 2 A schematic presentation of the rate of innovations during the history of mankind

- *Technology system.* Every country has a different capacity for absorbing types of technology. This capacity could attract foreign operations in either or both of two ways. A corporation may look for a country where a new technology would be workable and acceptable by all DMP factors, especially management and workers; thus, foreign corporations who have developed a more advanced technology may try to move to the U.S. Conversely, an organization which developed a new technology in one country, rendering its current technology locally obsolete, may look for less developed countries for continued operation of the latter.
- *Socio-cultural system.* This system includes not only the social structure of the country and its cultural values and norms of behaviour but also its political and geopolitical pattern, with the corresponding positive or negative ratings from the viewpoint of foreign organizations.

Intercultural operation leads to supranational attitudes

When a corporation competes with other corporations within the borders of its own country, its national loyalty is not at stake; it is, in fact, irrelevant. By contrast, the management of a corporation with a major part of its operations outside its home country is often faced with conflicts between this loyalty and its organizational responsibility.

At first, every national corporation turning international tends to subordinate its own interests to those of its nation state's but, as its operations expand, its attitude gradually changes. For one thing, it becomes more and more dependent on its foreign operations and, unless it puts its own interests first, it may jeopardize its economic existence. For another, its original national identity becomes blurred as its membership (owners, managers, workers, customers, etc.) is 'diluted' with foreigners. By this process, in fact, the organization acquires both main characteristics of a multinational corporation – namely, a multiple structure and a supranational approach.

Terminology has changed along with the transformation undergone by organizations operating in more than one country. Early 'international' companies always identified themselves with their home countries. Their operations (largely commercial) closely followed the colonial pattern of the country, adhering to the managerial structure and procedures which they found most appropriate at home.[12] Their national identity was even reflected in their names (e.g. U.S. Steel, British Petroleum, etc.); an organization with two 'home countries' to which it was equally committed and loyal duly used a double name – e.g. Royal Anglo-Dutch Shell, Anglo-American Tobacco Company, etc. By contrast, the more recent term 'multinational' implies that the corporation operates throughout the countries rather than transacts its operations between them. (Another term referring to the *supranational* character of such corporations is 'transnational', which some scientists actually regard as more appropriate than 'multinational'.)

Significantly, the advent of the multinational corporation coincided with the demise of the colonial empires. It could well be that, with the loss of its colonial outlets, the international company lost its sense of national affiliation. Moreover, now that some of the industrialized nation states (e.g. the Western European countries) are abandoning their independent economic positions, the way is open for the large corporations to move even further in their supranational attitudes.

Another boost to this supranational trend has recently been provided from some unexpected quarters. Certain national trade unions decided to start moving towards amalgamation and the creation of regional (e.g. European) or even world-wide trade unions, and in a different context Ralph Nader is advocating world-wide customer associations.[13] These developments fit into the conceptual scheme referred to earlier; each human factor in the

12. Some of these organizations applied home procedures to totally irrelevant situations. The story runs that one company circulated instructions in its Nigerian branch to the effect that on 1 October electric stoves were to be issued to all offices, and so they were!

13. The 'apostle' of such universal trade unions is Chemical Workers' Charles Levinson. There have been, in fact, several attempts in this direction. Louis Turner describes these efforts (Turner, 1973), and analyses their problems, successes and failures. Thus, for example, he points out that the International Transport Workers' Federation set a record in dealing with an international industry, in its coordination of shipping unions around the

DMP has its own objective and, vis-à-vis the management, would like to get the most out of its participation in the organization. An organization operating in different countries and facing different and mutually unrelated trade unions and customer populations has the advantage of being able to choose for a specific operation the country where it will encounter the least resistance in this respect. While coordinated action by trade unions, customers or any other factors would make things much tougher for the multinational corporation, it would strengthen its position vis-à-vis the nation state, as its dealings with the above factors would take place, so to speak, over the heads of the local government. In these circumstances, national groups of other factors (e.g. suppliers or bankers) would have to form a united front against the corporation, and eventually so would the governments.

Multinational corporations require multiple (multistructure) managerial structures

It has already been pointed out that, as a multinational corporation moves into more and more countries, the more it tends to operate within a so-called multistructure structure. This becomes especially necessary if the organization embarks on operations which penetrate deeper into the socio-cultural structures of the nation states. The multinational corporation finds out fairly soon that in order to move into, say, manufacturing operations, and achieve more or less similar results in two socio-culturally different countries, it has to control its operations in them through essentially different managerial structures. For example, organizations operating today in the countries of what used to be the British Empire no longer have to deal with identical political and financial frameworks, but are almost fully exposed to free interplay of distinct environmental systems. Fortunately (or perhaps inevitably), the multinational corporations started to employ local managers familiar with the effects of culture on management

world. In the same context, the most publicized success in achieving international parity of earnings was when Walter Reuther's United Auto Workers got Chrysler to concede equal pay for its U.S. and Canadian employees in 1967. Ralph Nader, the U.S. consumers' spokesman and leader, has recently spread his activities to the consumers of multinational corporations the world over (Armstrong, 1971).

in terms of both attitudes and relationships, which the earlier organizations (staffed almost exclusively with 'home country' managers) had mostly lacked.

One can regard the advent of multiple structures as an inevitable consequence of the dynamics of the effects of growth. In order to accommodate substantially different organizational sizes, the management has to operate in different structures according to the

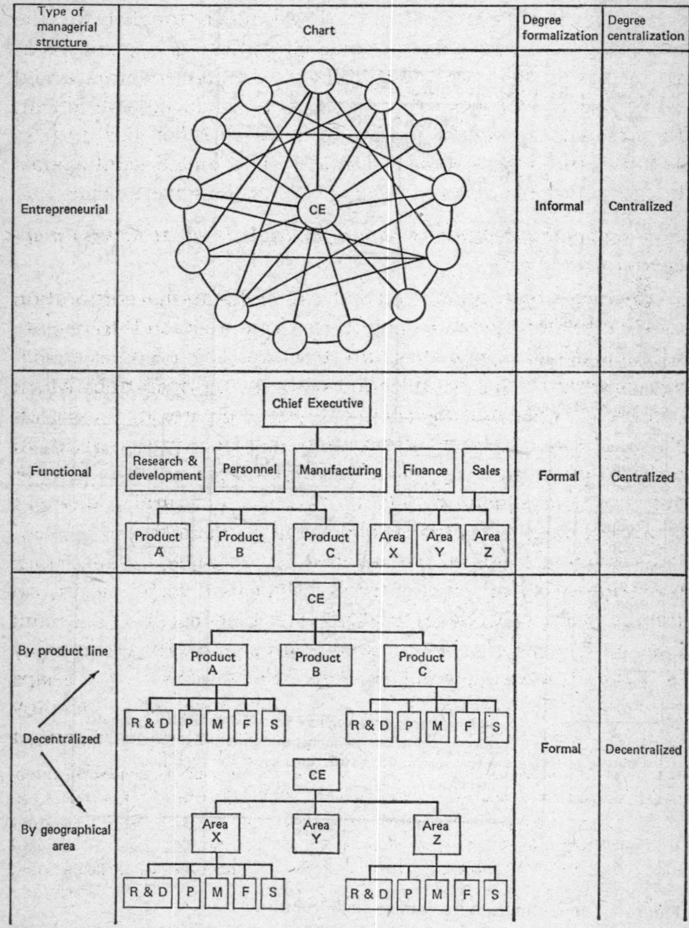

Figure 3 Examples of the basic managerial structures

actual and predicted situation of the organization. An organization would usually go through some or all of the following managerial structures which are also presented in the organigrams (organization charts) Figures 3 and 4:

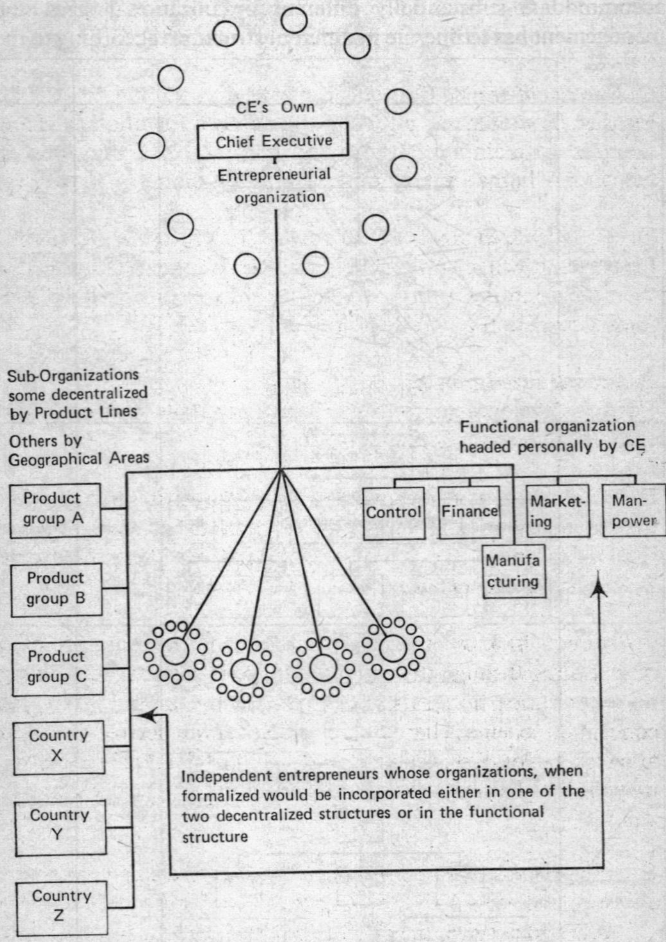

Figure 4 The multistructure managerial structure

A. *Entrepreneurial structure.* Entrepreneurial growth – the stage of foundation and establishment based on centralization and informal communications, with almost no formal structure.

B. *Functional structure.* Formalization of centralization – the stage of bureaucratization, i.e. methods, procedures and functions are introduced resulting in a functional organization.

C. *Functional growth* (formally centralized).
Further development, until the time comes for another change designed to maintain efficiency on the one hand, and meet the demands of human nature for maximum autonomy on the other.

D. *Decentralized structure.* Formalization of decentralization – the stages at which various functions are delegated to the heads of the implementing units, which thereby become self-sufficient (decentralization by product lines or by areas).

E. *Decentralized growth.*
Further development, with the secondary units passing in their turn through some of the above stages.

F. *Multistructure or multiple structure.* Multistructured growth – the secondary units no longer operate within identical structures but within one of the three basic alternatives – entrepreneurial, functional or decentralized.

Figure 5 is a schematic presentation of the progress of an organization through the various managerial structures. Although no organization necessarily proceeds exactly as per Figure 5, the conceptual scheme is based on principles either derived in systematic research or observed again and again in similar situations and may, in the absence of evidence to the contrary, be considered as valid:

- *The organization is bound on a long-range trend of growth* (in terms of scope of DMP). It has already been shown that, in order to survive, the organization has to follow (or lead) the growth pattern of the business field in which it operates. There may be reversals and lapses here and there, but in the long range the growth trend has an upper and a lower bound. In Figure 5 the growth pattern is linear, i.e. always at the same pace, represented by straight lines at the same angle with the time axis. This, of course, is never so in reality.

- *At certain points of its growth the scope of DMP requires a new managerial structure.* Generally speaking, such a point occurs when the organization is moving to essentially new technologies, and/or product/service lines, and/or geographical areas.[14]
- *A basic change in the managerial structure cannot be introduced during a period of rapid growth.* We shall presently see that such a change calls for new managers (whose leadership characteristics conform with those required by the new structure) and necessarily entails a slow-down in the growth in scope of DMP. Sometimes, when the latter has outgrown the capacity of the existing structure, the change actually calls

14. Jean Woodward was the first to show that the scope of DMP is directly related to the production system and, as such, correlates with the managerial structure, which she measured by way of the number of levels of managerial hierarchy and the span of control, i.e. the number of subordinates reporting to the same superior (Woodward, 1965). While Woodward looked at the relation between the scope of DMP from an industrial–sociology point of view, Stopford treated it from an economic and business-administration approach, and also discovered that the managerial structure correlates with the Level of Technology. However, he found that the two most important scope of DMP parameters with which the managerial structure correlated were the product/service diversity and the area diversity (Stopford and Wells, 1972).

It has already been pointed out (footnote 11 above) that new managerial structures had to be 'invented' when the scope of DMP outgrew the capacity of existing structures to control it. It was Weber's bureaucratic organization (Weber, 1967) and the work of the 'scientific management group' in the U.S. which led to the functional structure. The decentralized structure was invented and first introduced in four American corporations, Du Pont, General Motors, Sears Roebuck and Standard Oil of New Jersey (Chandler, 1962). The multiple structure in the Western world seems to have evolved itself, but a business historian like Chandler could perhaps trace the link between the U.S. and European multistructured corporations and those of the Japanese. (See following footnote 16.)

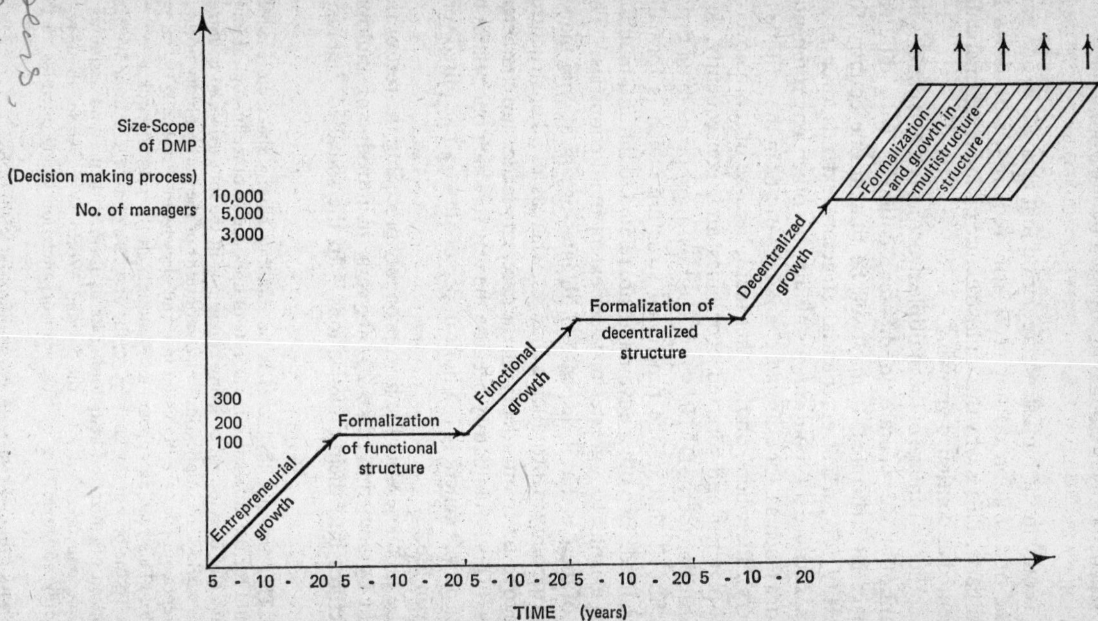

Figure 5 The effects of size on managerial structure

for reduction. Accordingly, structural change periods are schematically presented in Figure 5 by horizontal lines.

It is only in the multistructure period that changes in one part of the organization do not necessarily require a slow-down in other parts. This is why this multistructure period is schematically presented as continued growth.

Another advantage of the multiple structure is that it enables the organization to operate in different countries with different managerial structures. It may well be that in one country the necessity for an entrepreneurial structure extends over many years because of political instability or other environmental reasons (such as, for example, changing patterns in the attitude to bribery). Elsewhere, on the other hand, because of more government-planned and directed economies and, consequently, less competition for the D M P factors, the most appropriate managerial structure is that of the functional structure which is formally centralized. Two other advantages are related to the anti-mobility norm existing to a greater or lesser extent in all countries.[15] The first of these is that it dispenses with inter-organizational managerial mobility in introducing changes, whereas all other structures have to resort to outsiders with the necessary leadership characteristics. (This is mandatory because the way in which one relates to other people generally is a built-in personality trait acquired very early in life.)

The Japanese were the first, probably preceding the rest of the world by something like 20–30 years, in introducing multiple structures into their organizations.[16] In the so-called Zaibatsu,

15. This anti-mobility norm is outstanding among the factors which account for the differences in the rate of application of technological innovations and in standard of living conditions in the industrialized countries of the world. The implications and variations of the anti-mobility norm in different countries are discussed in detail elsewhere (Weinshall, 1973a, pp. 126–9). (This reading appears as Reading 7 in the present book.)

16. To the best of my knowledge, the first case of a large U.S. or Western European organization abandoning its uniform structure and assuming a multiple one occurred after the Second World War. Although there is probably no single U.S. or European organization which operates all the

internal mobility is combined with a systematic executive development programme.[17] Incidentally, this fact led to the mistaken impression that Japan's industry is governed by strict anti-inter-organizational mobility norms. In reality, in the smaller organizations, inter-organizational mobility is not only in existence, but recognized as necessary.[18]

The second additional advantage of the multiple structure is closely related to the one just described and is, indeed, conditional on no (or at least very little) mobility out of the organization. A multistructure organization with almost no mobility, which hires its people at a relatively early age, has an opportunity to learn to know each of them well. This enables top management to ascertain the managerial characteristics of its executives, and assign them

---

possible variants (see Figure 4), there exists today an ever-growing number of non-Japanese organizations which incorporate within them independent entrepreneurs as well as units connected to the centralized functional structure, and units connected to the geographically or the product/service line decentralized structure. Thus, for example, if a company like Nestlé acquires a new chocolate factory in Spain, it has three alternatives of incorporation. It can subordinate it either to the manufacturing function of the functional structure, or to the Chocolate Product Divison which is one of the decentralized structure product/service lines, or finally, to the Iberian Division, which is one of the decentralized structure-independent area operations.

17. The managers are drawn from that part of the organization in which they have served for several years, and undergo some form of re-training, depending on their characteristics: while the ones with bureaucratic leadership characteristics would probably go to the Japanese equivalent of business school programmes, others who are entrepreneurs or entrepreneurs' aides could be sent on a study tour in another country and/or business. Back from re-training, they are posted where their type of leadership (or followership) is required.

18. The legend that anti-mobility has always been part of the Japanese industrial creed probably originated from the first widely circulated book about Japanese business (Abegglen, 1958; see also Roberts, 1970, p. 340); in fact, Abegglen did not go into the history of this norm (reproduced from Japan's traditional family and caste structures), nor did he describe smaller enterprises where it does not exist. Actually, it came into being as late as 1912, following an economic crisis due in part to the high degree of inter-organizational mobility which ran in many cases up to hundreds of per cent annually (Yoshino, 1968).

Zabatsu

to posts where their leadership and followership traits[19] can be best utilized.

The most difficult staffing problem in the multistructure organization is, however, selection of the Chief Executive. It has already been emphasized that the way in which a person best relates himself to others in an organization is established quite early in life, along with other personality traits acquired in early childhood.[20] There are very few people to be found today who could relate themselves in different leadership styles to different people. However, it is exactly such a 'flexible' leader that is needed for the position of Chief Executive of the multistructure structure.

Let us figure out what the role of a Chief Executive of a multistructure organization (Figure 4) would be vis-à-vis his subordinates. The managers in his immediate vicinity, constituting part of his own entrepreneurial 'entourage', would expect him to interfere with them at will at any moment. The managers heading the various functions in the functional structure would be controlled by him usually not more than once a week. The heads of the decentralized product/service divisions and of the decentralized area divisions would report to him on a monthly or, say, a six-monthly basis – and in the meantime would be free to run their

19. The Zaibatsu organizations draw their managers directly from the universities once a year. There is no placement for university graduates at any other time of the year, except immediately after graduation. The large Japanese corporation hires a large number of managers (usually hundreds or thousands at a time) and always from the same university or group of universities. The newly-arrived managers are coached by specially appointed old-timers, who likewise keep an eye on them as to their managerial capacities and future promotional prospects (Drucker, 1971). Drucker credits these mentors with the success of the Zaibatsu organizations in promoting the right people to the top positions: according to him, all the chief executives of Mitsui (probably the largest corporation in the world) were most suitable choices for this highest post over a period of 300 years. Incidentally, he refers to the mentors as 'godfathers', a term which, although appropriate, was an unfortunate choice following the best-seller fiction about the Mafia by this name (Puzo, 1969).

20. There are several main types of leaders who can function properly only in one of the basic three structures. The same types of leaders (and followers) appear throughout the multiple structure, except for the Chief Executive.

sub-organizations as they see fit. Finally, the independent entrepreneurs would be free for periods of up to five or even ten years before the Chief Executive might want to find out whether their sub-organizations have reached a size necessitating formalization of the managerial structure.[21]

It is interesting to note that the 'span of control' of the Chief Executive, i.e. the number of people reporting to him directly, varies widely from one sub-structure to another. In his own entrepreneurial entourage he may have any number (up to 100 or more) of people with whom he is in constant direct contact. In his functional sub-structure he has up to ten heads of the functional departments, while in the decentralized sub-structure he may have several scores of heads of product/service divisions and/or area divisions.

Thus, the Chief Executive of a multiple structure may have to assume a supervisory position towards his subordinates ranging from every few hours, through every few days and every few months, to every few years. In these circumstances his personality traits must include the capacity for flexible leadership for establishing different interpersonal relationship patterns with different managers.

In spite of the fact that people with such characteristics are rare, no shortage of them has been felt to date, as each multistructure organization needs only one Chief Executive and the number of such organizations is not very large.

21. The so-called 'time-span of discretion' (Jacques, 1961) of the Chief Executive's subordinates thus ranges from a few hours to a few years. Although it is doubtful whether one would ever reach the ability to establish equitable remuneration for managers exclusively on this basis, Jacques's concept of equitable payment correlated with the time-span of discretion undoubtedly applies in principle to the managers subordinated to the Chief Executive of a multistructure organization, in that the longer the time-span, the higher the remuneration. Thus, the salary scale of these managers will range from high to low as follows:

Independent entrepreneurs
Heads of the independent product/service line or area divisions in the decentralized sub-structure
Heads of the functions in the functional structure
Entrepreneurs' aides surrounding the Chief Executive in his own entrepreneurial sub-structure.

The role and particular contribution of the multinational corporations

We have already established that multinational corporations are concrete and definable. We have also concluded that their advent in the middle of the twentieth century was inevitable and that they are here to stay, encompassing more and more of the industrial and business activities of the world. Now that it is clear that we and our descendants will have to live with this extraordinary phenomenon, let us speculate about their impact on humanity. In other words, are we facing a brighter, better and safer world, or are we headed for what George Orwell and Anthony Burgess have so vividly projected in *1984* and *A Clockwork Orange*?

The dominant fact is that the multinational corporations are taking over some of the basic roles hitherto traditionally regarded as the province of the nation states. The other implications may be summed up as follows:

- The multinational corporations constitute barriers to war.
- They move technology, capital, know-how and more advanced standards of living from the developed to the developing areas of the world, helping bridge existing economic gaps.
- They carry with them the most advanced managerial concepts and techniques.
- They induce less advanced nation states, through their mere presence, to change their cultural environments.

Encroachment on the authority and power of the nation states

Over the years, large corporations have undertaken more and more services for their employees, traditionally (at least, in the western world) considered as the province of the state.[22] Likewise, we have witnessed increasing manifestations of so-called 'public responsibility'. The latter usually starts with the organization

22. The degree of this so-called 'responsibility towards the employees' is closely linked to the socio-cultural system prevailing in the country. Its most extreme manifestation is in Japan, where many organizations provide not only housing and education for their staff, but also schooling and even marriage portions for their children (Abegglen, 1958).

contributing to the socio-cultural life of the community within which it operates. (This could be something like the Corning Glass Museum[23] in upstate New York, or the comprehensive schooling system, from elementary to university level, established by Philips in Eindhoven.) The next step is usually a contribution by the organization to some other aspect of life in the country where it operates – not excluding local political activity. The third step consists in the organization allowing, or perhaps even encouraging its managers to participate in, public activities of a variety of types, eventually assuming governmental positions, on a 'dollar a year' basis.

The degree of this 'public responsibility' of business corporations mainly depends on two factors – the size of the organization (its scope of DMP) and the socio-cultural system (including the political sub-system) of the country in which it operates. Thus, small and relatively poor organizations cannot afford it where the socio-cultural system is favourable, whereas even the largest U.S. corporations operating in a country like the U.S.S.R. are in no position to attempt it even if they wanted to.

Obviously, the larger the corporation, the more power and authority it tends to abstract from the government. From its own point of view, the latter does not mind so long as the corporations contribute towards the maintenance of the services which are within its own responsibility. However, the moment it feels that the corporation's actions run counter to its policies, it introduces suitable legislation against them. This becomes problematic when the government is dealing with a multinational corporation. The dependence of countries on multinational corporations is steadily increasing[24] and governments are becoming less able to discipline

23. The Corning Glass museum is not the only unique world example in its own field of operation. In the author's home town, Haifa, Dr Reuben Hecht, the entrepreneur of 'Dagon' (the largest grain site in Israel) established the only wheat and grain museum in the world.

24. As early as 1963, American firms, some of which were (or subsequently became) multinational corporations, owned the following industries in France: 40 per cent of the petroleum industry, 45 per cent of the rubber industry, 65 per cent of the telecommunications equipment, etc. (Servan-Schreiber, 1967, p. 25). According to the same source, the same American

them.[25] This is why one could predict, as we have already done, that in the not-too-distant future governments will get together to consider joint action against the manoeuvres of multinational corporations. (This has already happened in specific limited fields like that of currency flow and exchange.) Such collaboration between governments may turn out to be the best (albeit unintended) gift of the multinational corporations to humanity.

Prevention of wars

The topic of war and peace is as old as history and there is a real question whether wars are altogether unavoidable, considering that 'the imagination of man's heart is evil from his youth', (Genesis 8: 21). It is clear, however, that the more the world advances technologically, the more horror war could entail. This goes for localized wars too but, of course, it is the prospect of an atomic global war which hangs like the shadow of doom over the human race.

It is here that the multinational corporations make a significant contribution in preventing armed conflict and perhaps removing its causes, primarily the economic ones. A multinational corporation operating in several countries can ill afford to lose its assets, customer markets, manpower, supplier and capital sources, which would be in jeopardy if any of these countries were involved in a war among themselves. (An outstanding example is Fiat. Whether through licensing or straightforward ownership, the

---

organizations held, in 1967, the following shares in Europe's electronic industries:

50 per cent in the semi-conductor industry
80 per cent in the computer industry
95 per cent in the integrated-circuit industry

25. A grim example, recently disclosed (Sampson, 1973), of how far a multinational corporation may go in its 'supranational' behaviour is that of ITT (probably the first Western multinational corporation) which actually manufactured armaments in Germany before and during the Second World War, until its installations were destroyed by Allied bombing. All this in spite of ITT being an 'American' corporation.

Agnellis are directly connected with a major part of the car industry in several European countries, e.g. Italy, Spain, France and the U.S.S.R. Involvement of any of these countries on different sides of a war would probably mean a mortal blow to the corporation.)

The role of the multinational corporations in this respect goes far beyond that of a fire brigade. The recent détente between the U.S. on the one hand and China and the U.S.S.R. on the other owes much to the multinational corporations, who urged the U.S. government to open the way for them into these vast potential markets.

Narrowing the gap between the rich and poor parts of the world

One of the major problems of the world is the gap between its rich and poor parts. Although the nation states have been getting together and seeking solutions, the resulting plans fall short of the needs or are impracticable.[26] In fact, it seems that bringing the poorer nation states closer to the richer ones would primarily be achieved through pressures from the grass-roots rather than from the top.

The multinational corporations, searching for environments in which they could find new and (from their point of view) more suitable labour, trade unions, customers, suppliers, governments, etc., are also attracted to the poorer countries of the world, cutting across borders and tariff barriers. Their impact on the economies of these countries penetrates pressures for higher standards of living and levels of education. In this latter respect, in particular, government efforts have hitherto produced negligible results. For example, African and Indian university graduates returning to their countries found neither the jobs nor a congenial atmosphere for them to apply their education productively. Many of them stayed in the countries where they had been trained, or

26. One such plan was put forward by David Horowitz, then Governor of the Bank of Israel, who suggested that every rich nation state devote 1 per cent of its GNP to the poorer states (Horowitz, 1960). Robert McNamara, President of the World Bank, recently put forward a similar plan in which the proposed percentage was 5 per cent. None of these plans ever progressed beyond the academic stage.

returned to them following frustrating experiences. This situation is being remedied to some extent by the multinational corporations who provide the lacking employment opportunities while gradually raising the level of the positions staffed with local residents, training them themselves or sending them to appropriate universities.[27]

Using and spreading modern and advanced managerial concepts and technologies

Multinational corporations resort to the most sophisticated concepts and techniques available, both in their current operations and in planning for the future. They are the only organizations which try to forecast, as best they can, how the environment will develop during the next 10, 20, 30 or even 50 years, and take these forecasts into considerations in their own long-range planning. By contrast, democratic governments limit their 'future' to the period between one election and another and rarely exceed ten years. As for totalitarian régimes, although they speak in terms of 'eternity' (Hitler's 1,000-year Reich!), their practical life-span is mostly of the same order as that of their democratic counter-parts.[28] In the circumstances, governments often make use of the environmental forecasts and analyses of the corporations.[29]

As multinational corporations move from one country to

27. A more detailed discussion of the relation between the size of nations (in terms of their human and other resources) and the scopes of DMP is given in an earlier paper by the author (Weinshall, 1973b).

28. It is interesting to note that even in ancient days it was common practice for the more tyrannical rulers to speak of their régimes as being there to stay.

29. One example to the contrary is an African country in which one of the largest European corporations was operating on a large scale. On instructions from his headquarters, the local manager prepared periodical reports on the environmental conditions, to be used as bases for long-range planning. As a result, he was charged with espionage; and neutral organizational scientists had to testify on his behalf, to the effect that periodical reports on environmental conditions are part of the managerial technique of modern corporations.

another, they carry along with them their accumulated knowledge and know-how of managerial concepts and technologies. This does not mean, of course, that they introduce the most advanced concepts and technologies into every single country. They do, however, try to go as far as possible.

Inducing cultures to adapt to economic developmental needs

Multinational corporations are what one could refer to as 'change agents'. They are undoubtedly the most powerful carriers of the convergence of cultures[30] as a result of the effects of spreading technology and its attendant factors (education, standard of living, etc.).

The effects of the multinational corporations on nation states, in inducing their cultures to adapt to economic developmental needs, may be seen in what has happened in some European countries since the Second World War.

There is no doubt that Marshall Plan aid to Germany had contributed enormously to that country's post-war recovery. It seems, however, that its achievement in not only regaining its technological lead over other European countries but also adapting its managerial structures to the requirements of the ever-growing scope of DMP – is due to the multinational corporations rather than to U.S. government aid.

Germany was the country which opened its doors widest to the multinational corporations, at the same time opening its mind to its organizational culture – thanks, apparently, to its traditional ability to adapt relatively quickly to new behav-

30. The term 'convergence' is part of a terminology used by writers on the relation between culture and management. According to Ross Webber, the divergence and convergence dichotomy consists roughly of some people believing that cultural diversity is there to stay, and others maintaining that the cultures are drawing close together (Webber, 1970). Howard Perlmutter extends the terminology to include four different approaches to the predicted future of the cultures of industrialized countries – divergence, submergence, convergence and emergence (Perlmutter, 1969). Emergence is what Perlmutter himself believes to be the outcome of multinational corporations creating an integrated culture, which would dominate the industrial world (a belief shared by this author).

ioural trends. Take, for example, inter-organizational managerial mobility. The stereotype German manager had always been one entering an organization at the lowest level and slowly advancing, in an apprenticeship fashion, up the hierarchy, never moving to another organization. Today, the rate of inter-organizational mobility in Germany is higher than in any other European country and the relevant attitudes and norms are rapidly changing.[31]

The effects of the multinational corporations on the national culture are felt even in France, where behaviour is both more individualistic and more traditional than in Germany (one 'classical' contrast between the two nations is said to be that every German wants to buy what his neighbour has just bought, while every Frenchman wants something different from what his neighbour owns). Organizational behavioural changes could be discerned in France within the boundaries of subsidiaries of multinational corporations and, although only a few of these changes have spilled over into the environmental socio-cultural system, this is a beginning.

A research approach to the different aspects of the multinational corporations

The term 'measurement' applied to scopes of DMP and to managerial structures is bound to evoke a sceptical response. There is no claim in this article (nor, I am sure, in the work of the overwhelming majority of social scientists) that organizational behaviour lends itself to measurement at the same (let alone a higher) degree of precision as natural-science phenomena. Nevertheless, even

31. Studies comparing Chief Executives in the U.S. with their counterparts in six Western European countries (De Bettignies, 1970), in Scandinavia (De Bettignies and Evans, 1971) and in Israel (Margalit and Weinshall, 1972) include, inter alia, very illuminating inter-country comparisons as to differences in their inter-organizational mobility. A study at the international business school of INSEAD (European Institute for Business Administration), Fontainebleau, showed that the attitudes of German students towards the anti-mobility value changed more rapidly than those of their colleagues from other countries, as a result of the multinational business education they received (Weinshall, 1973a).

at this early and crude stage, both the scope of DMP and the managerial structure can be determined with the available measuring tools described below.

The use of these tools is of special importance for two main reasons:

- First, it would permit rapid identification of the need for running the organization as a multinational corporation, in other words determining whether its scope of DMP has reached the change level.
- Second, the managerial structure of the whole organization could be compared with that dictated by the total organizational scope of DMP, determined in the preceding step.

The general proposition is described in Table 1. The analytical steps are, in their order of sequence: decide what the scope of DMP is; determine the actual managerial structure; determine the leadership characteristics of the key managers.

The diagnostic alternatives for the same organization undergoing a growth process are (see Table 1):

Analytical Steps	*Diagnostic Alternatives*			
	A	B	C	D
1 Scope of DMP	+	+	+	+
2 Managerial Structure	+	–	+	–
3 Leadership Characteristics of Managers	+	–	–	+

Table 1 Four organizational situations – balance and imbalance between scope of DMP, managerial structure and leadership characteristics

(A) the actual managerial structure is the one required by the scope of DMP, and the key managers have the leadership (and followership) characteristics required by the managerial structure.

(B) the organization has 'outgrown' its managerial structure; this means that while the scope of DMP has increased, the key managers have not changed and the managerial structure is the same.

(C) at this point the scope of DMP could have somewhat increased or remained the same as above. The disparity between scope of DMP and managerial structure forces the organization to adapt the latter, without, however, bringing in new key managers. The leadership characteristics of the managers are thus not in line with the structure; they are either coerced into a behaviour incompatible with their personality traits, or voluntarily adopt an 'artificial' one.[32]

(D) a preferable solution lies in bringing in new key managers with leadership characteristics in line with the requirements of the scope of DMP. Once brought in, they rapidly transform the existing managerial structure and it is back to (A).

Let us now consider the measuring tools and some examples,

32. There is one exception which does not fall into the pattern of the three behaviour alternatives (personality-trait, coerced, and 'artificial' voluntary), namely periods of extreme emergency (e.g. war). On such occasions a person naturally adopts a leadership (or followership) behaviour not in line with his personality traits. Such behaviour, however, lasts only for the duration of the actual emergency.

Conceptually, this phenomenon could be explained by a sociological interpretation of Maslow's hierarchy of needs (Maslow, 1954, pp. 80–93). We are born into, and brought up for the first several years within, a certain behavioural environment which could be described in Maslow's terms as a search for physiological and safety needs (under war and/or hunger conditions), or for belongingness and love (in their absence), or for esteem (or social standing), or self-actualization (i.e. self-fulfilment). In the industrialized countries, the prevailing situation most of the time is that of search for social standing and recognition. So long as this situation prevails, voluntary behaviour which is affected by personality traits does not change. However, if a situation reverts to, say, war, the overwhelming majority of people will relinquish their personality-affected behaviour and *voluntarily* adopt a behaviour conducive to their environmental needs at the time (e.g. accept military discipline and routine). This will last as long as such needs are perceived and felt.

with special reference to multinational corporations and multiple structures.

Scopes of decision-making processes

We have already seen that, in order to establish the scope of DMP of an organization, we have to find out what are the technological, product/service lines and geographical areas of operations chosen by management in order to stand up to direct competition for its factors of DMP from other organizations. In a simplified procedure, the two last parameters suffice for relating the scope of DMP to the managerial structure. This method is a short cut, in which determination of the level and diversity of technology is circumvented. This is possible because there is a large degree of congruence between product/service diversity and technological diversity. In these circumstances, determination of the other two parameters becomes a relatively simple matter. This is done, according to Stopford, as follows:

The product/service lines of the organization are identified and related to an existing product/service classification, such as the U.S. Standard Classification.

The geographical areas in which the organization is selling its products and/or services are identified.

The total (i.e. sales) turnover is resolved into a matrix of the product/service lines by geographical areas.

The following two ratios are measures of the two parameters:

$$\text{Degree of Product/Service Diversity} = \frac{\text{Sales Turnover of Product/Service Line with Largest Turnover}}{\text{Total turnover}}$$

$$\text{Degree of Geographical Diversity} = \frac{\text{Sales Outside the Country with Largest Turnover}}{\text{Total Turnover}}$$

Stopford divides each of the two parameters into three grades, as follows:

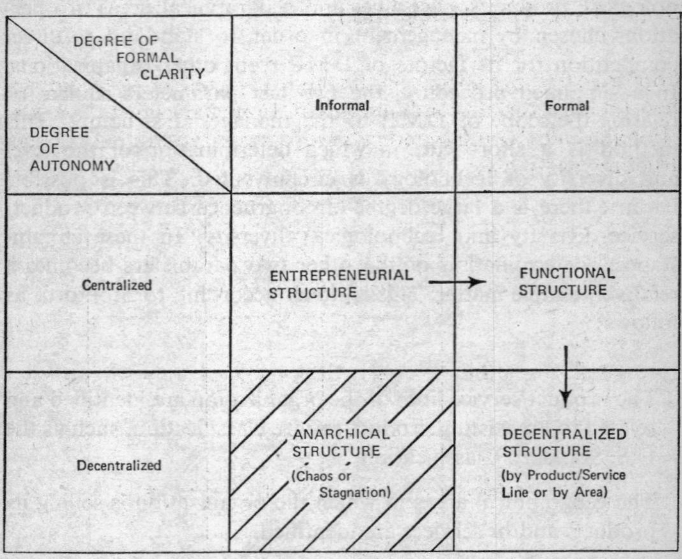

The three grades of Degree of Geographical Diversity are specific in the above matrix. The grades of None, Low and High of Degree of Product Diversity require some elaboration. This is how Stopford himself explains it:

A highly diversified product line is defined in this study by the condition that $n \times s$ is greater than 1 where:

n = number of two-digit industries represented in the product line

and s = proportion of total sales generated by products outside the major industry.

For example, a firm with sales divided in the percentages of 40, 30,

30 among three industries satisfies the condition of n × s greater than 1, since n = 3 and s = 0·60. Such a firm is, therefore, in a category of high product diversity. Similarly, low product diversity is defined by the condition that n × s lies between 0 and 1. Thus, a firm operating in two-digit industries is necessarily classified in the low category even if there is an equal share of the total sale in the two industries. Firms that have all their operations entirely within a single two-digit industry are classified as having no product diversity. (Stopford and Wells, 1972, p. 185.)

Stopford's findings appear on the table on page 416. According to these findings, certain combinations of 'Foreign Product Diversity – Foreign Sales' could be indicative of specific types of managerial structure, as follows:

Foreign product diversity (Degree of product diversity)	0-20%	21%-39%	Over 39%
High	7	8	9
Low	4	5	6
None	1	2	3

Foreign sales
(Degree of geographical diversity)

Type of Managerial Structure	Square-Numbers on 'Foreign Product Diversity – Foreign Sales' Matrix																		Totals			
	1		2		3		4		5		6		7		8		9					
	No. of Org.	%	No. of Org.	%	No. of Org.	%	No. of Org.	%	No. of Org.	%	No. of Org.	%	No. of Org.	%	No. of Org.	%	No. of Org.	%	No. of Org.	No. of R.O	% of Rel. Org.	% of Cov.
																				*	**	***
International Division (Functional Structure)	30	100	13	92			25	66											68	68	83	100
Area Divisions (Decentralized Structure)			(1)		10	100			(2)		(2)				(1)		(1)		17	10	100	59
World-wide Product Divisions (Decent. Struct.)							(9)		(2)				12	85	(7)				30	12	85	40
Mixed Structure (Multistructure Structure)							(4)		8	67	(1)		(2)		(6)		1	67	22	10	67	40
**** Grid Structure (Multistructure Structure)															(2)		1		3			
Total	30	100	14	100	10	100	38	100	12	100	3	100	14	100	16	100	3	100	140	100	83	71

*, **, ***, **** — appearing at the bottom of page 417

* These are the organizations next to which appear their percentages (and they do not appear in parenthesis)

** These are again the percentages of the number of Relevant Organizations out of the total number of organizations appearing in the same squares of the matrix. Thus, for example, for the International Division type:

$$\% \text{ of Relevant Organizations} = \frac{30 + 13 + 25}{30 + 14 + 38} \times 100 = \frac{68}{82} = 83\,\%$$

*** This is the percentage of the Relevant Organizations for every managerial structure, out of all the organizations which were found to have such a structure. Thus, for example, for the organizations with 'Area Divisions' managerial structure:

$$\% \text{ of Coverage} = \frac{10}{17} = 59\,\%$$

**** It is assumed that a so-called 'Grid Structure' cannot exist for a prolonged period of time and that it is an intermediary step towards a Multistructure Structure. This is why Stopford's Mixed Structure and Grid Structure were combined on this table.

The probabilities that organizations with the above 'Foreign Product Diversity – Foreign Sales' would indeed be according to the above specified managerial structures vary from 67 per cent to 100 per cent (percentage of relevant organizations). The above squares cover only 40 per cent of World-wide Product Divisions and Mixed and Grid Structure organizations and 59 per cent of the Area Divisions organizations. Only for the International Division organization there is a 100 per cent coverage in the above squares of the grid.

'Traumatic' Expansion in the Scope of DMP	*Required Change in Managerial Structure*	
	From	*To*
1 Moving from a simple technology to a more complex one (34)	Entrepreneurial Structure	Functional Structure
2 Diversifying from one product/service line to two or more (35)	Functional Structure	Decentralized by Product/Service Lines
'Traumatic' Expansion in the Scope of DMP	*Required Change in Managerial Structure*	
	From	*To*
3 Moving to operation in several countries, usually manufacturing in each of them only a few product/services. (Environment permitting operation within a Functional Structure.)	Decentralized by Product/Service Lines	Decentralized by Geographical Areas
4 Moving to operation in countries with markedly different environmental systems and adapting the product/service lines to the opportunities and constraints prevailing in each country. (Opportunities and constraints affected both by competing organizations and by environmental systems.)	Decentralized by Geographical Areas	Multiple Managerial Structure

So-called 'traumatic' stages in the scope of DMP (established by the parameters of technology, product/service diversification and geographical spread) related to different managerial structures are shown in Table 2.[33]

33. These are the results of John Stopford's study (Stopford and Wells, 1972) reported elsewhere (Weinshall, 1971) together with Worthy's study in Sears Roebuck (Worthy, 1949), Woodward's study in 100 industrial organizations in South Essex (1965), and a clinical study in one U.S. industrial organization (Weinshall, 1960). Other relevant studies are those of Burns and Stalker carried out in Scottish and English electronics organizations (Burns and Stalker, 1961) and of Lawrence and Lorsch, carried out in the organizations of the plastic materials, containers and consumer foods businesses industries in the U.S. (Lawrence and Lorsch, 1968). All of them are focused on the relation between the scope of DMP, the managerial structure and the leadership characteristics, although the terminology used and the coverage of the constituent elements differ from one study to another.

34. Several methods are available for measuring the level of technology. Two of these are Bright's typology of levels of mechanization (Bright, 1958) and Jean Woodward's typology of production systems (Woodward, 1965). Comparison of Bright's seventeen 'levels of mechanization' and Woodward's three production systems shows that the latter method is preferable for studying the effects of technology on management structure (Weinshall and Twiss, 1973, vol. 1, pp. 27–39).

35. It should be noted here the two-digit classification used by Stopford is far too broad for identifying 'traumatic' expansion. Even if a three-digit system is used, the difference between one product/service line and another would be quite large. For example, the three-digit groups within the two digit group 37 are:

Major Group 37 – Transportation Equipment
371 Motor Vehicles and Motor Vehicle Equipment
372 Aircraft and Parts
373 Ship and Boat Building and Repairing
374 Railroad Equipment
375 Motorcycles, Bicycles and Parts
376 Miscellaneous Transportation Equipment

Thus, addition of one or more product/service lines to an original three-digit line, within the same two-digit product/service line would still constitute a 'traumatic' change.

In addition to the above, the effect of each environmental system (Figure 1) must be determined separately. Of the above five systems, the first three (the employment-market system, the money-market system and the product/service supply-demand system) can be studied both qualitatively and quantitatively,[36] and the remaining two (the technological system, namely the environmental human capacity to absorb technology, and the socio-cultural system, which consists of the educational, legal, political and geopolitical aspects of the environment)[37] only qualitatively. The need for elaborate environmental analysis may be obviated by identifying, as early as possible, the 'bottleneck' system, namely the system which has the largest effect on the organizational scope of DMP.[38] Thus, for example, if the employment market is identified as the bottleneck system, it is this system which needs thorough analysis, while for the others superficial scanning will do.

However, if we are concerned with organizations operating in different countries, analysis of the technological and socio-cultural systems in each country is unavoidable. It is this analysis

36. Qualitative study of the three systems could best be done through case studies in which the effects of each environmental system on the organizational scope of DMP are described. Thus, for example, the fluctuations of the employment market pendulum (Weinshall and Twiss, 1973, vol. 2, pp. 167–70) in Israel were described through case studies written during the 1962–3 full-employment, the 1966 unemployment, and the 1970 over-employment periods (Blustein and Weinshall, 1972).

Quantitative analysis in the three systems could be based on statistical measurements. Thus, for example, the foreign manpower employed in the merchant navy of a country like Israel is a good indicator of the employment market system (Niego, 1962). Alternatively, the differences in the relation between pre-tax profit rates on the one hand, and the rate of bankruptcies and take-overs on the other could be indicative of the money market system of the country; Kuehn presented, in a paper to the 1973 TIMS Conference in Israel, a statistical analysis of such a relation for British firms (Kuehn 1973).

37. The technological and socio-cultural systems are interrelated to some extent. These are the most important systems to be studied by multinational corporations. Such analyses are usually available in books relating technology, culture and government to business and management, which are up-dated from time to time.

38. The term 'bottleneck analysis' is discussed in greater detail elsewhere (Weinshall, 1973b).

which provides an answer to the two questions posed in the last two 'traumatic' changes of Table 2, namely:

- Does the environment permit an operation within a functional structure?
- Do the environmental systems in one country differ from those in another to such an extent that, even with technology, product/service line diversity and geographical spread identical, the scope of DMP is so different as to necessitate different managerial structures?

The first question is a special case of the second. There are countries in which, because of the socio-cultural system, there is a need for many organizations to operate within an entrepreneurial structure – for example, countries in which governmental operation is based on personal deals and bribery.

In general, the scopes of DMP of organizations may differ from one country to another, because the environmental systems create different types of competitive 'laissez-faire'.

This is due not only to the degree of political control of the economy. Consider the Japanese environment, in which there is extensive linkage, coordination and support between organizations. The absence of inter-organizational mobility for managers reduces even further the scopes of DMP of organizations which on the face of it, judged by technology, product diversity and geographical dispersal – should be similar to their counterparts in the U.S. and Western Europe.[39]

To sum up, thorough analysis of the scope of an organizational DMP is an elaborate task. This is especially when one tries to extrapolate the scope of DMP into the future, i.e. combine environmental analysis with corporate planning. Approaches to

39. The effects of the environmental systems on the scopes of DMP are also vividly illustrated by the organizational behaviour of the Mafia, which ignores or defies four of them in all organizations under its control (including those with a 'respectable' façade) – the exception being the technological system.

such analysis and planning have already been conceptualized,[40] and the ideas as to measurement of the scope of DMP presented in this section could be considered as a rough substitute for more elaborate methods.[41]

Managerial structures

Managerial-structure measurements should be based on combined evaluation of the informal and formal structure of the management organization. This is achieved by comparing the managers' perceptions of their informal position in the organization with the requirements of the organigram (organization chart).

The practical procedure consists, on the one hand, in being asked to 'list the names of people with whom you generally work most closely, regardless of their position in the organization', and (on the other hand) in the Chief Executive being asked to draw an organigram.

The degree of formalization or informalization (the so-called 'clarity' of the formal structure) and comparison of the organigram with the working relationships as perceived, yield the degree

40. An outline of such concepts has been the basis of the work of John D. Glover and his colleagues at the Harvard Business School since the late 1950s (Glover, 1970). Glover divides the environment into four systems – 'Community', 'Culture', 'Habitat' and 'Product'. He perceives the business corporation as a system of productive agents converting various types of inputs into various types of outputs.

41. The ideas for measuring the scope of DMP presented in this article, are based on a static review. Glover's outline presents a more dynamic approach in that it suggests 'pro-forma' environmental analysis and corporate planning, which would take into account forecast conditions in the future.

A 'futurological approach', however, could sometimes be carried too far. Thus, Herman Kahn recently ventured a forecast as to France's relative economic position in Europe, conflicting with the evaluation of most scientists, French or non-French; it seems that Kahn based his forecast primarily on Gross National Product figures, overlooking some basic phenomena in the French socio-cultural system (Kahn and Weiner, 1967).

Managers outside the U.S. are in the fortunate position that much of what is done by 'futurologists' in relation to the U.S. can be done by themselves by observing what is happening there, the question they have to ask being essentially not 'what' but 'when'.

of centralization (or decentralization) of control, authority and responsibility in the hands of the Chief Executive (the so-called 'autonomy' of the sub-units).

Taken in conjunction, they provide in principle the matrix of managerial structures (see Figure 6) defined earlier in this paper. (The fourth situation – Anarchy – although possible, is inherently dysfunctional to the organization.) The technique by which the managerial structure is thus evaluated and based on action research studies in specific organizations is called the Informalogram.[42]

Among the thirteen organizations hitherto studied simultaneously by the informalogram and a clinical action research, one was found to have a multiple structure. This was a foreign-owned shipping organization operating in Japan and comprising two distinct parts – one running its shipping lines and the other serving as its shipping agents. It so happened that, while the shipping agency's management was exclusively Japanese, the two top levels of management in the shipping lines were non-Japanese – mostly nationals of the Western country where the owner company was located and to whose headquarters the operations centred in Japan were weakly linked. Analysis of the managerial structure in the two sub-organizations revealed different structures.[43] The

42. The degree of clarity and degree of autonomy are established through four so-called 'structural measurements', based on mutually-perceived working relationships (MPWRs) between pairs of managers who mention each other when listing the people with whom they work most closely:

Informal Activity	– average number of MPWRs per manager
Formal-Informal Coverage	– percentage of organigram relationships covered by MPWRSs
Individual Autonomy	– number of participants at least removed from the Chief Executive in terms of MPWRs
Inter-unit Independence	– ratio of intra-unit and rater-unit MPWRs

The informalogram background, the research findings during 1957–72 and the details of the technique appear elsewbere (Weinshall, 1973d). The informalogram has been used to date in Britain, France, Japan and Israel.

43. This use of the informalogram is described in a sociometric case study elsewhere (Weinshall, 1973c).

non-Japanese sub-organization had a functional structure, partially decentralized in the relationships between the Chief Executive and the management; a larger degree of decentralization was apparently impossible, due to an insufficient number of managers and other resources. In the Japanese sub-organization, while, on the one hand, the clarity of the formal structure and the mutual dependence of individuals and units indicated a functional structure, the informal activity of the managers did not. In fact, the managerial structure was characterized by Japanese culture-bound behaviour and, especially, of the so-called *ringi* decision-making process.[44] In these circumstances it was not surprising to discover through the action research that the Chief Executive was relating himself differently to the managers in the two sub-organizations.

Managerial attitudes

Of the wide spectrum of studies on managerial attitudes, we shall confine ourselves to two types, one determining the degree of satisfaction with the existing structure and the other describing attitudes in different cultures. Managerial attitudes should always be studied as part of an organizational research, in order to establish whether the leadership (and followership) characteristics of the managers are in line with the structure dictated by the scope of DMP and with the actual structure. This could be done by a set of standardized questions exploring the attitudes of the managers towards such things as formal organization, freedom and help in doing the job and, most of all, the degree of satisfaction with various aspects of the work and the organization. Managerial

44. The *ringi* process has been described by Mike Yoshino as follows:

> The word *ringi* consists of two parts – *rin*, meaning submitting a proposal to one's superior and receiving his approval, and *gi*, meaning 'deliberations and decisions'. The ringi system has, indeed, all of these features.
>
> . . . the lower-echelon managerial staff member must follow a certain procedure. He must draft a document known as a *ringisho*. In this document he must describe the matter to be decided and his recommendation as to what ought to be done.
>
> By complex and circuitous paths, the *ringisho* slowly works its way up to top management, eventually reaching the president. When the president approves the *ringisho* by affixing his seal, the decision is final. The *ringi* document is then returned to the original drafter for implementation.

(Yoshino, 1968, pp. 254–5).

satisfaction should, likewise, be explored through clinical research, i.e. non-directive interviewing.[45]

The importance of finding out how managerial attitudes vary from one cultural environment to another for the operation of multinational corporations in different countries is self-evident. Several international studies on managerial attitudes have been carried out since the early 1950s. However, until recently these studies did not necessarily involve specific organizations.[46] Eventually, similar studies were devised for groups of managers in specific organizations – sometimes from different countries within the same multinational corporation.[47]

For determining the supranational attitudes of the multinational corporation, two possible procedures are available.

The first is through a clinical research both at the top and at the country level, in order to corroborate the multinational behaviour expressed by top management. Interviewees should include not only managers but workers, customers, suppliers, owners, bankers and trade union and government people.

The second procedure is the so-called Group Feedback Analysis (GFA). The top management of the organization is divided into two levels – all those reporting directly to the Chief Executive (level 1) and those just below them (level 2). Each group is convened separately for two sessions. The first is a data-collecting

45. In an early work by the author, examples of a standardized questionnaire (Weinshall, 1960, Appendix A, pp. 3–6) and analysis of the responses are presented (Weinshall, 1960, pp. 100–110, and Appendix, pp. 3–6). The same source quotes numerous attitudes from non-directive interviews (Weinshall, 1960, pp. 37–66).

46. Two of the best-known projects of this type were carried out by Mason Haire and his team (Haire et al., 1963) and Bass and his team (Barret and Bass, 1970). Haire applied elaborate attitude questionnaires to samples from a variety of countries. He then carried out a cluster analysis on the responses and lumped together the countries in which the managerial attitudes were similar. Bass devised concrete business administration situations played by groups of managers in each country. The response of the participants to the situations serve as basis for his analysis of differences in managerial attitudes between the countries.

47. Two such studies come to mind: Sirota's study in IBM, designed in a similar way to Mason Haire's studies (Sirota and Greenwood, 1971), and Hesseling's study in Philips, which is in some ways reminiscent of the studies of Bass, utilizing role-playing situations for managerial-attitude research (Hesseling, 1970).

session, in which the participants are given a battery of short questionnaires one after the other. The data of some of these questionnaires is then summarized and after a short interval the group reconvenes and the participants discuss their own results, which are fed back to them; this discussion is taped and content-analysed. The questionnaires are almost identical at both levels in order to permit joint quantitative analysis and comparison. The GFA procedure thus enables us to study managerial attitudes both quantitatively and qualitatively.[48] When utilizing it, the main

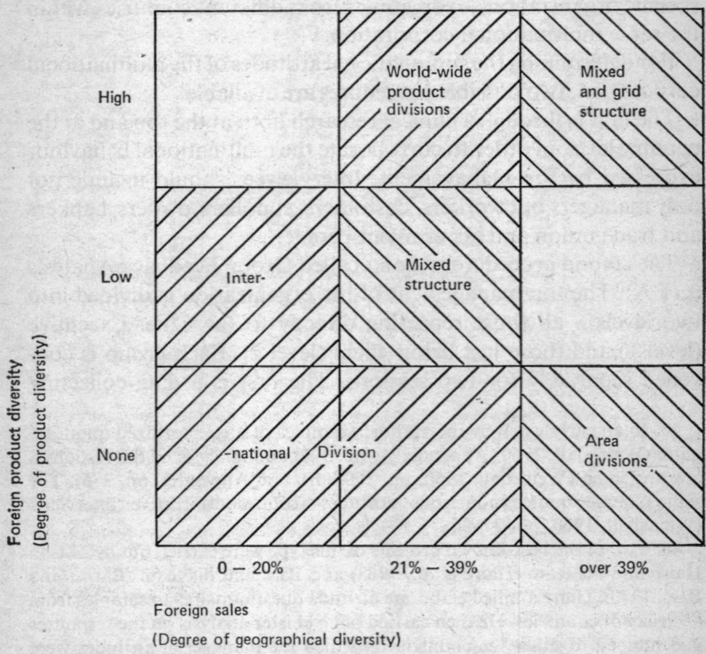

Figure 6 The three basic managerial structures – entrepreneurial, functional, and decentralized – related to the two parameters of clarity and autonomy

48. The GFA methodology was developed by Dr Frank Heller, who has already used it for completion of two studies on managerial decision-making studies in the U.S. and U.K. (Heller, 1971). Heller currently heads an international GFA research on managerial decision-making, conducted in Holland, Germany, Spain, France, Italy, Sweden, Israel and Japan.

problem is what kind of questionnaires to use in exploring supranational attitudes and tentative steps have been taken in recent years towards a special questionnaire for this purpose.[49]

Summary and conclusion

This paper presents the multinational corporations – their evolution, their present role in the world and methods for studying them.

The paper opens with the definition of multinational corporations – by way of their international scope of decision-making process, their multiple (multistructure) managerial structure and their supranational attitudes. Subsequently the paper explains how the inevitable organizational growth process evolved out of the Industrial Revolution, leading it through development and expansion in its technologies, product and service lines and, finally, in geographic spread of the organizational operations. This inevitable growth confronts the organization with the necessity of adapting its managerial structures, from time to time, to the ever-increasing scopes of decision-making processes. An organization would therefore start its operations in an entrepreneurial structure, possibly moving from there through different types of functional and decentralized structures, finally reaching multiple structure, a federation of several different types of structure.

However, international operations and a multiple structure are not by themselves enough for turning an organization into a multinational corporation. The organization has to acquire supranational attitudes to become one. It has, of course, to function within the constraints imposed on it by the governments of the territories within which it operates. The multinational corporation does not, however, abide to the interests of governments when operating outside their territories.

Next, the universal role of the multinational corporations is considered. They are compared with nation states, as to the contributions or damages they can bring to humanity. It is shown

49. This is done within the attitude study part of the Multinational Business Education project, conducted on students of INSEAD (the European Institute for Business Administration at Fontainebleau, France) since 1966 (Weinshall, 1971b).

that on such matters as ensuring peace and understanding between nations, bridging the gap between the rich and poor parts of the world, transfer of technologies and managerial practices, convergence of cultures to developments in technology and the rise in standard of living, etc. – the beneficial contributions of the multinational corporations outweighs, to a large extent, those of the nation states.

The identification of an organization as a multinational corporation is not a matter of black or white, but rather of degree. One has to establish the scope of decision-making process, the managerial structure and the managerial attitudes in order to find out how much of a multinational corporation the organization is. The last part of the paper therefore presents ways and means for researching the organizational size, structure and attitudes.

The main conclusion of this paper is that multinational corporations are here to stay, survive and grow. A closely related major conclusion is that the multinational corporations are taking over more and more power and responsibilities from the nation states of the world. The growing role of the multinational corporations, when compared to nation states, seems to be beneficial for the future of humanity.

References

ABEGGLEN, J. (1958), *The Japanese Factory*, The Free Press, Illinois.

AHARONI, Y. (1971), 'On the definition of a multinational corporation', *Quarterly Review of Economics and Business*, vol. II, no. 3.

ARMSTRONG, R. (1971), 'The passion that rules Ralph Nader', *Fortune*, May.

BARRET, G. V., and BASS, B. M. (1970), 'Comparative surveys of managerial attitudes and behaviour' (Comparative Management Teaching, Training and Research), from *Proceedings of the Comparative Management Workshop*, pp. 179–217.

BLUSTEIN, M., and WEINSHALL, T. D. (1972), 'Effects of 1965–67 unemployment and 1969 full employment on organizational behaviour of several industrial enterprises in Israel', *Organization and Administration*, vol. 18, no. 2, p. 114. (In Hebrew.)

BRIGHT, J. R. (1958), 'Does automation raise skill requirements?', *Harvard Business Review*, July–August.

BROOKE, M. Z., and REMMERS, H. L. (1970), *The Strategy of the Multinational Enterprise*, Longman.

BURNS, T., and STALKER, G. (1961), *The Management of Innovations*, Tavistock Publications.

CHANDLER, A. D. (1962), *Strategy and Structure*, M.I.T. Press.

DE BETTIGNIES, H.-C. (1970), 'Leaders across the ocean: comparing American and European chief executives', *European Business*, no. 26.

DE BETTIGNIES, H.-C. and EVANS, P. L. (1971), 'Europe looks north at the Scandinavian business elite', *European Business*, no. 31.

DRUCKER, P. F. (1971), 'What we can learn from Japanese management', *Harvard Business Review*, March–April.

FRANKO, L. G. (1971), 'Joint venture divorce in the multinational company', *Columbia Journal of World Business*, vol. VI, no. 3.

GLOVER, J. D. (1954), *The Attack on Big Business*, Division of Research, Graduate School of Business Administration, Harvard University.

GLOVER, J. D. (1970), 'Outline of a system of concepts for environmental analysis and corporate planning', in *La Empresa Multinacional*, Barto Roig-Amat (ed.), Coleccion IESE, Serie AC-3, Ediciones Universidad de Navarra, pp. 75–106.

HAIRE, M., GHISELLI, E., and PORTER, L. (1963), *Cultural Patterns in the Role of the Manager*, vol. 2, Institute of Industrial Relations, pp. 95–117.

HELLER, F. (1971), *Managerial Decision-Making – A Study of Leadership Styles in Power Sharing Among Senior Managers*, Tavistock Publications.

HESSELING, P. (1970), 'The uses of auto-observation of interactions in a multinational product centre', in *La Empresa Multinacional*, Barto Roig-Amat (ed.), Coleccion IESE, Serie AC-3, Ediciones Universidad de Navarra, pp. 383–405.

HIRSCH, S. (1971), *The Export Performance of Six Manufacturing Industries: A Comparative Study of Denmark, Holland and Israel*, Praeger Publications, New York.

HOMANS, G. C. (1959), *The Human Group*, Routledge and Kegan Paul.

HOROWITZ, D. (1960), Statement at the Bank's Annual Discussion, 1960 Annual Meeting's Board of Governors, International Monetary Fund, Press Release no. 27, Washington, D.C.

JACQUES, E. (1961), *Equitable Payment*, Heinemann.
KAHN, H., and WEINER, A. J. (1967), *The Year 2000: A Framework for Speculation on the Next 33 Years*, Macmillan.
KUEHN, D. A. (1973), 'An empirical analysis of capital market discipline on poor performance and its implications for the theory of the firm', presented to the TIMS Conference, Tel-Aviv, May.
LAWRENCE, P., and LORSCH, J. W. (1968), *Organization and Environment*, Harvard University Press.
MACDONALD, A. (1972), 'Conflict at the summit: a deadly game', *Harvard Business Review*, March – April.
MARGALIT, Y., and WEINSHALL, T. D. (1972), 'The Israeli Presidents', *Organization and Administration*, vol. 18, no. 4, p. 116. (In Hebrew.)
MASLOW, A. H. (1954), *Motivation and Personality*, Harper and Bros., New York.
NIEGO, S. T. (1962), 'The effect of full employment on what goes on in industrial enterprises', unpublished M. Sc. dissertation, Department of Industrial Management and Engineering, Technion - Israel Institute of Technology. (In Hebrew.)
PENROSE, E. T. (1959), *The Theory of the Growth of the Firm*, Basil Blackwell, Oxford.
PERLMUTTER, H. V. (1969), 'Emerging East – West ventures: the transideological enterprise', *Columbia Journal of World Business*, vol. IV, no. 5. (And see this volume, pp. 140–62.)
PUZO, M. (1969), *The Godfather*, Heinemann.
REMMERS, H. L. (1970) 'Direccion financiera en la empresa multinacional', in *La Empresa Multinacional*, Barto Roig-Amat (ed.), Coleccion IESE, Serie AC-3, Ediciones Universidad de Navarra, pp. 249–62.
ROBERTS, K. H. (1970), 'On looking at an elephant: an evaluation of cross-cultural research related to organizations', *Psychological Bulletin*, vol. 74, no. 5, pp. 327–50. (And see this volume, pp. 56–104.)
SAMPSON, A. (1973), *The Sovereign State: A Secret History of I.T.T.*, Hodder and Stoughton.
SERVAN-SCHREIBER, J. J. (1967), *Le Défi Américain*, Editions Denoël, Paris.
SIROTA, D., and GREENWOOD, M. J. (1971), 'Understand your overseas workforce', *Harvard Business Review*, January–February 1972, pp. 53–60. (And see this volume, pp. 261–76.)
STOPFORD, J. M., and WELLS, L. T. (1972), *Managing the Multinational Enterprise*, Longman.

TURNER, L. (1973), 'Trade unions and the multinational company', in *Fabian Industrial Essays*, L. Klein (ed.), The Royal Institute of International Affairs.

VERNON, R. (1971), *Sovereignty at Bay: The Multinational Spread of U.S. Enterprises*, Longman.

WEBBER, R. A. (1970), 'Convergence or divergence?', *Columbia Journal of World Business*, vol. IV, no. 3. (And see this volume, pp. 39–55.)

WEBER, M. (1967), *Theory of Social and Economic Organization*, William Hodge.

WEINSHALL, T. D. (1960), *The Effects of Management Changes on the Organizational Relationships and Attitudes*, unpublished doctoral dissertation, Harvard University.

WEINSHALL, T. D. (1971a), 'Applications of two conceptual schemes in case study and general organizational research', *Papers in Management Studies*, Ashridge Management College.

WEINSHALL, T. D. (1971b), 'Multinational business education – research methodology and attitudes study', *Management International Review* nos. 2–3, pp. 87–110.

WEINSHALL, T. D. (1971c), *Economic and Organizational Consequences of the Size of Nations and other Aspects of Size*, mimeographed working paper no. 130/71, Leon Recanati Graduate School of Business Administration, Tel-Aviv University.

WEINSHALL, T. D. (1972), *The Bible as Pioneer in the Fields of Management and Organizational Behaviour*, mimeographed working paper no. 156/72, Leon Recanati Graduate School of Business Administration, Tel-Aviv University.

WEINSHALL, T. D. (1973a), 'Overcoming the differences in communication and other cultural characteristics through education of multinational managers', *The Multinational Company in Europe: Some Key Problems*, Michael Brooke and Lee Remmers (eds.), Longman. (And see this volume pp. 163–211.)

WEINSHALL, T. D. (1973b), 'Study of organizational size and managerial structure', in *The Organization of Management Research*, Desmond Graves (ed.), Elsevier Publishing Co., Amsterdam.

WEINSHALL, T. D. (1973c), 'Managerial structure of a nationally mixed organization in Japan', *Journal of Organization and Administration Sciences*, 1977.

WEINSHALL, T. D. (1973d), '*The Informalogram as an Indicator of Managerial Structure*, mimeographed working paper no. 167/73,

Leon Recanati Graduate School of Business Administration, Tel-Aviv University.
WEINSHALL, T. D. and SHIMSHONI, D. (1973), *A Total System Research Programme for a Whole Industry*, mimeographed working paper no. 144/73, Leon Recanati Graduate School of Business Administration, Tel-Aviv University.
WEINSHALL, T. D., and TWISS, B. (1973), *Organizational Problems in European Manufacturing*, (2 volumes), Longman.
WOODWARD, J. (1965), *Industrial Organization: Theory and Practice*, Oxford University Press.
WORTHY, J. C. (1949), 'Democratic Principles in Business Management', *Advanced Management*.
YOSHINO, M. (1968), *Japan's Managerial System*, M.I.T. Press.

Selected Bibliography

M. Ajiferuke and J. Boddewyn, 'Culture and Other Explanatory Variables in Comparative Management Studies', *Academy of Management Journal*, June 1970, pp. 153–63.
J. Boddewyn, 'Comparative Management Studies: An Assessment', *Management International Review*, 1970.
G. Caplan, 'Some Comments on Problems of Community Psychiatry and Technical Co-operation in Israel', contribution to conference on *Economic Planning and Social Policy in Israel*, Harvard University Centre for Middle East Studies, 1958.
S. M. Davis, *Comparative Management: Organizational and Cultural Perspectives*, Prentice-Hall Inc., New Jersey, 1971.
M. Haire, E. E. Ghiselli, L. W. Porter, *Managerial Thinking: An International Study*, John Wiley and Sons, New York, 1966.
E. T. Hall, *The Silent Language*, Fawcett Publications Inc., Connecticut, 1970.
W. J. Lederer and E. Burdick, *The Ugly American*, Gollancz, 1959.
R. Nath, 'A Methodological Review of Cross-Cultural Management Research', *International Social Science Journal*, vol. XX, no. 1, pp. 35–62.
A. R. Negandhi and B. D. Estafen, 'A Research Model to Determine the Applicability of American Management Know-How in Different Cultures and/or Environments', *Academy of Management Journal*, December 1965, pp. 309–18.
H. Schollhammer, 'The Comparative Theory Jungle, *Academy of Management Journal*, March 1969, pp. 81–97.
W. F. Whyte, 'An Intercultural Center for Organizational Research', *Organizational Behavior: Theory and Application*, Richard D. Irwin, Illinois, 1969.
J. Woodward, *Industrial Organization Theory and Practice*, Oxford University Press, 1965.
W. L. Zwerman, *New Perspectives on Organization Theory*, Greenwood Publishing Corporation, Connecticut, 1970.

Acknowledgements

Permission to reproduce the following Readings in this volume is acknowledged to these sources:

1. *Academy of Management Journal*
2. *Columbia Journal of World Business*
3. Institute of Industrial Relations
4. McGraw-Hill Co. Inc.
5. Mr E. Russell Eggers.
6. *Columbia Journal of World Business*
7. Longman Group Ltd
8. McGraw-Hill Co. Inc.
9. John Wiley and Sons
10. *Harvard Business Review*
11. *European Business*
12. Institute of Industrial Relations
13. (a) *Occupational Psychology*
    (b) Tavistock Institute of Human Relations
14. *Sociology*
15. The Leon Recanati Graduate School of Business Administration

Author Index

Subject Index